mathematics
for the young child

mathematics for the young child

Editor
Joseph N. Payne

Managing Editor
Charles C. E. Clements

Design and Illustration
Jody Braun Graphic Design

National Council of Teachers
of Mathematics

Copyright © 1990 by
THE NATIONAL COUNCIL OF TEACHERS OF MATHEMATICS, INC.
1906 Association Drive, Reston, Virginia 20191-1593
All rights reserved

Third printing 1999

Library of Congress Cataloging-in-Publication Data

Mathematics for the young child / editor, Joseph N. Payne ; managing
    editor, Charles C.E. Clements ; design and illustration, Jody Braun
    Graphic Design.
            p.   cm.
    Includes bibliographical references and index.
    ISBN 0–87353–288–0
    1. Mathematics—Study and teaching (Primary)   2. Mathematics—
Study and teaching (Preschool)   I. Payne, Joseph N. (Joseph Neal)
QA135.5.M3692   1990
372.7—dc20   90–42418
                                                                  CIP

The publications of the National Council of Teachers of Mathematics present
a variety of viewpoints. The views expressed or implied in this
publication, unless otherwise noted, should not be interpreted as official
positions of the Council.

Printed in the United States of America

Table of
Contents

Preface

Mathematics for the Young Child is a book for teachers of children in preschool through grade 4, ages three through nine. The book is designed to help teachers make important decisions about the mathematics curriculum and give them some effective ways to help children attain the mathematical power needed both for everyday use and for careers in the twenty-first century.

The foundation of the mathematics needed for personal affairs and for careers must be well laid by the end of grade 4. Consequently, a major effort is needed to improve both the curriculum and the instructional methods used with children at these early levels.

Relevant research in each chapter provides a framework and dependable justification for the suggested curriculum and instructional strategies. Instructional activities are interwoven to furnish practical and useful ideas that teachers can modify and expand. The intent is to combine research results with proved classroom practice.

Effective teaching, viewed as an interactive activity, is a major goal of this book. The intent is to help teachers understand the spirit of this interaction, the way tasks should be presented, the kind of questions to ask, the way manipulatives should be used to stimulate and develop thinking, and the way children's responses should be used to make instructional decisions. The teacher is viewed as a planner of mathematical experiences—experiences to be executed with a balance between teacher direction and child initiation.

Chapter 1 identifies nine themes of the book related to learning and teaching:

1 Developing conceptual knowledge is a major goal.

2 Procedural knowledge is developed from sound conceptual knowledge.

3 Applications and problem solving using the child's own experiences are integral components for all mathematics topics.

4 Children construct their own knowledge and understanding.

5 Construction of knowledge requires active cognitive effort by the child.

6 Mathematical content and teaching methods should be developmentally appropriate.

7 Diagnosis and assessment are ongoing parts of teaching.

8 Calculators should be available at all times as instructional tools.

9 Preschool mathematics encompasses a broad range of content, as indicated in various chapters of this book.

These themes are described more fully at the end of chapter 1 and are reflected in the content chapters of the book. Chapter 1 also contains an overview of major national documents and makes reference to initiatives of various states and provinces. The framework for the book is developed further in chapters 2 and 3, with in-depth presentations on how mathematical knowledge is developed in the young child and how problem-solving abilities and attitudes can be a central focus. The teaching and learning of specific mathematical content is covered in chapters 4 through 12. The role of technology is evident throughout the chapters with many suggestions on calculator use, and chapter 13 concentrates on using microcomputers for mathematics learning. Chapter 14 focuses on the teacher as a planner of mathematics instruction.

Special attention has been given to preschool and kindergarten throughout the book. Each author made special effort to address the needs of children and teachers at these early levels. It should be clear that the mathematics curriculum for early-age children is much more than just counting.

Mathematics for the Young Child is designed to be used by teachers independently, by teachers in continuing education, by preservice teachers in courses on teaching mathematics to children, and by graduate students in seminars on mathematics teaching and learning. The book should be helpful to states and provinces and to school systems active in curriculum development for preschool through grade 4. It is hoped that the many practical suggestions will make the book a reference of continuing use to a teacher in the classroom.

The Editorial Panel met first in January 1987. At that meeting we identified the major directions for the book and chose authors for the chapters. Authors were chosen on the basis of their knowledge of research and effective classroom practice as well as their ability to write and convey information to teachers. The authors chosen agreed to write the chapters and meet the deadlines set for timely publication. Each author prepared an outline, revised the outline, wrote a first draft, and then produced final copy based on comments and suggestions from the Editorial Panel at each stage. I am especially appreciative of the high quality of their work and of their patience and understanding in working through the final manuscript with me. This group provided the substance of the book.

The many other people who have freely contributed a rich array of talents in the production of this book include the following:

Editorial Panel
Patricia F. Campbell   Edward C. Rathmell   Marilyn N. Suydam   John A. Van de Walle
Thomas P. Carpenter   DeAnn M. Huinker, *Assistant*

National Council of Teachers of Mathematics Staff
Charles Clements   Jo Handerson   Lynn Westenberg   Mollie Cox   Cynthia Rosso

Photography
D.C. Goings *Photo and Campus Services University of Michigan*
Ernie York (chapter 13) *Educational Technology Center University of Maryland*
Kevin Fitzsimmons (chapter 14) *University Communications Services Ohio State University*

Typing and Manuscript Manager
Helen Candiotti *School of Education University of Michigan*

To all these people, I express my sincere appreciation for excellent work. I extend special thanks to—

Charles Clements, for outstanding and sensitive editorial work on the book in his quiet and gentlemanly manner and for his consistent commitment to producing a quality book, and his exceptional editorial staff, Jo Handerson, Lynn Westenberg, and Mollie Cox;

Cynthia Rosso, for her support and help with business and printing matters;

Jody Braun, not only for the quality of her design and illustration but also for her commitment to their functional use in achieving the educational goals, often improving the presentation of the content;

Don Goings, for his ability to capture both the spirit of the children and the spirit of learning mathematics with his photographs;

Giannine Perigo, principal of Carpenter School in Ann Arbor, for her organization and help in making arrangements for the photographs taken by Don Goings, and to the teachers and students at Carpenter School who were so cooperative and photogenic (Giannine Perigo was formerly an outstanding third-grade teacher with whom I worked daily for two years in her mathematics class and learned much about what a truly outstanding teacher of young children does);

Chapelfield Elementary School of Gahanna, Ohio, for photographs in chapter 14, and the Center for Young Children at the University of Maryland, for photographs in chapter 13;

Christian Hirsch, former chair of the Educational Materials Committee, for his genuine support of my initial proposal and for his help in the early stages of the planning;

John Dossey, past president of NCTM, for his help in getting NCTM Board approval for the book;

John Van de Walle and Marilyn Suydam, for reading my draft of chapter 1 and giving many helpful suggestions;

DeAnn Huinker, who served as a genuine member of the Editorial Panel by reading and reacting to all manuscripts and by making many suggestions for instructional activities;

Charles Hucka, for his major contribution to the 1975 book, *Mathematics Learning in Early Childhood*, and for his gentle coaxing over several years that led me to make a proposal for this book as its successor;

George E. Hollister and Agnes G. Gunderson, authors of *Teaching Arithmetic in Grades I and II*, published by D. C. Heath in 1954, for writing such an interesting and helpful book, serving somewhat as a prototype for the 1975 book, *Mathematics Learning in Early Childhood* (Gunderson was also the author of the reference to fractions in the primary grades quoted in chapter 9);

Gordon Rapp, for photographs used in figures 2, 3, and 4 in chapter 6;

Lee Polisano, partner, Kohn Pederson Fox Associates, for supplying the photograph of 70 East 55th Street, NYC, used in the window of our geometry chapter;

Helen Candiotti, my ever-helpful secretary, who cheerfully did much of the typing, duplicating, and numerous mailings for the book;

Ruth Payne, for sharing her successful teaching experience at the primary level and her delight with, and love of, teaching young children;

many outstanding teachers, for being enthusiastic about new directions for content and teaching methods, including my students at the University of Michigan and experienced teachers in special classes in Detroit and Lenawee County.

It has been fun to work on this book. I hope that it will elicit for the reader some of the same feelings of excitement and satisfaction that have gone into its production.

Joseph N. Payne, Editor

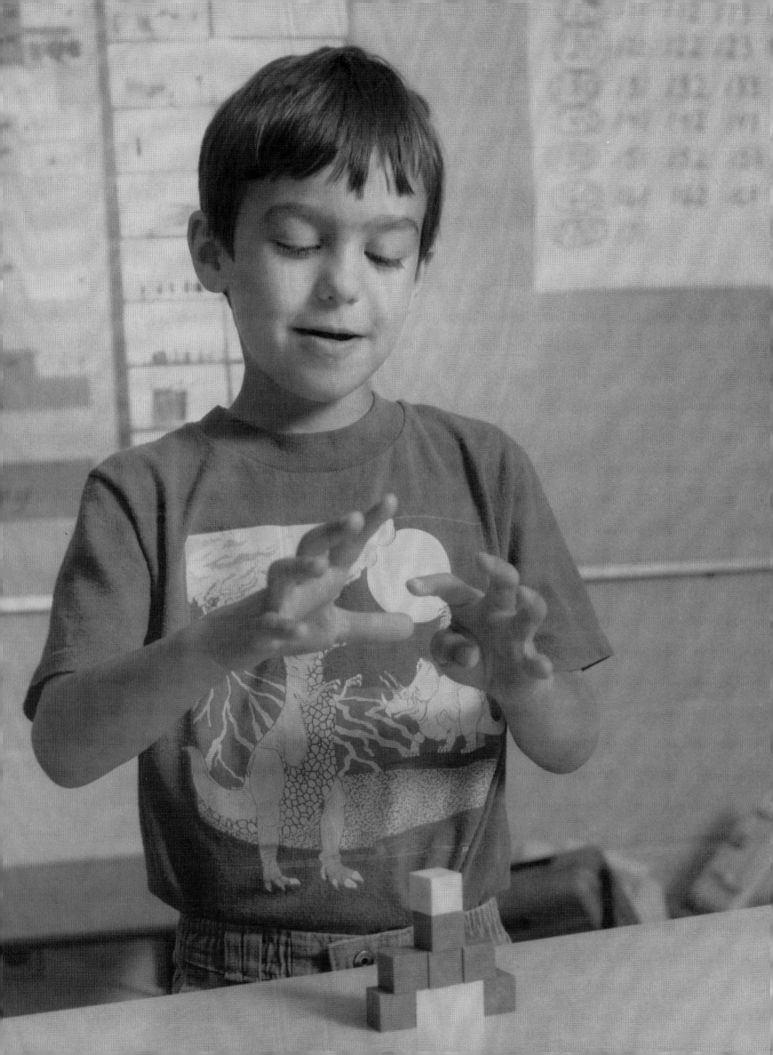

1

new directions in mathematics education

joseph payne

Work on this book began in 1986 at a time when major efforts were under way to chart sweeping new directions in mathematics education. The impetus for change came from the relatively poor performance in mathematics of our young people, especially when compared with results from other industrial countries, and from the new needs of people in our technological society. No longer were basic computational skills sufficient for either personal or career needs. Businesses and industries were already finding it difficult to fill positions with persons possessing adequate thinking, problem-solving, and quantitative reasoning skills.

This book was developed with the firm conviction that the changes required in mathematics education must begin with our young children. In the preschool years through the fourth grade, the age span for which this book is written, children can and must understand mathematical concepts and relationships and develop mathematical reasoning and problem-solving skills.

This chapter provides a framework and an overview for the book. The reasons and directions for change in the mathematics curriculum and the way it should be organized and taught are summarized using major reports. Then themes for this book are identified, and special attention is given to calculators and to preschool mathematics.

everybody counts

A stimulating and thoughtful publication, *Everybody Counts: A Report to the Nation on the Future of*

Mathematics Education (National Research Council 1989), provides an informative and motivating report of the status of mathematics education in the United States. It gives suggestions, in the views held by many people about mathematics, for the type of major changes that are needed—broad changes in the curriculum and in instructional methods at all levels, preschool through college.

opportunity for everyone

"Mathematics is the key to opportunity" (p. 1) is the opening sentence of the report. Jobs require workers who can perceive patterns and solve unconventional problems. All citizens need mathematics to make informed decisions. These needs, not calculations now done mostly with machines, are the ones that make mathematics a prerequisite for many jobs and essential for enlightened citizenship.

The report highlights the negative effects of existing practice. "Mathematics is the worst curricular villain in driving students to failure in school. When mathematics acts as a filter, it not only filters students out of careers, but frequently out of school itself" (p. 7). The report also attacks the often-held attitude that differences in innate ability are the cause of poor achievement. Instead, differences are attributed to individual effort or to the opportunity to learn. The report is critical of an attitude sometimes heard from a parent and often directed to a child: "I never could do math myself."

Nor is gender or race a reason for poor performance in mathematics. Although women receive only one-third of university degrees in science and engineering, there is almost no difference in the performance of male and female students who have taken equal advantage of similar opportunities to study mathematics. The lack of a good mathematics foundation shuts out many blacks, Hispanics, and American Indians from scientific and business careers. "Inadequate preparation in mathematics imposes a special economic handicap on minorities" (p. 21).

teaching and construction of knowledge

Mathematics is viewed too often as being about getting right answers rather than about clear creative thinking. The rules and procedures of mathematics are too often learned without any real understanding. The report decries the dominant practice of teachers explaining and students listening. Rather, the report presents a different alternative that emphasizes the *construction* of one's own mathematical knowledge.

In reality, no one can teach mathematics. Effective teachers are those who can stimulate students to learn mathematics. Educational research offers compelling evidence that students learn mathematics well only when they construct their own mathematical understanding. (P. 58)

To help students with the construction of their mathematical knowledge, the report suggests that students work in groups and engage in discussion. Students are encouraged to make oral and written presentations themselves and in other ways take charge of their own learning.

When students explore mathematics, their invented,

creative strategies often bear little resemblance to the examples found worked out in the textbook. Not only are powerful processes developed when they truly explore mathematics rather than absorb preformed rules, but an all-important confidence level also emerges. "There is no way to build this confidence except through the process of creating, constructing, and discovering mathematics" (p. 60).

broader curriculum

A broader curriculum is essential, including not only arithmetic but estimation, measurement, geometry, statistics, and probability (p. 46).

Although paper-and-pencil computation constituted the objective of mathematics for the ordinary citizen fifty years ago, today's needs are very different.

The major objective of elementary school mathematics should be to develop number sense. . . . It is not mindlessly mechanical, but flexible and synthetic in attitude. It evolves from concrete experience and takes shape in oral, written, and symbolic expression. Links to geometry, to chance, and to calculation should reinforce formal arithmetic experience to produce multiple mental images of quantitative phenomena. (Pp. 46–47)

Mathematics is viewed as the science of pattern and order (p. 31). Children's natural curiosity about patterns should be reinforced by their school experience. Patterns should include shapes, numbers, and chance.

The regular use of calculators and computers is a recurring theme in the report.

Using calculators intelligently is an integral part of number sense. Children should use calculators throughout their school work, just as adults use calculators throughout their lives. More important, children must learn when to use them and when not to do so. . . . Calculators create whole new opportunities for ordering the curriculum and for integrating mathematics into science. (P. 47)

In summary, the report provides a rationale and suggestions for new directions for a mathematics curriculum with a broader scope of content with different emphases, consistent use of calculators, and improved teaching methods.

curriculum and evaluation standards

In 1986, the Board of Directors of the National Council of Teachers of Mathematics (NCTM) established a commission that produced the 1989 publication, *Curriculum and Evaluation Standards for School Mathematics*. The *Standards* provides a wide-ranging examination of the status of mathematics education in schools. A call for major change occurs in the initial background section.

Inherent in this document is a consensus that all students need to learn more, and often different, mathematics and that instruction in mathematics must be significantly revised. (P. 1)

One of the major tasks of the commission was to—

create a coherent vision of what it means to be mathematically literate both in a world that relies on calculators and computers to carry out mathematical procedures and in a world where mathematics is rapidly growing and is extensively being applied in diverse fields. (P. 1)

Societal goals are described, including a call for opportunity for all people, similar in tone to the call in *Everybody Counts*.

Creating a just society in which women and various ethnic groups enjoy equal opportunities and equitable treatment is no longer an issue. Mathematics has become a critical filter for employment and full participation in our society. We cannot afford to have the majority of our population mathematically illiterate. Equity has become an economic necessity. (P. 4)

goals for students

The *Standards* document lists five general goals reflecting the importance of mathematical literacy for all students (pp. 5–6):

1 Learning to value mathematics

2 Becoming confident in their ability to do mathematics

3 Becoming mathematical problem solvers

4 Learning to communicate mathematically

5 Learning to reason mathematically

To attain these goals, the *Standards* recommends as did *Everybody Counts,* an active, constructive view of learning. The best teaching methods were viewed as being more child-centered than teacher-centered. Opportunities for active student involvement include projects, group and individual assignments, and discussion between teacher and students and among students.

The *Standards* recommends that calculators be available to all students at all times and noted the lack of evidence that the availability of calculators makes students dependent on them for simple calculations. Students should be able to select and use the most appropriate tool for the mathematical task at hand (p. 8).

k–4 standards

The first of four major sections deals with standards for curriculum and instruction in kindergarten through grade 4. There is a call for a shift away from the prevalent concentration on paper-and-pencil computational topics, which yields a curriculum narrow in scope. The emphasis on rote computational activities has had especially bad results not only on narrow curricula but on children's beliefs. "Children begin to lose their belief that learning mathematics is a sense-making experience. They become passive receivers of rules and procedures rather than active participants in creating knowledge" (p. 15).

The K–4 recommendations from the *Standards* are based on the assumptions that the mathematics curriculum should (pp. 17–19)—

1 be conceptually oriented;

2 actively involve children in doing mathematics;

3 emphasize the development of children's mathematical thinking and reasoning abilities;

4 emphasize the application of mathematics;

5 include a broad range of content;

6 make appropriate and ongoing use of calculators and computers.

A summary of the changes in content and emphasis in K–4 mathematics (NCTM 1989, pp. 20–21) is given in figure 1.

Each of the thirteen standards in the K–4 section contains clear examples that illustrate these shifts in content emphases. Suggestions are given for instruction, including examples of activities and sample dialogues with students. The authors of this book, several of whom served on the *Standards's* K–4 writing team, have reflected and amplified the general themes found in the *Standards.*

Increased Attention

Number

Number sense
Place-value concepts
Meaning of fractions and decimals
Estimation of quantities

Operations and Computation

Meaning of operations
Operation sense
Mental computation
Estimation and the reasonableness of answers
Selection of an appropriate computational method
Use of calculators for complex computation
Thinking strategies for basic facts

Fig. 1. Summary of changes in content and emphasis in K–4 mathematics

Geometry and Measurement

Properties of geometric figures
Geometric relationships
Spatial sense
Process of measuring
Concepts related to units of
measurement
Actual measuring
Estimation of measurements
Use of measurement and geometry
ideas throughout the curriculum

Probability and Statistics

Collection and organization of data
Exploration of chance

Patterns and Relationships

Pattern recognition and description
Use of variables to express
relationships

Problem Solving

Word problems with a variety
of structures
Use of everyday problems
Applications
Study of patterns and relationships
Problem-solving strategies

Instructional Practices

Use of manipulative materials
Cooperative work
Discussion of mathematics
Questioning
Justification of thinking
Writing about mathematics
Problem-solving approach to
instruction
Content integration
Use of calculators and computers

Decreased Attention

Number

Early attention to reading, writing,
and ordering numbers symbolically

Operations and Computation

Complex paper-and-pencil
computations
Isolated treatment of
paper-and-pencil computations
Addition and subtraction without
renaming
Isolated treatment of division
facts
Long division
Long division without remainders
Paper-and-pencil fraction
computation
Use of rounding to estimate

Geometry and Measurement

Primary focus on naming
geometric figures
Memorization of equivalencies
between units of measurement

Problem Solving

Use of clue words to determine
which operation to use

Instructional Practices

Rote practice
Rote memorization of rules
One answer and one method
Use of worksheets
Written practice
Teaching by telling

evaluation standards

The last of the four major sections deals with evaluation. The Evaluation Standards emphasize the need to change existing tests. "Many existing tests cannot measure the student outcomes identified in the *Standards*. . . . Tests must change because they are based on different views of what knowing and learning mathematics means" (pp. 189–90). The Evaluation Standards proposed that "student assessment be integral to instruction; multiple means of assessment methods be used; all aspects of mathematical knowledge and its connections be assessed; and instruction and curriculum be considered equally in judging the quality of a program" (p. 190). The evaluation emphases in the *Standards* (NCTM 1989, p. 191) are summarized in figure 2.

Clearly it is the intent of the *Standards* to set a direction for evaluation that is different from the

Increased Attention	Decreased Attention
Assessing what students know and how they think about mathematics	Assessing what students do not know
Having assessment be an integral part of teaching	Having assessments be simply counting correct answers on tests for the sole purpose of assigning grades
Focusing on a broad range of mathematical tasks and taking a holistic view of mathematics	Focusing on a large number of specific and isolated skills organized by a content-behavior matrix
Developing problem situations that require the applications of a number of mathematical ideas	Using exercises or word problems requiring only one or two skills
Using multiple assessment techniques, including written, oral, and demonstration formats	Using only written tests
Using calculators, computers, and manipulatives in assessment	Excluding calculators, computers, and manipulatives from the assessment process
Evaluating the program by systematically collecting information on outcomes, curriculum, and instruction	Evaluating the program only on the basis of test scores
Using standardized achievement tests as only one of many indicators of program outcomes	Using standardized achievement tests as the only indicator of program outcomes

Fig. 2. Emphases of the Evaluation Standards

existing multiple-choice format of standardized tests with a relatively narrow view of both the mathematical content and the instructional objectives. Standardized tests existing in 1990 do not measure the goals as set forth in these national reports and in forward-looking state and provincial documents.

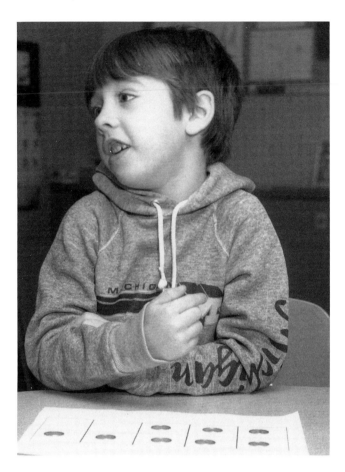

state
and
province initiatives

As reports from NCTM and other major organizations have highlighted the need for, and the direction of, change in mathematics education, it is the states and provinces—and local educational agencies—that have the major responsibility for bringing about change. At all levels, new objectives reflect a more enlightened view of the mathematics curriculum and the way mathematics can be taught. By 1990, only one year after the publication of the NCTM *Curriculum and Evaluation Standards,* most states had developed plans for implementation. These plans frequently include new objectives, curriculum guides, teaching suggestions, programs for teacher training, and parent awareness programs. Changes in objectives at this level often result in mandated tests, giving added importance to the objectives.

As one example, in 1988 the Michigan State Board of Education approved the *Michigan Essential Goals and Objectives for Mathematics Education* (Michigan Department of Education 1988). These objectives were prepared by a committee organized by the Michigan Council of Teachers of Mathematics as a replacement for a minimal set that had been in effect since the early 1970s. The 1988 objectives reflected a broadened framework of content strands and mathematical processes. A subsequent publication contained examples for the objectives, suggestions for teaching, and sample assessment items (Michigan Department of Education 1989).

In the Michigan Framework, each content strand is addressed under a series of mathematical processes. Features of the Michigan Framework are similar to ones in the NCTM *Standards.* As objectives for the content strands were written, a decision was made on the process that went with the objective, in fact, the way the objective would be assessed. The content and process strands are shown in figure 3.

The following were set as major new directions in the overview to the objectives (Michigan Department of Education 1989, p. ix):

1 Conceptualization of mathematical topics receives much greater attention. [About one-half of the total number of objectives at the K–3 level are conceptualization objectives.]

2 Problem solving permeates all content strands.

3 Graphical representation and interpretation are strengthened.

Mathematical Content Strands	Mathematical Processes					
	Conceptualization	Mental Arithmetic	Estimation	Computation	Applications and Problem Solving	Calculators and Computers
Whole Numbers and Numeration						
Fractions, Decimals, Ratio, and Percent						
Measurement						
Geometry						
Statistics and Probability						
Algebraic Ideas						
Problem Solving and Logical Reasoning						
Calculators						

Fig. 3. Framework: Michigan mathematics objectives—content and process strands

4 The needs of students in a technological society are reflected. The objectives reflect the value of the calculator as a teaching tool and as a tool for students in solving problems beginning in the early grades.

5 Mental arithmetic and estimation receive more attention and are given greater importance. [Complex paper-and-pencil computation is reduced substantially.]

6 Spatial visualization and geometry are broadened.

7 Algebraic concepts and symbolism are introduced earlier.

Of major importance in Michigan is the every-pupil test given near the beginning of each year in grades 4, 7, and 10. The Michigan objectives were written with the agreement that calculators would be available for use on most of the test. In the pilot version, calculators were permitted on about three-fourths of the K–3 test, on all parts except mental arithmetic, paper-and-pencil computation, and some estimation items. It was the

view of the committee that prepared the objectives that the use of calculators on tests was essential in providing time and incentive for a broader range of content and different instructional objectives. The Michigan initiative is just one example of a state-level organization leading the curriculum, instructional methods, and assessment framework in the direction of the Standards.

Many local schools, particularly larger school districts, have launched similar efforts in writing objectives. There is wide variation in the quality of the local objectives. Some districts provide outstanding objectives; others appear merely to have been copied from existing textbooks.

Although textbooks may have features that seem to reflect new directions, the real content often does not show an adventurous spirit in pointing to new directions for curriculum and teaching. Excessive numbers of exercises, in teacher-prepared materials as well as in textbooks, require only paper-and-pencil computation, making it difficult to accomplish what is needed. Good instructional strategies demand such things as interactive cooperative group work, student discussions, and a greater reliance on manipulative models and calculators. Textbooks and worksheets are only small tools in a comprehensive teaching toolbox.

The new directions being set at the national level provide a challenge for states, provinces, and local schools. It is important for both teachers and administrators alike at any of these levels to look carefully at any new proposals for mathematics curriculum and instruction and to evaluate these proposals in the light of widely accepted recommendations such as the Michigan objectives and the NCTM *Standards*.

mathematics for the young child

In the early discussions that led to the development of this book, the Editorial Panel identified several themes that were to be integrated into all the chapters. These themes reflect new directions for mathematics education consistent with the changes suggested in the NCTM *Standards* and in the initiatives of various states and provinces. The following sections highlight and summarize the major themes of this book.

conceptual development

Developing conceptual knowledge is a major goal. Chapter 2 deals in depth with the meaning of conceptual knowledge and contrasts it with procedural, or algorithmic, knowledge. Deficiencies resulting from giving excessive attention to procedures are identified and discussed. Attention is given to the need to relate procedural knowledge to conceptual knowledge. Suggestions are given for organizing instruction to enhance concept development.

The major foundation for K–4 mathematics consists of sound concepts of whole numbers, whole number operations, measurement, geometry, space, graphical representation, fractions, decimals, and probability, all reflected in the content chapters of this book. Research and practical experiences show with certainty that these major concepts require a substantial amount of time for their development, a wide variety of examples, and experiences from the real world of the learner.

As will be evident from all the chapters, concept development requires frequent use of concrete models and diagrams. The perceptual and quantitative dimensions of mathematical knowledge are related carefully to the child's natural language and the child's way of perceiving and thinking. Consistent attention is given to avoiding a premature introduction of symbols and algorithms.

relating conceptual and procedural knowledge

Procedural knowledge is developed from sound conceptual knowledge. Chapter 2 provides an overview of this major task. The goal is to develop meaningful algorithms rather than rote procedures that too often characterize mathematics curricula and instructional methods. In all chapters of this book where procedural knowledge is developed, it should be clear that the procedures are developed from sound concepts.

The pitfalls of a curriculum that concentrates solely on algorithms and procedures are highlighted. Suggestions are given for effective classroom instruction to develop concepts and relate procedures to concepts.

applications and problem solving

Applications and problem solving using the child's own experiences are integral components for all mathematics topics. The role of a child's own personal experiences is evident in the development of conceptual knowledge. Personal experiences are of equal

importance for problem solving. Chapter 3 deals with the development of problem-solving strategies for children in preschool and early grades. A perusal of that chapter will make clear the connections between the real-life experiences of students and their work with problem solving.

Chapter 3 also provides a framework for approaching much of the work in mathematics, a framework that should be evident in the remaining chapters of the book. It is easy to see how promoting a problem-solving attitude, furnishing practical experiences, and giving concrete examples can lead children to develop a wide range of mathematical ideas.

knowledge construction

Children construct their own knowledge and understanding of mathematical concepts and procedures. Providing concrete manipulatives and diagrams helps in this process. The active use of oral language is also a powerful tool as children work to construct ideas and relationships. The construction of knowledge depends and builds on the experiences the child has already had with a given mathematics topic. A child-centered approach, always attentive to children's current ideas and experiences, is desirable in planning units of work and specific lessons. Each of the content chapters in this book uses the experiences of students, concrete representations, and oral language as major tools in the construction of mathematical knowledge by the child.

active involvement

The construction of knowledge requires active cognitive effort by the child. The previous themes in fact incorporate this role of active involvement. This idea is singled out for amplification more than anything else. The construction of conceptual knowledge requires the active cognitive effort of the child. It is the child who does the learning. It is the child who processes the information and builds on it. It is the child who should do the talking and the explaining. Although this active role of the learner in the acquisition of mathematical knowledge is the most difficult idea to get across in printed form, we have attempted to do so.

It is impossible to keep children from doing things with manipulative materials. Some of these actions may be cognitively constructive, some not. Nevertheless, there is action, and it is this action that forces some kind of thinking and reaction.

One way to think about the use of manipulatives is as catalysts for thinking. It is not the pretty colors or the feel of manipulatives that makes them valuable; rather, it is that manipulatives help to promote and focus the reflective thought of the young child—and even the adult. Usually manipulative materials require that a teacher or knowledgeable adult interact with the learner; otherwise, the manipulatives become nothing more than pieces of wood or plastic. The role of conversation is to bring out the desired mathematics.

The importance of active involvement is illustrated by the numerous activities throughout the book, identified with a special logo, a large **a**. These activities are intended to be done by a teacher with children. Suggested questions are included along with sample student responses. The actual responses of children may not parallel the samples. What is important is not to get children to respond as in the samples but to listen to the content of a child's reply and build on those ideas. It is children's answers and explanations that tell the perceptive teacher what the next instructional move should be.

developmentally appropriate

Mathematical content and teaching methods should be developmentally appropriate. In *Developmentally Appropriate Practice,* the National Association for the Education of Young Children (NAEYC) uses two

dimensions to describe developmental appropriateness —age appropriateness and individual appropriateness (NAEYC 1986):

Knowledge of the age span served by the program provides a framework from which teachers prepare the learning environment and plan appropriate experiences. . . . Learning in young children is the result of interaction between the child's thoughts and experiences with materials, ideas, and people. These experiences should match the child's developing abilities, while also challenging the child's interest and understanding. (P. 2)

In guidelines produced for developmentally appropriate practice, suggestions for curriculum include the following (NAEYC 1986, pp. 3–5):

■ An integrated approach that provides for all areas of a child's development—physical, emotional, social, and cognitive

■ Basing curriculum on teachers' observations and recordings of each child's special interests and developmental progress

■ Emphasizing learning as an interactive process with children learning through active exploration and interaction with adults, other children, and materials

■ Learning activities and materials that are concrete, real, and relevant to the lives of young children

■ Provision for a wider range of developmental interests and abilities than the chronological age range of the group would suggest

■ Increasing the difficulty, complexity, and challenge of an activity as children are involved with it and as children develop understanding and skills

In *Mathematics for the Young Child,* using developmentally appropriate teaching means that the child is the center of concern—the child's thoughts, the child's words, the child's actions. Instructional activities throughout this book encourage teachers to take a child-centered approach to instruction. Interactive discussions are frequently suggested. Not only are active discussions a valuable vehicle for learning; they are, for teachers of the young child, the best window to the young mind. The focus of this book is on the development of children's thinking, not on the production of sterile answers.

diagnosis and assessment

Diagnosis and assessment are ongoing parts of teaching. Initially, a separate chapter on diagnosis and assessment was planned. As the content chapters developed, it became clear that the authors were incorporating diagnosis and assessment as integral parts of teaching. All chapters include ideas for diagnosing students' strengths and weaknesses, and suggestions for using the diagnostic results in instruction are given. Consequently, the separate chapter was dropped, since the content chapters related diagnosis and assessment to the daily and ongoing process of planning and instruction.

calculator use

The view taken in this book is that *calculators should be available for use by children at all times and at all ages, even preschool and kindergarten.* Calculators can be superb instructional tools, there is no evidence at all that they do any harm, and they are an ever-present part of the society in which we live.

An ordinary four-function calculator is the best choice

for use in classes for young children. A great variety of these calculators are available. Some are a bit more useful than others for classroom instruction. Most are relatively inexpensive, making it feasible for each classroom to have its own set. One major advantage of a classroom set, especially for young children, is the ease in giving instructions on how to use the calculator.

In selecting calculators, teachers should consider their durability, ease in reading displays, ease in key stroking, and power source. Solar calculators seem to have universal appeal because battery replacement is not necessary.

Beyond the usual keys for addition, subtraction, multiplication, and division, it is especially important that calculators have a constant function for addition and subtraction. It is easy to check for this. Press 1 $\boxed{+}$ $\boxed{=}$ $\boxed{=}$ $\boxed{=}$ and see if the calculator "counts by ones." If it does not, it probably does not have the constant function. Do not choose a calculator without this constant function for addition and subtraction. The other keys, such as $\boxed{M}$ (for memory), $\boxed{\%}$, and $\boxed{\sqrt{\ }}$, are not likely to be used by grade 4, although some teachers do use the memory keys in teaching order of operations.

Calculators are useful in teaching many mathematical concepts. They help children in preschool, kindergarten, and grade 1 learn to count orally. They help children count on, count back, skip count, recognize the value of digits in multidigit numbers, practice basic facts, search for patterns, and solve problems. Many of these require the constant function feature.

The constant function is usually activated with an operation key and the equal sign, as shown by the examples in figure 4.

There are examples throughout this book showing the uses calculators have in instruction. Calculator use should lead to the reduction of tedious aspects of paper-and-pencil computation, providing more time for developing concepts and for teaching a much broader range of mathematical topics. As has been noted from major documents, much of the paper-and-pencil

	Key Strokes	Display
Count by ones	1 + = = =	1, 2, 3
Count by fives	5 + = = =	5, 10, 15
Count by twos from 1	1 + 2 = = =	3, 5, 7
Count back	10 − 1 = = =	9, 8, 7
Add 8 to any number	+ 8 =	8
	7 =	15
	100 =	108
Subtract 7 from any number	− 7 =	7 −
	10 =	3
	42 =	35
Multiply any number by 8	8 × =	64
	7 =	56
	12 =	96
Divide any number by 6	÷ 6 =	0
	18 =	3
	600 =	100
Multiply by 3 repeatedly	3 × = = =	9, 27, 81
Divide by 4 repeatedly	800 ÷ 4 = = =	200, 50, 12.5

Fig. 4. Calculator keystrokes using the constant function

computation now taught is rarely used in everyday affairs or in careers. The use of calculators can—and should—have a major impact on the mathematics curriculum.

preschool mathematics

Preschool mathematics encompasses a broad range of

content, as indicated in the various chapters of this book. All too often the mathematics done with children in preschool consists only of counting, usually in a rote fashion. Counting may extend to real objects, but rarely does one find a program with mathematics of any breadth and depth.

Young children need a program that expands and deepens their conceptual knowledge, already substantially developed by age three. They don't need worksheets—they need a mathematics world that is immersed in concrete materials, heavy with children's language, and almost devoid of symbolic, formal procedures.

Although the content of this book extends to topics for grade 4, a concerted effort was made to address the needs of preschool and kindergarten teachers. A substantial portion of most chapters includes content and strategies for children aged three to five:

■ Chapter 2 provides a rationale and suggestions for developing conceptual knowledge, applicable to content for preschool children.

■ Chapter 3 on problem solving contains many examples that can be used with preschool children. The overall approach is one that could and should characterize instruction at these early levels.

■ Chapter 4 is replete with excellent examples for concepts of number. This kind of number work should supplant the excessive attention paid to counting by ones that has characterized most preschool programs. Of special importance is building an understanding of numbers in relation to 5 and 10 and of part/whole ideas.

■ Chapter 6 presents an approach to solving practical problems using manipulatives as an initial strategy. It is clear from this chapter that preschool children can do substantially more work with practical problems than what is usually planned.

■ Chapter 9 includes suggestions for activities related to fractions that can and should be done with children in the everyday activities of almost any preschool or kindergarten.

- Chapter 10 has a variety of interesting geometric activities that extend beyond the usual practice of only naming the simple plane figures.

- Chapter 11 presents ideas that precede formal instruction in measurement, beginning with body units and moving to arbitrary units. Many of the activities can be used easily with preschool and kindergarten children.

- Chapter 12 has suggestions for beginning work with graphs, using examples from the preschool classroom.

- Chapter 13 gives suggestions for using the computer with Logo and criteria for choosing software that should be especially helpful to teachers of children three to five years of age.

- Chapter 14 presents suggestions for planning for instruction with helpful ideas on organizing and storing materials and classroom organization. Many suggestions are useful for preschools and kindergarten.

A sound preschool program is one that has all the major mathematical components from the chapters listed above. Sound mathematical concepts and good reasoning by thoughtful preschool students are good predictors for future success in mathematics. The overall goal of this book is to provide a developmental sequence for each of the content areas beginning with the knowledge of three-year-olds and extending through grade 4.

The points of view developed for preschool children are just as valid for kindergarten. Too often kindergarten has become an "early first grade" with a plethora of work sheets, desks in a row, and "serious math work." Such a program is counterproductive. Kindergarten mathematics must embody all the traits of a sound early-age program adapted for the maturing and growing child. If goals are set only in terms of children writing their numerals and counting to 30, or 100, it is probably true that the kindergarten program is barren and without merit. The kindergarten child can and should be heavily involved in an oral, interactive, broadly based program in mathematics with consistent use of manipulatives.

summary

Major forces are helping set new directions for mathematics education at the national, state and province, and local levels. The changes are necessary in preparing students who will spend their adult lives in the twenty-first century. We can no longer tolerate a curriculum and teaching methodology that were adequate fifty or a hundred years ago and are still prevalent in 1990. We must produce a curriculum and teaching methods that give learners mathematical power for use both in their own everyday affairs and in the careers they choose. With the efforts of many people, we can produce a much improved and enlightened mathematics education literacy. Our country, our states and provinces, our schools, and especially our young people deserve nothing but our best efforts. It is in response to this challenge that this book was prepared.

references

Michigan Department of Education. *Michigan Essential Goals and Objectives for Mathematics Education.* Lansing, Mich.: The Department, 1988.

————. *An Interpretation of the Michigan Essential Goals and Objectives for Mathematics Education.* Lansing, Mich.: The Department, 1989.

National Association for the Education of Young Children. *Developmentally Appropriate Practice.* Washington, D.C.: The Association, 1986.

National Council of Teachers of Mathematics. *Curriculum and Evaluation Standards for School Mathematics.* Reston, Va.: The Council, 1989.

National Research Council. *Everybody Counts: A Report to the Nation on the Future of Mathematics Education.* Washington, D.C.: National Academy Press, 1989.

james hiebert

mary lindquist

2

developing mathematical knowledge in the young child

Several first graders are sitting around a table at school. The teacher suggests that they pretend they are at a birthday party and need to share the treats. The teacher gives Susan twenty balloons and asks her to share them with three friends so that each receives the same number of balloons. Susan gives the balloons one by one to each child in turn, making several rounds until she runs out of balloons. Then she counts each friend's pile to make sure that each friend has the same number.

Later in the day, the same first graders are working in their mathematics workbooks. They are to write answers to problems like these:

```
  15        14        8        15
+  2      +  5      -  5     +  7
```

Susan remembers working these kinds of problems

before. She remembers the teacher telling the class how to write the answers for each kind of problem. She tries hard to recall the rules and remembers that the "+" sign means to add the numbers and the "−" sign means to take away. She does the first three problems quickly and then pauses momentarily on the last one. She figures that this must be like the others:

```
  15        14        8        15
+  2      +  5      -  5     +  7
  17        19        3       112
```

These two snapshots from a first-grade classroom illustrate two different types of knowledge that children acquire about mathematics. In the first episode, Susan was drawing on many experiences, both in and out of school, to solve the problem of sharing the balloons. She used her knowledge of sharing and of counting to invent a partitioning strategy to distribute the balloons. Although she may not have solved a problem just like this one before, it was similar to other situations she had experienced and it seemed solvable to her by using skills she had already developed, such as counting. An important feature of this problem is that Susan understood it. What is more, she understood the strategy that she used to solve it, in part because she devised it herself. We shall call the kind of knowledge that Susan demonstrated in this situation *conceptual knowledge.*

In the second episode, Susan was drawing on a different kind of knowledge to solve the problems. In the first place, the problems themselves were different from the one about sharing balloons at a party. These were problems that Susan had seen only in school, only in her mathematics book. Each problem was presented in its entirety with a few symbols written on paper. No stories or objects were involved. Then, too, the teacher had told them exactly what the problems meant and had given them some rules to solve them. In fact, the teacher had solved some problems exactly like these on the chalkboard. So Susan did not need to invent her own strategies; she had only to recall the rules she had been taught. It is important to note that Susan did not completely understand these problems, but she got most

of them right because she remembered the correct rule. We shall call the kind of knowledge that Susan used in this situation *procedural knowledge.*

Conceptual and procedural knowledge are two different kinds of knowledge that children acquire about mathematics. It is important to think about these two kinds of knowledge to understand how children learn mathematics and the reasons for their successes and failures in mathematics.

If students are to be successful, they must connect the two kinds of knowledge. We must help students build conceptual and procedural knowledge, we must be aware of what kinds of knowledge children are acquiring, and we must help them *connect* conceptual and procedural knowledge. To tell the whole story, we must back up a bit.

conceptual and procedural knowledge

Many noted psychologists and educators have found that in their study of children's learning, it is useful to

distinguish among different kinds of knowledge. Children learn very different kinds of things. They learn how to tie their shoelaces, and they learn what fairness means. These are different kinds of knowledge, and if we throw them together, it is easy to get confused about what happens when children learn. Piaget (1978), for example, identified two kinds of knowledge—conceptual understanding and successful action—and Vygotsky (1962) suggested the distinction between spontaneous concepts and scientific concepts.

Those who have focused on children's learning of mathematics have also found it useful to distinguish among different types of knowledge. In many instances, the distinctions capture the differences between the knowledge illustrated by the two snapshots of Susan's activities. For example, Ginsburg (1982) suggests that children acquire much *informal* knowledge of mathematics through a variety of experiences, both inside and outside school. Children cannot always express their informal knowledge precisely, but such knowledge is useful because it helps them solve problems. It is made up of intuitions, perceptual information, invented strategies, and other knowledge that has been acquired in dealing with everyday quantitative situations. *Formal* knowledge, however, is acquired largely from direct instruction in school. Formal mathematical knowledge consists of methods, procedures, or rules for solving school mathematics problems. Much of children's formal knowledge tells them how to manipulate written symbols according to step-by-step prescriptions.

A related distinction is described by Skemp (1978), who suggested that mathematics teachers often use the word *understanding* in two ways. On the one hand, its meaning is the one commonly used outside of school— students understand something if they know how and why. For example, Susan apparently understood the sharing problem. She was able to develop an appropriate strategy, and she probably knew why her strategy would work. She understood that if she distributed the balloons one by one, she would keep the numbers equal at the end of each round. Skemp refers to this kind of understanding as *relational* understanding because we can relate what we are learning to other things we know. On the other hand,

mathematics teachers sometimes say that students understand something if they just know how or if they can get the right answers. Skemp calls this *instrumental* understanding. Susan got correct answers to all problems like

$$14 \qquad \text{and} \qquad 8$$
$$\underline{+\ 5} \qquad\qquad \underline{-5}$$

because she knew the rules for these kinds of problems and applied them correctly. The rule was used like an instrument, or a tool, to solve the problems. But it appears that Susan did not understand this situation relationally because she did not understand what the problems meant or why the rules worked. If she had understood the rules, she could have adjusted them for 15 + 7. Perhaps Susan had not yet connected the rules she had memorized to other things she knew about addition, such as simple addition stories and various counting strategies.

When thinking about learning and teaching mathematics for young children, we believe it is useful to distinguish between *conceptual knowledge* and *procedural knowledge* (Hiebert and Lefevre 1986). Conceptual knowledge is knowledge that is rich in relationships. It can be thought of as a connected web, where every piece of information is related or connected to other pieces of information. Students acquire conceptual knowledge if they can fit a new piece of information with something they already know or if they suddenly recognize a connection between things that they previously learned as isolated pieces of information. When Susan was introduced to 15 + 7, it is likely that she was pretty good at counting and that she could solve problems like "John has 15 balloons. He gets 7 more. How many does John have then?" (Carpenter and Moser 1984). If Susan had recognized the connections among 15 + 7, the story situation, and counting on 7 from 15, she would have acquired a new piece of conceptual knowledge and then solved the problem correctly.

Procedural knowledge, in contrast, is made up mostly of rules, procedures, or algorithms for performing mathematical tasks. Procedures are step-by-step prescriptions that generate correct answers for particular kinds of problems. Some procedures are simple one- or two-step prescriptions, and others are quite complicated. As an example of a simple procedure, students might learn that to solve all problems like $3 + 5 = \square$, they add the first two numbers and write the result in the box. This becomes part of their procedural knowledge even if they have no idea what situation the number sentence represents or what the $+$, $=$, and $\square$ symbols mean. In other words, procedures can be learned in isolation from other things the students might know.

Both conceptual knowledge and procedural knowledge are important, and both can be learned in school. The kind of knowledge that is acquired depends to a great extent on the kind of instructional activities that are provided. Instruction can be designed to help students build conceptual knowledge, or it can be designed to help students acquire procedures. We believe that instruction should do both. But more than that, instruction should be designed to help students see connections between the two kinds of knowledge.

consequences of not connecting concepts and procedures

The evidence from research reported in the past decade suggests that we are not doing enough to help students connect concepts with procedures. Most students acquire procedural knowledge separately from conceptual knowledge. Large-scale surveys (Hart 1981; Kouba et al. 1988a, 1988b) and close-up analyses of individual topic areas (Davis and McKnight 1980; Hiebert and Wearne 1986; Schoenfeld 1986; VanLehn 1983) converge toward the same conclusion: *Many students learn rules and procedures for performing tasks with virtually no idea of what the problem means, why the procedure works, or whether the answer is reasonable.* Two examples from the most recent mathematics results from the National Assessment of Educational Progress (Kouba, Carpenter, and Swafford 1989) illustrate the point. First, fewer third graders could name the number that is 10 more than 98 (61% correct) than could add two-digit numbers with regrouping (84% correct). This finding suggests that

some students are learning rules for manipulating symbols without understanding the quantitative meaning of the symbols. A second example is shown in figure 1. About half the third graders believed that $49 + 83 = 132$ is equivalent to $49 = 83 + 132$, and fewer than one-third recognized the inverse relationship between addition and subtraction. Clearly, students were working with symbolic expressions that they do not understand.

Why should we worry if students memorize rules and procedures without connecting them to their conceptual knowledge? If students can apply a rule to solve a problem and get a correct answer, do they need to know why the rule works or what the rule is doing for them? It happens that learning rules and procedures without understanding them has many serious consequences. Many of these consequences are long term and do not show up immediately. It might look as if students are doing well, but it is likely that they are experiencing as yet undetected difficulties. These difficulties will eventually cause serious problems. Difficulties showing up by the seventh grade on items in the National Assessment (Kouba et al. 1988a, 1988b), for example, may have begun much earlier, possibly in the primary grades. Research in the psychology of learning offers some explanation for these difficulties.

If $49 + 83 = 132$ is true

which of the following are true?

	percentage of third graders responding
$49 = 83 + 132$	52
$49 + 132 = 83$	13
$132 - 49 = 83$	29
$83 - 132 = 49$	7

Fig. 1. Performance on a number-sentence item in NAEP

memory

Isolated procedures are difficult to remember. One reason that learning procedures without connecting them to meaningful conceptual knowledge causes problems is that procedures are more difficult to remember for very long if they are learned as isolated pieces of information. A well-documented finding in psychology is that it is easier to remember things that make sense (Chase and Simon 1973; Chi 1978). What this means is that it is easier to remember things that are connected to other knowledge one has already acquired. They are easier to remember because there are more ways to retrieve the information from memory. For example, suppose students are learning to add decimal numbers and the teacher says, "When you add decimal numbers, you must first line up the decimal points." If this information is all that students acquire about setting up decimal-addition problems, the "line up the decimal points" rule will be stored in memory as an isolated piece of information. Remembering it will depend on retracing a single mental path from the perceptual recognition of a written addition problem involving decimals, for example, 3.4 + 2.17, to the rule prescribing how to set up the problem. However, if students also learn that the concept underlying the procedure is the adding together of things that are alike, and if they recognize how this procedure is the same as what happens when they add whole numbers or common fractions, they are more likely to remember the rule. Several mental paths lead to the rule for adding decimals: for example, thinking about ideas of place value, common denominators, or the relative sizes of quantities. In fact, if students recognize these kinds of connections to conceptual knowledge, they probably could "reinvent" the rule if they forget it.

transfer

Isolated procedures do not transfer well. A second reason that students experience difficulty if they acquire procedural knowledge separately from conceptual knowledge can be illustrated with another example. Imagine that students are learning multidigit subtraction

for the first time. If only procedures are taught, lessons might be developed as shown in figure 2.

Then a problem like 40 − 24 might be presented, along with a somewhat different procedure for handling this type of problem. Different procedures would also be described for solving problems like 302 − 185, 300 − 42, 413 − 189, and so on. The trouble with this kind of instruction is that if the rules are taught as prescriptions for manipulating symbols, with little discussion of their meaning or how they are

46 − 21 = ☐

Write 21 under 46.   46
Subtract right to left.   − 21
6 − 1 = 5.   5

                                   46
                                 − 21
4 − 2 = 2. Write 2.   25

63 − 28 = ☐

This problem is different
and requires different rules:

                                   63
Write 28 under 63.   − 28

You can't do 3 − 8.   5
Cross out 6.   ̶6̶3
Take 1 from 6 and make it 5.   − 28

                                   51
                                   ̶6̶3
Put 1 with 3 to make 13.   − 28
Subtract 8 from 13. Write 5.   5

                                   51
                                   ̶6̶3
                                 − 28
Subtract 2 from 5. Write 3.   35

Fig. 2. Example of teaching only procedures

alike, students will tend to link each rule to the specific kind of problem for which it was developed. If the procedures are taught as different rules for different problems, it is likely that students will use a particular rule only for one kind of problem. They will not see how a rule can be changed or modified to solve a related problem. This means that when a new problem is encountered, 4123 − 581, for example, students will not be able to use what they already know to solve the problem but will need to be taught a new rule.

An alternative instructional approach that promotes transfer of procedures is to connect a whole set of related procedures to the conceptual ideas that lie behind them. All the subtraction examples just cited can be viewed as taking away one set of hundreds, tens, and ones from another set, with some "trading" where needed (see fig. 3). The different subtraction procedures can be connected to the basic conceptual ideas of place value and subtraction.

In general terms, the reason that this alternative instructional approach encourages the transfer of a procedure from one problem to another is that it helps students understand why the procedure works. It has been recognized for some time that if procedures are understood or learned in a meaningful way, they transfer more easily to related problems (Brownell 1947; Dewey 1910). But we now understand a little more about why this is true. Problems that are related share some conceptual components. For example, all two-digit subtraction problems involve taking tens and ones away from tens and ones. If we say that students understand a procedure, we usually mean that they see the connection between the procedure and its conceptual basis. In 63 − 28, changing 3 to 13 and 6 to 5 is just a record of what happens when you trade a 10 for ten 1's in order to take away some more 1's. Students then are able to see how the procedure they learned for one form of a problem might be used for another form. They can mentally follow the conceptual paths that connect the different forms of problems (Greeno 1983). So the procedure becomes linked to a variety of problems—it "transfers" from one problem to another. Conceptual knowledge releases the procedure from the surface context or the form in which it was learned and encourages its use on conceptually related problems.

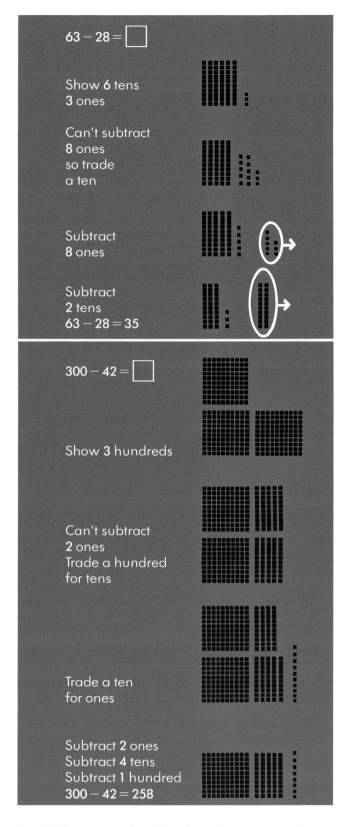

Fig. 3. Relating procedures for subtraction to conceptual ideas

many individual procedures

There are too many procedures to learn them individually. A direct consequence of learning procedures as isolated rules that are locked to specific kinds of problems is that different rules must be learned for different problems. If, for example, the procedure for solving 63 − 28 is taught as a narrow rule for only that kind of problem, students probably will not see how to use the rule to solve 40 − 24 or 413 − 189. Then, as student move from one kind of problem to another, for example, from 63 − 28 to 40 − 24, they must recall and apply different rules. But there are simply too many different kinds of problems in mathematics for students to learn and remember different rules for each kind.

The alternative instructional approach suggested previously alleviates this difficulty by actually reducing the number of separate rules that must be learned. Instruction can be designated to show how all the different subtraction problems can be solved by the same "core" procedure. The different rules can then be seen as minor variations of the core procedure. Organizing procedural knowledge in this way

increases the likelihood that it will be remembered because there is less to remember.

choosing correct procedures

It is difficult to remember when to use which procedure. A fourth reason that students experience difficulty when they learn only procedures is that it is difficult for them to remember which procedures go with which problems. Even if students remember the rule itself, they may have trouble deciding when to use it. If they have not established connections between a procedure and the concepts on which it is based, their conceptual knowledge is of no help. This is unfortunate because students' conceptual knowledge can serve as a useful monitor by prompting them about which procedure is appropriate for a given problem (Gelman and Meck 1986; Piaget 1978) and by warning them that a procedure about to be used is inappropriate (Gelman 1982; Greeno 1980). Consider again our student who is learning to subtract. Suppose the student encounters

$$\begin{array}{r} 50 \\ -26 \end{array}$$

The most common error is to write a 6 in the ones place and subtract 2 from 5 to get 36 for the answer (Ashlock 1986; Brown and Burton 1978). This procedure would be rejected, however, if the student understood the appropriate procedure because the incorrect procedure does not represent the action of removing 26 items from 50 items. The same conceptual knowledge that would warn against using the inappropriate procedure also would reinforce the choice of the appropriate procedure. To begin removing 26 items from 50 items, we can unbundle or trade a set of 10 and remove 6 items.

power of procedures

Procedures are sometimes too powerful. One reason that we teach students procedures and rules for manipulating symbols is that these techniques are very powerful. We can solve time-consuming and difficult real-world problems with relative ease by representing the problem with symbols and manipulating them. Indeed, the real power of mathematics lies in the fact that we can work with very complicated ideas by moving a few symbols around on paper. For example, suppose we are planning a field trip for all the second-grade classes and need to ask enough parents to drive cars. We know that 98 students are in the second grade and that each car will hold 4 students. How many cars do we need? One way to figure this out would be to bring all the students onto the playground and count them off in groups of 4. Another way is to write 98 ÷ 4 and work the problem on paper or on a calculator. This second method is quicker and more convenient. In some situations, the problems get so complicated that not only is it quicker to solve them with symbols but it is nearly the only way to solve them.

Because procedures for symbols are so powerful and because they can be learned separately from conceptual knowledge, procedures can take students far beyond their level of understanding. Students can memorize rules for solving problems that they don't understand. The trouble is that if students do not understand the problem or exercise and why the rule they are using works or what it is doing for them, they have no way of knowing when to use the rule. They have no way of knowing whether their answer makes sense or of monitoring their own performance.

If students have not connected procedures with their conceptual knowledge, the procedures can quickly take them beyond their conceptual understanding. In the primary grades, addition and subtraction algorithms encourage students to solve number problems larger than those they have had an opportunity to think about in a real-world or conceptual context. Later, when students are asked to do long-division problems, even simple ones like 98 ÷ 4, many students have little idea of what the quotient means or how to interpret the remainder (Silver 1986). Teachers probably can think of many situations in which students memorize rules for completing exercises and solving problems and even get correct answers but have little idea what the problem means or whether their answers are reasonable.

Sending students ahead procedurally without making sure their conceptual knowledge is progressing equally well widens the gap between the kinds of knowledge and reinforces the damaging effects described earlier.

attitudes and beliefs

Destructive attitudes and beliefs are promoted. Up to this point, we have been talking about the cognitive effects of separating conceptual and procedural knowledge. It appears that such a separation has important affective consequences as well. Doyle (1983; 1988) points out that the kind of work students do in classrooms determines how they think about the subject and what they recognize as being important. If students are asked to spend much of their time learning and practicing procedures for manipulating symbols, independent of conceptual considerations, we might expect students to believe that mathematics is a matter of remembering the right rules and checking the answer key. Apparently, this is exactly what many of them believe. Many students see mathematics only as symbols on paper (Mason 1987) and believe that their job is to remember and follow the rules for operating on the symbols (Kouba et al. 1988a). They believe that symbols and rules have little to do with their intuitions, their ideas of what makes sense, or their conceptual understanding (Hiebert and Wearne 1986; Schoenfeld 1986).

These beliefs are destructive because they take mathematics away from students. Mathematics becomes something that cannot be understood, a subject that is separated from real life and from things outside the classroom that make sense. It is a subject for which they become completely dependent on someone else. Mathematics class is a time when students are given problems by the teacher or in the text that they don't entirely understand, when they recall and apply little-understood rules to solve them, and when their answers are checked by an authority. Students feel little control over anything mathematical, and that, they believe, is the nature of mathematics. Think again about Susan distributing the balloons and then working the addition and subtraction problems. We hope that it is clear that although destructive beliefs may not be promoted by the context of the party problem, they might be promoted in the symbolic context. Whether or not such problems are created depends on how well students are able to connect their conceptual knowledge to the procedures they are asked to learn.

instruction to build concepts and relate concepts to procedures

Students do not connect concepts and procedures automatically. In fact, it appears that they are naturally inclined to keep things separate. The human mind has a strong tendency to associate something recently learned with the context in which it is learned (Bruner 1973). Things learned in a particular context are often tied initially to surface features of that context. This means that the knowledge is not accessed or applied unless the current context matches that in which it was acquired. This learning phenomenon results in a tendency for students to store knowledge in separate "mental compartments" and to recognize a particular

compartment's knowledge as useful only when they see problems just like those for which they originally acquired the knowledge. This compartmentalization is illustrated well by Lawler's (1981) description of a six-year-old child learning to add and subtract. During the course of the year, the six-year-old encountered addition and subtraction problems in different situations both in and out of school. She learned to add and subtract in school using the standard procedures for working problems on paper. She added and subtracted numbers in her head when she worked with Logo in an after-school program, and she sometimes added and subtracted with money in the toy store. Different methods were learned or invented in each context, and the methods remained faithful to the context in which they were acquired. Money methods were used only with money, Logo methods with Logo, and paper-and-pencil methods with paper and pencil.

The tendency to compartmentalize knowledge seems to affect procedural knowledge especially hard. Conceptual knowledge, by definition, is knowledge that is not overly compartmentalized but rather is connected in various ways. Procedural knowledge, however, is knowledge that *can* be acquired as isolated bits. Because students do not automatically connect procedures with concepts, special attention must be given during instruction to building conceptual knowledge and connecting it to procedures.

building conceptual knowledge

Teaching students to build their conceptual knowledge means teaching in a way that helps them connect new information with things they already know. This requires that opportunities be provided for students to recognize relationships between the new information they are learning and ideas that they already understand. Discovering relationships and making connections is time consuming and requires a good deal of mental effort. So, more instructional time is needed to help students build conceptual knowledge of major mathematical ideas.

Many important concepts in elementary school

mathematics are related, which means that spending time on developing one concept will help students construct knowledge that can be connected to other concepts. For example, an important idea about numbers, developed in kindergarten and first grade, is that they can be decomposed into smaller numbers, each of which can be thought of as *part* of the *whole*. The number 9 can be thought of as composed of 5 and 4, or 2 and 1 and 6, or many other combinations (see chapter 4). The concept of part and whole is important not only for students' understanding of smaller numbers but also because of its connection to later concepts of numbers, such as place value (see chapter 5), operations (see chapter 6), and fractions (see chapter 9). Other major ideas in elementary school mathematics include concepts of geometry, such as the variety of attributes on which figures can be compared (see chapter 10) and concepts of measurement, such as the crucial role of the unit in all measuring situations (see chapter 11).

Instruction that helps students build these concepts has some important common characteristics. As noted earlier, the goal of such instruction is to provide opportunities for students to recognize connections between the new ideas they are encountering and familiar ideas with which they are comfortable. But, we can be more specific than this.

One way of thinking about how connections between ideas are made is to think of the number of ways in which mathematical ideas can be represented. Lesh, Post, and Behr (1987) suggest five ways in which mathematical ideas are commonly represented: (1) through language; (2) through real-life experiences that occur inside and outside of school; (3) by physical materials, such as base-ten blocks, craft sticks, and fraction bars; (4) by pictures; and (5) by written symbols. Often a particular mathematical concept can be represented in all five ways, but sometimes some representations are more helpful than others to students who are trying to see relationships between a new concept and concepts they already understand. Representations that draw on real-life experiences or that use physical materials connect most easily to young children's prior knowledge. Therefore, instruction designed to help children build their conceptual knowledge should initially present concepts by placing them in familiar real-life contexts and by representing them with physical materials.

Children's conceptual understanding of an idea grows as they see how the idea can be represented in all five ways. As different ways of representing the idea are created (by the teacher *and* students), the students should see the connections among the representations and be able to translate from one representation to another. The written symbol is an especially important and powerful form of representation in mathematics, but it should be presented only within the context of other representations. Connections between the written symbols and the other forms of representation should always be clear.

Tasks that encourage or require students to connect representations of a mathematical idea involve higher-level cognitive processes than tasks that aim to increase the efficiency of performing with a single representation. For example, looking for ways in which the method of solving 43 − 19 with craft sticks is the same as (and different from) solving 43 − 19 with written symbols requires considerable thought and reflection. But practicing written problems like 43 − 19 so that one can become faster at executing the algorithm makes fewer demands on higher-level processes. This means that teachers must encourage students to spend the time and mental effort needed to make connections and must actively support their attempts to do so.

In summary, instruction can help students build their conceptual knowledge by considering the ways in which concepts are represented in instructional lessons. New concepts should be presented in familiar real-life situations and with physical materials so students can connect the new ideas with things they already know. Concepts should then be developed by representing them in different ways. Instruction should focus on helping students think about the different representations, discuss their differences and similarities, and translate from one to the other. Such instruction takes more time than is usually allowed for presenting new concepts, but it has powerful consequences in the long run.

connecting concepts and procedures

Procedures in school mathematics often are rules that prescribe how to manipulate symbols to get correct answers. These are the procedures that students often learn by rote, unconnected to concepts they already understand. But instruction can be designed to help students connect procedures and concepts.

Connections to concepts can be made at three points in the execution of a procedure (Hiebert 1984, 1988). Consider an example, such as 4 × 23. To complete this problem, first we interpret the symbol and decide what rule or procedure to use, then carry out the procedure, and finally present our answer. At each of these points we can connect procedural knowledge with conceptual knowledge. At the first point, we can connect the written symbols with the quantities or actions they represent. Perhaps the second numeral is connected with a mental image of 2 groups of ten and 3 individual blocks, and the "×" symbol is connected with the action of making groups of 23 (see fig. 4).

Connections between numerical symbols and concrete representations of quantities will already have been made if instruction helped students build conceptual knowledge of place value and multidigit numbers when they were first introduced. At the second point, connections can be made between the manipulations of the written symbols and parallel actions on physical materials that represent the quantities. For example, connections can be made between the actions of making 4 groups of 23 blocks and regrouping the blocks to count the total and the action of multiplying the written symbols

        23
    ×   4.

When these connections are made, students understand why the written procedure works. At the third point, connections can be made between the written answer and estimates of a reasonable answer. Because 23 is almost 25, the answer to 4 × 23 is close to 4 × 25. Students might think of 4 quarters and realize that the answer to 4 × 23 must be close to 100. Connections at this point help students monitor their own performance.

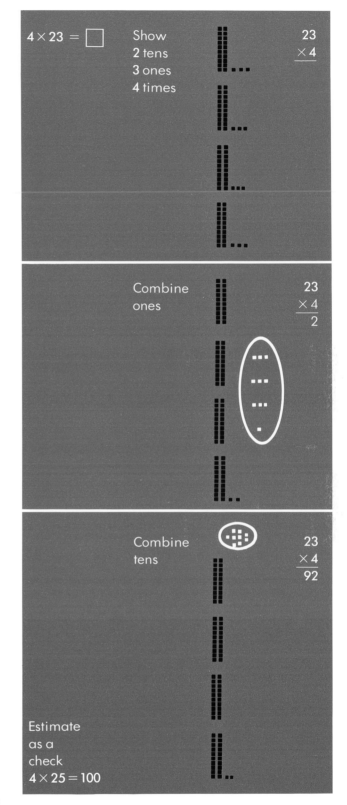

Fig. 4. Relating multiplication procedures to conceptual ideas

Connections between conceptual and procedural knowledge result in procedures that can be used meaningfully and that are not easily forgotten. The connections produce procedures that avoid the pitfalls of procedures that are memorized in isolation. Connections between conceptual and procedural knowledge also ensure a solid foundation from which children can continue to develop competence in mathematics.

We have suggested some general guidelines that can be used for designing instruction that assists students in building conceptual knowledge and in connecting their conceptual knowledge with mathematical procedures. To help the reader begin thinking about the specifics of these guidelines and how they might work in classroom settings, we shall suggest some particular features of instruction that are consistent with the guidelines.

effective classroom instruction

What are classrooms like if the primary goal is to help students build and connect conceptual and procedural knowledge? The features presented here that describe such classrooms are not independent of each other. The blending of these features is as important as the features themselves.

concepts

Concepts are developed. A central theme of this chapter is the importance of connecting conceptual and procedural knowledge. But students must possess a rich base of conceptual knowledge to make connections to procedures. Often conceptual knowledge is neglected or underemphasized in the mathematics classroom. It is not a simple task to help children gain the needed conceptual knowledge and all the required conceptual knowledge is not necessarily acquired before related procedural knowledge. The process is often interactive. Nor is all conceptual knowledge directly related to procedural knowledge. Many concepts are not tied to

procedures. For example, much of the geometry learned in the early years is conceptual with few, if any, procedures to be learned.

Since building conceptual knowledge is a high priority, classes are filled with activities that allow children to develop a wide variety of concepts. Number activities are still the heart of the curriculum. Since children need to develop a strong number sense, they spend time developing many meanings of, and relationships among, numbers. For example, "eight" means eight separate objects, 5 plus 3, one more than 7, or a number less than 10. Larger numbers have similar meanings but also have meanings related to place value. Similarly, operations have a variety of meanings. Children not only solve the sentence $8 - 3 = \square$ but also can tell what the sentence means or what types of situations it represents.

Children need to have the opportunity to develop spatial sense as they learn geometric concepts. Today, children are often able only to name selected examples of geometric figures. In place of this superficial learning, children in conceptual development classes identify and produce exemplars and nonexemplars of geometric concepts, compare and contrast geometric

figures, examine relationships among sets of figures, and explore properties of given figures.

This type of learning is exemplified by the following vignette from a second-grade classroom. Each child compares a four-sided geoboard figure with another child's and tells one way the shapes are alike and one way they are different. Look at figure 5 and listen to the class as they discuss Brad's and Jill's shapes.

- "Jill's has more pegs on it."
  "They both have one peg inside."
  "Jill's is bigger. It's four squares and Brad's is two, three, three and a half."
  "The sides of Jill's are all the same. Brad's aren't."
  "Brad's has one square corner. Jill's has four."
  "Brad's slants. Jill's is straight up and down."
  "Jill's is in the center. Brad's is on the side, sort of."
  "If you turn Jill's upside down it looks the same, but Brad's would point down rather than up."
  "Brad's has a side longer than Jill's."
  "Neither uses any pegs in the bottom row. Or in the right column."
  "It would take three 'moves' to make Brad's look like Jill's."
  "But it wouldn't be in the same place as Jill's."
  "Does Brad's have a special name?"

It is evident that the children in this class have had many opportunities to look at geometric figures and their properties and that the teacher is receptive to many observations.

Experiences must also be provided to develop concepts in measurement, probability, statistics, and other topics. These topics, as well as number, operations, and geometry concepts, are elaborated on in other chapters of this book.

models

Models are used. One of the initial meaningful ways for children to represent mathematical ideas is with

physical materials. Thus, it is essential that classes for the young child provide such materials and appropriate experiences with the materials. This means that the preschool is alive with materials to help children develop concepts. There are common, everyday materials that children can sort, count, and otherwise investigate. Some materials, such as different-sized blocks and containers, enable children to develop

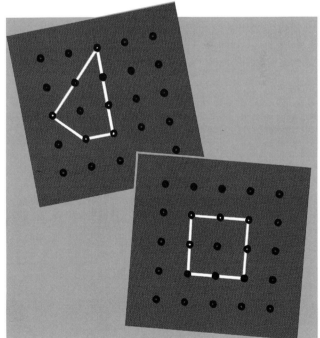

Fig. 5. Geoboard activity in grade 2

measurement concepts, and other materials, such as shapes and puzzles, can help develop geometric concepts. In preschool, the purpose of many activities is determined by the child.

In the early years of school, materials can also be used to model mathematical concepts and procedures. At these levels, some materials are special models or manipulatives that directly characterize the mathematical ideas involved. Children should feel free to use the models to explore mathematical ideas, but often the purpose is structured by the teacher. For example, children can be asked to find different ways to represent 37 with base-ten blocks. Figure 6 shows some ways that children found when challenged to make at least two different representations. The purpose of this activity is to build flexibility in the way 37 (or any other number) can be seen.

Although concrete or physical materials generally are more powerful than pictures at an early age, pictures are also one of the common representations of mathematical ideas. Children are encouraged to draw and to interpret pictures as they are developing concepts and procedures.

oral language

Oral language is encouraged. As children represent mathematical ideas with models, it is natural for them to talk about these models and what they are doing with them. This process leads to the representation of the mathematical ideas through language. In our mathematics classroom, children talk, listen, write, and read. Along with the visual or perceptual images they build with physical materials, they develop a language to describe mathematical concepts and procedures. This language begins with, and grows from, experiences; instruction does not begin with words alone without the experiences that give meaning to the words. Gradually, mathematical language is developed. For example, children might begin by describing a given figure as a square "pushed over" and later learn that it is a rhombus.

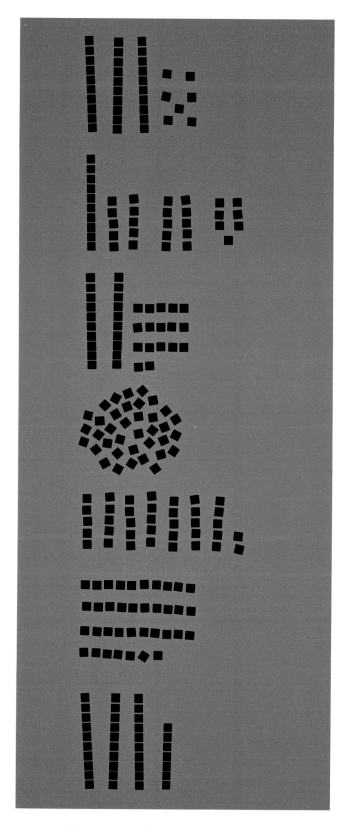

Fig. 6. Different ways to show 37 with base-ten blocks

In the classroom we have described, questions are central to instruction. The questions are designed to help children make connections and think through problems and to help a teacher ascertain the knowledge of the children.

The children, as well as the teacher, are actively asking questions of themselves and of each other. One type of question concerns the reasonableness of answers. For numerical computations, this judgment of reasonableness relies on number and operation sense, not solely on a set procedure such as rounding. Another type of question concerns whether similarities or differences exist among problems. Another type of question is a self-monitoring process: "Am I on the right track? Do I have enough information? Have I seen a problem like this before?"

symbols

Symbols are developed carefully. Symbols are introduced as a way to describe something a child already knows. Too often, a symbol is introduced without sufficient prior experiences, and children do not understand what is being represented. This makes the symbol just a mark on paper, without a referent, and children must rely on a multitude of procedures to handle it. Consider, for example, the equal sign. It is often introduced with addition as a replacement for the implied phrase "find the answer." Little time is spent building the concept of equality or helping students understand that the equal sign is a way to represent the same amount on each side. The lack of this understanding alone would present students with difficulty in solving a sentence such as $2 + \square = 8$. Without a conceptual knowledge of equality, students cannot link the procedures they know with the sentence they are solving.

Children need a variety of experiences in representing the ideas they are learning. For example, in the modeling of 37, it is important to describe the different representations with words and then with symbols or with a mixture of words and symbols, as shown in figure 7.

Teachers can help children understand that the same symbol or groups of symbols can represent many different ideas. For example, $2 + \square = 8$ can represent a comparison (Jim has 2 marbles. Ed has 8 marbles. How many more marbles does Ed have than Jim?), a joining situation (Lois had 2 toy horses. Her father gave her some more. She now has 8. How many did her father give her?), or a part-whole situation (There are 8 marbles. Two of them are green and the others are red. How many are red?). Later, children come to understand that regardless of the situation represented by $2 + \square = 8$, they can

3 tens and 7 ones *or*
$3 \times 10 + 7$

1 ten and 27 **ones** *or*
$1 \times 10 + 27$

2 tens and 17 ones *or*
$2 \times 10 + 17$

37 ones

7 groups of five
and 2 more

3 groups of 10
and 7

4 groups of 10
less 3

Fig. 7. Representing base-ten blocks with written symbols

Developing Mathematical Knowledge in the Young Child   31

operate on the symbols mathematically. Without this careful development of the symbols, mathematics will continue to be a series of rules, and even tricks, for many children.

By using the concrete models to guide the development of procedures with symbols, students are likely to connect concepts and procedures—they are also likely to see why the procedures work.

procedures

Procedures are connected to concepts. The previous discussion makes it clear that the curriculum should include more than procedures, but in the teaching of procedures, the connections to conceptual knowledge need to be made explicit and students need opportunities to establish these connections for themselves. The succeeding chapters will give a variety of illustrations of how to do this. In setting the scene for these chapters, we want to highlight several important principles that should guide the teaching of procedures, especially computational procedures.

First, students should learn a procedure by performing actions on the same physical models or referents used to develop the meaning of the symbols. For example, if multidigit numerals have been associated with sticks bundled in tens and hundreds, then the addition algorithm should be discussed using bundled sticks.

Second, the moves that are made with the models to solve the problem should parallel those made with the symbols. That is, as children work with the models, their actions should be represented, at each step, by the symbols. Children should see that the actions on the symbols are merely a way to tell what they are doing with the models. For example, in adding 38 + 24, the first step is to represent the numbers with manipulatives. This is recorded by writing each of the numerals 38 and 24 next to its concrete representation. The next step is to combine the individual blocks, trading 10 of them for a long stick, and place the long stick on top of the other tens. This action is recorded by writing a 2 for the remaining individual blocks in the ones place and writing a 1 for the long stick at the top of the tens column. Of course, discussion would make clear that 12 is the sum of 8 and 4 and that 12 means 2 ones and 1 ten. Parallel actions on the blocks and sticks and the symbols are continued until the problem is solved.

relationships and connections

Relationships and connections are sought and encouraged. A rich environment, along with the encouragement of investigation, helps young children see relationships and make many connections. For example, they begin to understand that pouring a large container of water into a smaller container, no matter what the size of the containers, makes the smaller one overflow. This, in turn, is like trying to fit a long, skinny block into a short space. For older children, more emphasis should be placed on looking for relationships among ideas, contrasting them, and looking for similarities.

Let's look at an example. A small group of third-grade children were trying to solve a real-life problem as they planned for a district-wide carnival.

■ *Al:* Mrs. Lyle said there were 3294 third-grade students and 2973 fourth-grade students in our school district.

Bea: And suppose we sell one balloon to each. How many will we need? Do you think we can sell one to everyone?

Tran: We need to add, but we haven't added numbers like that.

Bea: But we know 3294 is more than 3 thousand and 2973 is almost 3 thousand. So I say we need 6 thousand.

Al: Are you sure that's enough? Let's see—we can add 294 and 973. [Stops to add with pencil and paper.] That's 1267. So it's 1 thousand and 267 more. So it's 3 thousand, 2 thousand, and this, or 6 thousand and 267 more. So we better order 7 thousand.

Tran: How much will that cost?

Sue: Well, it says we can get 500 balloons for $21. But what about 7000?

Al: We could ask Mrs. Lyle.

Bea: But she said we should figure it out.

Tran: Let's draw a picture. (See fig. 8.) Oh, that means 1 thousand is $42. And we need 7 thousand.

Sue: That's seven of the $42. I wish I had a calculator. (She stops to add 42 + 42 + 42 + 42 + 42 + 42 + 42.) Wow, that's $294. Maybe we shouldn't buy that many.

Notice how the children were relying on their

Fig. 8. Picture to help solve a problem

conceptual knowledge of number and operations. They were making relationships between this problem and simple, similar ones they had solved before.

involvement

Children are actively involved. If children are actively involved, they do and talk about mathematics and, more important, they are active thinkers. They know why procedures work and how to use them. Reconsider the example of the third-grade students who were trying to determine the cost of the balloons. At each step the children were thinking actively.

Encouraging children to think in mathematics has many long-term benefits. There will be times when a group of children does not make much progress with a problem such as the balloon problem, and they will need the teacher's help. However, it is essential for teachers to expect all young children to think and even to struggle some. There are students in middle schools and secondary school mathematics who do not believe they have to think in mathematics class. They have been conditioned to "tell me how," to want only a rule, and to give immediate, quick answers. Young children can and do think, and it is the responsibility of teachers to keep them thinking.

Management in such a classroom can be more challenging because it is not always clear in what direction the child will proceed. This does not mean, however, that no goals or plans can be established. On the contrary, the teacher must take an active role in structuring experiences that will lead to the desired outcomes.

assessment

Assessment includes concepts, not just procedures. In such a classroom, it is essential to know how children are thinking. For example, do they understand the procedures? Can they link one representation of a mathematical idea with another representation of that idea? Assessment is an integral part of instruction.

Teachers can use a variety of techniques—asking many oral questions, observing the actions of students working with models, and having children show or tell why a procedure works.

Consider this short interchange between a child and her teacher.

- *Cathy:* Nine minus four, that's five, isn't it?

  Mr. Barker: How did you think about this?

  Cathy: Well, I thought about getting blocks, but then I thought—it's nine, seven, five.

What do we know about Cathy? Does she have a concept of subtraction? Even in this brief encounter, the teacher can learn much about her knowledge. Is she beyond counting all the blocks? Does she have a way to think about nine? Is she confident? Do you think that Mr. Barker was helping to build her confidence?

Assessment of children's mathematical competencies must evaluate children's conceptual knowledge and the connections they have made between concepts and procedures. It is tempting to test only procedures, such as computational skills, because the items are easy to make up and the answers can be marked quickly.

It is more difficult to design tasks that measure conceptual knowledge and the links between concepts and procedures. Teachers might need to talk with children, perhaps individually or in small groups, to probe their understanding of concepts and procedures. Asking students to explain what they are thinking with the aid of familiar concrete representations reveals much about their conceptual knowledge. Some students, like Cathy, can reveal their thinking with simple verbal explanations. The point is that if we value conceptual knowledge and its connections with procedures, we must convey its importance to students by assessing it as well as teaching it.

We have described several features of a classroom in which children build and link concepts and procedures. In such a classroom, children know what it means to do mathematics. This does not imply that they always have a procedure at hand or even that they have an answer for every problem. But it does imply that the children

know how to approach problems and are willing to think, try, and ask why. They are confident children who know they *can do* mathematics.

summary

Before entering school, young children engage in a variety of activities that involve quantities and spatial relations. Through these everyday experiences, children develop many simple but useful mathematical understandings. They also develop simple procedures or strategies for solving problems. A striking feature of children's knowledge at this point is that the procedures they develop are based on their understanding. Young children don't solve problems they don't understand.

Children's intuitive informal strategies and procedures have some limitations. Although children understand their self-invented procedures and those procedures are useful for solving simple problems, they are cumbersome and sometimes inadequate for solving more complex problems. School instruction in mathematics should help students develop more powerful and efficient ways of representing and solving problems. Think about Susan one last time and her problem of sharing twenty balloons with her friends. Her invented strategy of sharing one by one and checking by counting worked fine for this problem. But suppose that in sixth grade, she is put in charge of distributing treats for a school party. There are 346 students and the school has purchased 23 bags of candy, 12 of which have 75 pieces each and 11 of which have 100 pieces each. Susan needs to share them equally. Although Susan's one-by-one sharing strategy would work, it would be very tedious. Mathematics instruction in school is about assisting Susan in developing efficient procedures for solving problems like this one.

The danger is that if the new, more powerful and more efficient procedures are introduced apart from what is meaningful for children, their benefits are lost. If Susan learns the procedures for multiplying and dividing numbers on paper or on a calculator but does not see that these procedures can be used to solve her candy-distribution problem, they are of no use. To be useful, children must understand what the procedures do for them. In other words, children must understand the concepts that lie behind the procedures, and they must connect these concepts to the procedures.

During the primary grades, the knowledge students acquire is the foundation for later learning in mathematics. We believe that activities that help students acquire conceptual and procedural knowledge in a tightly connected way are most beneficial.

Helping students connect conceptual and procedural knowledge requires an investment of time up front, and the really significant payoffs may not become evident immediately. This means that teachers must take a long-term view. But it is not always easy to see the long-term benefits of good instruction. Most teachers teach in graded schools and see their students only for a year. Often, they teach the same grade every year, and it can be difficult to expand one's view and see beyond the boundaries of the nine-month term. It can also be difficult to spend time helping students to understand something, to invent and develop solution strategies, and to see why a particular procedure works, when these efforts may not produce their most visible results until the students are sitting in another class, several years later. It is natural for teachers to want to see immediate results. A change of mind and a certain courage are required to invest time now for the long run. It is hoped that this chapter and this book provide the encouragement and support for doing just that.

In this chapter, we have provided a rationale for setting up a classroom that assists students in building and connecting conceptual and procedural knowledge. But more than that, we have tried to provide support for teachers who have the courage to design such a classroom, a classroom with long-term benefits for their students. The other chapters in this book continue this process by describing instructional strategies and acivities with the same goals.

references

Ashlock, Robert B. *Error Patterns in Computation.* 4th ed. Columbus, Ohio: Merrill Publishing Co., 1986.

Brown, John S., and Richard R. Burton. "Diagnostic Model for Procedural Bugs in Basic Mathematical Skills." *Cognitive Science* 2 (1978): 155–92.

Brownell, William A. "The Place of Meaning in the Teaching of Arithmetic." *Elementary School Journal* 47 (January 1947): 256–65.

Bruner, Jerome S., *Beyond the Information Given.* New York: W. W. Norton & Co., 1973.

Carpenter, Thomas P., and James M. Moser. "The Acquisition of Addition and Subtraction Concepts in Grades One through Three." *Journal for Research in Mathematics Education* 15 (May 1984): 179–202.

Chase, William G., and Herbert A. Simon. "The Mind's Eye in Chess." In *Visual Information Processing,* edited by William G. Chase. New York: Academic Press, 1973.

Chi, Michelene. "Knowledge Structures and Memory Development." In *Children's Thinking: What Develops?* edited by Robert Siegler, pp. 73–96. Hillsdale, N.J.: Lawrence Erlbaum Associates, 1978.

Davis, Robert B., and Curtis McKnight. "The Influence of Semantic Content on Algorithmic Behavior." *Journal of Mathematical Behavior* 3 (Autumn 1980): 39–87.

Dewey, John. *How We Think.* Boston: Heath, 1910.

Doyle, Walter. "Academic Work." *Review of Educational Research* 53 (Summer 1983): 159–99.

_____. "Work in Mathematics Classes: The Context of Students' Thinking during Instruction." *Educational Psychologist* 23 (Spring 1988): 167–80.

Gelman, Rochel. "Basic Numerical Abilities." In *Advances in Psychology of Human Intelligence,* edited by Robert J. Sternberg, pp. 181–205. Hillsdale, N.J.: Lawrence Erlbaum Associates, 1982.

Gelman, Rochel, and Elizabeth Meck. "The Notion of Principle: The Case of Counting." In *Conceptual and Procedural Knowledge: The Case of Mathematics,* edited by James Hiebert, pp. 29–58. Hillsdale, N.J.: Lawrence Erlbaum Associates, 1986.

Ginsburg, Herbert P. *Children's Arithmetic.* Austin, Tex.: PRO-ED, 1982.

Greeno, James G. "Analysis of Understanding in Problem Solving." In *Developmental Models of Thinking*, edited by R. H. Kluwe and H. Spada, pp. 199–212. New York: Academic Press, 1980.

_____. "Conceptual Entities." In *Mental Models,* edited by Dedre Gentner and Albert L. Stevens, pp. 227–52. Hillsdale, N.J.: Lawrence Erlbaum Associates, 1983.

Hart, Kathleen M., ed. *Children's Understanding of Mathematics,* pp. 11–16. London: John Murray, 1981.

Hiebert, James. "Children's Mathematics Learning: The Struggle to Link Form and Understanding." *Elementary School Journal* 84 (May 1984): 497–513.

_____. "A Theory of Developing Competence with Written Mathematical Symbols." *Educational Studies in Mathematics* 19 (1988): 333–55.

Hiebert, James, and Patricia Lefevre. "Conceptual and Procedural Knowledge in Mathematics: An Introductory Analysis." In *Conceptual and Procedural Knowledge: The Case of Mathematics,* edited by James Hiebert, pp. 1–27. Hillsdale, N.J.: Lawrence Erlbaum Associates, 1986.

Hiebert, James, and Diana Wearne. "Procedures over Concepts: The Acquisition of Decimal Number Knowledge." In *Conceptual and Procedural Knowledge: The Case of Mathematics,* edited by James Hiebert, pp. 199–223. Hillsdale, N.J.: Lawrence Erlbaum Associates, 1986.

Kouba, Vicky L., Catherine A. Brown, Thomas P. Carpenter, Mary M. Lindquist, Edward A. Silver, and Jane O. Swafford. "Results of the Fourth NAEP Assessment of Mathematics: Measurement, Geometry, Data Interpretation, Attitudes, and Other Topics." *Arithmetic Teacher* 35 (May 1988a): 10–16.

_____. "Results of the Fourth NAEP Assessment of Mathematics: Number, Operations, and Word Problems." *Arithmetic Teacher* 35 (April 1988b): 14–19.

Kouba, Vicky L., Thomas P. Carpenter, Jane O. Swafford. "Number and Operations." In *Results of the Fourth Mathematics Assessment of the National Assessment of Educational Progress,* edited by Mary M. Lindquist, pp. 64–93. Reston, Va.: National Council of Teachers of Mathematics, 1989.

Lawler, Robert W. "The Progressive Construction of Mind." *Cognitive Science* 5 (January-March 1981): 1–30.

Lesh, Richard, Thomas Post, and Merlyn Behr. "Representations and Translations among Representations in Mathematics Learning and Problem Solving." In *Problems of Representation in the Teaching and Learning of Mathematics,* edited by Claude Janvier, pp. 33–40. Hillsdale, N.J.: Lawrence Erlbaum Associates, 1987.

Mason, John H. "Representing Representing: Notes following the Conference." In *Problems of Representation in the Teaching and Learning of Mathematics,* edited by Claude Janvier, pp. 207–14. Hillsdale, N.J.: Lawrence Erlbaum Associates, 1987.

Piaget, Jean. *Success and Understanding.* Cambridge: Harvard University Press, 1978.

Schoenfeld, Alan H. "On Having and Using Geometric Knowledge." In *Conceptual and Procedural Knowledge: The Case of Mathematics,* edited by James Hiebert, pp. 225–64. Hillsdale, N.J.: Lawrence Erlbaum Associates, 1986.

Silver, Edward A. "Using Conceptual and Procedural Knowledge: A Focus on Relationships." In *Conceptual and Procedural Knowledge: The Case of Mathematics,* edited by James Hiebert, pp. 181–98. Hillsdale, N.J.: Lawrence Erlbaum Associates, 1986.

Skemp, Richard R. "Relational Understanding and Instrumental Understanding." *Arithmetic Teacher* 26 (November 1978): 9–15.

VanLehn, Kurt. "On the Representation of Procedures in Repair Theory." In *The Development of Mathematical Thinking,* edited by Herbert P. Ginsburg, pp. 201–52. New York: Academic Press, 1983.

Vygotsky, Lev S. *Thought and Language.* Cambridge: MIT Press, 1962.

3

developing problem-solving abilities and attitudes

joan worth

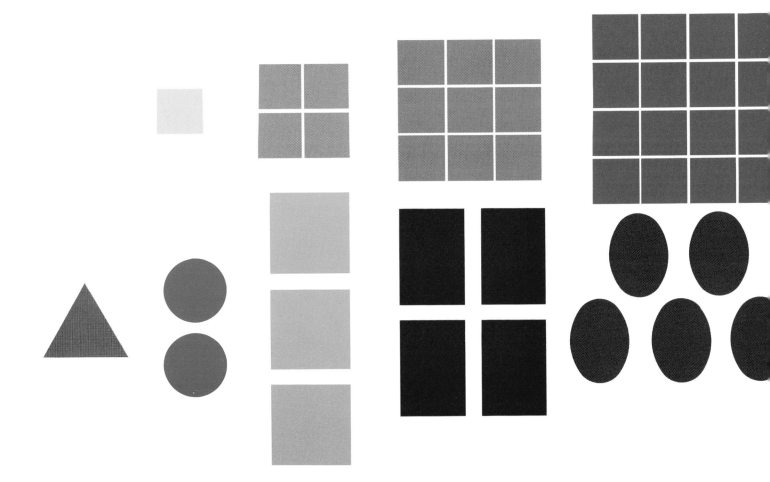

1223334

In grades K–4, the study of mathematics should emphasize problem solving so that students can—

- use problem-solving approaches to investigate and understand mathematical content;
- formulate problems from everyday and mathematical situations;
- develop and apply strategies to solve a wide variety of problems;
- verify and interpret results with respect to the original problems;
- acquire confidence in using mathematics meaningfully.

Curriculum and Evaluation Standards for School Mathematics (NCTM 1989, p. 23)

The preceding statement is explicit about the role of problem solving for the young child, extending the recommendation of *An Agenda for Action* (NCTM 1980) that problem solving be the focus of school mathematics. Teachers of young children have the difficult task of relating these broad goals to the mathematics curriculum on a daily, weekly, and yearly basis, and they may raise such questions as these:

- Why must I spend time on problem solving when the children are only beginning to learn to read and write and to develop mathematical concepts?

- Where do I fit problem solving into an already full curriculum?

- What kinds of problem-solving experiences should young children have?

- How can I make these experiences an integral part of the mathematics activities that the children already do?

- How can I evaluate problem-solving progress?

The aim of this chapter is to offer ideas and activities to answer these questions.

reasons for problem-solving experiences

One of the major reasons for studying mathematics is to develop the ability to solve problems. This ability is critical not only to children's future needs and uses of mathematics but also to productive citizenship and even human progress. To develop problem-solving abilities, appropriate experiences must begin with the young child's first "formal" encounters with mathematical ideas. Teachers of young children have always known that the mathematical ideas that children develop in early childhood form the foundation for all the mathematics they will study later and that during these early years children develop attitudes toward mathematics and beliefs about their ability to learn mathematics. So it is with problem solving—children's future success in solving problems depends directly on their beginning problem-solving experiences. These experiences include problem solving both as a process and as an approach to concepts.

Problem solving as a process is a means of finding solutions in unfamiliar situations. We want young children to begin to develop the ability to think through a new and unusual situation or problem and reach their own conclusions. This "thinking through" involves using previously learned concepts and skills appropriately and applying them to the new situation.

When the teaching and learning of mathematics is approached from a problem-solving perspective, concepts and procedural skills are developed on the basis of problem settings that require those concepts and skills. A problem-solving approach helps young children make sense of the concepts, skills, and relationships that are essential in an early childhood mathematics curriculum.

the nature of problem-solving experiences

Problem-solving experiences for young children should be consistent with their developmental level and be based on what we know about young children and how they learn.

We know that from their earliest years, children exhibit a natural sense of wonder and a desire to learn. To survive, they had to become problem solvers. Bombarded by a multitude of sensations and objects in a rapidly changing environment, young children try to bring some order and meaning to their day-to-day activities by watching, analyzing, using trial and error, and drawing conclusions. Because they have no learned responses to recall, these behaviors lead to the generation of new solutions; children invent mathematics as explanations for their experiences. They experience frustration and learn to persevere. They explore the unknown and learn to take risks. Thus, they have been successful problem solvers all their lives and have developed problem-solving skills that are based on their real-world experiences. As noted by Carpenter (1985, p. 417), "Children enter school with quite well-developed informal systems of mathematics. Young children are very good at solving simple word problems and their solutions are often creative and involve relatively sophisticated problem-solving processes." In a comment on strategies, Hiebert (1984, p. 497) made a similar point: "Most children enter school with reasonably good problem-solving strategies. A significant feature of these strategies is that they reflect a careful analysis of the problems to which they are applied."

It is generally accepted that children require experiences with concrete materials in the initial stages of learning. This is because sensory learning is the foundation of experience and learning is based on experience. Children must actively participate both mentally and physically as they learn. This active participation can take many forms, the most common being hands-on experiences with concrete objects (see fig. 1). Active involvement also includes interacting with other children and the teacher through watching,

Fig. 1. Using manipulatives

talking, listening, reading, imitating, practicing, and following directions.

Problem-solving experiences should also be based on what we want young children to learn, that is, on the broad goals of problem-solving instruction.

We want children to develop confidence in their ability to solve problems because the belief that they can solve problems will influence their performance. "All too often, children enter first grade with enthusiasm, anxious to try any mathematical problem and confident of their success, only to become 'turned-off' by mathematics before entering third grade, firmly convinced they cannot do it" (Bruni 1982, p. 10).

We want children to take risks, to tackle unfamiliar tasks, and to stick with them—in short, to try and persevere. We want children to be flexible in their thinking and to know that many problems can be modeled, represented, and solved in more than one way.

We want children in a particular problem situation to explore, examine, and make observations about the situation; to interpret information correctly; to discuss their ideas; to make decisions and plans by considering alternative strategies; to test and verify their ideas; and to express their conclusions.

It is important to keep in mind that achieving such goals

is a long-range undertaking, not a lesson's—or even a year's—objective. Solving problems and using problem solving to develop concepts and procedural skills take time.

implementing problem-solving experiences

Teachers are the primary figures in a child's mathematical education, so what they do and how they do it are vital aspects of developing the problem-solving abilities of children. What can a teacher do to nurture and develop children's problem-solving skills and attitudes? The suggestions that follow partially answer this question.

create a positive atmosphere for problem solving

Because problem solving is a way of thinking—partly cognitive and partly affective—and because of the uncertainty inherent in problem-solving situations, a positive classroom climate is essential to build children's confidence in their ability to solve problems. Generally, if pupils leave the primary grades without a positive attitude, we know they are not likely to develop one later. Young children respond most favorably in an environment that is warm, free of anxiety, and oriented toward success. The most important factors affecting the classroom atmosphere are the attitudes and actions of the teacher. The following are some important ways for teachers to create a positive classroom atmosphere:

- *Be enthusiastic.* Enthusiasm is contagious. Let children see that a teacher can be excited about problem solving.

- *Provide time.* A great deal of time must be allowed for children to learn and practice problem solving. Making problem solving a regular and frequent part of the mathematics program is also another way of communicating to children the importance of problem solving.

- *Reinforce willingness to take risks.* Let children know how important it is for them to be willing to try and to take risks, even though they are not sure what they are trying is "right." Children need a great deal of security to risk being "wrong." When they begin to appreciate that they often learn as much from a "wrong" attempt as they do from a correct answer and that their attempts are valued, their sense of commitment to the process is strengthened. Children must not be afraid to make a mistake, to be different, or to think independently.

- *Reward perseverance.* Minor failures or a sense of frustration are inevitably part of doing and learning mathematics. Encouraging children to keep on trying will pay large dividends in their future study of mathematics.

- *Use children's experiences.* As often as possible, base problem situations on children's everyday experiences in school and at home. Children are interested in problems that they can relate to their lives and deal with on a personal level. This connection helps them apply the mathematical ideas they are learning as well as helping them interpret their world.

- *Accept unconventional solutions.* There is often more than one way to solve a problem. Encouraging children to use their natural, instinctive problem-solving skills will not only enhance those skills but also lead to some very creative solutions to problems.

- *Emphasize process as well as the answer.* If the teacher regularly discusses with children how and why they did certain things, they will learn to value the process as well as the answer.

teaching processes

One of the more important ideas for young children to accept is that a problem is any situation for which they do not have an immediate solution or do not know instantly how to get one. We do not want young children to develop the belief that when they are solving a problem, they must find *the* single correct answer immediately, and if they cannot find it immediately, they will never find it. Children need to be convinced that problem solving is not a simple, clear-cut procedure and that solutions are not found instantly. We want those children whose first response to a problem is a raised hand and a cry of "I don't know how to do this!" to accept a response of "Of course not! If you knew how to do it, it wouldn't be a problem." Once children accept this notion, they need help on how to begin—that is, what to do when they don't know what to do.

problem-solving model

"Systematic instruction based on a problem-solving model enhances students' success" (Suydam 1987, p. 101).

A general model is usually not introduced directly to children before third grade. However, a model can be useful as a framework for approaching problem-solving situations with young children, organizing activities, and posing questions to get children started. Thus many topics can be taught from a problem-solving perspective. The most commonly used framework is Pólya's model. This model has four stages. Although the stages are often called by different names, they have the same purpose. One way of describing the stages is as follows:

1 Make sure you know what the problem is about.

2 Think of strategies to try.

3   Solve the problem and answer the question.
4   Think and talk about your solution.

It is important to note that these stages are not fixed steps—they are not always used, or used in the order given. However, they do provide a starting point. An awareness of the stages and the purpose of each will help in organizing instruction and in asking questions.

The purpose of the first stage, understanding the problem, is to get children used to the idea of thinking about the problem before they use manipulatives or pencil and paper to try to solve it. Children can be helped to accept this part of the problem-solving process by asking them questions that focus on the information in the problem and on what the problem is asking them to find. At this stage, questions are asked that can be answered mentally or without models or pencils. Although questions would be specific to a particular problem, some general questions follow:

■ What does [a particular word or phrase] mean?

■ What are you asked to find?

■ What do you know about . . .? (What information is given?)

■ Can you tell the problem in your own words?

The second stage is the planning stage. Here, the focus is on developing plans for what children might do to solve the problem by guiding them to consider strategies such as those discussed later in this chapter. Strategies can be suggested until children become familiar with the process. In both the first and second stages, questions are posed, but the ultimate goal is for children to ask questions themselves.

During the third stage, children are using the strategy they chose to solve the problem. The role of the teacher is to observe, help, and encourage.

In the fourth stage, children generalize their thinking and consider not only what they did but why they did it. "Discussion of the nature of the problem, the strategies used, and the reasons for using them may be vital to the successful teaching of problem solving. Knowing not just 'what to do' but 'why to do it' promotes transfer to new problems" (Suydam 1987, p. 103).

The focus on the processes as well as the answer is strengthened by questions such as these:

■ Does your answer fit the question?

■ Can you explain how you solved this problem?

■ How did you decide what to do?

■ Does this remind you of any other problem?

■ Could you have solved this in other ways?

■ Can you think of another question for this problem?

■ What would happen if . . .?

When questions are posed for discussion, it is important to include open-ended questions like the last three above. Such questions can have a variety of appropriate responses that show that some problems have many solutions and some have no solution. Open-ended questions also encourage divergent thinking—a valuable problem-solving tool. Cliatt, Shaw, and Sherwood (1980) reported that at the kindergarten level, children's ability to think divergently was increased when they were repeatedly exposed to divergent-thinking situations. The researchers concluded that divergent thinking "should be encouraged at an early age so that it becomes a natural and accepted part of children's intellectual functioning" (p. 1063).

Discussions with children at any of the stages, and encouraging them to verbalize their thinking, can be valuable in developing mathematical language. They find that representing and talking about a particular situation can be done in many ways. The importance of developing oral language skills at the early childhood level is noted by McClinton (1981) in a report of a study on young children's verbal problem solving.

Many examples of the informal use of this general model are included in the activities described later in this chapter. A description of the use of a similar model with second graders is found in Spencer and Lester (1981).

specific strategies

"Teaching students a range of strategies increases their options when attacking problems. If one way doesn't work, they know other ways that might" (Suydam 1987,

p. 101). As the strategies are developed and used, it is important that they be labeled problem-solving strategies so that children know they are solving problems and think of themselves as problem solvers. The strategies described here are general enough to be used with a variety of mathematical topics in teaching from a problem-solving perspective. They are also specific enough to be used alone or in combination as children practice problem solving. A familiarity with a variety of strategies allows children to model or represent problems in many ways. Many of these strategies also will be used in later years.

act it out

Children act out situations that illustrate operations or that model a particular problem. This strategy has its beginnings in the "dramatic play centers" of many kindergarten classrooms and continues through the grades. The following activities can serve as both a learning and a diagnostic function, since the children's responses to questions will reveal if ideas are understood.

Dishes for a party. When the setting at a dramatic play center is a house, pose a problem like this one for the group of children at that center (see fig. 2):

"There will be 5 people at Bryan's party. Are there enough dishes to set the table for everyone at the party?"

Children must then decide what they need and place things on the table. As they think and talk about their solution, ask, "How did you decide what dishes you needed? How do you know you have enough? What will happen if 2 more people come to the party?" **a**

Nursery Story. Use a familiar nursery story such as the Three Little Pigs and add questions about the number of sticks or bricks and the number of huffs and puffs. One group of children can act the story out as it is told and the rest of the children give the solutions to the problems posed. **a**

No words allowed. Read a problem aloud and have a group act it out without speaking (see fig. 3). The rest of the children then give the solution.

"Four people get on the bus at the first stop. At the second stop, three people get on and two people get off. How many people are on the bus then?"

Children might decide to set chairs up to represent seats on the bus, or just sit on the floor. In talking about the solution with children, ask, "Can you think of another question for this problem? What would happen if the bus made two more stops and three more people got on at each stop?"

Another time, change the setting to a train or airplane with questions about the number of seats occupied or empty or the number of tickets needed or used. **a**

Several other suggestions for problems that can be acted out appear in Coombs and Harcourt (1986).

use manipulatives

Since children at the early childhood level constantly use manipulatives as they learn mathematical concepts, it is a natural extension for them to use manipulatives to solve problems. This strategy is similar to "acting" in that children go through the actions, but here they manipulate objects rather than themselves. Problem situations should involve more than the number combinations they are learning. The purpose is for children to learn that they can use manipulatives to model problems and count to find solutions. At these early stages children should not be asked to write the mathematical sentence. Only when children have learned to write number sentences associated with the operations should they be asked to keep written records of their observations or maneuvers.

Numbers story sheet. Provide each child with counters (beans, blocks, chips, etc.) and a sheet of paper to be used as a story sheet. Demonstrate initially on an overhead projector or magnetic board what the children are to do. Tell a story, possibly related to the current theme in your classroom or to some story you are reading together.

Fig. 2. Dishes for a party

Suppose, for example, the theme is the circus. Have the children draw a ring on their story sheets to represent the ring at the circus and tell them their counters represent clowns:

"Three happy-face clowns drove into the ring in a small car. [You and the children put 3 counters into the ring.] As they were driving around the ring, a sad-faced clown ran in to join them. [Put another counter into the ring.] When the sad-faced clown jumped into the car, the car stopped. Immediately 2 more sad-faced clowns ran into the ring to help fix the car. [Put 2 more counters into the ring.] How many clowns are in the ring now? [Children should count 6 counters.] When the car was fixed, the 3 happy-faced clowns jumped in and drove out of the ring. How many clowns are left in the ring?" [Children should remove 3 of their counters and respond that 3 clowns are left.]

Children enjoy telling their own stories to a partner or a group of children, who then use the counters to represent the problem (fig. 4).

Fig. 3. Strategy—act it out

Fig. 4. Representing a problem

Developing Problem-solving Abilities and Attitudes   45

Paper-bag problems. Paper bags help make use of children's imaginations. Hold up a bag and illustrate this story.

"You may think this is a brown bag, but it's really a barn! You may think these are blocks, but they are really cows. There are 3 cows inside the barn [put 3 blocks in the bag], and then 4 more cows go into the barn. [Put 4 blocks in the bag.] One cow leaves the barn [take 1 block out]. How many cows are left in the barn?"

After doing one or two problems like this, children will want to make up their own. The bag can become an elevator, a mud puddle, or a bookshelf. The cubes or blocks then become people, tadpoles, or books. Children can share problems with small groups or partners, who then solve them using their own paper bags (fig. 5). **a**

Fig. 5. Paper-bag problems

a *Chart-paper problems.* These problems help children make the transition from orally presented problems to word problems. The familiar strategy of using manipulatives provides a sense of security because children can use their counters to solve the problems before they can read or symbolize. By saving the charts, children can use them later when they can read for themselves. Provide an appropriate number of counters and a background or story sheet for each child.

"What did you do on the playground this morning?" [Suppose someone says she was playing on the swings.] "Let's make up a problem about playing on the swings. How many children were on the swings? What happened next—did more come or did some go away?" [Continue in this manner, printing the problem as children describe the situation. Then have children solve the problem using their counters on their story sheets, and ask one child to explain how he or she solved it.]

Children will be eager to make up other problems, which can be recorded as they tell them (see fig. 6). As the class solves each problem, ask appropriate questions to make sure children understand the problem and guide them in thinking and talking about their solutions. **a**

Specific directions for twenty problem-solving activities based on manipulative materials are detailed in Castaneda, Gibb, and McDermit (1982).

draw a diagram

Making a diagram is a powerful problem-solving strategy that children (and adults) often use quite naturally. It can help in understanding a problem as well as in solving it. When this strategy is introduced, it is important to emphasize to children that they do not need to draw a "picture" similar to a photograph. Initially, children can make a drawing of what they did with manipulatives as a way to transfer their actions with manipulatives to the pictorial stage. Eventually, a drawing replaces the use of objects.

a *Tallies on a story sheet.* Provide appropriate story sheets, or have children sketch their own. Read or tell a story while children listen. Then tell the story a second time, having the children make a mark on their story sheets for each object or item mentioned and counting the marks to answer the question posed in the story. In the next example, children should have a story sheet showing a tree with two branches.

"Terry was watching some birds in a tree in the park.

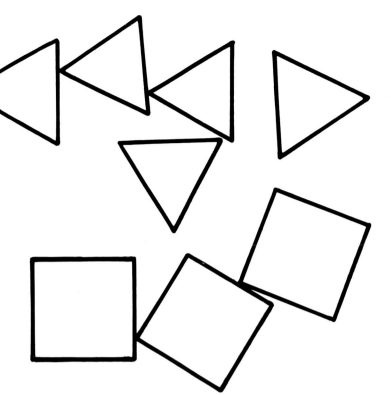

Fig. 6. Writing problems as children say them

There were 3 birds sitting on the first branch and 2 birds sitting on the second branch. [Children make a mark for each bird.] Then 2 more birds came to sit on the second branch. [They make 2 more marks.] How many birds were sitting in the tree then? [Children count the marks made.] Then 3 birds flew off the second branch. [They cross out a mark for each bird that flew away.] How many birds were left in the tree?" [They count the marks that are not crossed out.]

Figure 7 shows a story sheet a child might do for this problem. If any children have trouble doing it, they could show the actions with their counters first, then draw what they did.

When children can make marks on their papers to represent objects, problems such as the following can be presented.

a *Tell and print a story.* Tell a story and print it on chart paper so children can refer to it. "Ajmal got a box of blocks for his birthday. The blocks were shaped like squares, triangles, and circles. He got 1 more square block than circle blocks, 1 more circle block than triangular blocks, and 5 square blocks. How many blocks did Ajmal get?" To help children "understand the problem," ask, "What shapes were Ajmal's blocks? How many more squares than circles were there? How many more circles than

triangles? How many squares?" You might have to suggest they first draw a diagram to show how many of each kind of block Ajmal got, then count the blocks

a

Fig. 7. A child's story sheet

they drew. (See fig. 8.) When thinking and talking about their solutions with them, ask, "Which blocks did you draw first? Why? Suppose there had been 5 triangular blocks—how many blocks would Ajmal have received?" **a**

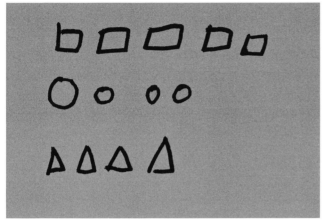

Fig. 8. Sample of drawing done by child

Problems about position illustrate the need for a diagram:

a *Drawing diagrams.* "In a race, Bella finished ahead of Peter. Rosa finished beind Peter. Ted finished ahead of Bella. Who won the race?" Before children start, ask, "How many were in the race? Could Bella have won the race? What do you have to find? What could you draw to represent each person?" When thinking and talking about the solution with children, ask, "Who did you draw first? Why? Who did you put in next? Could you have solved this any other way?" **a**

Practice in making and using drawings to help solve problems is given in Greenes et al. (1982).

guess and check

Much of preschool learning is based on guessing and checking, yet it is often difficult to get children to accept this as a legitimate "school" strategy because of their concern about "being correct." Children need to be encouraged first to make guesses, then to make better guesses based on knowledge and experience. They can move beyond wild or random guessing by considering

the information in a problem and what a reasonable outcome might be. Having them keep some kind of record as they check their guesses lets them refine their guessing skills to use in solving problems.

a *Target games.* These games provide excellent guess-and-check situations. Use an overhead transparency or provide copies similar to the one in figure 9. Tell the children a story such as this one: "Kelly was throwing bean bags at this floor target. She threw two bean bags and got a score of 6. Which squares could her bean bags have landed on?" To make sure children understand the problem, ask someone to explain the game Kelly was playing. Then ask, "How many bean bags did Kelly throw? What was the sum of the numbers in the two squares her bean bags landed in? Could they have landed in squares 3 and 4? What do you have to find?" Then suggest that they try different pairs of numbers, or guess and check, and keep a record of the pairs they tried. Help children think and talk about their solutions and tell about their guesses. Then ask, "Which two squares could the bean bags have landed on if Mary had a score of 7? [2 and 5, or 3 and 4.] If Billy had a

Fig. 9. Strategy—guess and check

score of 8? [6 and 2, or 3 and 5]." Discuss the possibility of both bean bags landing in the same square. **a**

Buying toys. Prepare an overhead transparency or individual sheets similar to figure 10. Using names from the class, say, "Mike spent 9 cents at the toy sale and bought 2 toys. What did Mike buy?" Ask questions for understanding similar to those suggested for the bean-bag game. After discussing the children's solutions with them, change the number of toys bought to 3 and the amount spent to 12 cents, which gives two solutions [3, 4, and 5; and 1, 4, and 7]. **a**

Game: What are my numbers. As the game is played, write the data on the chalkboard. "I'm thinking of three numbers. When added, their sum is 17. They are all greater than 2 and less than 9. What are they?" To make sure children understand the problem, ask, "How many numbers do you have to find? What is their sum? Could one of the numbers be 2? 9? Might there be more than one set of three numbers?" When thinking and talking about the solution with children, make sure they find all three sets [3, 6, 8; 4, 5, 8; and 4, 6, 7]. **a**

Number puzzle. Draw six circles on the chalkboard in a triangular shape, as shown in figure 11. Ask children to put the numbers 1 to 6 in the circles so the sum on each side of the triangle is 9. To make sure they understand the problem, ask, "How many circles are there? How many numbers can you use? Can you use a number more than once? What do you know about the numbers in the corner circles? How many numbers will you add to get a sum of 9? How many times? Try guessing and checking, and keep a record of your guesses." When thinking and talking about the solution, discuss why starting with 4, 5, or 6 in a corner circle would not check out. With older children you might talk about making a list of the sets of three numbers with a sum of 9 [6, 2, 1; 5, 3, 1; 4, 3, 2]. Note which numbers appear twice in the list, and thus go in the corners. **a**

Problem situations that make use of guessing and checking appear in Charles and Lester (1985).

Fig. 10. Buying toys

Fig. 11. Number puzzle

sound like, feel like, smell like, look like? Tell me about its size. What is it used for? What else? What other things are used for the same thing? Where might you find it? Where else? What else would you find there?" These questions should be followed by observing and describing two or more things. To begin to develop comparisons, ask, "How are these the same? How are they different?" Provide pictures of a *set* of objects, such as (*a*) an orange, apple, and banana or (*b*) a car, truck, and bicycle, and ask, "What is the same about all these pictures? What else? What is different about these pictures? What else?   **a**

a *Alike and different.* Provide children with sets of pictures such as those shown in figure 12 and pose problems like these: Which one is different? Which two are the same? Ask questions as suggested above to help children get started.   **a**

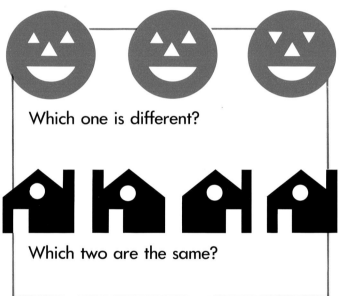

Which one is different?

Which two are the same?

use logical thinking

What you want your pupils to do when you ask them to "think about it" is to think logically. The foundation of logical thinking is identifying likenesses and differences. Children need many opportunities to use their senses to observe and describe various attributes of objects. One way of accomplishing this is to play Tell Me about It, as described by Harcourt (1988).

a *Observe and describe.* Show an object (a piece of clothing, a toy, a fruit, an empty box, a crayon, etc.) and pass it around for children to look at. Then have each child make one statement about the object, asking questions that focus on various attributes: "What color is it? What does it

a *"Who am I?" logic problems.* Clues are given as questions are asked. Three series of pictures are shown in figure 13. Questions to help children understand and solve the first problem might be: "What is the first clue? Cross out the flowers that do not have 5 petals. Which flowers are not crossed out? What is the next clue? Cross out the flowers that do not have 4 leaves. Which flower is left?"   **a**

				I have 5 petals and 4 leaves.
				I have 3 legs, 1 eye, and 4 arms.
				I have a smile, a hat, and curly hair.

Fig. 13. Who am I?

Logic problems. A logical thinking problem for older children is shown in figure 14. Ask, "How many girls played soccer? What color are their shirts? What do you have to find out? Could Carol's shirt have been green? How might you keep a record of your thinking?" After children have solved the problem, talk about what they did to solve it. Some might have written the colors down and put the names beside them, or vice versa. **a**

Problems designed to be solved using this strategy are contained in Immerzeel and Thomas (1982).

Carol, Betty, and Helen all play soccer. Each one plays on a different team and wears a different colored shirt. Their shirts are green, blue, and red. Helen does not like blue. Carol's shirt is red. Who wears the green shirt?

	Carol	Betty	Helen
red	yes	no	no
blue	no	yes	no
green	no	no	yes

Fig. 14. Logic problem

use calculators

Calculators can help children focus directly on the processes of problem solving rather than merely on computation. Children must learn at an early age that calculators will not think for them—they must tell the calculator what to do. (Of course, when the computing necessary to solve a problem is easily within children's ability, they should be encouraged to use the "calculator" in their heads.) "Calculators can enhance students' problem-solving achievement and can certainly widen the choice of problem-solving strategies" (Suydam 1987, p. 108). If children make up their own problems using calculators, as suggested later in this chapter, they are able to use larger numbers, which they enjoy. Some specific problem-solving activities using the calculator are suggested below. Detailed directions on calculator use are found in chapter 1.

Count on, count back. Have children solve problems by counting both forward and backward.

How many numbers can you count between 13 and 25? Ask, "What is the first number you count between 13 and 25? The last number? What are you asked to find? How can you use your calculator to help you count?" (Enter 13 $\boxed{+}$ 1 $\boxed{=}$ $\boxed{=}$ $\boxed{=}$; continue to press $\boxed{=}$ and count the number of times the $\boxed{=}$ is pressed.) What 5 numbers come just before 29?" Enter this as 29 $\boxed{-}$ 1 $\boxed{=}$ $\boxed{=}$ $\boxed{=}$ $\boxed{=}$ $\boxed{=}$. **a**

Skip counting. Explore number patterns by having children skip count by 2, 3, 4, 5, and 10 using different starting points. "What numbers do you say when counting by 2 from 11 to 21?" Enter this as 11 $\boxed{+}$ 2 $\boxed{=}$ $\boxed{=}$ $\boxed{=}$ . . . . **a**

Find my number. Ask children to find specific numbers with their calculator: "What number will appear if you enter 10 $\boxed{+}$ 1 and press the $\boxed{=}$ key 10 times?" [20] "How many ways can you make 25 using two numbers and one $\boxed{+}$ sign?" [13 if reversals are not allowed; 26 if allowed]. **a**

Many activities requiring calculators to be used as a problem-solving tool are contained in Reys et al. (1980) and Coburn (1988).

Developing Problem-solving Abilities and Attitudes   51

problem-solving orientation

Much of young children's early learning of mathematical concepts and skills presents opportunities for problem solving. Therefore, much of the everyday instruction in mathematics can be done from a problem-solving perspective. This also allows problem solving to be integrated into all aspects of the program.

Many common activities in the mathematics program can be transformed into problem-solving situations by posing questions and having children talk about their solutions. By saying, "Here is a problem for you to solve," children know they are solving problems and begin to think of themselves as problem solvers. The tasks set for children in these common activities are problems because the children do not immediately know the solution. The problem-solving strategies suggested above can be used singly or in combination as children solve the problems posed. The activities that follow are meant to illustrate a problem-solving approach with traditional early childhood topics. Other chapters in this book also contain problem-solving activities.

sorting and classifying

Sorting and classifying are very basic skills that children have used before entering school or in their early school years. They are also skills children will use as they study patterning, number, graphing, geometry, and measurement. The teacher will usually ask children to put together things that are the same in some way, to identify or describe how they are the same, and to put them together in a different way. Figure 15 shows a child sorting by wood and nonwood. Another typical activity is outlined below.

a *Button sort.* Present a collection of buttons (or pieces of paper, counters, small toys, or keys). Say, "I have a problem for you to solve. How can you sort the buttons into two groups so the buttons in each group are the same in one way?" Before children do the sorting, ask, "How many groups

do you have to make? What has to be in each group? [Buttons that are the same in one way] Can you see two buttons that are the same? How are they the same? Are there any others like this?" After children have sorted, talk about their solution. "Why do the buttons in this group belong together?" Show another button and ask, "Where would this button belong? Can you think of a different way to sort these buttons? Could you sort them so they are the same in more than one way? Could you sort them into three groups?" (See fig. 15.) **a**

Children should practice sorting many different collections of materials, including themselves. As activities are discussed, children are asked which problem-solving strategies they used to solve their sorting problems. They will likely mention acting it out, using manipulatives, drawing diagrams, guessing and checking, using logical thinking, or some combination of these.

Fig. 15. Sorting by wood and nonwood

ordering

Ordering activities also lay a foundation for later work with number and measurement and provide problem-solving experiences involving the creation of logical sequences. Children should practice ordering objects using many different attributes. Their first experiences will likely involve comparing two things and identifying which one has more or less of an attribute such as height, width, depth, mass, color, or sound. Then they should work with three items and begin sequencing; finally, they should be able to place another item in the correct position in an existing sequence. The box-ordering activity below can be repeated with many other sets of objects having a variety of attributes.

a *Boxes in order.* Show children a collection of boxes and tell them the problem is to put the boxes in order. Before they begin work, ask, "What is one way you might arrange the boxes?" They may suggest height, for example. Then choose two of the boxes and say, "How can you put these two boxes in order by height?" Pick another box and ask, "Where would this one fit?" After the children have put all the boxes in order, talk about how they did it, letting them describe their order. Then give them another box to fit into their sequence. Finally, discuss other ways the boxes could have been arranged in order—shortest to tallest or widest to narrowest, for example. (See fig. 16.) **a**

Children can order nearly any collection of similar items using many of the problem-solving strategies: they can put themselves in order by acting it out and guessing and checking; put objects or pictures in order by manipulating or drawing; or put sequences of pictures in order using logical thinking.

patterning

Patterning is often described as an important component of mathematical thinking. Finding, extending, and creating patterns requires analyzing and reflecting as well as noticing similarities, differences, and essential features—all involving many aspects of problem solving. Looking for a pattern is a problem-solving strategy children will use as long they continue their study of mathematics. Thus, labeling patterning activities as problem solving gives children an early start. Some examples of problem-solving patterning activities follow.

a *Read my pattern.* Have children practice "reading" patterns presented on an overhead projector or made with objects. Make a pattern of Popsicle sticks or straws similar to that shown in figure 17. One way children might read this is *up, across, up, across, up, across.* Let children copy your pattern using their own sticks. Then ask, "What comes next? Then what?" If any children have difficulty, suggest that they look back: "What comes after the *up* stick?" Finally, give the children the problem of making up their own pattern and have other children read it. **a**

The preceding activity can be repeated using a variety of materials, such as colored pasta, buttons, bottle caps, colored blocks, or interlocking cubes. The patterns may occur in the positioning, as in the activity above; be based on color, as in red, blue, green, red, blue, green, red, blue, green; or be based on number,

Fig. 16. Ordering by size

Fig. 17. Pattern of sticks

as in 2 cubes, 3 cubes, 2 cubes, 3 cubes, 2 cubes, 3 cubes. Children will enjoy recording their patterns by drawing and coloring or by pasting sticks or paper strips onto a background sheet. The patterns can be held up for others to see and describe and can make an attractive display when posted (see fig. 18). Children also enjoy using themselves to make "people patterns" based on clothing items (long sleeves, short sleeves), hair color, body position (sit, stand), or number (2 girls, 2 boys), having the rest of the class identify and describe the pattern.

Fig. 18. Making patterns

You can extend children's activities by providing patterns that can be felt and heard as well as seen. Smooth and rough surfaces, hand clapping, musical tones, and songs can all be used in problem-solving patterning tasks. An example of a physical education activity follows.

Movement patterns. Perform a few repetitive movements such as step, hop, clap; step, hop, clap. Ask children to describe your pattern, then have them repeat and extend your pattern. Finally, let them create their own action sequences for others to describe, repeat, and extend. Follow up by encouraging children to find the patterns in any folk or circle dances they are learning. **a**

Art, music, and science activities often offer many other opportunities for identifying and describing patterns. The skills children develop in solving problems by pattern recognition will contribute not only to the development of their number sense and skills but also to the development of their ability to analyze and reflect

on situations, in other words, their ability to solve problems.

Many activities using patterning as problem solving are found in Burton (1983), Van de Walle and Thompson (1985), Van de Walle and Holbrook (1987), Baratta-Lorton (1976), and Harcourt (1988).

solving story problems

Story or word problems with direct applications of the four operations have always been a part of the school mathematics curriculum. In fact, for some time the problem-solving component of mathematics programs, particularly at the early childhood level, was limited to solving story problems with addition and subtraction.

In recent years it has been generally accepted that finding answers to the usual story problems is not necessarily problem solving. If children can immediately see either the answer or the operation needed to find it, they have not really solved a problem—they had no problem to solve.

This is not to say that story problems have no role in the early childhood mathematics curriculum. Indeed, they do provide settings both for developing the concepts of the operations and for practicing the operations, as detailed in chapter 6.

Story problems are also the vehicle used to help children learn to write number sentences to represent addition, subtraction, multiplication, and division situations. Although these number sentences are not usually necessary to solve the simple word problems with manipulatives, the translation of story situations to number sentences is an important step for children in learning to represent situations mathematically. This ability to use mathematical symbols to model a problem is most useful and important throughout the study of mathematics.

Before they can use symbols, children need to be able to identify which operation a story problem calls for. "Choose the operation" activities can help children make the transition from manipulatives and counting to symbolizing addition and subtraction situations. Two such activities are suggested below.

a *Game: Whom would you hire?* In this game, name one child as the "adder" and another as the "subtracter," then tell story problems to the class. After each one, ask "Whom would you hire to solve this problem for you, Billy or Mary? Why?" **a**

a *Plus and minus using "some."* Provide children with two cards, one of which has a large plus sign on it, the other a large minus sign. Tell a story problem using the word *some* instead of numbers. When children hear an action in a problem, they hold up the sign symbolizing which action they hear. For example, you might say, "There were some cookies on the plate, and Raj's mother put some more cookies on the plate. [Children hold up the plus sign.] Then Raj and his friends ate some of the cookies. [Children hold up the minus sign.]" Children enjoy telling their own "some" stories to the class or a small group. **a**

a *Number sentences for manipulatives.* Tell children they will be "record keepers", by writing number sentences that record what was done with manipulatives (see fig. 19). Present a story problem such as this one: "Tony had 4 toy cars. He got 3 more for his birthday. How many toy cars did Tony have then?" After children have shown the problem with their counters and answered the question, say "Now let's show this problem with a number sentence. How many toy cars did Tony have before his birthday? [Children show 4 counters, and write "4" on their papers.] Then what happened? [Children might say, "He got some more—that is addition", and write " + ."] How many more did he get? [Children write "3".] Then how many toy cars did he have? "[Children write " = 7."] **a**

This activity can be repeated several times.

The same procedure can be followed for story problems involving subtraction situations. Then, children can tell stories about number sentences or draw pictures for number sentences. Note that these number sentences directly model the action of the problems (Carpenter,

Fig. 19. Writing a number sentence

Moser, and Bebout 1988). Because children most naturally write sentences that represent the action, the previous activity can be repeated with situations that are described by open sentences.

a *Open-number sentences.* Present a problem such as this: "Five children were playing on the swings. Some more children came to play, and then eight children were on the swings. How many more children came to play?" Then ask, "How many were playing on the swings to begin with?" [Children write "5."] "Then what happened?" [Children write " + ."] "How many more came?" [Children might say "We don't know"; have them make a line, box, or circle.] "How many were playing on the swings then?" [Children write " = 8."] Children solve such open sentences as $5 + \underline{\quad} = 8$ by thinking of what is added to 5 on the swing to get 8 on the swing. The meaning of " = " is essential. **a**

At later stages, some children may take different points of view about the action in a problem and write different but equivalent number sentences for the same problem. This should be encouraged as long as children can justify or explain their thinking.

A wide variety of story problem activities can be found in Coombs et al. (1987).

These are but a few mathematics curriculum examples that can be taught and labeled as problem-solving activities. Many more are included in this book. Remember that teaching and labeling these concept-developing experiences as problem solving can give children confidence in their ability to solve problems.

everyday activities

Many of the ordinary classroom management situations can be opportunities to develop and refine problem-solving skills. Indeed, many of the best problem-solving situations at the early childhood level come from these everyday situations. Taking advantage of these helps children see the need for, and uses of, mathematics in their lives. Ask questions as children take part in activities such as these:

■ Help arrange enough chairs, desks, or tables for different activities: "Are there enough chairs here for Billy's group? How many more do we need? How many should sit at this table?"

■ Sort books and other objects for use in particular ways: "Which of these books should you use? How can you sort and share these jars of paint? How many blocks will each person need?"

■ Distribute materials to each group or each child: "How many pieces of paper do you need for your story sheets? Are there enough at this table for everyone? How many extra are there? How many more do you need?"

■ Form teams to play games: "How many teams of four can we make? How many should be on each team for this game?"

The planning of such class activities as parties, field trips, or track meets offers many possibilities for problem solving. Questions need to be posed and children encouraged to consider possible needs, make decisions, and discuss the results of their actions.

creating problems

There is likely no better way to extend children's ability to solve problems than by having them create their own problems. In doing so, they must consider the amount of information to include as well as how to pose the question. Very young children can create oral problems for a group or the whole class to solve. For older children, writing their own problems provides a setting for them to practice the writing skills they are learning in language arts. Knowing they are writing for a purpose and that others will be reading what they write motivates children to be careful with spelling and punctuation. Some activities to help children get started follow:

a *Choosing names and numbers.* Provide kindergarten children with sheets on which to fill in names and numbers, such as those shown in figure 20. Children can use their own names or copy the names of friends from cards displayed around the room. Initially, let children "read" their own sheets and pose such questions as, "Who ate more cookies? How many more? How many cookies were eaten all together?" Children can solve them by using manipulatives. Eventually, let children pose their own questions orally.   **a**

Fig. 20. A problem sheet

What's the question? This is an activity that provides oral practice in posing problem questions. Give children some data and have them ask a question about the data. For example, "4 cars and 5 trucks" might produce responses like "How many toys all together?" "How many more trucks than cars?" This activity can be followed by giving children two numbers and having them write a complete problem using those two numbers. **a**

 What's the problem? Use the pages from a catalog or advertisements, or prepare transparencies or sheets similar to figures 10 and 21. Give an answer, and have children tell a problem that has that answer. For the example shown, you might say, "The answer is 9 dollars. What's the problem?" Children could respond, "I bought a book and a toy car. How much did I spend?" or "How much more than the ball does the baseball glove cost?" If

children have copies of the illustrations, they can create and write their own problems on the back of the sheet. **a**

 Cut out pictures. Pictures from magazines or catalogs can be cut out and pasted and a problem written about them. Some children might enjoy drawing a picture instead of cutting them out. **a**

Have children print their problems on index cards or separate sheets of paper. The student's name should be written on the front, with the problem, and a worked-out solution should go on the back (see fig. 22). Children can then exchange and solve one another's problems. If they have questions about the suggested solution, they can be checked with the author of the problem.

Each time children write a problem, it provides an

Fig. 21. What's the problem?

"instant" set of new problems that children enjoy solving. Keep problems on index cards in an "Our Own Problems" box; sheets can be posted for all to see and then kept in an appropriately labeled file folder. Sometimes let children choose problems to work on independently. At other times distribute the problems to the class for a problem-solving practice session. As a special project have children write and illustrate problems that you duplicate and make into a "Problems by Our Class" booklet for each child to take home.

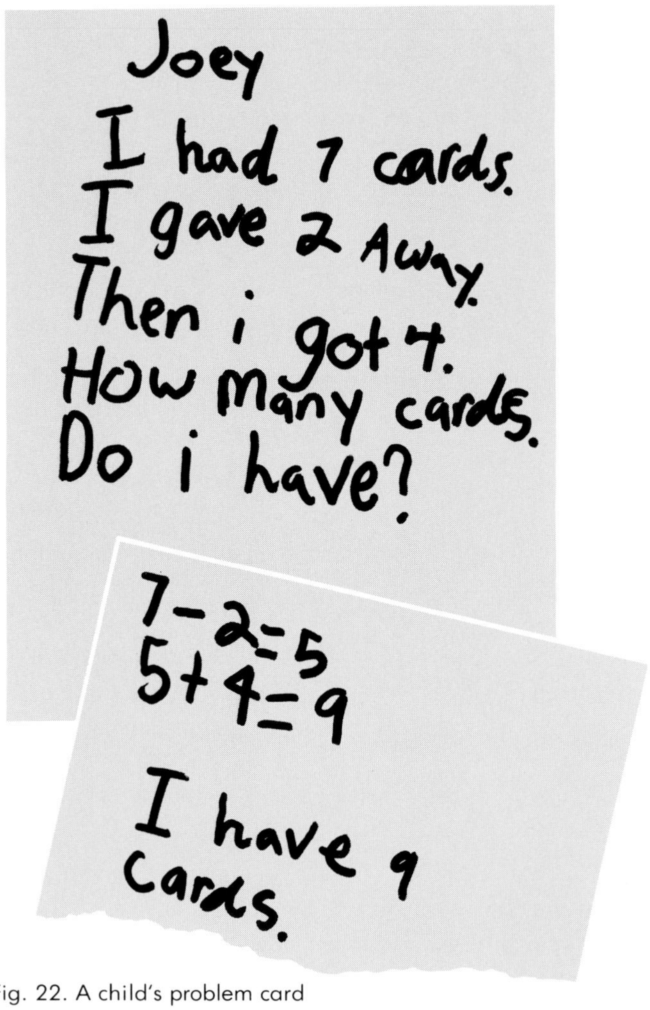

Fig. 22. A child's problem card

grouping procedures

The way in which a classroom is organized for problem solving depends on the purpose of a particular activity, on the needs of children, and on the teacher's own interests, abilities, and teaching style.

Whole-class discussions about problem solving allow a focus on the process by directing children's attention to what the problem is about and to different ways they solved the problem. Work with large groups is effective when introducing a new strategy or problem and when demonstrating and modeling appropriate vocabulary.

When children are solving problems, working in small groups provides for maximum interaction. Learning seldom takes place in isolation, and the opportunities children have to interact will help them become aware of different points of view. They will learn to express their ideas, validate facts, ask questions, and explain and justify their own reasoning processes. They will also learn to listen to each other. Small groups provide a supportive environment that can help children become more confident and less dependent on the teacher. There is time to observe, talk with individuals or the group, and evaluate.

Finally, children should have the opportunity to work individually on problems at their own rate, to work independently, and to take responsibility for their own work. The problems children create are continuing sources for independent work.

evaluating both attitudes and skills

The evaluation of problem solving must be more than a check for correct answers. Getting correct answers is important—it is the reason we solve problems. However, answers alone provide little information about *how* children solve problems, important information needed in making instructional decisions.

To help make effective decisions about methods, content, and management, evaluation practices should be based on goals for teaching problem solving. Each goal, as well as the relationships among them, will have an important effect on the development and improvement of children's problem-solving performance. Thus, it is essential that beliefs, attitudes, and thinking processes be evaluated, as well as correct answers. Evidence of children's self-confidence or belief in themselves as problem solvers can be seen in such behaviors as being willing, even eager, to try; persisting if first efforts fail; representing and solving some problems in more than one way; and realizing that some problems may have more than one answer.

An assessment of what children think and do when they solve problems is most effective if it is based on information collected in a variety of ways. Some techniques are observing, interviewing, marking written work, and testing.

observing

Observing children as they work is likely the most efficient and effective evaluation technique at the early childhood level. Observations can provide information about behaviors difficult to assess in any other way, such as willingness and perseverance, flexibility, and the systematic use of problem-solving skills. An observation of a child working at an activity identifies not only what the child can do but, equally important, what the child cannot do.

Much of the time that children are engaged in problem-solving activities the teacher is moving around the classroom, watching, listening, and assisting. For evaluation purposes, it is important to remember that every child is not evaluated each time. Rather, only a few children are chosen, three or four at the most. Observations are limited by selecting specific aspects of the children's problem-solving performance or attitudes to observe and record. Over several months all children are observed several times. Occasionally children being observed are questioned to get a clearer picture of their thinking. These questions are different from those asked to help children get started on, or even solve, a problem because the purpose is different; the questions are more like those asked to help children learn to think and talk about their solutions. Such questions might begin, "How did you [do, try, or know] . . .?" "Why did you . . .?" "What happened

when you . . .?" The answers to these questions can be unusual and, if pursued, may indicate a misunderstanding or an interesting and creative approach to a problem.

If possible, record observations immediately, rather than trying to remember them later. To do this, as well as to avoid being overwhelmed by paper, recorded observations need to be short and to the point. Records can be kept in a variety of ways. Some suggestions follow.

a *Observation notes.* Index cards can be kept in a box with dividers listing each child's name. Use one card for each of the three or four children to be observed, with the name and the date on the top of the card. The cards are easy to carry with you around the class, and you can jot down your observations as you move from group to group. When you file the cards, you can note children who have not been observed recently and plan your next observation session accordingly. An example is shown in figure 23. **a**

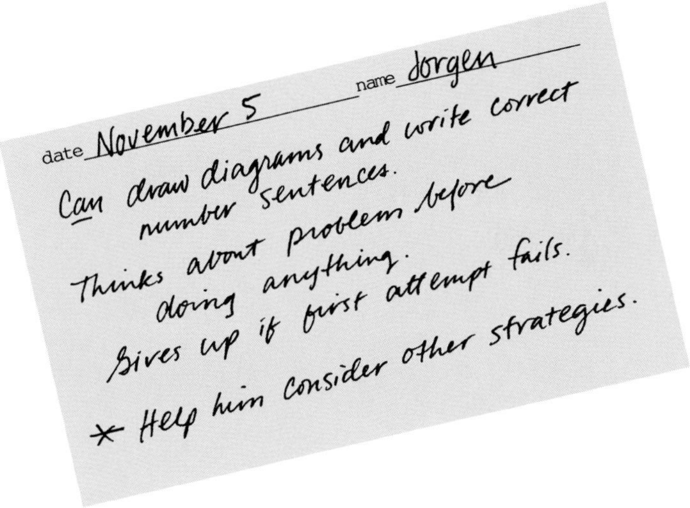

Fig. 23. Observation notes

a *A checklist.* Checklists provide a record of the development of specific skills and attitudes over time. Prepare a short checklist of the behaviors you are most interested in and duplicate one for each child. An example is given in figure 24. You can keep these checklists in a three-ring binder with a section for each child or in individual file folders. **a**

name_____
                                    _date_____
                         Usually Occasionally Rarely
1) Is willing to try
2) Perseveres   ___   ___   ___
3) Makes an effort to   ___   ___   ___
   understand a problem   ___   ___   ___
4) Chooses appropriate
   stategies   ___   ___   ___
5) Successfully carries
   out strategies   ___   ___   ___
6) Explains solutions   ___   ___   ___
7) Appears self-confident   ___   ___   ___

Fig. 24. Skills and attitudes checklist

Class charts. Class charts are helpful in keeping track of which children you have observed. Use two sheets of paper and make about fifteen rectangles on each sheet. Print children's names in the rectangles, and use the space remaining to write observations and the date. When each child has been observed once, cut the sheets and add the small rectangles to the file box or record book. Blank peel-off stickers can be used on the chart to save time.

Making such observations and records is time-consuming, however, the information about each child's performance is invaluable in planning the next stages in a problem-solving program.

interviewing

Individual interviews undoubtedly provide the best information about children's attitudes and thinking processes but are too time-consuming to be the primary evaluation technique. However, in a quiet corner an occasional interview of a child who is having trouble solving problems is revealing. Present a problem and ask the child to "think aloud" as he or she solves it. Ask "What?" "Why?" "How?" questions for clarification. As soon as possible after the interview, record the date, a description of the child's behavior, interpretations of it, and note the help the child may need.

written work

Once children are able to show their solutions to problems in writing, their written work can help evaluate their problem-solving performance. Of course, one of the things you check is to see if the answer is correct, but written work can also be used as a check on the problem-solving process. One way of doing so is to encourage children to record as much of their work as possible, to provide maximum information about their thinking. To emphasize your interest in the solution process as well as in the solution itself, assign marks to each stage of the problem-solving process, as well as to their answers. Several scoring scales are detailed in Charles, Lester, and O'Daffer (1987). Once children realize that their efforts as well as their answers are valued, they take more care with their written records. The procedure not only provides more information about their thinking but helps them learn the importance of keeping a record of what they do.

testing

Paper-and-pencil tests are probably the most common means of evaluating older children's ability to get correct answers. However, tests can also be used to assess children's thinking. One way is to ask for things other than the correct solution. For example, present a problem and ask one of the following questions: "What do you have to find out in this problem?" "What information in this problem would you use to find the solution?" "What operation(s) would you use to solve this problem?" "What strategy might you try to solve this problem?"

When evaluation is a regular part of the problem-solving program, children learn that problem solving is important. With a combination of techniques, you can evaluate all four goals for problem solving. Using the information from evaluation to plan appropriate activities, you can meet children's needs and help them improve their problem-solving performance.

concluding comments

The suggestions and activities in this chapter are not meant to be exhaustive but rather ones on which a teacher can build. The challenge is to make problem solving the central focus of children's mathematical learning so that they can develop the abilities and attitudes necessary to become confident and successful problem solvers. The encouraging fact is that what the teacher chooses to do will make a difference:

> What you teach about problem solving does have an effect. If problem solving is treated as "apply the procedure," then the students try to follow the rules in subsequent problems. If you teach problem solving as an *approach,* where you must think and apply anything that works, then students are likely to be less rigid. (Suydam 1987, p. 104)

references

Barratta-Lorton, Mary. *Mathematics Their Way.* Palo Alto, Calif.: Addison-Wesley Publishing Co., 1976.

Bruni, James V. "Problem Solving for the Primary Grades." *Arithmetic Teacher* 29 (February 1982): 10–15.

Burton, Grace M. "Problem Solving: It's Never Too Early to Start." In *The Agenda in Action,* 1983 Yearbook, pp. 20–32. Reston, Va.: National Council of Teachers of Mathematics, 1983.

Carpenter, Thomas P. "How Children Solve Simple Word Problems." *Education and Urban Society* 17 (August 1985):417–25.

Carpenter, Thomas P., James M. Moser, and Harriet C. Bebout. "Representation of Addition and Subtraction Word Problems." *Journal for Research in Mathematics Education* 19 (July 1988): 345–57.

Castaneda, Alberta M., E. Glenadine Gibb, and Sharon A. McDermit. "Young Children and Mathematical Problem Solving." *School Science and Mathematics* 82 (January 1982): 22–28.

Charles, Randall I., and Frank Lester, Jr. *Problem-solving Experiences in Grade 1 Mathematics.* Menlo Park, Calif.: Addison-Wesley Publishing Co., 1985.

Charles, Randall I., Frank K. Lester, and Phares G. O'Daffer. *How To Evaluate Progress in Problem Solving.* Reston, Va.: National Council of Teachers of Mathematics, 1987.

Cliatt, Mary Jo Puckett, Jean M. Shaw, and Jeanne M. Sherwood. "Effects of Training on the Divergent-Thinking Abilities of Kindergarten Children." *Child Development* 51 (December 1980): 1061–64.

Coburn, Terrence. *Calculate! Problem Solving with Calculators: Whole Number Operations.* Palo Alto, Calif.: Creative Publications, 1988.

Coombs, Betty, and Lalie Harcourt, *Explorations 1.* Don Mills, Ont.: Addison-Wesley Publishing Co., 1986.

Coombs, Betty, Lalie Harcourt, Jennifer Travis, and Nancy Wannamaker. *Explorations 2.* Don Mills, Ont.: Addison-Wesley Publishing Co., 1987.

Greenes, Carole, George Immerzeel, Linda Schulman, and Rika Spungin. *TOPS: Beginning Problem Solving.* Palo Alto, Calif.: Dale Seymour Publications, 1982.

Harcourt, Lalie. *Explorations for Early Childhood.* Don Mills, Ont.: Addison-Wesley Publishing Co., 1988.

Hiebert, James. "Children's Mathematics Learning: The Struggle to Link Form and Understanding." *Elementary School Journal* 84 (May 1984): 497–513.

Immerzeel, George, and Melvin Thomas, eds. *IDEAS from the Arithmetic Teacher, Grades 1–4 Primary.* Reston, Va.: National Council of Teachers of Mathematics, 1982.

McClinton, Sandra L. "Verbal Problem Solving in Young Children." *Journal of Educational Psychology* 73 (June 1981):437–43.

National Council of Teachers of Mathematics. *An Agenda for Action: Recommendations for School Mathematics of the 1980s.* Reston, Va.: The Council, 1980.

_____. *Curriculum and Evaluation Standards for School Mathematics.* Reston, Va.: The Council, 1989.

Reys, Robert E., Barbara J. Bestgen, Terrence G. Coburn, Harold L. Schoen, Richard J. Shumway, Charlotte L. Wheatley, Grayson H. Wheatley, and Arthur L. White. *Keystrokes: Calculator Activities for Young Students: Counting and Place Value.* Palo Alto, Calif.: Creative Publications, 1980.

Spencer, Patricia J., and Frank K. Lester. "Second Graders Can Be Problem Solvers!" *Arithmetic Teacher* 29 (September 1981): 15–17.

Suydam, Marilyn. "Indications from Research on Problem-solving." In *Teaching and Learning—a Problem-solving Focus,* edited by Frances R. Curcio, pp. 99–114. Reston, Va.: National Council of Teachers of Mathematics, 1987.

Van de Walle, John A., and Helen Holbrook. "Patterns, Thinking, and Problem Solving." *Arithmetic Teacher* 34 (April 1987): 6–12.

Van de Walle, John A., and Charles S. Thompson. "Let's Do It: Promoting Mathematical Thinking." *Arithmetic Teacher* 32 (February 1985): 7–13.

4
concepts of number

john van de walle

A rich understanding of number sense includes a collection of integrated relationships. Number is not a singular concept. Figure 1 shows seven relationships, each based on the global ideas of connections between quantity, or cardinality, and counting. "More" and "less" relations are refined to include the useful idea of one more or two more and one less or two less. A new relationship is perceived by viewing numbers in terms of the important anchors, or benchmarks, of five and ten. Spatial relationships, including instant recognition of quantities in patterned sets, provide a global understanding of quantity as a special gestalt, or singular entity, going beyond counting. As larger numbers are learned, the relative size of numbers becomes a new relationship of interest. A significant but quite different relationship is that between parts and the whole. When children are able to interpret a quantity in terms of its parts, concepts of number become more flexible and applicable to such new ideas as addition, subtraction, and place value. Number sense, or concepts of number, encompasses all these relationships.

Informal experiences outside school contribute much to the central foundations of number sense for young children. Some primitive notions of quantity develop as early as one or two years of age (Gelman and Meck 1986; Fuson and Hall 1983). Structured or formal activities at home and in school can help children build on this foundation and eventually develop "rich" concepts of number.

There are many reasons for an added emphasis on number sense. Number sense contributes directly to problem-solving abilities (see chapter 6) and flexible thinking in numerical situations. The self-confidence and

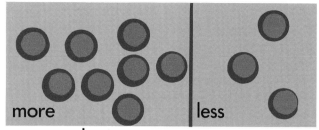

more or less

counting/cardinality

1 more, 2 more...1 less, 2 less

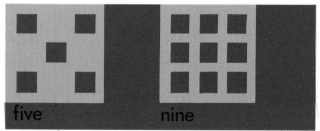

spatial

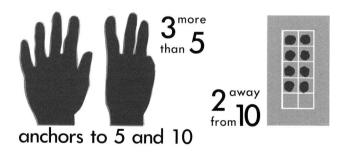

anchors to 5 and 10

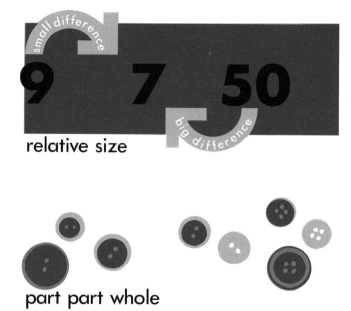

relative size

part part whole

Fig. 1. Relationships for concepts of number—number sense

positive attitudes displayed by children with good number concepts are in stark contrast to the insecurities of many upper-grade children and adults who still rely on finger counting. An understanding of number relationships is an important prerequisite for developing basic-fact strategies, as shown here and in chapter 7. Relationships for numbers through ten are used to develop concepts of numbers through 20 and are extended through place value to larger numbers. Chapter 8 presents a broad view of computation that includes estimation and mental computation, skills that directly depend on number relationships. Traditional mathematics in the early grades focuses on getting answers with counting as the most readily available, although least efficient, means of doing it. Without a major commitment by a curriculum to experiences that develop number sense, many children will never understand number in any way other than by counting.

The goal of this chapter is to map the general development of number concepts and suggest activities that can enhance that development. Informal diagnostic suggestions are made to help build instruction on children's existing level of understanding.

early
number concepts

two types
of number knowledge

Chapter 2 distinguishes conceptual and procedural knowledge. Procedural knowledge—knowledge of symbols, syntax, and procedural rules—includes reading and writing numerals, oral or rote counting, oral counting on and back, and accurately counting sets of objects. For many years instruction in number focused almost exclusively on this procedural knowledge with the implicit assumption that it is the same as conceptual knowledge. The conceptual knowledge of number relies on procedural knowledge but is much more encompassing. A central element of conceptual knowledge of number is an understanding of quantity, cardinality, or "how much−ness." The basic concept of cardinality is expanded through the construction of other relationships based on quantities. As outlined in figure 1, these relationships help us deal with more than the question of "how many." They offer us flexibility in thinking about number by relating one quantity to another logically as well as visually or spatially.

interaction:
the role of oral counting

A complete conceptual knowledge of number is not constructed before the procedural knowledge of oral counting is acquired. A knowledge of counting interacts with a knowledge of number concepts, with counting playing a significant role in the early development of beginning number concepts.

Gelman and Gallistel (1978) refer to counting as a *scheme* in the Piagetian sense. That is, children use counting as a means of assimilating and developing their understanding of quantity. Preschool children are frequently encouraged to use counting to answer a wide array of questions about *how many*. Their earliest notion of number, acquired at age one or two, probably includes some concept of "one," possibly of "two," and then of "many." Collections of three and more are not clearly differentiated. The counting process is the means by which children can reflect on, and give more differentiated meaning to, the basic concepts of quantity and the broader concepts of number.

counting principles

Three rules, or principles, have been identified as necessary prerequisites for accurate counting: the *stable order rule,* the *one-to-one rule,* and the *abstraction rule* (Fuson and Hall 1983; Gelman and Gallistel 1978; Gelman and Meck 1986; Baroody and Ginsburg 1986). A brief examination of these principles provides some insight into the complexity of the counting process.

The stable order rule says that the words used in counting must be the same string of words from one count to the next. This principle of counting develops before children learn the correct string of counting words. That is, children who use an incorrect string of counting words, such as "one, two, three, five, seven," will repeat that same sequence each time they count. Of course, the standard counting sequence must be learned before counting will produce a result viewed by adults as correct.

The one-to-one rule states that each counting word must be paired with exactly one object being counted. Parents and teachers are familiar with counting errors in which children skip over an object in counting or count some objects more than once. Evidence suggests that children as young as three years are aware of the need for the one-to-one rule but may not be able to apply it consistently. Small sets of movable objects and sets arranged in a row are less likely to cause one-to-one errors than randomly arranged, unmovable objects. For pictured objects, marking objects as counting is done will reduce the number of errors.

The abstraction rule states that any collection of objects can be counted; the collection does not have to exhibit uniformity. Even children between the ages of two and three apply counting procedures to collections of dissimilar physical objects. The ability to perform logical classification tasks, such as identifying groupings with a common characteristic, does not seem to be a prerequisite to meaningful counting.

These three counting principles and a mastery of the standard sequence of number words are sufficient for children to "count," albeit in a strictly procedural manner. With the development of two additional principles, the *cardinality rule* and the *order-irrelevance rule,* the construction of the conceptual knowledge of number begins. Each rule represents a significant step in learning to count meaningfully.

The cardinality rule states that when a set is counted, the last counting word said indicates the numerosity of the set. The cardinality rule represents the all-important connections that a child makes between the counting procedure and the naming of the cardinality, or "how much—ness," of a set. The following two diagnostic activities are designed to assess these connections.

diagnosing
cardinality-counting connections

 Hide a number. Ask the child to count a set of objects. After the set is counted, even if done incorrectly, immediately cover the set with a box lid. Then ask, "How many counters are under the lid?" If the child responds with the last counting word used, it can be assumed the counting-cardinality connection has been made. **a**

 Last number named. Present a set of objects and ask the child, "How many?" If the last count is strongly emphasized or repeated, as in "One, two, three, four, five; *six* (there are six)," it can be inferred that the child is using the cardinality rule. To be certain, again ask "How many?" If the child recounts the set each time you ask, he or she probably does not understand the cardinality rule. **a**

Teachers should be aware that the following tasks may be interpreted differently by different children: "Tell me how many." "Count these for me." "Count to tell me how many." Before a count-cardinal connection is developed, the first two tasks appear to be very different to a child. By first grade, some children who are asked "How many?" may believe that counting is not permitted and attempt it only by looking, and thus make errors in the process.

Children who understand the order irrelevance rule know they can count a set in any order and get the same result. At about four to five years of age, children can count sets in different orders, from left to right and then right to left, but in most instances they are unable to anticipate that the result will be the same. The following activities can serve both a diagnostic and a learning function for children beginning to connect counting with early number concepts.

diagnosing
the order irrelevance rule

 Count both ways. Line up six counters and count them with the child. "What if we count them again but start from the other end?" (See fig. 2.) If the child responds "Six" without counting, he or she is using the order irrelevance rule. Regardless of the response, avoid trying to explain. Rather, suggest that the child test out his or her ideas by counting. Discuss the result and repeat the task with a larger set, such as ten. **a**

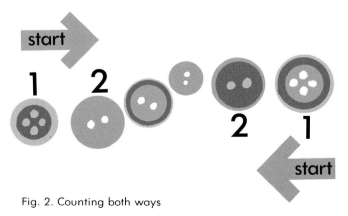

Fig. 2. Counting both ways

early counting activities

By kindergarten, most children demonstrate use of all five counting principles. However, all preschool and kindergarten children will likely benefit from additional counting activities, such as the following:

 Catch the mistake. Use a hand puppet to count objects on a flannel board or a table. Make different types of counting errors and ask children to catch the mistake and to explain what the puppet did wrong. For example, have the puppet count "one, two, four, five, . . ."; count one item twice; or count orally faster than it points to the objects. Include errors in the one-to-one rule and the use of the correct counting sequence. Talk with the puppet to include prediction errors. "How many do you think there will be if we count the red circles first?" **a**

 Show my number. Give children counters and fifteen or twenty small paper plates. Say a number, such as "Seven," and then say, "Show my number." Children put seven counters on each plate. With a partner, each child can take turns and count aloud. Some children may benefit from a tape recording that repeats the counting sequence to the specified number. **a**

cardinality rule activities

The following activities are appropriate for students who are beginning to demonstrate use of the cardinality rule.

 Count and rearrange. Have students count a set of objects. Then rearrange them (e.g., spread, stack, or shove together) and have students predict how many counters are present. Discuss their ideas and then recount. **a**

 Same, more, less. Have students make sets that have the same number of counters, more, or less counters than a given set. See figure 3. **a**

Fig. 3. Making sets with more, less, and same.

When children use counters to make a set, their opportunities to count, recount, count on, and reflect on these actions are much greater than if they simply counted orally or compared pictured sets. However, it is also worthwhile for children to select sets of matching quantities of three to ten objects from a wide array of sets of different configurations or patterns.

 Dot cards. Prepare a set of fifty or more cards about 5 cm square. On each card draw a set of three to ten dots, squares, or triangles in easily countable arrangements. These cards can be used in a variety of matching activities:

- Mix the cards and have students sort them into piles that show the same number of objects.
- Use the cards to play the traditional card game of war.
- Select a single card as the target and sort the remaining cards into three piles: those with more, less or the same number of objects.
- Make lotto boards with 15 squares slightly larger than the cards. On each square draw a set of objects similar to those on the cards. Each player has a different board. To begin, all the cards are

turned facedown. Players turn up one card at a time and try to match it with a square on their boards. If they cannot match the card to a square on their board, the card is turned over again. The first player to fill his or her board with matched cards is the winner. **a**

abstraction of the cardinality concept

The counting-cardinality connection eventually helps children construct a concept of cardinality that is separate from the objects that are counted. On the basis of their work with first-grade children, Steffe, von Glasersfeld, Richards, and Cobb (1983) offer some insight into this gradual construction of an abstract concept of number through counting.

At the lowest level, children are able only to apply their counting skills to sets that can be seen. At higher levels, children can apply a count to less concrete things, such as spaces where covered objects might be, finger point, or use number words. At the highest level, children can reflect on the result of counting as an entity in itself without its being tied to any other representation. These children are referred to as "abstract counters."

abstract counting activities

Counting tasks. Three similar activities are illustrated in figure 4. In each, a mat is used so that some counters are covered and some are not.

In the first, the abstract counter points to the cover, says "Six," and proceeds to count on. At lower levels, children may not be able to do the task, may first count by ones up to six, or perhaps use their fingers to create an image of the first six.

In the middle one, an abstract counter can switch from a counting use to a cardinality use of the number word *nine* (Fuson and Hall 1983).

In the last one, the child must count from the three showing up to the total of nine and keep track of the number of counts. The ability to "double count" or to count how many counts are being made is the clearest indication of an abstract counter. **a**

counting on and counting back

The meaningful use of counting on or counting back and simultaneously keeping track of the counts

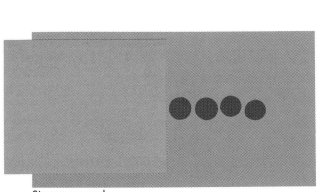

Six are covered.
How many are on the board?

I counted all of the disks
on the board. This one (point) was nine.
How many are on the board?

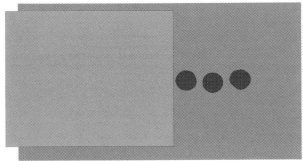

There are nine disks on the board.
How many are covered?

Fig. 4. Three abstract counting tasks

represents a significant growth in numerical understanding.

counting-on activities

Cover part and count on. Have children line up twelve small counters. Next have them slide four counters under their left hand as in figure 5. Now say, "Point to your hand. How many are there?" [Four] "All right, let's count like this: Four . . .,

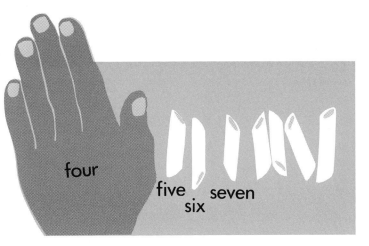

Fig. 5. A counting-on activity

[children point to their left hand], five, six, . . ., twelve." Repeat with other amounts under the left hand. **a**

Counting with children. Line up about ten children, each in front of a chair. Together, count four children at one end of the row and have them sit. "How many children are sitting? Let's count on to find how many in all." Together, they count "five, six, . . ., ten." Repeat with other numbers. **a**

Counting on can be done with a worksheet but perhaps not as meaningfully. Leutzinger (1979) found that activities such as those illustrated in figure 6 are progressively more difficult and should be preceded by activities involving real counters.

counting-back activities

Counting back is useful but significantly more difficult than counting on, but the following activities can help children develop this skill.

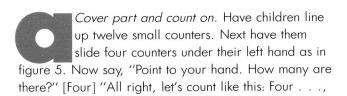*Take off/put on.* Have children line up eight counters on their desks. Say, "Take off one." Children then remove one counter, and say, "Seven!" Repeat taking off one counter until three counters remain. Then switch to "Put on one counter," returning to eight. Continue counting up and back. **a**

Stand up, sit down. Seat eight children in a row. As the class counts forward, have the children stand one at a time. When the last

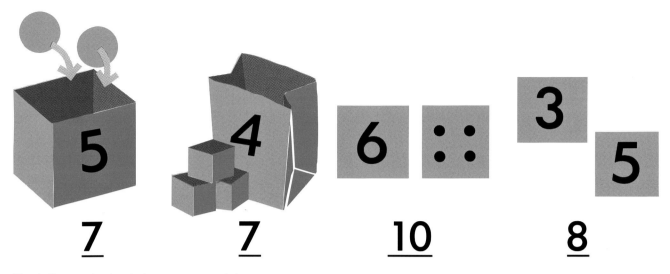

Fig. 6. Progressive levels for count-on worksheets

child is standing, reverse the counting sequence as the children sit down one at a time. Continue counting up and back. A regular cadence can be kept by clapping.

a

reading, writing, and using numerals

As children acquire number concepts, they must connect them to the numerals representing those concepts. This connection can be achieved by incorporating numerals into familiar activities. An effective method of incorporating numerals is to make collections of small numeral cards about 4 cm square. Children can place the cards on sets or pictures of sets and thus avoid the need for pencils or crayons or hard writing surfaces. Errors can be easily corrected without messy erasures. When children become proficient in forming numerals, cut paper into small squares and let them write the numeral they need on the paper and place it with the set. (This method still eliminates erasures.)

The calculator is an important vehicle for connecting counting activities with numerals. To make the calculator count, press ⊞ ① ⊟ ⊟ ⊟ . . . . The display will show 1, 2, 3, . . . , going up by one with each press of ⊟. To count backward from 10, press ① ⓪ ⊟ ① ⊟ ⊟ . . . . As children work on counting activities

with a calculator, they should say the numbers aloud as they press the keys. This helps them to coordinate the counting act, the counting words, and the numerals. (Because not all calculators have this "automatic constant" feature for ⊞ and ⊟, purchases of calculators should have this specification, as described in chapter 1.)

Count up and back. Count up and back between 4 and 8 with a calculator:

Press	Say	Display
4	four	4
+	plus	
1	one	1
=	five	5
=	six	6
=	seven	7
=	eight	8
−	*minus*	
1	one	1
=	seven	7
=	six	6

a

It has been common practice to teach numeral (and letter) recognition through a variety of drill-and-practice activities, which are generally effective. Teaching children how to write numerals presents a greater difficulty. Children who can read a correctly written numeral may write the same numeral reversed or in some other incorrect manner. Such activities as "writing" large numerals in the air, tracing them in a sandbox, or forming them with clay have all been used with good results.

Baroody (1987) makes a strong case for taking a cognitive approach to the reading and writing of numerals. The idea is to help children reflect on the shapes of numerals through verbal descriptions. In the writing of numerals, he suggests emphasizing a "motor plan": where to start, in which direction, round or straight, etc. For the numeral 7, for example, the plan might be to start at the top and go straight across to the right. Next make a slanted line all the way to the bottom. The motor plans should be practiced aloud by the children as they form the numerals. Children can use their own wording as long as it describes a correctly formed numeral.

 Make my number. One child gives oral directions to other children for drawing a secret numeral. The direction giver should not see what the others are doing. The children who are writing should try to do exactly what the direction giver is saying. **a**

Say your plan. Incorporate the use of verbal motor plans into more traditional numeral writing tasks. For example, have children say their motor plan each time they trace the numeral, as they make the numeral with a "snake" of modeling clay, or as they "paint" the numeral with water on the sidewalk. **a**

It is not necessary to wait until number concepts are developed to begin teaching children to read and write numerals. Practice activities can be done before and during work on counting and number concepts. In any event, difficulties that a child has in writing numerals should not be a major concern. Regardless of the approach, nearly every child masters these skills completely by third grade.

elaborating cardinality and new relationships

It has been traditional for the mathematics curriculum to move from relatively simple counting activities directly to addition and subtraction. This leap from beginning concepts of cardinality to addition and subtraction is enormous and premature. When children with limited number concepts attempt to master the various combinations of addition and subtraction, they must rely on counting as their sole means of solving problems. Children require a prolonged opportunity to engage in a variety of activities that will direct their immature counting skills toward the development of more useful relationships among numbers. The activities in this section are appropriately begun in kindergarten and continued at least through the second grade. The goal is broader, richer, and more flexible concepts of number.

instant recognition of patterned sets

Most adults and many children easily recognize dot patterns, such as those on dice and dominoes, without counting. When children first encounter patterned arrangements, they must count the objects to determine the number. With continued exposure to, and reflection on, the makeup of a pattern, its spatial configuration becomes familiar and the number is quickly recognized.

Recognizing dot patterns is a significant expansion of number concepts. For example, a child sees a two-by-three arrangement of dots and, without counting, recognizes six. But he or she has also counted this set many times. The dots are more than an abstract symbol for six. The spatial arrangement is intimately associated with the concept of six developed through counting. Since the patterned six does not require counting, the concept of six as a single entity is enhanced (Labinowicz 1985). A child is much more likely to count on from six if the set of six is in a recognizable pattern, or represents a well-known whole. Furthermore, a new idea of six as two groups of three is inherent in the pattern and supported by the visual gestalt. A three-by-three pattern for nine dots is learned in a similar manner. A knowledge of the two patterns leads to the obvious relationship between six and nine. Such relationships between numbers cannot be developed through counting.

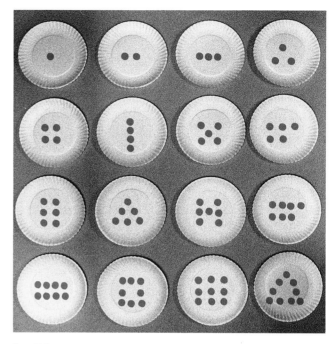

Fig. 7. Dot patterns to nine

patterns in less than a second. Children love to see how fast they can go. Make additional sets so that children can use them in pairs or small groups. **a**

Dot patterns. Make patterned dot sets on luncheon-sized paper plates using one color for each pattern, as shown in figure 7. Compact dot arrangements are best. When first introducing a pattern, give children counters and a construction-paper mat. Display a pattern for about three seconds. Then ask, "How many dots did you see? Can you use your mat and make what you saw?" Discuss the pattern and count various parts of it. For example, the domino five has four dots in a square and one in the middle. Add a few new patterns each day. As children become more familiar with the patterns, flash them more quickly. Soon they will recognize the

Dominoes. Make a set of 4-cm-by-8-cm dominoes from posterboard using the dot patterns in figure 7. (It is possible to make over 300 different dominoes but a set of about 60 is sufficient.) Use the dominoes for a variety of activities. Play dominoes using the standard rules. Let two or more children see how fast they can make a "train" using all the dominoes. Separate the dominoes into piles for three players and see who can make a domino train first. **a**

The patterns in figure 7 should be frequently used in any activities involving sets of objects. Later, the dot patterns can be expanded to include patterns in two or more parts; all the patterns will be incorporated into activities for developing other number relationships.

five as a benchmark

Another powerful way to think of numbers up to ten is to think of them in relationship to the number five. Five is chosen since two fives make the very important number ten. The idea is to think of the number eight, for example, as five and three more. Four is one less than a group of five. Japanese children are taught to make extensive use of the benchmark five in their representations of numbers, and evidence suggests that the approach pays off in students' mastery of basic facts and greater flexibility of numerical thinking (Hatano 1982; Kroll and Yabe 1987).

 Five-frames. Provide children with a construction paper mat with a five-frame and some counters. Numbers are shown on the five-frame by filling in the spaces from left to right (with no space left between), as in figure 8. For the numbers six to nine, counters are placed on the mat just under the five-frame. Call out numbers between one and nine in random order and have children represent the numbers on their five-frame mats. **a**

Five-bar cards. Make sets of five-bar cards for each child as in figure 9. Note that the card for five is a bar of five connected

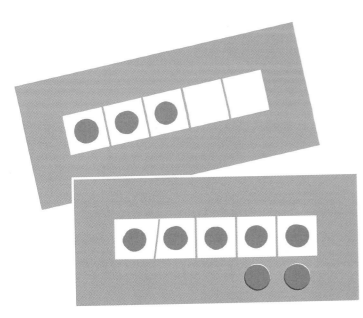
Fig. 8. A five-frame for three and seven

Fig. 9. Five-bar cards

squares but the squares on the other cards are separated. Ask the students to hold up seven. Emphasize the use of the five bar to show the numbers from five to nine. Five-bar cards can be used in any activity in which the students are to respond with the numbers one through nine. **a**

The two activities just described introduce children to the notion of five as a benchmark. Other materials can also illustrate this important relationship and be used for any number or basic-fact activity. Plastic connecting cubes can be used by making a bar of five and using four loose cubes. Japanese-style posterboard "number tiles" can also be made. Use strips of posterboard 3 cm wide and mark 3-cm squares on the strips. Cut 10 single squares and make two five-bars, storing individual sets in plastic bags. Finally, the dominoes or dot plates described earlier can be used by children to match each dot pattern as it is shown or drawn.

five and ten as benchmarks

It is just as important to think of seven as three away from ten as it is to think of it as five and two more. The use of ten as a benchmark is a natural progression from the activities just described (Thompson and Van de Walle 1984b). A construction paper mat with a ten-frame and two five-frames that form a two-by-five rectangles can be used in the same way as a five-frame. Numbers are represented on a ten-frame by first filling in, from left to right, the top row and then the bottom row, as shown in figure 10. Each number is then seen simultaneously in relationship to five and ten.

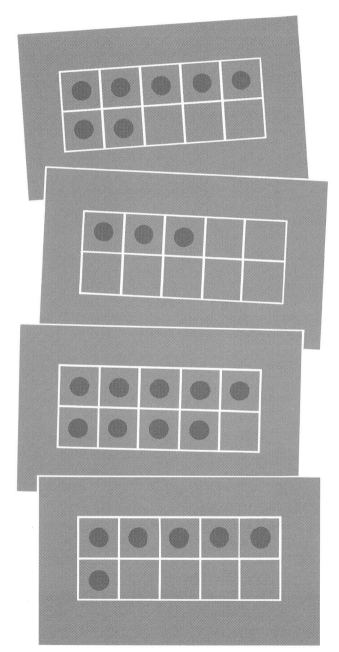

Fig. 10. Ten-frames for 3, 6, 7, and 9

Crazy mixed-up numbers. This activity is adapted from *Mathematics Their Way* (Baratta-Lorton 1976) and is similar to the first five-frame activity. Each child has a ten-frame and counters. The teacher calls out numbers from zero to ten. After each number, the children say "plus _____" or "minus _____" [whatever amount is required to change their ten-frame to the new number]. They then add or remove counters accordingly. Small groups of children can use long strips of paper with a list of about 15 "crazy mixed-up numbers." A student playing "teacher" can read off one number at a time to the rest of the players. **a**

ten-frame cards

Ten-frame cards provide more variations. Make cards about the size of small index cards from posterboard. Draw a ten-frame on each card using dots to show different amounts. A set of twenty cards consists of a zero card and a ten card and two each of the cards for one through nine. The following activities reinforce the concept of ten:

Flash ten-frames. Flash ten-frame cards to the class to see how fast they can tell how many dots are shown. Spend three to five minutes with this activity frequently. Encourage speed—children love to see how fast they can go.

Two important alternatives to saying the number of dots are to say the number of spaces instead of the dots or to say the "ten-fact," for example, "Seven and three." **a**

Games. Draw a large ten-frame on the chalkboard or an overhead transparency and encourage the children to think in terms of the ten-frame for the following two verbal activities:

1. Play "Five And" by calling out a number between five and ten. Children respond with "five and _____" using the appropriate number. For example, the teacher calls "Eight," and the children respond, "Five and three."

2. In "Make Ten," the teacher calls out a number between zero and nine. The children respond with the

74   Chapter Four

later and require special attention. Even children who can count on and count back must connect this procedural knowledge with the conceptual ideas of "more than" and "less than."

a *Dot pattern.* Add the dot patterns shown in figure 11 to the collection of dot plates described in figure 7. The single or double dots added to a basic pattern are in a contrasting color. Discuss with the children the "one more than" and "two more than" relationships between these new patterns and the original patterns. **a**

a *Dots, any form.* Present children with sets of objects in any form (dot patterns, ten-frames, numerals) and have them make or draw sets that are one more than the set given. The same can be done with one less than, two more than, and two less than. **a**

a *Flash dots.* If the dot plates or ten-frames are flashed as in earlier activities, have children respond with the number that is one more than the number shown. Repeat for the three other relationships. **a**

number required to make ten. For example, if you call "Four," the children respond with "Six." **a**

Numerals or dot patterns can be matched with ten-frames drawn on paper, or children can draw dots into small ten-frames. Once introduced, the ten-frame becomes a powerful way to represent and construct numbers and can be used interchangeably with dot patterns and other number representations.

one or two more, or less

Although virtually all kindergarten children can compare two obviously different sets (Baroody 1987), the more specific relationships of one more and two more, and one less and two less are constructed much

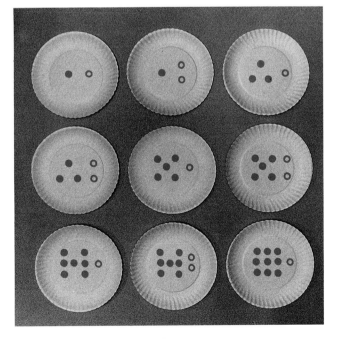

Fig. 11. Dot patterns: one more and two more

Domino trains. Have the children make "one more than" domino trains. Each new domino must be played so that the new square is one more than the last square. When a ten is played, the next domino can be any number (fig. 12). Similar rules are used for the three other relationships.　　**a**

Calculators. A strictly symbolic activity that gives children practice with these four special relationships can be done on a calculator. For a two-less-than exercise, students begin by pressing $\boxed{-}$ $\boxed{2}$ $\boxed{=}$, then any number. Students try to predict the result before they press $\boxed{=}$.

Press	Say two less	Press $\boxed{=}$
$\boxed{8}$	"six"	6
$\boxed{4}$	"two"	2
$\boxed{7}$	"five"	5

a

Double five-card. Add a double five-card to the five-bar cards described in figure 9. A double five-card is simply an empty ten-frame or two five-bars. These six cards can now be used as response cards for any activity in which the answers range from one to nineteen. For example, call out numbers and have the children use the five-bar cards to show the number that is one more than the number you call.　　**a**

Two more than. Call out numbers one at a time. Pause for a few seconds and then ask someone to say the number that is two more than the number called. This strictly verbal activity

profitably fills those spare minutes before lunch or between lessons. An overhead calculator can be used to "call" the numbers and confirm the responses, making this a very quiet activity.　　**a**

difference between numbers

The last three sections have suggested activities that help children focus on some special relationships between numbers, that is, numbers have been related to five and to ten and to one or two more or less. Those relationships are easier for children to construct than a more general knowledge of differences between numbers. In this section, activities are presented that help children determine how much more or less one number is than another, ideas closely related to basic addition and subtraction facts. The idea is to explore such relationships apart from symbolic addition and subtraction.

Difference war more. Use any dot cards or the number cards from a standard deck of cards. All cards are dealt to the two players who turn them facedown as in the familiar game of war. A "kitty" with approximately 50 counters is also prepared. On each play both players turn up a card from their decks. The player whose card is more wins a number of counters from the kitty equal to the difference between the cards. Both players keep their cards. Ties are ignored because the difference is zero.

Fig. 12. Domino train for one more

The game is over when the kitty is empty. The player with the most counters wins.

In "Difference War Less" the player whose card is less wins the counters.

Make the difference. In this activity students spread out about ten to fifteen dominoes and then place counters next to each to show the difference between the two sets on the domino.

Bar graphs. "How much more?" and "How much less?" questions should always be a part of the discussion that follows the construction of a simple bar graph. For example, if the class has just finished making the graph shown in chapter 12, ask questions such as these (notice the pairing of "more" and "less" questions):

How many more children have cats as favorite pets than have dogs?

How many less have snakes than have birds as favorite pets?

Difference game. Two children sit side by side and work on one number during the activity (Thompson and Van de Walle 1984a). For example, for seven, two bars of seven connecting cubes each are used. (A row of squares or wooden cubes are good substitutes.) One bar is placed on a mat. The first child takes part of the other bar and places it to the right of the first bar, as in figure 13. The second child examines the two bars (or rows of cubes) and describes the situation: "The difference between seven and two is five." The bars can be moved next to each other to verify the result. The short bar is removed and another example displayed. After several turns, the two students switch roles.

For a challenge version the first bar, after being counted, is placed under the mat and out of sight.

Chapter 6 describes children solving addition and subtraction story problems with countable objects. Of the fourteen types of story problems possible, six involve differences between two amounts. These stories can be explored even before the formal introduction of addition and subtraction. Modeling difference story problems with counters is an excellent way to help children construct difference relationships between small numbers.

Fig. 13. The difference game for 7 and 2

part-part-whole concepts

a new conceptualization

The early number concepts and relationships that have been discussed so far are constructed principally through the counting process. Through counting, children develop and use a *successor schema,* or "mental number line," for understanding quantity (see fig. 14 [Resnick 1983]). Although counting is an important learning tool, many number relationships are difficult to construct with only a successor schema. For example, a count of 9 objects in no way signals the fact that 9 is composed of 6 and 3 or 3 and 4 and 2. Even the difference relationships described in the previous section are difficult to construct with counting alone, especially for larger quantities and larger differences.

Fig. 14. The number line schema for numbers

A more sophisticated schema allows one to consider two or more quantities as separate entities and also as parts of a larger whole. Two models for this part-part-whole schema, shown in figure 15, illustrate how a quantity can be thought of in terms of its smaller parts.

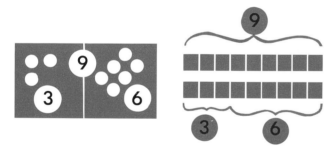

Fig. 15. Two part-part-whole models

A part-part-whole understanding of number marks a major advance in the child's understanding. Resnick (1983, p. 114) states that "probably the major conceptual achievement of the early school years is the interpretation of numbers in terms of part and whole relationships. . . . This enrichment of number understanding permits forms of mathematical problem solving and interpretation that are not available to younger children." At the very least the part-part-whole schema is in some way related to children's understanding of addition and subtraction connections (Baroody, Ginsburg, and Waxman 1983), the solution

of addition and subtraction word problems (Riley, Greeno, and Heller 1983), and an understanding of place value (Resnick 1983).

The fact that many children do not exhibit part-part-whole understanding until some years after they learn to count suggests that an aspect of this construct may be related to maturation. Some think that the classic Piagetian class-inclusion task (shown a bouquet of three daisies and eight roses the child is asked if there are more roses or more flowers) is an indicator of children's ability to construct part-part-whole constructs (e.g., Kamii 1985). The task is not solved by most children until age seven or eight. It can certainly be argued that the class-inclusion task has a heavy linguistic burden that is not involved in understanding that a set of seven can consist of a set of two and a set of five.

Many children apparently fail to develop a part-part-whole conceptualization of number and continue into the upper grades or even adulthood relying almost entirely on less efficient counting techniques. A failure to use the part-part-whole construct imposes a serious burden on further number development. The position of this chapter is that children can be aided in construction of the part-part-whole schema by engaging in, and reflecting on, meaningful activities emphasizing the part-part-whole relationship. The activities already presented focus children's attention in this direction.

part-part-whole activities

Many part-part-whole activities have children focus on a single number at a time. The idea is to see that the number seven, for example, can be thought of in terms of parts: two and five, six and one, three and two and two, and so on.

Part-part-whole mat. Give pairs of children a part-part-whole mat and counters (fig. 16). In working on six, one child puts six counters on the mat with some in each section. The other child

Fig. 16. Part-part-whole mat for six

a *Number stations.* In these activities, children make designs, collections, or drawings with a specified number of elements in each. One to three children use one set of materials to form ten or more patterns, each having the same number of items. They then return to the patterns and say a "number sentence" for each. A pattern or design may be seen in more than one way, and children should be encouraged to look for more than one combination, as the examples in figure 17 show. **a**

An entire class can work on number stations with different groups using different materials. You will need to interact with the children to encourage them to "read" their designs and look at them in different ways.

a *Two-part dot patterns.* Add two-part dot patterns to the dot plates described earlier. Some possibilities are shown in figure 18. A different color should be used for each part. (Patterns with parts of 1 and 2 have already been introduced.)**a**

dot-card activities

A set of small dot cards with a variety of configurations for each number can profitably add to a number development program. Make a master for a set of cards; each card should be about 5 cm square. These can be duplicated on construction paper or card stock, laminated, and cut apart. In figure 19, nine dot cards for eight are shown. These include each pattern suggested earlier, one that requires counting, and ten-

"reads" the mat: "Two and four is the same as six." After several combinations the children reverse roles. Six and zero is an important and legitimate combination. **a**

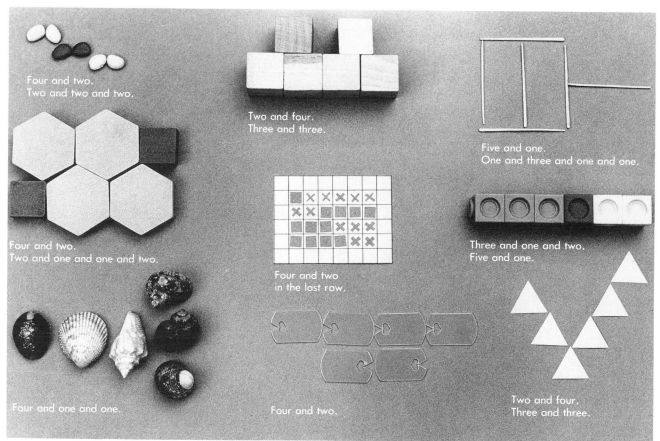

Fig. 17. Number station examples

frame cards with standard and unusual configurations. Similar cards can be devised for each number from one through ten. Four or five cards for the smaller numbers are sufficient. An assortment of cards is shown in figure 20.

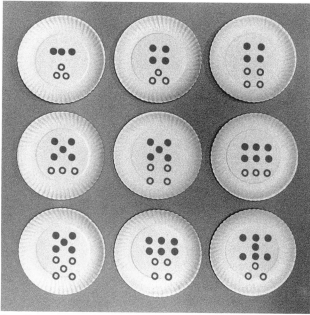

Fig. 18. Two-part dot patterns

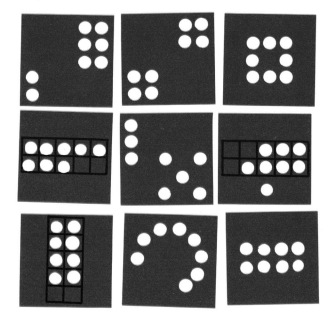

Fig. 19. Dot cards for eight

Fig. 20. An assortment of dot cards

a *Double war* (Kamii 1985). The game is played like war but on each play two cards are turned up by each player instead of one. The winner is the one with the larger total. In playing, children begin to use relationships among the cards to determine the winner and do not necessarily find the totals. **a**

a *Match me.* Select one card at random. Find another card that has the same number of dots (or one more than, two less than, etc.). Put that match aside and repeat until no further matches can be made. **a**

a *Two-part-numbers.* Specify a number between five and ten and have students work together to find pairs of cards that total the specified number. While the rest of the children close their eyes, one player turns down one card in each pair. In turn, the other players try to determine how many dots are on each facedown card.

For a variation, give each player three cards with fewer dots than the target number. The players then race to find another card that, together with the initial cards, totals the target number. **a**

missing-part activities

In the activities involving two parts, children begin to think about numbers in terms of a missing part, for example, three and what will make seven? This type of activity is not restricted to dot cards. Number strips and two-column strips (fig. 21) can be used in the earlier number-station activities as well as in the following missing-part activities. Materials can be easily made by cutting tagboard that has been printed with a 2-cm grid. Both should include pieces with one to ten squares, with more of the smaller sizes than the larger ones. With the two-column strips, odd numbers have an "odd" square on one end, providing yet another relationship for children to explore. Sets can be made for the overhead projector by punching a hole in each square.

The dot cards incorporate many of the relationships that have already been discussed as well as the part-part-whole construct. As children search through a pile of dot cards for a particular number or use a card in a game, different configurations tend to induce mental shifts from one type of relationship to another. The dot cards can be profitably used in many activities already described as well as those that follow.

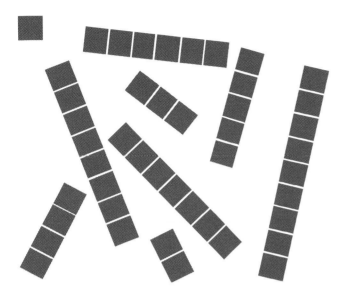

class directed by the teacher. This game can be played in a similar manner using ten-frames, dot cards, numeral cards, or even oral-number names presented by the leader. In the beginning it is best for each student to have his or her own set of materials. **a**

a *Two-part cards.* Sets of "two-part cards" can be made for each number from five through ten, or even higher. A set for eight has sets of dots for the numbers zero through eight on one side and the other part of eight shown on the reverse. Color-code the cards so that the sets for each number do not get mixed up. The cards are used like flashcards. Children see one side and try to name the part on the other side. Numerals can be included along with the dots. Later, sets can be made that have only numerals. **a**

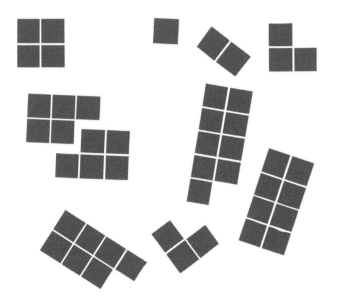

Fig. 21. Number strips and two-column strips

a *I wish I had.* This game focuses on one number. The teacher or leader shows a number strip or a two-part strip and says, "I have three. I wish I had eight." The rest of the children respond by holding up the other part of eight (five) that they find in their own set of materials. Alternatively, they can simply say the other part orally. The game can be played by two children, a small group, or an entire

addition and subtraction symbolism

The use of a part-part-whole schema has been shown to be related to students' ability to solve certain types of addition and subtraction word problems (Cobb 1987; Carpenter 1986).

As children begin to learn about addition and subtraction concepts, they can also begin to *encode* part-part-whole and missing-part activities by writing addition and subtraction equations. For example, when working at a number station (fig. 17), children can write a corresponding addition equation besides saying a number sentence for a design. Equations can be written on small pieces of paper and placed with each design. Children write the relationships they have constructed, thought about, and said aloud. They write mathematics, not just do worksheets.

When one part is removed or missing, the situation can be encoded as a subtraction sentence. One way to do so is to make the known, or visible, part the "take away" number, or the subtrahend. For example, in the "I Wish I Had" games, if the target number is eight and the number shown is five, it would be encoded as

8 − 5 = 3. In a similar manner, children can count out eight counters on one side of a part-part-whole mat and then cover them with a piece of tagboard. Next they reach under the cover and move some counters to the other side of the mat. Then they can write a subtraction fact as shown in figure 22. By encoding the known part as the take-away amount, the child is encouraged to think in terms of addition or a missing part to determine the result. Examine the subtraction-fact strategies suggested in chapter 7. In almost every instance, the child is taught to work from the subtrahend to the minuend. In part-part-whole terminology, children can master subtraction facts by thinking, "What is the missing part?" For example, for the fact 9 − 6 = □, the child who is using a part-part-whole construct can think, "Six and what makes nine?"

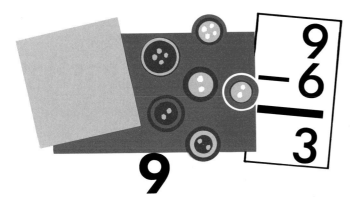

Fig. 22. Missing parts for subtraction

numbers to twenty

So far, this chapter has focused on developing concepts and relationships for numbers through ten. Numbers larger than ten can be understood principally by making connections between relationships among smaller numbers and similar or analogous relationships among larger numbers. For example, the "two more than, two less than" relationship between five and seven can be extended to fifteen and seventeen. These and similar extensions of previously constructed relationships are not automatically transferred to larger numbers. In this section, suggestions are made for helping children extend relationships among smaller numbers to the teens and beyond.

counting

Counting beyond ten and even well beyond twenty is not uncommon even for the kindergarten child. As with smaller numbers, much can be gained from counting. Some effort should be made to help children see the oral pattern in the teens so that they can connect knowledge of the earlier sequence to the higher numbers. Counting-on and counting-back activities can be conducted into the teens in the same way as with smaller numbers. The calculator is useful for counting (see chapter 1).

pre-place-value relation with ten

It is tempting for adults to explain the numbers between ten and twenty in terms of place value; that is, to explain the 1 in 16 as representing one ten and the 6 as representing six ones. This place-value conceptualization of 16 involves two ideas that are difficult for the young child to construct: first, the idea of counting sets of ten as single entities (as in one ten, two tens, etc.), and second, using a positional-value numeration system to represent them (e.g., the digit in the second place records how many tens).

The number ten should, however, play a significant role in helping children conceptualize the teens and extend earlier relationships to these numbers. After children have begun to use a part-part-whole schema to understand smaller numbers, a special part-part-whole relationship for numbers greater than ten can be developed. Specifically, emphasis should be placed on numbers having two parts, where one of the parts is ten. Children learn that the easiest way to think about seventeen is that "seven and ten is the same as seventeen." No attempt is made to relate the 1 in 17 to the ten part of this representation. The set of ten does not have to be to the left of the set of seven. Models for ten should be the familiar dot patterns and ten-frames that were used earlier (see figure 23). Place-value materials that are designed to help with the construct of *one* ten rather than *a set of ten* are not suggested at this level.

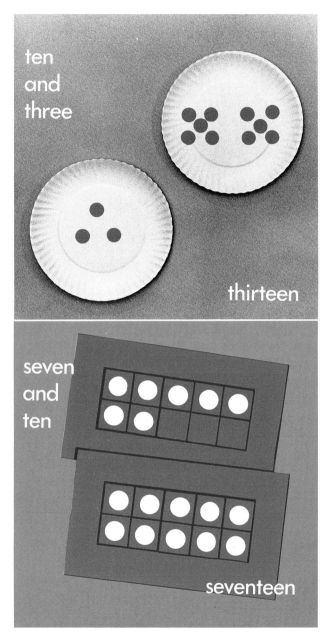

Fig. 23. Part-part-whole for the teens

 Part-part-whole for teens. On the overhead projector place ten counters in one part of a simple part-part-whole mat. Count them with

the class. Place a set with fewer than ten counters in the other part and count them. Next count the entire set, both parts, by ones. Have the class chorus the combination: "Ten and five is fifteen." Turn the mat around and say the combination in the reverse order. Change only the side with fewer than ten counters and repeat several times. **a**

 *Crazy mixed-up numbers.* Extend the "Crazy Mixed-Up Numbers" game but give each player two ten-frames drawn on construction paper, one under the other. A new rule is that for numbers ten or greater, one of the ten-frames must be completely filled (it is not important which one). Stop periodically on numbers between five and twenty and have children say the part-part-whole combination. For numbers greater than ten, one part is always ten: "Ten and three is thirteen." For numbers less than ten, one part is always five. **a**

Make it a point to represent frequently numbers greater than ten with a distinct set of ten using a dot pattern or ten-frame. It is not necessary to use a left-to-right orientation to show the ten part.

As noted earlier, the relationships of one more than, one less than, two more than, and two less than should be extended to the teens.

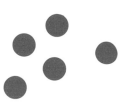 *One or two more or less.* On the overhead projector show a set of four counters, and ask children what is one more than or two less than, and so on. After each response, add a filled ten-frame to the display and repeat the question (fig. 24). **a**

"how many?" (five)
"and one more is?" (six)

"how many?" (fifteen)
"and one more is?" (sixteen)

Fig. 24. Extending relationships to teens

doubles and near doubles

The double (e.g., sixteen is "double eight") and the near-double relationships (seventeen is "double eight and one more") are frequently viewed as tricks or strategies for mastering addition and subtraction facts (see chapter 7). However, these relationships provide a powerful conceptualization of the numbers from ten through twenty and, as such, are well worth developing before mastery of the basic facts begins.

Calculator doubles. Use the "double maker" on a calculator by pressing [2] [×] [=] (the display will then show 4). A press of any digit key followed by [=] will give the double of the number pressed. Children can work in pairs to try to say the double before the [=] key is pressed.

This activity, along with such visual representations as double dot patterns and such simple verbal drills as "Double seven is _____" can supplement fact practice. **a**

estimation of quantities

Another important kind of numerical relationship is that of approximation. Children need to develop intuitive feelings for quantities that they see in various visual arrangements and forms.

Ten or twenty? Each student is given two squares of construction paper, one yellow and one green. On the green square, have each student write a large "10" and on the yellow square a large "20." The teacher then places between five and thirty countable objects in a random display on the overhead projector while it is turned off. Students' attention is directed to the screen, and the light is turned on for about one second. Students hold up the square of paper showing the number closer to the number of objects they saw on the screen. The colored paper will allow you to see at a glance how well your students are estimating. Count the objects with the class and let them determine which number is closer. Be sure to use a wide variety of objects such as grains of rice, paper clips, plastic chips, pencils, buttons, pasta, and toothpicks. **a**

Occasionally you can arrange the items in an array of rows and columns or in groups of equal amounts. If the

Concepts of Number   85

objects—beans, centimeter cubes, toothpicks—are mixed together, the challenge is quite different.

Preschool and kindergarten children can play "Five or Ten?" in the same way. Older children can play "Ten or Thirty?" or Fifty or a Hundred?" Having children try to guess the exact number is not recommended since they might think that they are supposed to get an exact answer.

Encourage children to estimate through the use of fixed choices. This method is more effective with younger children than if they are asked to estimate or guess.

Children's estimates of measures are directly related to their understanding of quantities. It makes sense, therefore, to correlate number development with measurement. Activities in chapter 11 suggest the relationship between estimates of quantities and estimates of measures.

summary

Number concepts consist of many relationships. Children's understanding grows slowly over time as they construct new relationships between and among simple concepts of quantity. Although counting is the vehicle that children use initially to understand number, an emphasis only on counting is a serious curricular error. Children must be given opportunities to develop ideas beyond simple counting and matching of sets with numerals. Activities that develop spatial patterns; establish connections to the benchmarks of five and ten, one or two more or one or two less; and highlight differences of five and ten, differences between numbers, and part-part-whole relationships should have a major place in the mathematics curriculum for children of ages three through nine.

In the traditional primary-level curriculum, counting skill is generally viewed as the ultimate goal of number development rather than the initial step. Therefore instruction moves directly from counting to the introduction of symbolic addition and subtraction. The result is that many, if not most, children fail to develop

number sense characterized by a rich variety of relationships. Instead they continue to count their way through elementary school.

Mastery of addition and subtraction facts is now developed through the use of strategies. These strategies are the application of the relationships discussed in this chapter, as are concepts of larger numbers.

For basic facts, mental computation, estimation, measurement, and problem solving, a strong argument can be made that number sense, represented by an understanding of the many relationships, provides flexible ways to think about numbers. Such flexibility enhances students' performance and understanding. Spending significant amounts of time early in the curriculum on the development of the number relationships presented here deserves serious attention.

references

Baratta-Lorton, Mary. *Mathematics Their Way.* Menlo Park, Calif.: Addison-Wesley Publishing Co., 1976.

Baroody, Arthur J. *Children's Mathematical Thinking: A Developmental Framework for Preschool, Primary, and Special Education Teachers.* New York: Teachers College Press, Columbia University, 1987.

Baroody, Arthur J., and Herbert P. Ginsburg. "The Relationship between Initial Meaningful and Mechanical Knowledge of Arithmetic." In *Conceptual and Procedural Knowledge: The Case of Mathematics,* edited by James Hiebert. Hillsdale, N.J.: Lawrence Erlbaum Associates, 1986.

Baroody, Arthur J., Herbert P. Ginsburg, and Barbara Waxman. "Children's Use of Mathematical Structure." *Journal for Research in Mathematics Education* 14 (May 1983): 156–68.

Carpenter, Thomas P. "Conceptual Knowledge as a Foundation for Procedural Knowledge." In *Conceptual and Procedural Knowledge: The Case of Mathematics,* edited by James Hiebert. Hillsdale, N.J.: Lawrence Erlbaum Associates, 1986.

Cobb, Paul. "An Analysis of Three Models of Early Number Development." *Journal for Research in Mathematics Education* 18 (May 1987): 163–79.

Fuson, Karen C., and J. W. Hall. "The Acquisition of Early Number Word Meanings: A Conceptual Analysis and Review." In *The Development of Mathematical Thinking,* edited by Herbert Ginsburg. New York: Academic Press, 1983.

Gelman, Rochel, and C. R. Gallistel. *The Child's Understanding of Number.* Cambridge: Harvard University Press, 1978.

Gelman, Rochel, and Elizabeth Meck. "The Notion of Principle: The Case of Counting." In *Conceptual and Procedural Knowledge: The Case of Mathematics,* edited by James Hiebert. Hillsdale, N.J.: Lawrence Erlbaum Associates, 1986.

Hatano, G. "Learning to Add and Subtract: A Japanese Perspective." In *Addition and Subtraction: A Cognitive Perspective,* edited by Thomas P. Carpenter, James M. Moser, and Thomas A. Romberg. Hillsdale, N.J.: Lawrence Erlbaum Associates, 1982.

Kamii, Constance K. *Young Children Reinvent Arithmetic.* New York: Teachers College Press, Columbia University, 1985.

Kroll, Diana Lambdin, and Toshiaki Yabe. "A Japanese Educator's Perspective on Teaching Mathematics in the Elementary School." *Arithmetic Teacher* 35 (October 1987): 36–43.

Labinowicz, E. *Learning from Children: New Beginnings for Teaching Numerical Thinking.* Menlo Park, Calif.: Addison-Wesley Publishing Co., 1985.

Leutzinger, Larry. "The Effects of Counting-on on the Acquisition of Addition Facts in Grade One." Ph.D. diss., University of Iowa, 1979.

Resnick, Lauren. "A Developmental Theory of Number Understanding." In *The Development of Mathematical Thinking,* edited by Herbert Ginsburg. New York: Academic Press, 1983.

Riley, M. S., James G. Greeno, and J. I. Heller. "Development of Children's Problem-solving Ability in Arithmetic." In *The Development of Mathematical Thinking,* edited by Herbert Ginsburg. New York: Academic Press, 1983.

Steffe, Leslie P., Ernst von Glaserfeld, J. Richards, and Paul Cobb. *Children's Counting Types: Philosophy, Theory, and Application.* New York: Praeger Publishers, 1983.

Thompson, Charles S., and John A. Van de Walle. "Let's Do It: Modeling Subtraction Situations." *Arithmetic Teacher* 32 (October 1984a): 8–12.

_____. "Let's Do It: The Power of Ten." *Arithmetic Teacher* 32 (November 1984b): 6–11.

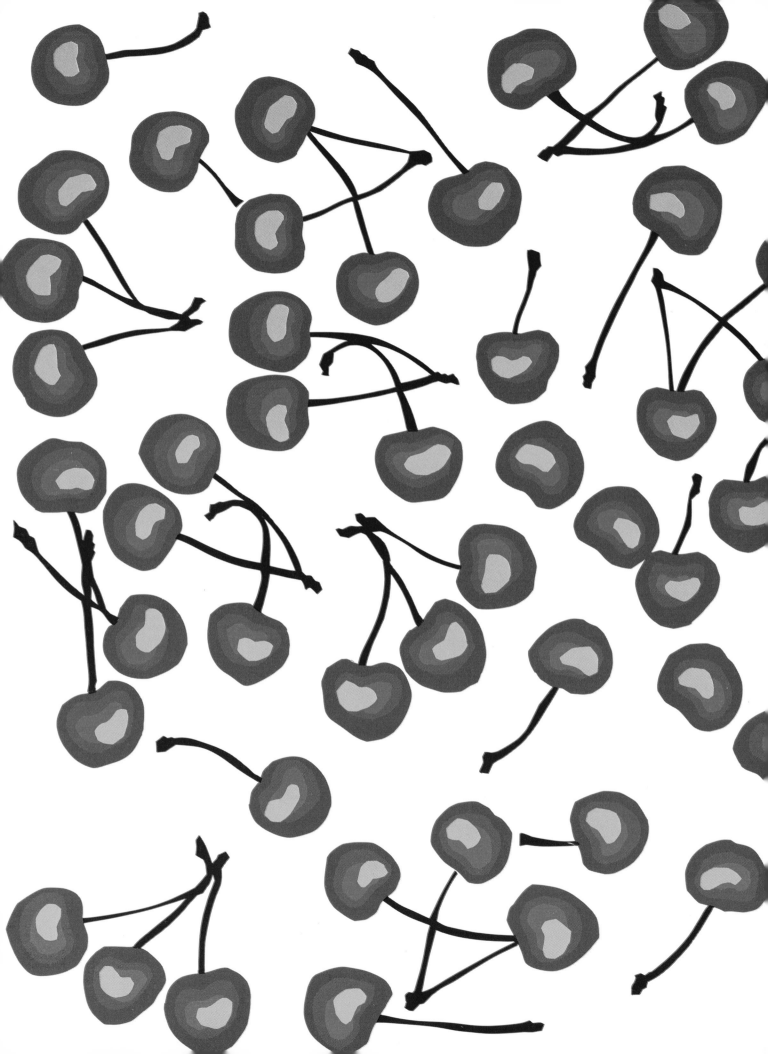

5
place value and larger numbers
charles thompson

A sound understanding of numbers with two or more digits includes thinking of each number in terms of its component parts, its relation to other numbers, relative magnitudes, and practical experiences. For example, think of 265—

■ as component parts—
265 singles
   2 hundreds 6 tens 5 ones
26 tens 5 ones
   5 fifties and 15 more;

■ in relation to other numbers—
   15 more than 250
   65 more than 200
   35 less than 300;

■ as relative magnitudes—
large compared to 13
about the same as 273
small compared to 894;

■ from practical experiences—
number of children in the auditorium
weight of a large adult in pounds
cost of a video recorder in dollars
not as the number of children in class.

The major goal of this chapter is to delineate the conceptual structure of two-, three-, and four-digit numbers and to give suggestions on how these ideas can be built effectively with children. The concepts developed in chapter 4 are extended here to reflect the major place-value ideas to be taught from kindergarten through grade 4.

This chapter begins with a description of the three major components of place-value knowledge. Then ungrouped and pregrouped materials are used to illustrate developmental activities for children. Special attention is given to counting by ones, by groups, and by tens and ones. Included are equivalent representations, sequential grouping, comparison, rounding, and estimating. Similar attention is given to three-digit numbers, and then some suggestions are given for larger numbers. The chapter concludes with suggestions for diagnosis.

place-value knowledge

Three basic components of place-value knowledge are represented in the triangular structure shown in figure 1, an elaboration of a similar diagram presented by Payne and Rathmell (1975). At the top of the structure are conceptual models, materials that embody or represent base-ten conceptual knowledge for children. The two lower corners are oral and written representations of those concepts. To understand place value means to have conceptual knowledge, represented by the models at the top, and to be able to connect this knowledge to oral and symbolic representations of that knowledge. These connections are depicted by the solid lines on the sides of the figure.

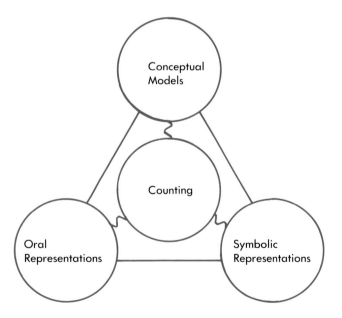

Fig. 1. Components of place-value knowledge

The activity of counting is central to developing conceptual knowledge and is also a principal way to make the connections with the oral and written forms. As the models and associated concepts become more elaborate, the method of counting changes accordingly. For example, if a collection of twenty-three objects is grouped in tens, then the child might count, "Ten, twenty, twenty-one, twenty-two, twenty-three," to make the connection between the model (the objects) and the oral name (twenty-three). Counting, "One, two (tens), and one, two, three (singles)," helps to make the connection between the two groups of ten, the three singles, and the symbolic form, 23. If the child changes the model and represents 23 as 1 ten and 13 ones, the counting leads to different oral and symbolic forms. The coordination of these different counts and representations constitutes a complete and flexible understanding of place-value knowledge (fig. 2).

A guiding principle for instruction on place-value concepts is that early developmental work should focus on concrete models and oral representations of those models. This emphasis on the connections indicated by the left side of the triangular structure in figure 1 should continue until the concepts are firmly established. Having students mechanically put numerals in columns is of no value if the complex and difficult grouping concepts have not already been constructed by the students. There is little doubt that young children can count the number of sets of ten sticks and write that number in a box labeled TENS and similarly count single sticks and write that number in a box labeled ONES. But such activity does not help students construct the relationships between tens and ones or the concept of representing larger quantities by using groups of ten and singles.

place-value materials

Two basic kinds of materials are used for place-value instruction, *ungrouped materials* and *pregrouped materials.*

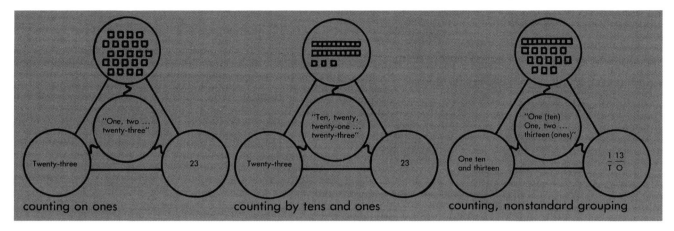

Fig. 2. Coordinating grouping and counting

ungrouped materials

Ungrouped materials, shown in figure 3, are simply individual items such as beans, cubes, or straws that children form into groups. For example, if a child has enough beans to form a group of ten, those ten beans can be placed in a plastic bag or a small cup, and used as a unit, a single group of ten. Ten cups or bags of ten beans, ten groups of ten, can be formed into a new group and become the next unit, called a hundred.

pregrouped materials

Pregrouped materials, by contrast, are formed into groups before the child uses them. When the child has enough single items to form a group, those items are *traded* for a different item, which replaces or represents the group of items traded in.

There are two types of pregrouped materials, proportional and nonproportional. Examples of proportional materials include base-ten blocks, or equivalent models cut from tagboard, and beans glued in tens to Popsicle sticks (fig. 3). The essential feature of proportional materials is that each piece is physically ten times as large as the next smaller piece. The *tens* piece is ten times as large as the *ones* piece, and the *hundreds* piece is ten times as large as the *tens* piece. Nonproportional materials, such as colored chips, abacus, and coins, are not related by size. For example, a blue chip may be worth ten yellow chips because it was defined to be so, not for any intrinsic reason. Any exchange relationships must be imposed on the materials by the children.

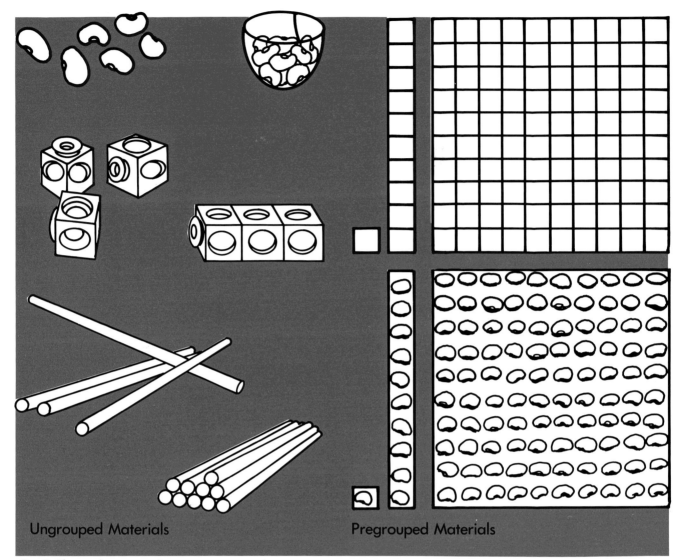

Ungrouped Materials

Pregrouped Materials

Fig. 3. Place-value materials

advantages and disadvantages

The advantage of ungrouped materials is that the children actually form and break apart the groups themselves, helping them construct mental relationships between ones and tens and between tens and hundreds. Ungrouped materials would be the best type of model if not for disadvantages from practical use. With ungrouped materials, it is tedious and time consuming to count tens and to build models for

hundreds. A bundle of ten bundles or a tub of ten cups of ten is impressive and useful for demonstration but not practical for use at children's desks.

By using pregrouped materials, however, it is relatively easy to build numbers in the hundreds and even thousands. But pregrouped materials have disadvantages, too. Pregrouped proportional materials are built to exemplify the grouping relationship by making each piece proportionally larger than the next smaller piece. However, even though this relationship exists in the materials, there is no guarantee that it exists in the mind of the child. Many children learn to refer to a wooden ten-stick as a "ten" but still count to find how many ones cubes are needed to build it. Pregrouped nonproportional materials have an even more serious disadvantage. Because the pieces are not related by size, the child must already understand the exchange relationships that the pieces are defined to possess. That is, the child must already understand base-ten relationships. For this reason, nonproportional materials will not be used in activities in this chapter and are not recommended for the development of place-value concepts.

Because of the nature of place-value materials and of place-value concepts, it is important to choose and sequence the use of materials carefully. Children developing the concept of a group as a single entity simultaneously consisting of ten singles should be using ungrouped materials. After initial grouping ideas and place-value concepts are firmly established, pregrouped proportional materials can be introduced. Given sufficient experience with ungrouped materials, most children are ready to use proportional pregrouped materials and can understand the equivalences in trading ten of one item for one of a different item, and vice versa.

concepts for two-digit numbers

Counting groups of objects as single entities and naming those groups with counting words like *ten* and *hundred* are significant hurdles in the construction of base-ten conceptual knowledge.

making and counting groups

Before beginning with ideas of tens and ones, children can benefit from separating a set into groups of a specified size and then counting these groups as single units.

Groups of 4, 5, or 6. Use three different types of counters, such as shells, macaroni, and chips. Place from 20 to 30 counters in each bag. Have children make as many groups of 4 as possible and record the results as in figure 4. "How many fours do you have? How many extras? Write the number on the sheet." Repeat for groups of 5 and 6.

Use the record sheets and have students estimate the number of counters. Have students put the counters back in the bag and exchange their record sheets and bags with a partner. "Look at the record sheet. Now estimate the number of counters in the bag for that record sheet." After estimating, have them count them by ones to see how close they were with their estimates.

Attachable plastic cubes can also be used to show groupings. Begin with a long stick and separate it into groups of 4. Count the groups of 4 and see how many singles are left.   **a**

Fig. 4. Making and recording groups

Counting groups represents a developmental advance for children and prepares them for work with groups of 10. Smaller groups are less tedious to count and avoid the issue of calling a group a "ten."

three
ways to count

Initial conceptual activities should focus on making and using groups of ten and counting by tens and not on writing numerals. Research by Rathmell (1969), Barr (1978), and Hong (1987) shows the value of oral counting and the use of concrete materials in learning place-value concepts. When a set of objects has been grouped into sets of ten, there are three different ways that the set can be counted:

a   Count by ones: One, two, three, . . ., forty-two, forty-three.

b   Count by groups and singles: One, two, three, four *sets of ten,* and one, two, three *singles.* (The italic words may vary.)

c   Count by tens and ones: Ten, twenty, thirty, forty, forty-one, forty-two, forty-three.

The "count by ones" method (fig. 5a) uses the understanding of numbers that children have before they begin to construct base-ten concepts and illustrates cardinality as they have learned it.

The other two counting methods are based on counting groups of tens as individual units. Counting by groups and singles (fig. 5b), although more direct and more easily understood, does not result in a single number name for the total. The more sophisticated and standard method of counting by tens and ones (fig. 5c), can be coordinated with counts of groups and singles. Counting by groups and singles, the middle triangle in figure 5, is a link between counting by ones and the desired place-value concepts. Many activities should involve counting grouped sets using both forms so that the word *fifty,* for example, is associated with five groups of ten and the word *fifty-seven* with five groups of ten and seven singles.

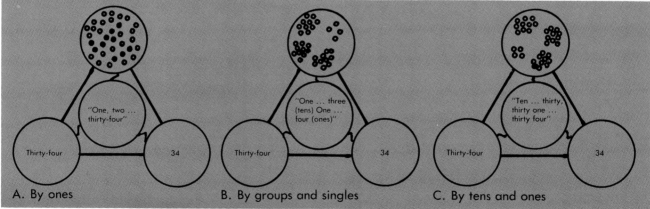

Fig. 5. Ways to count

a *Count by groups and by tens.* Have children make sets of ten and count them two ways. For example, have children place ten shells in individual plastic bags, make bundles of ten coffee stirrers or Popsicle sticks, or make macaroni necklaces with ten pieces each. "Show me six bags of ten and let's count groups. One, two, . . ., six. Now let's count the regular way by tens. Ten, twenty, . . ., sixty." Repeat for other tens, giving special attention to the more difficult names, *twenty, thirty,* and *fifty.*

Extend both types of counting to include groups of ten and singles. "Show me five bundles of ten and three singles. Can you count like this? Ten, twenty, . . ., fifty, fifty-one, fifty-two, fifty-three." **a**

a *Count three ways.* Ask children to stand, extend their fingers, and count by ones until there is a total of seventy-eight fingers extended. "How many groups of ten fingers are there? Let's count the groups. [7] How many single fingers? [8] Let's count the fingers by tens and ones to make sure there are seventy-eight. What are three ways we can find the total?" It may be useful to have children open their hands when the focus is on the total number of fingers but close their fists, hiding their fingers, when the focus is on groups of ten. **a**

a *Tens from oral names.* "If I count a set by ones and get thirty-four, how many groups of ten can I make? [3] How many extras will there be? [4] If I make four groups of ten and have seven extras, what will I get if I count by ones? [47] How do you know? What will I get if I count the same set by tens and ones? Why?" **a**

Children need ample opportunities to make a connection between counts by ones and less familiar counting by groups and by tens and ones. These activities provide an opportunity to focus on the dual meanings of the word *ten* as a number of objects and as the name of a group of objects. It is a gradual move from, "How many *groups of ten* are there?" to "How many *tens* are there?" The same transition to the use of ten as a group name can be made from bundles of ten, cups of ten, or bars of ten. The important thing is to realize that the word *ten* as a single entity is a

difficult concept for children, and it should be connected gradually with language and ideas that children already know.

Counting by groups and singles (or extras) is different from counting by tens and ones, especially for children, and both of these are different from counting by ones. Children need more experience connecting these three different kinds of counting than most adults realize.

tens and ones sequentially

Partitioning existing sets into groups of ten and extras as in the previous activities is important. It develops the essential grouping concepts of a base-ten system. However, it does not model the sequential way in which two-digit numbers are formed as one counts nor the right-to-left orientation of the place-value positions. Children should actually accumulate objects one at a time on a place-value chart to model the way that numbers are created sequentially and to establish the left-to-right orientation of tens and ones.

without numerals

The basic sequential grouping activities, and many others involving multidigit numbers, require a place-value mat similar to the one shown in figure 6. Mats can be made from a 12″ × 18″ sheet of construction paper and laminated after the two ten-frames are drawn. The ten-frames help children organize materials on their mats and eliminate tedious counting. For uniformity, counters are placed on a ten-frame from left to right, filling the top row of five squares before beginning the second row, as shown in chapter 4. Figure 6 shows the place-value mat for 2 tens and 7 singles. The following activities connect all three types of counting.

a *Sequential grouping game.* Give children a place-value mat and a supply of counters and cups. Each time you say, "Plus one," children place a counter in the top ten-frame and announce the total on their mats in this form, "Zero tens and one." As

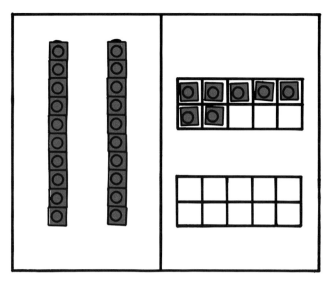

Fig. 6. Place-value mat for 2 tens and 7

you continue to say, "Plus one," children add counters each time to their top ten-frame. Each time the ten-frame is filled, children put the ten counters in a small cup and place the cup in the middle column. This sequential building of cups of ten continues until ninety-nine counters have been placed. Throughout, children announce each new total in the groups and singles form, "Two cups of ten and three." Frequently ask the children to state the total number of counters in standard form, "Twenty-three," and to verify the total by counting. Initially, children will count by ones, but soon they will count by tens and ones. To help them focus on making the groups of ten, occasionally ask, "How many more counters do you need to make a cup of ten?"　a

Count back. Play the game in reverse. Begin with nine cups of ten and nine singles, and remove one each time as you say, "Minus one." Observe what children do when there are no singles and only groups of ten on their mats. "Why don't you want to take one from a cup? [Leaves only nine in the cup, not ten.] Why do we want to keep ten in each cup? [It's much easier to count with groups of ten.] What do we do?" [Empty one cup onto a ten-frame.]　a

Sequential grouping both forward and backward demonstrates important aspects of place value for two-digit numbers and provides readiness for regrouping in addition and subtraction. Children must coordinate counting by ones, counting by tens and ones, building and breaking apart groups of ten, the place-value names for numbers (two tens and three), and the standard names for numbers (twenty-three).

There are several variations of sequential grouping:

- Add or remove two counters at each turn instead of just one.
- Roll a die and add or remove as many counters as the number shown on the die. This can be modified and made into a two-player game by taking turns rolling the die. The goal is to be the first player either to build 99 or to remove all 99 counters, depending on whether the counters are being added or removed from the mats.
- Use a variety of counters. For example, have children use sticks that can be bundled or interlocking cubes that can be connected to make bars of ten.

connecting to numerals

The previous grouping activities help children develop an understanding of place-value concepts for numbers up to 99. The following activities help children connect numerals to the concepts they have already developed. The conceptual connections between models and oral representations (the left side of the triangular structure in figure 1) should be firmly established before beginning to connect those ideas to symbols (the right side of the triangular structure). A premature emphasis on symbolism will only create difficulties.

Number cards. Make a stack of number cards labeled 0 through 9 and loop them together. Place them at the top of each place-value column as shown in figure 7. Do the same sequential grouping activities just described. As counters are added or removed from the mats, change the cards to indicate the number of units, both ones and tens, in each column.　a

The next activity provides opportunities to reason and to develop strategies as in counting on by ones and tens.

Fig. 7. Number cards with place-value mat

 Place-value nim. The materials needed are a place-value mat, two stacks of 0–9 number cards, ten single counters, and nine groups of ten. Each player in turn chooses to add 1, 2, or 3 single counters *or* 1, 2, or 3 groups of ten to the mat, announces the new total, and shows it with the number cards. The winner is the player who makes the mat total exactly 100 counters. The game can also be played in reverse starting with 100. The winner is the player who removes the last counter.

Calculators can be very useful for counting by ones and by tens. See chapter 1 for calculator specifications.

a

Calculator counting. Have children press 1 ⊞ and then press ⊟ repeatedly, saying the numbers as they are displayed. The display will show counting by ones. "Can you predict what the next number will be before you press the equal key? Check now by pressing the key."

Have students count to a number such as 23. "Now cover the display. Press the equal key three times. What number do you think is hidden?" Have them check by looking.

Let the students count on from a number such as 34 by pressing 34 ⊞ 1 and then pressing the equal key repeatedly.

Start at 100 and count back by ones. Press 100 ⊟ 1 and then press ⊟ repeatedly. Again have them cover the display and press the equal key three times and predict the hidden number.

Counting by tens is done the same way.

10 ⊞ ⊟ ⊟ ⊟ ⊟ shows counting by tens.

23 ⊞ 10 ⊟ ⊟ ⊟ ⊟ shows counting on from 23 by tens.

60 ⊞ 1 ⊟ ⊟ ⊟ ⊟ shows counting on from 6 tens by ones. **a**

estimating with tens

As children become proficient in working with numbers up to 99, they need to develop intuitions about the magnitudes of those numbers. One way to do this is to estimate quantities using groups of ten as a visual guide.

Estimate the number of objects. Place between 15 and 99 objects, such as popcorn or paste sticks, on a paper plate, on the overhead, or on a poster. Next to this display place exactly 10 of the same objects. Show children how to use the set of 10 as a visual guide to estimate the number of objects. Have them make their estimate using tens. To check, make sets of ten and count by tens and ones.

Do similar estimating experiences throughout the year, varying the size of the objects—leaves, Valentine cards, paper clips, grains of rice—as well as number. **a**

using pregrouped materials

It is possible to use ungrouped materials for all two-digit number work, but it is cumbersome. To model 89, for example, eighty-nine objects must be counted out. It is much simpler to use pregrouped materials. Figure 8 shows base-ten blocks for the number 89.

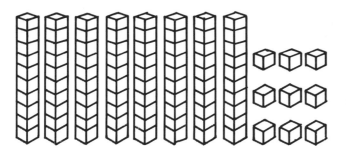

Fig. 8. Base-ten blocks for 89

 Explore materials. Explore base-ten blocks showing that 10 singles make one ten-piece. "Place the singles along the ten-piece. How many singles do you need to make a row just as long as the ten-piece?"

Count out seventeen singles. Place a ten-piece and seven singles next to them. "Which is more? [Both the same.] There are more pieces of wood in the group of seventeen pieces, but the ten-piece and seven singles are just the same. Is it easier to show twenty-five by using only singles or by using two ten-pieces and five singles? Which way is easier to count?" **a**

trading activities

Introduce the idea and language of *trading*, a single word that means both *building groups* and *breaking groups apart*.

Trading game. Provide base-ten blocks and a die. Roll the die, and choose that many singles. Repeat, trading singles for ten-pieces when possible. If two people play, the winner is the first to reach 100.

The reverse of this activity is challenging. Begin with 9 ten-pieces and 9 singles. Roll a die to determine the number to remove. When there are fewer singles on the mat than need to be removed, ask, "How can we

remove 5 ones when only 2 are here? Is there any way we can keep the same total amount on our mats but have more ones?" **a**

Two related activities help prepare children for regrouping in addition and subtraction. Children use materials to illustrate examples on worksheets.

Can you trade? Use a worksheet with a sticks-and-dots picture (fig. 9). Tens are represented by drawing sticks and ones by dots. (Children can make these simplified drawings as early as second grade.)

Have children put ten-pieces and singles on their place-value mats to match the worksheets. "Are there enough ones to trade for another ten? Circle Y for yes or N for no. Draw the new sticks-and-dots picture. Write the number." **a**

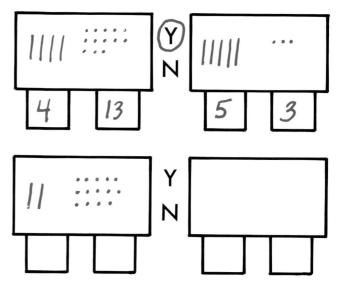

Fig. 9. Can you trade for a new ten?

The next activity prepares children for subtraction.

Do you need to trade? Use a worksheet as shown in figure 10 and model with base-ten blocks. "I want to remove 6 so I can give one to each child at this table. Do I need to make a trade? Why? Circle Y or N. If you circle Y, draw sticks and dots and write the number." **a**

98   Chapter Five

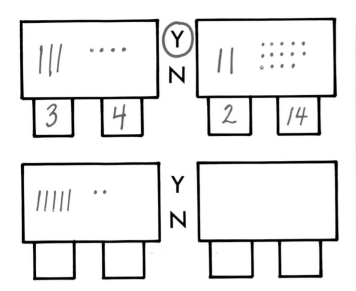

Fig. 10. Do you need to trade to remove 6?

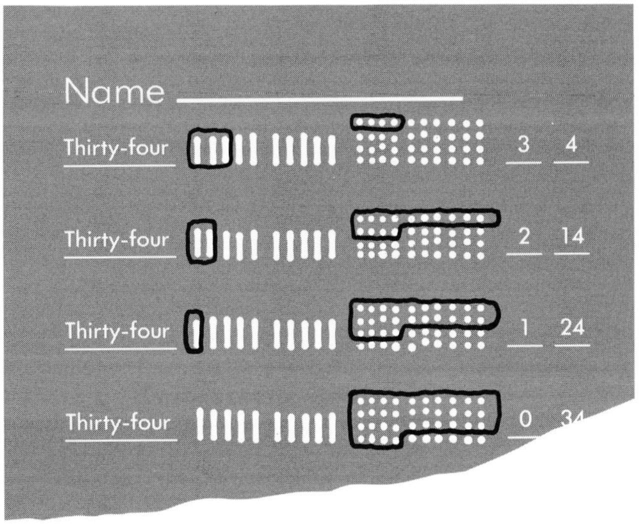

Fig. 11. Equivalent representations for 34

equivalent representations

Children need to develop flexibility in representing two-digit numbers. In the following activity they find all possible ways to model a two-digit number using ten-pieces and one-pieces. Counting is done as shown in figure 5 each time a ten is traded for ones.

Four ways to show 34. Have children use their ten-pieces and one-pieces and show the number 34. "Let's count to show we have thirty-four. Ten, twenty, thirty, thirty-one, thirty-two, thirty-three, thirty-four. How can we write the number? What does the 3 show? [3 tens] What does the 4 show?" [4 ones]

"Can you find another way to show 34? Explain it by counting." Show two ten-strips and fourteen singles. Count, "Ten, twenty; one, two, three, . . ., fourteen; twenty and fourteen is thirty-four, two tens and fourteen ones." Students can write 2 | 14 in a simple tens and ones chart. Further exploration will lead to the other ways to model 34, 1 | 24 and 0 | 34.

A worksheet version of this same activity is shown in figure 11.

Figure 12 shows a variation of this activity. The first column is a number word, a version of the oral name for a number; the middle column is a model; and the third column is a symbolic representation. The worksheet shows one of these three representations. The task is to determine the other two representations.

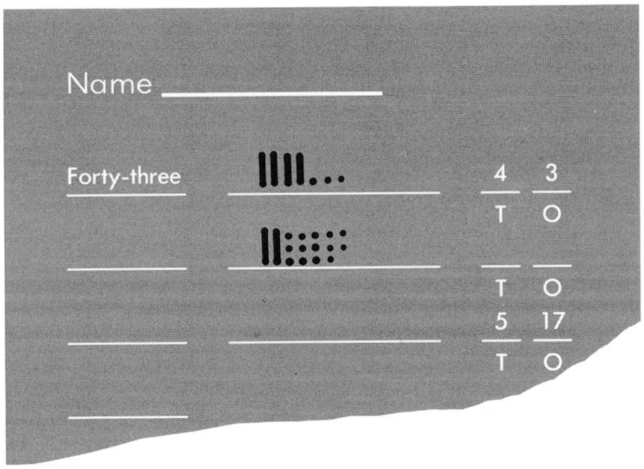

Fig. 12. Writing the other two representations

comparisons

Children need to acquire the ability to compare any two two-digit numbers in order to decide which is larger. For children who can count and write the numbers to 100, this skill is deceptively easy. They pick the smaller or larger on the basis of which number comes first in the counting sequence. However, "comes after" is not the same as "greater than." Place-value materials should be used so that children base their decision on the magnitudes of the two numbers.

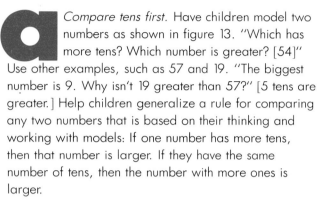 *Compare tens first.* Have children model two numbers as shown in figure 13. "Which has more tens? Which number is greater? [54]" Use other examples, such as 57 and 19. "The biggest number is 9. Why isn't 19 greater than 57?" [5 tens are greater.] Help children generalize a rule for comparing any two numbers that is based on their thinking and working with models: If one number has more tens, then that number is larger. If they have the same number of tens, then the number with more ones is larger.

Do a challenging extension. "Which is greater, 4 tens and 17 ones or 5 tens 3 ones? Can you explain using ten-pieces? Do you need to trade first?" **a**

rounding

One way to estimate in computation is to round two-digit numbers to the nearest ten. Instead of rotely teaching a symbolic rule, we can help children understand rounding by using base-ten blocks and a meterstick marked in centimeters.

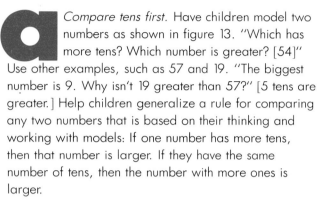 *Meterstick rounding.* Pick a two-digit number such as 74. "How many tens are in the number? What tens are just below and just above the number? [7 tens and 8 tens]. Is 74 nearer to 7 tens or to 8 tens?" Place the ten-pieces and singles for 74 along a meterstick, as in figure 14. "Which number of tens is nearer to 74 on the meterstick?" There should be a lively discussion on how to round 75 because neither 70 nor 80 is closer. Point out that generally it is rounded to the higher ten. Help children to generalize. "Can you tell how to round any two-digit number?" **a**

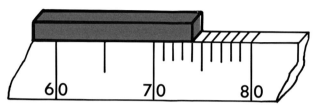

Fig. 14. Using a meterstick to round

three-digit numbers

Activities for three-digit numbers are similar to those for two-digit numbers. The place-value triangular structure (fig. 1) that depicts the relationships for two-digit numbers also depicts them for three-digit numbers. See

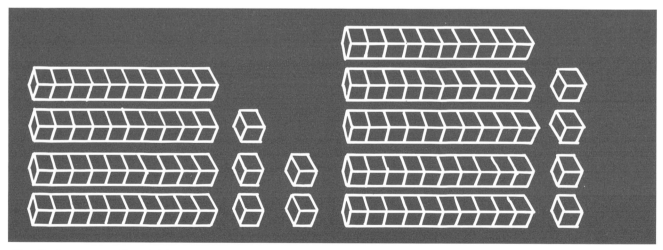

Fig. 13. Comparing 45 and 54

There are fewer viable choices for models for three-digit numbers. The preferred materials are base-ten blocks, which are centimeter cubes for ones, decimeter rods for tens, and decimeter squares for hundreds. These materials enable children to model numbers up to 999 effectively and efficiently, and they embody a 10 to 1 size ratio between tens and ones and between hundreds and tens. A worthy substitute for the wooden blocks, at a fraction of the cost, is a set of tagboard centimeter squares for ones, decimeter strips for tens, and decimeter squares for hundreds.

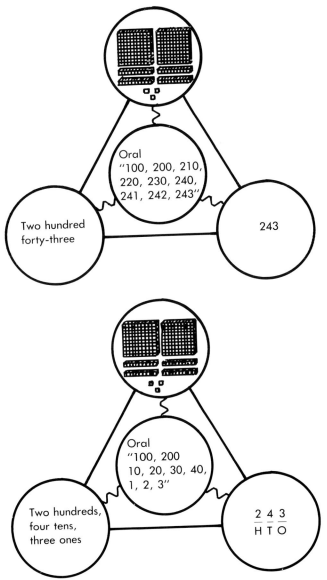

figure 15. As with smaller numbers, activities should focus initially on relating models with their oral names. The appropriate numerical symbols can be added later. However, three-digit numbers are more complex, and there are difficulties that do not occur with two-digit numbers.

- The word *hundred* must be understood as 100 singles, as 10 tens, and as a single group.

- "Double trades" are frequently encountered, as in adding 5 to a mat showing 397 or removing 4 from a display of 402.

- Establishing number sense for numbers up to 999 is a new challenge. Many children have not seen collections of 750 items, for example, and do not have good intuitions about the magnitudes of large numbers.

Fig. 15. Place-value relationships

sequential grouping

Initial activities for three-digit numbers should focus on helping children use counting to connect models with the appropriate oral names.

a *Making hundreds from tens.* Use a place-value mat with three places. "Show me ninety. Now add ten more. Put the ten-pieces together. What is the name for this bundle? [Hundred]" Move the bundle to the third column on a place-value mat. (The bundled rods are being used here as an ungrouped place-value material for *hundreds*.) Continue by adding 10, 20, or 30 at a time and saying each total. "Can you prove your total by counting by tens? By counting by hundreds and tens? How many tens did we use to make 270? [27] How is this like putting ten ones together to make a ten?" After reaching a total such as 350, reverse and remove 10, 20, or 30 each time. **a**

There are several important extensions to this activity.

■ Have children trade ten tens for a hundred square each time it is possible, modeling numbers to 990.

■ Include the use of ones. Begin with numbers such as 398, 307, or 517, and add five ones successively. Adding five ones to 398 leads to double trading. The numbers 307 and 517 involve zero tens or teen numbers that children find difficult, especially when done orally. Do the activity in reverse, removing ones.

■ Place a stack of number cards labeled 0–9 at the top of each place-value column as shown in figure 16. The number cards help children learn why *three hundred twelve* is written with numerals as 312 rather than 30012.

■ Use a calculator with a constant feature in conjunction with work on place-value mats. For example, model 268 on the mats and prepare the calculator to count by tens by pressing 2 6 8 [+] 10. Then, as children add a ten to their mats, have them press [=] each time to see the corresponding symbolic representation. Focus on the patterns of the digits as they change, especially when a trade is made.

Fig. 16. Number cards for place value

Throughout their work with numbers to 999, ask children to think about the total number of tens needed to build the numbers. Using the number cards will help children see the relationships between the number of tens and the first two digits of the three-digit numeral; for example, the number of tens needed to build 785 is 78.

readiness for addition and subtraction

The sequential grouping activities for numbers up to 99 can be modified to provide readiness for column addition and subtraction.

a *Place-mat addition and subtraction.* Use a cube with faces marked 1 ten, 2 tens, . . ., 6 tens and another cube marked 1, 2, . . ., 6. Roll both cubes to determine the amount to be added to the place-value mat. Record the initial amount, the amount added, and the net result on a strip of three-column paper as shown in figure 17. The written record shows the changes and results. The goal is not to teach the computational algorithms but to develop an understanding of trading. The trades for

ones, tens, or hundreds are not recorded. Do
subtraction in a similar way.   **a**

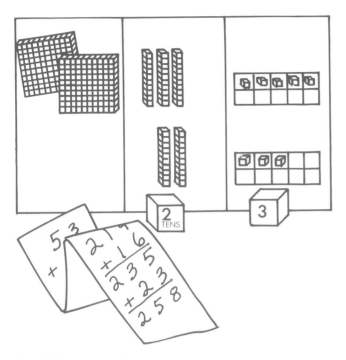

Fig. 17. Place-mat addition

Knowledge of equivalent representations prepares
children for addition and subtraction involving trading
and enables them to think of three-digit quantities in a
variety of ways.

a *Group in different ways.* Choose a number
such as 524. Have children model the
number, first in the standard way and then in
other ways. "Can you show the number with fewer
tens? With fewer hundreds?" Have children use base-
ten blocks and record their results by using squares,
sticks, and dots as shown in figure 18.   **a**

To use three-digit numbers, children need to extend
their oral counting skills to include counting by
hundreds, tens, and ones. In the example in figure 19,
children count and record the values by writing the
number words.

It is important that children know the value of each digit
in a three-digit number, especially for work with
computation. The following activity makes use of a

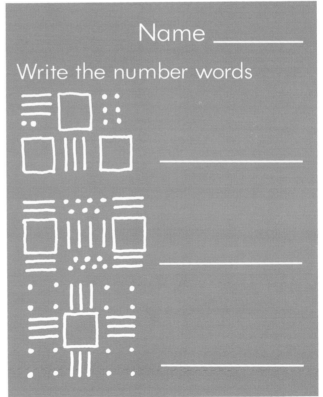

Fig. 18. Different groupings for a number

calculator and requires children to understand the value
of each digit.

Fig. 19. Counting and writing number words

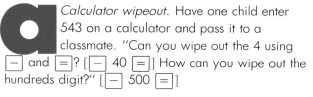

Calculator wipeout. Have one child enter 543 on a calculator and pass it to a classmate. "Can you wipe out the 4 using [−] and [=]? [[−] 40 [=]] How can you wipe out the hundreds digit?" [[−] 500 [=]]

A variation is "digit change" where the challenge is to *change* a digit to a new value. In this case the second player must decide first whether to press [+] or [−]. **a**

estimation and relative magnitude

Too frequently children learn to add and subtract numbers between 100 and 1000 without any real concept of how big these quantities are or their relative size.

Estimate hundreds. Have children estimate quantities between 100 and 999. Instead of using a group of 10 items as an estimating guide as was done with two-digit numbers, make a group of 50 or 100 to use as a reference. Peanuts in a bag, beans in a jar, shells in a box, or a stack of paper are examples of things to estimate. **a**

Closest to 400. Have each child make three lines as places for a three-digit number (__ __ __). Roll a die three times, allowing students to choose the space to put each number. Once a digit is placed, it cannot be changed. The goal is to create a number closest to 400. "Where would you put a 3 to show the greatest value? [Hundreds place] The least value?" [Ones place] **a**

Children who develop a mental number line for the numbers 0 to 1000 are developing good intuitions of the relative magnitudes of these numbers.

Super number line. Measure 10 meters of string and tie a ribbon at each meter mark. Place ten-pieces end to end and count

centimeters by tens. After reaching the first ribbon at the end of the first meter, count by hundreds and tens. "Where is 600? 860? 480? How is 600 on the super number line like 6 hundred-pieces? How is it different?"

Use the super number line to round three-digit numbers to the nearest hundred. Use the same procedure that was used for two-digit numbers. **a**

Guess my number. One child, the selector, secretly writes down a three-digit number; the other children try to guess it. Two children act as pointers, one on each end of the number line. If the secret number is 587 and a child guesses 700, the selector says, "Too high." The right-end pointer holds a finger at 700. Similarly, the pointer at the other end would move in to locate the most recent guess that was "Too low." In this way the two pointers always bracket the range of remaining possibilities. **a**

problem-solving puzzles

The following puzzles use place-value concepts and require logical reasoning:

- I am more than 930. I have twice as many tens as ones. Who could I be? [942, 963, 984]

- I am in the 400s. I am less than 430. I have more tens than ones. Who could I be? [410, 420, 421]

- I am just as much as 34 tens and 17 ones. Who am I? [357]

- If you put 2 tens and 12 ones with me, I'll be 2 less than 700. Who am I? [666]

- I am in the 600s. I have as many tens as 234. If you count by tens starting at 506 you will name me. Who am I? [636]

- I am built from seven base-ten blocks. I am more than 500. Who could I be? [502, 511, 520, 601, 610, 700]

four-digit numbers and beyond

The ideas that children have developed for numbers up to three digits need to be extended carefully to four digits and beyond. Children need to see and manipulate models for larger numbers to establish that the 10 to 1 ratio between hundreds and tens applies to any two adjacent place-value positions. (The pattern for naming numbers through hundreds is repeated in each of the next three place-value positions.) Perhaps even more important, children need to develop a number sense for larger numbers.

There are several possibilities as models for a thousand. The most logical approach is to group together ten of whatever items children have been using for hundreds. If children have been using tagboard decimeter squares, simply make a stack of ten of them and bundle them with an elastic band. If children have been using base-ten blocks, stacking ten of the wooden squares to make a decimeter cube is a good approach. Either of these models can be used to represent numbers up to 10 000. As with other numbers, children need to count to establish connections among the elements in the three corners of the place-value triangular structure (fig. 2). Many of the activities for two-digit and three-digit numbers can be extended or modified to apply to four-digit numbers.

generalizing the base-ten system

Using the model chosen to represent a thousand, arrange a *one,* a *ten,* a *hundred,* and a *thousand* in order, right to left. Help children see the simple pattern that ten pieces make one of the next larger size. At the same time, notice that the difference in size between one piece and the next is *not* the same. There is a very big difference between one *hundred* and one *thousand* but a relatively small difference between a *one* and a *ten.* What would the next piece look like—the piece for

a ten thousand? Perhaps you could build one from cardboard or draw one on a sheet of butcher paper.

Explain how numbers with four or more digits are named in groups of three. Each new group of one to three digits is read the same way numbers up to 999 are read. The only difference is that a new name for each group is attached, as shown in figure 20 for 548 063 702.

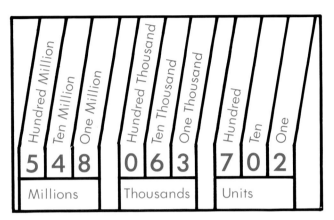

Fig. 20. Reading larger numbers

Turn the card and read. Make a set of nine cards, each with a 0 on one side and a digit from 1 to 9 on the other side. Shuffle the cards and place seven in a row with the 0s showing. Make a space between groups of three.

Turn the cards over one at a time in random order. Have children read the resulting multidigit numeral each time. Leading zeros are ignored.

a

referents for larger numbers

Children should develop referents for special large numbers like a thousand, ten thousand, hundred thousand, and million. To assist in this development, have children use what they know to think about thousands and millions.

■ How long will a chain of a thousand paper clips be? Ten thousand paper clips? A million?

- What would ten thousand one dollar bills look like? Children can cut "bills" from newspaper (at home) and pack them in bundles of 50 or 100.

- How far would a thousand children holding hands stretch?

- How long would it take to count to a thousand? To write the numbers to a thousand? To make a calculator count to a thousand? How long would it take the computer to count to a million?

Other activities use interesting problems that will make large numbers personally relevant.

- How many centimeter cubes will fit in a cubic decimeter? How many will cover a square meter? How many will fit in a cubic meter?

- Using a typewriter, how many dots (periods) can be put on a standard sheet of paper? How many sheets of paper will it take for a thousand dots? A hundred thousand dots? A million dots?

- How many printed characters are there on a white page of a standard telephone directory? How many pages are needed to have ten thousand characters? A million?

- How many candy bars would it take to cover the floor of your classroom? What about the floor and the walls and the ceiling?

- How many dimes stacked flat on top of each other would it take to reach from the floor of your classroom to the ceiling? From the ground to the top of the flagpole? To the moon?

- How many times do you breathe in a minute? An hour? A day? A year? In your lifetime? How many heartbeats in a minute? An hour?

diagnosis of place-value understanding

Place value is both important and complex. Frequently students learn how to do activities with place-value materials but do not construct all the corresponding ideas. In this section assessments are suggested to help

determine children's understanding. Each gives a slightly different view of a child's conceptual development.

meanings of individual digits

The following task, designed by Labinowicz (1985), provides an easy way to determine the meaning students give to individual digits in a multidigit number:

- Write a numeral, such as 67 or 324, but do not say it. Ask the child to write the number that is ten more. If the correct numeral is written within two or three seconds, then the child knows the value of the tens digit. The child who must count up ten by ones does not understand that, for example, the 6 in 67 represents sixty.

Children in the assessment above who must count would benefit from instruction that involves adding alternately 1, 2, or 3 ones or 1, 2, or 3 tens to a place-value mat and naming and writing the total after each change.

A digit correspondence task determines if a child connects individual digits in a numeral with subsets of ten. The following version of the task is similar to those used by Kamii (1984) and Ross (1988):

- Present the child with a collection of twenty-five counters and have the child count them and write the numeral that tells how many counters there are. If the child writes "25," circle the 5 and ask, "Does this part of your 25 have anything to do with how many counters there are? How?" Then, circle the 2 and repeat the question. The form of the question is important. Try not to give clues to the correct answer by the way the question is asked.

On the basis of Ross's work, children's responses to this task can be classified into three levels of understanding:

Level 1. The child is able only to write the 25 and does not match the 2 or the 5 with any items (fig. 21a). There appears to be no knowledge of the meaning of the individual digits as part of the numeral 25. The 25 is viewed as a single symbol that refers to the entire collection of counters. Level 1 children benefit from activities that involve counting a set of objects, separating it into tens and ones, counting the number of groups of ten and the number left over, and recounting by tens and ones to confirm the total number of counters.

Level 2. The child matches the 5 with five counters and the 2 with two counters (fig. 21b). Meanings for the digits are based on simple one-to-one correspondence. Note that eighteen of the counters are not matched with either digit. Level 2 children benefit from separating sets into tens and ones, counting by tens and ones to determine the total number of counters, and then matching the individual digits representing the total with the sets of tens and ones.

Level 3. The child matches the 5 with five items and the 2 with the twenty remaining items (fig. 21c). An appropriate understanding of the value of the digits is present. As a follow-up question, ask, "Can you tell me why the 2 goes with these counters?" A child with even greater understanding will arrange the twenty counters into two groups of ten to demonstrate the meaning of the 2.

equivalent representations

For children to think flexibly and understand computational procedures involving regrouping, they need to be able to give equivalent representations of quantities.

■ Provide the child with about twenty-five loose beans and four index cards, each with ten beans attached. First, make certain the child understands there are ten beans on each card. Then say, "Show me forty-six beans." After this has been shown, usually by using four cards of beans and six loose ones, say, "Show me forty-six beans in another way." (Note that there are not enough individual beans to use only the loose beans.) If the child cannot represent 46 in another way, then additional activities involving equivalent representations such as those presented earlier in the chapter would be appropriate.

place value in a problem-solving context

The final task presented here is designed to determine if a child uses place-value concepts in a problem-solving situation. The problem can be solved by counting by ones, but the child who understands place value will surely use place-value ideas and count by tens to solve the problem, because those ideas make the process much simpler and faster (Labinowicz 1985).

■ Place twenty-eight counters on one side of a divided mat as shown in figure 22. Say, "There are twenty-eight counters on this side. I'd like to add enough counters to the other side so that there will be fifty-

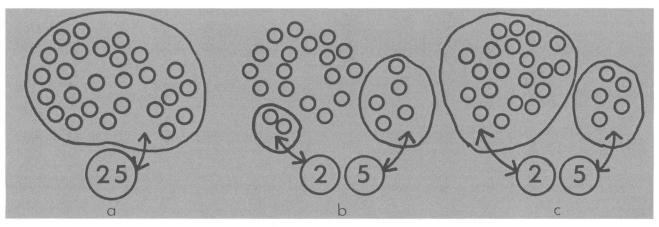

Fig. 21. Digit correspondence task

three altogether. I'd like for you to count, beginning with twenty-eight, to figure out how many counters I need to add to the other side." Some children count on by ones all the way to fifty-three. Others count by ones to thirty, then by tens to fifty, and then by ones to fifty-three. A few count like this: "Twenty-eight, thirty-eight, forty-eight, forty-nine, fifty, fifty-one, fifty-two, fifty-three." Almost all children use their fingers to keep track of how many they have counted. If a child counts by ones, then that child would profit from adding (and subtracting) sets of ten to (and from) collections of objects and verbalizing the total after each addition (or subtraction).

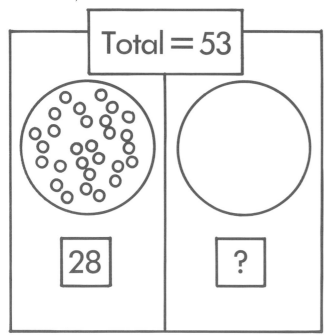

Fig. 22. How many more to make 53?

conclusion

Helping children develop the concepts and skills of place value is a formidable task. Children need opportunities to learn to coordinate a number of different ideas: grouping collections of objects, counting the grouped collections, saying the oral names, and recognizing and writing the symbols. Considerable planning is required, and more instructional time must be allocated than in traditional textbook programs.

After a conceptual approach to place-value instruction has been adopted and after ample time has been provided for children to develop place-value concepts, children will better understand the regrouping processes in addition and subtraction. Furthermore, they will be able to use numbers more meaningfully, especially in situations requiring estimation and number sense. The additional time and effort spent on place-value instruction is well invested.

references

Barr, David C. "A Comparison of Three Methods of Introducing Two-Digit Numeration." *Journal for Research in Mathematics Education* 9 (January 1978): 33–43.

Hong, Haekyung. "Effects of Counting by Tens on Numerical Abilities of Young Children." *Dissertation Abstracts International* 49 (1988): 2089A. University Microfilms No. 88-21538.

Kamii, Constance K. *Young Children Reinvent Arithmetic.* New York: Teachers College Press, Columbia University, 1984.

Labinowicz, Ed. *Learning from Children: New Beginning for Teaching Numerical Thinking.* Menlo Park, Calif.: Addison-Wesley Publishing Co., 1985.

Payne, Joseph N., and Edward C. Rathmell. "Number and Numeration." In *Mathematics Learning in Early Childhood,* edited by Joseph N. Payne, pp. 125–60. Reston, Va.: National Council of Teachers of Mathematics, 1975.

Rathmell, Edward C. "The Effects of Multibase Grouping and Early or Late Introductions of Base Representations on the Mastery Learning of Base and Place-Value Numeration in Grade One." *Dissertation Abstracts International* 30 (1969): 1084A. University Microfilms No. 69-14685.

Ross, Sharon H. "The Roles of Cognitive Development and Instruction in Children's Acquisition of Place-Value Numeration Concepts." Paper presented at the Annual Meeting of the National Council of Teachers of Mathematics, Chicago, April 1988.

**thomas carpenter
deborah carey
vicky kouba**

a problem-solving approach to the operations

What will children do if they are given the following problems during the first few weeks of school?

- Robin had 8 cookies. He ate 3 of them. How many cookies does Robin have left?

- Megan has 3 dollars to buy cookies. How many more dollars does she need to earn to have 8 dollars?

Here is how two beginning first-grade children solved the problems. For the first problem, Roy got out a group of counters and made a collection of 8 counters. He then took 3 counters away, counted the ones remaining, and said that the answer was 5. For the second problem, he first put out 3 counters and then added counters to them until there were 8 altogether. By keeping track of the number of counters he had added, he knew the answer was 5.

Melissa solved both problems without counters. For the second problem, she counted from 3 to 8, keeping track of the count on her fingers. By counting the number of fingers extended, she knew the answer was 5. She used a similar strategy to solve the first problem but counted backward from 8.

Neither Roy nor Melissa had learned these strategies in school nor had they spent much time in school solving word problems. Their responses are typical of children of this age. A number of studies of young children's problem solving show that young children enter school with the ability to solve a variety of word problems with modeling and counting strategies that they have learned informally or have invented for themselves (Carpenter 1985; Carpenter and Moser 1983; Fuson 1988; and Riley, Greeno, and Heller 1983). It is often assumed that word problems are difficult for students of all ages and that computational skills must be learned before children can solve problems. This research suggests, however, that young children can solve problems before they learn formal arithmetic and that, in fact, solving word problems can be used to develop and give meaning to the operations of addition, subtraction, multiplication, and division. The National Council of Teachers of Mathematics has recommended that problem solving be a major focus of instruction in mathematics (NCTM 1980, 1989). What we know about young children's problem-solving abilities and concepts of arithmetic provides a basis for implementing the NCTM proposals.

This chapter has three related themes:

- Children enter school with a great deal of informal knowledge about arithmetic and problem solving. We should nurture it and build our formal instruction on it.

- To build on children's knowledge, a regular assessment of their knowledge and the processes they use to solve different problems is necessary.

- Symbols should be introduced to represent concepts that children already know. We should not start with the symbols $+$, $-$, $\times$, and $\div$ and then attempt to give them meaning.

The program of instruction we are advocating is built on a thorough knowledge of students. The first step is to understand how young children think as they solve different types of problems. Thus, we look first at addition and subtraction, then at multiplication and division and how children's abilities evolve. Both sections are based on careful analysis of critical distinctions among problems and children's solutions of them. The concluding section contains specific implications for instruction and suggested activities.

addition and subtraction

Most adults would solve the two problems given at the beginning of this chapter by subtracting 3 from 8. To

young children, however, these are completely different problems, which they solve using very different strategies. For children, there are distinctions among different types of addition problems and different types of subtraction problems (Carpenter and Moser 1983).

A useful way of classifying addition and subtraction problems focuses on the actions or relationships described in the problems. This approach corresponds to the way that children actually think about the problems. As a consequence, this classification scheme distinguishes among problems that children solve with different strategies and serves as a framework for identifying the relative difficulty of problems.

We use four basic classes of problems: Join, Separate, Part-Part-Whole, and Compare. Join and Separate problems involve actions. In Join problems, the elements are added to a given set. In Separate problems, elements are removed from a given set. Part-Part-Whole problems involve the relationship between a set and its two subsets. Compare problems involve comparisons between two disjoint sets. All problems within a class involve the same type of action on quantities or relationships between quantities, but within each class there are several types that depend on which quantity is unknown. When the unknown is varied within each type of problem, eleven types of problems can be constructed. Examples of each type of problem are presented in figure 1. These eleven problems represent different interpretations of addition and subtraction.

This classification scheme is not intended to be something that children should learn. It is important, however, that teachers understand the distinctions among problems, because children respond differently to different kinds of problems, and understanding the differences among problems helps in understanding children's responses and why they may have difficulty with a particular problem. This scheme also insures that children are given experiences with problems that present a variety of addition and subtraction situations.

Textbooks often include only Join (Result Unknown) and Separate (Result Unknown) problems. This practice gives children a limited perspective of addition and

Join

Result Unknown

Connie had **5** marbles. Jim gave her **8** more marbles. How many marbles does Connie have altogether?

Change Unknown

Connie has **5** marbles. How many more marbles does she need to have **13** marbles altogether?

Start Unknown

Connie had some marbles. Jim gave her **5** more marbles. Now she has **13** marbles. How many marbles did Connie have to start with?

Separate

Result Unknown

Connie had **13** marbles. She gave **5** marbles to Jim. How many marbles does she have left?

Change Unknown

Connie had **13** marbles. She gave some to Jim. Now she has **5** marbles left. How many marbles did Connie give to Jim?

Start Unknown

Connie had some marbles. She gave **5** to Jim. Now she has **8** marbles left. How many marbles did Connie have to start with?

Part-Part-Whole

Whole Unknown

Connie has **5** red marbles and **8** blue marbles. How many marbles does she have?

Part Unknown

Connie has **13** marbles. **Five** are red and the rest are blue. How many blue marbles does Connie have?

Compare

Difference Unknown

Connie has **13** marbles. Jim has **5** marbles. How many more marbles does Connie have than Jim?

Compare Quantity Unknown

Jim has **5** marbles. Connie has **8** more than Jim. How many marbles does Connie have?

Referent Unknown

Connie has **13** marbles. She has **5** more marbles than Jim. How many marbles does Jim have?

Fig. 1. Classification of addition and subtraction word problems

subtraction. It encourages them to use superficial problem-solving strategies like looking for key words to decide, "Is this a plus or a take away?" The problems in figure 1 illustrate how such superficial strategies distort problem solving and are not uniformly effective. The different types of problems within each class contain the same key words but cannot be solved with the same operation.

children's solution strategies

Children use a variety of strategies to solve addition and subtraction problems. Children's solutions usually correspond to the action or relationships in a problem. Initially, children use physical objects or their fingers to model the actions or relationships directly. Direct modeling strategies are replaced first by more advanced counting strategies and later by the use of number facts. Transition stages occur between modeling, counting, and using number facts. Children who generally use modeling or counting strategies may also use selected number facts they have memorized.

direct modeling

To solve a simple addition problem, children use objects to represent each of the addends and then count the union of the two sets, starting with 1. This *counting all* strategy is illustrated in the following example:

■ *Teacher:* Robin had 4 toy cars. Her friends gave her 7 more toy cars for her birthday. How many toy cars did she have then?

Karla makes a set of 4 cubes and a set of 7 cubes. She pushes them together and counts, "1, 2, 3, 4, 5, 6, 7, 8, 9, 10, 11," pointing to a cube with each count. She then responds, "Robin had 11 cars." (See fig. 2.)

Although there is one basic modeling strategy for addition problems, there are several distinct strategies that children use to solve subtraction problems.

The strategy that best models the Separate (Result Unknown) problem is a *separating* action. The larger quantity in the subtraction problem is represented initially and the smaller quantity is then removed.

■ *Teacher:* Colleen had 12 guppies. She gave 5 guppies to Roger. How many guppies does Colleen have left?

Karla makes a set of 12 cubes and removes 5 of them. She counts the remaining cubes and responds, "She has 7 left." (See fig. 3.)

Fig. 2. Counting to solve a Join problem

Fig. 3. Direct modeling to solve a Separate problem

The strategy for a Join (Change Unknown) problem is an additive action. The child makes a set equivalent to the initial quantity and adds objects to it until the new collection is equal to the total given in the problem. The number of objects added is the answer. This *adding-on* strategy is illustrated in the following example:

■ *Teacher:* Robin has 4 toy cars. How many more toy cars does she need to get for her birthday to have 11 toy cars altogether?

Karla makes a set of 4 cubes. She puts other cubes next to this set (counting, "5, 6, 7, 8, 9, 10, 11") until she has a total of 11 cubes. The cubes that are added are kept separate from the initial set of 4 cubes. She then counts these 7 cubes. Karla responds, "She needs 7 more."

Compare (Difference Unknown) problems describe a matching process (see fig. 4). The strategy for solving these problems is constructing a one-to-one correspondence between two sets until one set is exhausted—counting the unmatched elements gives the answer. The following example illustrates this *matching* strategy:

■ *Teacher:* Mark has 6 mice. Joy has 11 mice. Joy has how many more mice than Mark?

Karla counts out one set of 6 cubes and another set of 11 cubes. She puts the set of 6 cubes in a row. She then makes a row of the 11 cubes and places it next to the row of 6 cubes. (See fig. 4) She then counts the 5 cubes that are not matched with a cube in the initial row. Karla responds, "She has 5 more."

counting

Counting strategies are more efficient than direct modeling with physical objects. Two related counting strategies are often used to solve addition problems.

Ann's example illustrates *counting on* from the first number, and George's example illustrates *counting on* from the larger number:

Fig. 4. A matching strategy to solve a Compare problem

■ *Teacher:* Robin had 4 toy cars. Her friends gave her 7 more toy cars for her birthday. How many toy cars did she have then?

Ann: 4 [pause], 5, 6, 7, 8, 9, 10, 11. She had 11 cars.
[As Ann counts, she extends a finger with each count. When she has 7 fingers extended, she stops counting and gives the answer.]

George: 7 [pause], 8, 9, 10, 11. She had 11 toy cars. [George also moves his fingers as he counts, but only slightly, so it is easy to miss that he is using them to keep track. (See fig. 5.)]

Fig. 5. Counting on from the larger number

A similar strategy is used to solve Join (Change Unknown) problems, but the number of the steps in the counting sequence is the answer.

■ *Teacher:* Robin had 8 toy cars. Her parents gave her some more toy cars for her birthday. Then she had 13 toy cars. How many toy cars did her parents give her?

Ann: 8 [pause], 9, 10, 11, 12, 13. [She extends a finger as she says the sequence from 9 to 13 and then looks at her extended fingers.] They gave her 5.

To reflect the action in the Separate (Result Unknown) problems, a backward counting sequence can be employed.

■ *Teacher:* Colleen had 11 guppies. She gave 3 guppies to Roger. How many guppies did she have left?

Ann: 11, 10, 9, [pause], 8. She gave 8 to him. [As

with the counting-on and counting-up strategies, Ann uses her fingers to keep track of the steps in the counting sequence.]

number facts

Children's solutions to word problems are not limited to modeling and counting strategies. Children learn number facts both in and out of school and apply this knowledge to solve word problems, although knowledge of the appropriate number fact does not mean that modeling or counting will not be used. Some children use a small set of memorized facts to derive solutions for problems containing other number combinations. Doubles (4 + 4, 7 + 7, etc.) are usually learned before other combinations, as are sums of 10 (7 + 3, 4 + 6). Children's use of derived facts is illustrated in the following example:

■ *Teacher:* Six frogs were sitting on lily pads. Eight more frogs joined them. How many frogs were there then?

Rudy, Denise, Theo, and Sandra: 14.

Teacher: How do you know there were 14?

Rudy: Because 6 and 6 is 12, and 2 more is 14.

Denise: I know that 8 and 8 is 16. But this is 8 and 6. That is 2 less, so it's 14.

Theo: Well, I took 1 from the 8 and gave it to the 6. That made 7 and 7, and that's 14.

Sandra: If 8 and 2 more is 10, then 4 more is 14.

Derived-fact solutions are based on an understanding of relations between numbers so it might be expected that only a handful of very bright students use them. However, even without specific instruction, a number of children use derived facts before they can recall all their number facts (Carpenter and Moser 1984).

The strategies children use to solve problems are based on their conceptual knowledge. They are not skills that are specifically taught but ones that emerge as children have many problem-solving experiences. These experiences can be designed to encourage the use of different strategies if appropriate word problems are selected. Classroom activities can also encourage the use of more efficient strategies. (See chapter 7.)

development
of strategies

The ages at which children use different strategies vary greatly. When they enter kindergarten or first grade, most children can solve at least some word problems with direct modeling using physical objects even though they have had little or no formal instruction in addition or subtraction. Some entering first graders are able to use counting strategies, and a few use number facts or derived facts consistently.

Children begin solving problems by using concrete objects to model directly the action in problems. Younger children are limited in their modeling capabilities—they do not plan ahead and can only think about one step at a time. This is no problem with the counting-all and separating strategies, but it can cause difficulties in modeling Change Unknown problems.

■ *Teacher:* Robin had 5 toy cars. How many more cars does she have to get for her birthday to make 9 toy cars?

Mike makes a set of 5 cubes and then adds 4 more cubes to the set, counting, "6, 7, 8, 9," as he adds the cubes. After adding the new cubes, he cannot distinguish them from the original set of 5 cubes. He hesitates for a moment and then counts the entire set of 9 cubes and responds, "9?"

Children at a basic direct-modeling level can apply their modeling strategies only one step at a time. As their problem-solving ability increases, they can reflect on their modeling strategies and plan their solutions to Join (Change Unknown) problems. By the middle of first grade, most children can solve Join (Change Unknown) problems by direct modeling, and with experience, they can solve Compare problems by matching the two sets.

Children progress to a level where they rely primarily on counting strategies, although they may occasionally go back to direct modeling. Virtually all children use counting strategies at some point in developing addition and subtraction concepts and skills. Although most texts present a sequence that goes from direct modeling with objects or pictures to the learning of number facts, children do not make that transition directly. Children at this level are generally more flexible in their use of strategies and can choose among several different strategies for the same problem.

Two basic principals allow children flexibility in choosing strategies for Join and Separate problems: an understanding of *part-whole relationships* and an understanding that *actions can be reversed.* By applying the part-whole principle, children learn that all problems in which both parts are known can be solved with an additive strategy. All problems in which one part and the whole are known can be solved using any of the subtraction strategies (counting-up, counting-down, or separating). Applying the action-reversal principle, children see that the act of joining objects to a set can be undone by removing the objects from the resulting set. For example, the following Start Unknown problem can be solved by reversing the action:

■ Colleen had some guppies. She gave 3 guppies to Roger. She had 5 guppies left. How many guppies did she have at the start?

If the 3 guppies that were given away are put back with the 5 guppies that are left, the original set of guppies is restored. (See Van de Walle's discussion of Part-Part-Whole in chapter 4 and Thornton's in chapter 7.)

For older children in the third or fourth grade, an analysis of problems based on part-whole relationships may be effective. Rathmell and Huinker (1989) propose that as children gain experience with Join, Separate, and Part-Part-Whole problems, their thinking becomes more flexible. They suggest that children at this age can deal with problems within a broader classification in which Join, Separate, and Part-Part-Whole problems are mapped into a part-whole structure. Younger children, however, have difficulty dealing with the part-whole relationship in a problem and do not solve problems in terms of this analysis.

In a class that focuses on problem solving, different types of problems are used and children's solution strategies are discussed. The following example shows children solving a problem in a number of ways:

A Problem-solving Approach to the Operations   117

■ *Teacher:* There are 3 clowns in the circus ring. Eight more clowns join them. How many clowns are in the circus ring altogether? [The teacher observes direct modeling and counting strategies and calls on a child who used direct modeling.] Brian, how did you solve the problem?

Brian: Well, I made 3 chips and then I made 8 chips, 'cause that's how many you said. Then I counted them up and got 11. Eleven clowns.

Teacher: Nice job. Did any one solve the problem another way? [The teacher calls on a child who had been counting on her fingers.]

Nell: I didn't use my chips. I just counted 3 [holds up 8 fingers], 4, 5, 6, 7, 8, 9, 10, 11. That's how I got 11.

Sam: I counted like Nell but I used the big number first and got 11. See, 8 [holds up 3 fingers], 9, 10, 11.

Brian: I can do that with my chips. This is 8 [points to the set of 8 chips] and 9, 10, 11 [points to each chip in the second set].

Teacher: Good thinking. Let's try another problem like that one.

The strategies do not have to be taught explicitly but can develop naturally within a problem-solving environment. In discussing strategies, children can validate their own thinking and influence the thinking of other children. Providing children with the opportunity to discuss their strategies may encourage more efficient problem solving.

multiplication and division

There are three major types of multiplication and division problems that can be introduced to the young child:

Multiplication: There are 4 eggs in each of 3 baskets. How many eggs in all?

Measurement Division: If there are 12 eggs, and 4 eggs in each basket, how many baskets are there? (See fig. 6.)

Fig. 6. Measure division

Partitive Division: Altogether there are 12 eggs and 3 baskets. If the same number of eggs is in each basket, how many eggs are in 1 basket? (See fig. 7.)

Fig. 7. Partitive division

In the multiplication problem, the unknown is the product, the total number of eggs. The number 4 shows how many eggs are in each group and 3 shows the number of groups. The roles of 3 and 4 are not interchangeable because 3 eggs in 4 baskets is a different situation.

In the measurement-division problem, the unknown is the number of groups or baskets. In the partitive-division problem, the unknown is the number of eggs.

Many children view these three types of problems as quite different and do not make the connections between multiplication and division. Nor do children readily view multiplication as commutative, and consequently, they do not solve measurement-division problems in the same way they solve partitive-division problems. Beginning in the second grade, young children are able to distinguish among the three types of word problems, although they do not use the technical vocabulary. Children are able to model or act out the word problems, showing that they understand the roles of the numbers in the problems. Children need this level of understanding and modeling before they are introduced to multiplication and division symbols, especially if we expect them to see that 12 ÷ 4 can represent either 12 eggs with 4 in each basket or 12 eggs split equally among 4 baskets.

Beyond problems with equivalent sets, word problems involve scalars (e.g., A toy truck is 2 feet tall. The real truck is 3 times as tall. How tall is the real truck?) and cross products (e.g., There are 3 flavors of ice cream and 2 kinds of cones. How many different combinations of ice cream and cones can you make?). These types are more difficult for young children and are usually delayed until later grades.

Multiplication and division word problems with equivalent sets are modeled in several ways; the most common are illustrated in figure 8.

Groups

Arrays

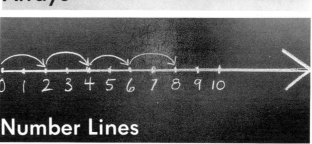

Number Lines

Fig. 8. Models of multiplication and division problems

children's solution strategies

Children use a variety of strategies to solve multiplication and division problems. The development occurs somewhat later but generally parallels the development of addition and subtraction strategies (Kouba 1989). Direct modeling strategies are replaced by counting strategies or additive and subtractive strategies, which later are replaced by multiplication and division facts.

direct modeling

The most common direct modeling strategy that first and second graders use to solve a multiplication problem is to create equal groups either with physical objects or tally marks and then count the total number. This strategy is similar in structure to a counting strategy used for addition problems.

■ *Teacher:* Nan had 4 flowerpots. She planted 3 flowers in each pot. How many flowers did Nan plant altogether?

Jean counts out 3 chips ("1, 2, 3") and sets them aside. She then counts out 3 more chips and makes a second group. After making the fourth group, she points to each group, counting, "1, 2, 3, 4," then counts the total starting with the first chip: "1, 2, 3, 4, 5, 6, 7, 8, 9, 10, 11, 12," to find the total.

To solve a measurement-division problem such as putting 15 into groups of 3, children count out 15 objects and use them as a pool to make groups of 3. When the pool is exhausted, the groups are counted and the result is reported as the answer. Alternatively, rather than making a pool of 15 objects, some children begin by forming groups of three while counting out the total number of objects, stopping when the count reaches 15.

■ *Teacher:* You have 15 cookies altogether to put on plates. You put 3 cookies on each plate. How many plates do you need?

Kevin counts out 15 chips, starting from 1. He then places 3 of the 15 chips in a pile, counting, "1, 2, 3." He continues to make piles in the same manner until the 15 chips are gone. Pointing to each pile, Kevin counts, "1, 2, 3, 4, 5—five plates."

Molly counts out 3 chips and puts them in a pile. She then takes 3 more chips and counts, "4, 5, 6," and puts them in a second pile. She continues until she has reached a count of 15. Molly then counts the number of piles she has made.

To solve a partitive-division problem, children may use either a partitioning (dealing) strategy or a grouping strategy. Children who use a dealing strategy make a set of 15 objects, deal them one by one in 5 piles until all the objects are dealt. To get the answer, they then count the number of objects in one pile. Children who use grouping strategies may do guess-and-test versions of the two grouping strategies described for measurement division. For example, when putting 15 objects into 5 groups, some children count out 15 objects, make a guess as to the number of objects in each group and then form the groups on the basis of their guess. If too many or too few objects are in the pool to form exactly 5 groups, the pool is reformed and another guess is made and tested. Similarly, some children guess at the number of objects in a group and begin forming groups while keeping a running count of the total number of objects. If, after 5 groups are formed, the total number of objects in the running count does not equal 15, another guess is made and tested.

■ *Teacher:* There are 24 marbles in the bag. If we share them equally among 4 children, how many marbles will each child get?

Anna begins by making a group of 4, counting, "1, 2, 3, 4. That's one. 5, 6, 7, 8. That's two." She continues until she has made 4 groups. She realizes that the running total is only 16 and she has to share 24, so she starts again. This time she begins with 5 in a group, then finally 6 in a group.

Carlos uses both a guess-and-test strategy and a dealing strategy to solve the problem. He begins by counting out 24 chips. He makes one group of 3, a second group of 3, and so on, until he has 4 groups of 3. He realizes that he has chips left over and checks to make sure he has made 4 groups by counting them, "1, 2, 3, 4." Then he deals out the extra chips one by one until they are all dealt to a group and counts the chips in one group, "1, 2, 3, 4, 5, 6." (See fig. 9.)

counting

Some children calculate answers to multiplication and measurement-division problems by multiple counting or skip counting, for example, finding 3 groups of 5 by counting, "5, 10, 15." Children keep track of the number of multiples counted usually with fingers, nods

Fig. 9. Guess and test for a partitive-division problem

of the head, or other kinesthetic devices. For multiples whose sequences they do not readily know they combine counting by multiples with counting by ones.

- *Teacher:* Pretend you are a squirrel. There are 6 trees. You find 4 nuts under each tree. How many nuts do you find altogether?

  Darla says, "Okay, 6 trees," and then extends one finger while saying, "4," a second finger while saying, "8," and a third finger while saying, "12." She pauses, looks up into the air and counts, "13, 14, 15, 16." As she says each numeral, she nods her head. She also moves her eyes and head slightly from left to right as she counts. When she says, "16," she puts up a fourth finger. She moves her head and eyes back to the left and continues, "17, 18, 19, 20." As she says, "20," she puts up a fifth finger. She announces "24 nuts" as her answer.

  Teacher: What were you doing when you were looking above your head?

Darla: Well, fours are hard so I was counting four marks.

Teacher: I didn't see any marks.

Darla: No, I was pretending.

Children often become confused if they use their fingers both to count the number of multiples and to serve as a reference for the set to be counted repeatedly. Most often, children use different means for keeping track of different counts, as Darla did. When children use skip counting to solve partitive-division problems, they guess at the number in each group and skip count by that guess. Thus they do not apply commutativity.

addition and subtraction

In additive or subtractive strategies, the child clearly identifies the use of repeated addition or subtraction to calculate the answer. Intermediate sums or differences are reported and incremented. Again, the number of times an addend is used is kept track of mentally or with objects kinesthetically.

This strategy can be applied successfully to the solution of multiplication and measurement-division problems where the number of objects in a group is known. However, within the context of a partitive-division problem, the quantity that is given is the number of groups. The number of objects to be added or subtracted for each group is not known. Therefore, the solution strategy for partitive-division problems is more naturally a direct modeling strategy; for multiplication and measurement-division problems the strategy may be additive or subtractive.

implications for instruction

We suggest a sequence of instruction in which children first develop general concepts of addition, subtraction, multiplication, and division; then learn the symbols for the concepts; and later memorize number facts and learn algorithms. At each step, the new knowledge or skill should be related to established knowledge and skills. By carefully assessing children's thinking at each step, teachers can facilitate these relationships.

The natural development of strategies through sharing and class discussion is a primary feature of a problem-solving environment. A variety of strategies should be recognized and discussed, rather than just one strategy. Lessons that are designed for whole-group instruction must allow for the variety of solution strategies that children use. Therefore, the teaching of specific strategies in the whole-group setting may only be beneficial to a small group of students. Lessons on word problems let children talk about appropriate strategies in an informal way. These discussions then become the context for dealing with more efficient strategies.

assessment of children's thinking

The first part of this chapter has emphasized our belief that instruction should build on what the children already know. Assessing children's thinking is the key to planning instruction. The analysis of children's solutions of different problems provides some perspective on what questions to ask and what to listen for.

It is important to assess not only whether a child can solve a particular problem but also how the child solves the problem. Children solve problems in many ways. The fact that two children give the correct answer to a problem does not mean that they solved the problem in the same way or that they had the same understanding of the problem. A child who solves addition and multiplication problems by directly modeling the problem has different concepts, skills, and needs than another child who solves the same problems by recalling number facts. The ability of a child to give a correct answer to a problem does not necessarily mean that the child has an advanced level of skill or understanding. For example, some children develop

very efficient counting strategies and can respond rapidly to many problems. As a consequence, even a timed test of number facts will not reveal that this child has not memorized the facts.

The most effective way to determine how a child solves a problem is to watch the child solve it and listen to the explanation of the process used. Ongoing assessments can be conducted by consistently listening to how children solve problems. Each interaction with a child is an opportunity to find out something about the child's thinking. The following classroom episode illustrates the assessment of children's problem-solving ability.

■ Mr. Day walks around the room while the children are working at their desks. Some children are using counters to help them solve problems.

Mr. Day: Good thinking on the last problem. Now let's try this one. Robin picked 4 apples. Bob gave her some more apples. Now she has 9 apples. How many apples did Bob give her?

Some of the children begin to make a set of 4 objects. He notices other students are counting on their fingers and some children already have their hand raised. Mr. Day isn't quite sure how several students solved the previous problem, so he asks a few to explain their solution to the class. (See fig. 10.)

Fig. 10. Assessment of problem-solving ability

Jean: I just counted. I knew 4 plus 4 is 8, and 1 more is 9. So 4 and 1 is 5.

David: I used my counters to count 4, then I needed

some more. [Pauses, then looks at his counters to retell the story.] Then I counted 5, 6, 7, 8, 9 [makes a second group with the counters].

Mr. Day: Then how many apples did Bob give Robin? [David isn't quite sure when he looks at his groups.] David, which group shows how many apples Robin had to start with?

David: This one, 4 [points to the first group].

Mr. Day: How many in the other group?

David: [Counts 1, 2, 3, 4, 5.] 5.

Mr. Day: Did Bob give Robin 5 more apples?

David: Yes.

Mr. Day: How do you know that?

David: Well, because she had 4 to start with [points to the first group of 4 chips]. Then Bob gave her these, so 5, 6, 7, 8, 9 [points to the second group of 5 chips], and that's 5.

Mr. Day: Nice explanation. Did anyone else solve the problem like David?

Mr. Day decided that David would benefit from more experience solving the same type of problem. He noted that several other children were also using a direct-modeling strategy. Mr. Day realized that although Jean did not recall the number fact, her derived-fact strategy was very efficient. He also thought that several children in the group could work together with Jean on more difficult types of problems.

Within one class period, this teacher was able to assess the thinking of many of the students in the class by observation and discussion in an informal setting. At the same time, the children were all working on the same type of problem using a variety of strategies. By asking the children how they solved the problem, the teacher could maintain their interest and emphasize the importance to the class of their contributions.

initial instruction

Children should solve word problems by counting and modeling before they are introduced to addition, *subtraction, multiplication, and division symbols and before they memorize number facts.* Children entering kindergarten and the first grade can solve simple addition and subtraction word problems by using modeling and counting. Some first-grade children and many second-grade children can also solve multiplication and division word problems with modeling and counting strategies. It is desirable to give children an opportunity to consolidate these strategies through extended practice with simple word problems before the symbols for the four basic operations are introduced.

Children should be provided experiences with a variety of problem situations as early as kindergarten and first grade. The purpose is *not* for them to distinguish among the problems or classify them in some way. If problems are selected with care, children will invent ways to solve them on their own; thus, it is unnecessary and even counterproductive to emphasize the distinctions among problems.

Overall levels of difficulty for problems of various types are shown in figure 11. In kindergarten and first grade, start with problems for level 1. Once children demonstrate that they can solve these problems, they can move to problems at level 2, and then to basic Compare problems at level 3. The rest of the problems

Difficulty Levels	Problem Type
1	Join, Result Unknown Separate, Result Unknown Part-Part-Whole, Whole Unknown
2	Join, Change Unknown
3	Compare Part-Part-Whole, Part Unknown
4	Join, Start Unknown Separate, Start Unknown

Fig. 11. Problem types clustered by level of difficulty

at level 3 and level 4 might be deferred until later in the school year.

Multiplication word problems can be introduced in first grade. After the children are familiar with number lines, multiplication problems involving equal-sized "jumps" on the number line can be introduced. Measurement-division and partitive-division word problems can be introduced later in first grade starting with simple situations involving small numbers.

Children who readily solve easy problems can move on to more difficult types of problems or learn some of the more advanced counting strategies. At the same time, less able children can be developing basic competence with easier problems. Small numbers might be used initially, but children can solve problems with larger numbers as long as the numbers are within their counting ranges. The following example illustrates how several types of problems can be incorporated into one lesson.

■ *Teacher:* Nina had 5 stamps. She collected 7 more stamps. How many stamps does she have altogether? [Children are given some time to solve the problem and are asked for their solutions.]

  Bob: 12. I know 7 and 3 are 10, and 2 more are 12.

  Teacher: [Alternative strategies are discussed and the class moves to the next problem.] Let's try this problem. Nina has 12 stamps to paste in her stamp collection. If she pastes 3 stamps on each page, how many pages will she fill? [Children are given a few minutes to solve the problem. After the strategies are discussed, the teacher extends the problem.] Nina bought 6 more stamps. How many stamps does she have now? How many more pages can she fill, if she pastes 3 stamps on each page?

In any worksheet include at least two types of problems. Many textbook pages contain only one type of problem. Children quickly pick up on this pattern, and it discourages them from reading and thinking about the problems. In most classes, it is appropriate to introduce only one new type of problem in a given lesson, but the new problems should be mixed in with ones that the children already can solve.

Children's responses to problems determine the types of problem they need. If a child cannot figure out how to solve a problem with modeling and leading questions by the teacher, it is appropriate to give easier problems until the child is ready to solve the more difficult problem. Attempting to force a strategy on a child or develop tricks for getting the answer can inhibit a child's problem-solving abilities. The following example illustrates decision making by the teacher:

■ *Teacher:* Luz had 8 stickers. She bought some more stickers. Now she has 12 stickers altogether. How many stickers did she buy?

  Sam: 12. [Has one group of 12 on his desk.]

  Penny: That's what I got.

  Teacher: Sam, tell us how you figured that out.

  Sam: Well, first she had 8, so I counted 8 of these [chips]. Then she got some more and now she has 12. She got 12.

  Teacher: Yes, she has 12 stickers altogether but the story already told us that. Let's listen again. [Reads the story again.] Sam, what is the story asking us to find?

  Sam: How many she bought.

  Teacher: How many stickers did Luz have at the beginning?

  Sam: 8.

  Teacher: First you said you counted out 8. Where is your group of 8?

  Sam: [Makes a group of 8 chips.] Here's 8.

  Teacher: [Models what Sam is doing by making a set of 8 on the overhead projector.] Is that how many she had altogether?

  Sam: No, she needs some more.

  Teacher: How many more would she need to have 9 stickers altogether?

  Sam: One more, 8, 9. [Adds another chip.]

  Teacher: [Places another chip on the overhead to form a second group.] How did you know that?

  Sam: I just added on 1 more to 8 and got 9.

  Teacher: If Luz had 8 stickers to begin with, how many more would you add on to make 12? [Reconstructs the set of 8 chips on the overhead.]

Sam: Oh. [Whispers the counting sequence.] 9, 10, 11, 12. [Counts the set.] 4.

Teacher: How many more stickers did Luz buy?

Sam: 4.

Teacher: OK, let's try another problem. [Gives the children another problem with the change set unknown and focuses on Penny, the other child in the group who responded incorrectly to the first problem.] Pat had 7 shells in her bucket. Her brother gave her some more shells. Now Pat has 11 shells in her bucket. How many shells did her borther give her?

Penny: 11.

Sam: No, it's 4. See, 8, 9, 10, 11. [Points to a group of 4 chips on his desk.]

The teacher has Penny model the problem as she reads each step. Penny responds correctly to each question and is then given another problem to solve independently but is not successful. It seems that unless Penny has help in representing the problem situation, she cannot solve it. Although she knows the procedure for making sets, she can focus only on the counting task. As a result, she cannot plan her strategy in advance and identify the solution set. The teacher decides that Penny is not ready to solve this type of problem and provides her with more experience solving different, less difficult, problems.

Children's reading ability should not prevent them from having a variety of problem-solving experiences. Reading is not a prerequisite to problem solving. Children can work on word problems through activities and oral reading that compensate for low reading level.

*Variety of experiences.* Problem solving can be done with the whole class with the teacher reading or telling the story. Readers and nonreaders can be paired to work cooperatively by sharing their solution strategies. One child can read the problem, and the other child can record the solution. Volunteers (older students, parents, grandparents) can be readers for children. This is another opportunity for children to share their thinking about problems and explain their solutions. Rebus reading and the use of

the students' names in a word problem can facilitate the reading of problems, as in figure 12. Word problems can be tape recorded and set up at a mathematics "listening center." Record problems of equal difficulty on several tapes. Label the tapes, and supply counters and recording sheets. The children can select a tape, listen, solve the problem, and record their answers. **ɑ**

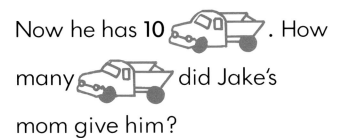

Fig. 12. Rebus problem to minimize reading

developing a problem-solving environment

Problem solving should not be limited to mathematics lessons. The meaning of addition, subtraction, multiplication, and division can be developed as problems are encountered naturally throughout the school day. For example, imagine the beginning of a school day and visiting Ms. Frances's first-grade class to find out how she is generating so much enthusiasm for problem solving. All the children are gathered to discuss the day's activities.

■ *Ms. Frances:* Can someone circle today's date on the calendar? [Sue marks a ring around 17 as in figure 13.] OK. Our field trip to the aquarium is on the 21st day of the month. How many more days before we go? [Children spend a minute or so figuring out the problem. Ms. Frances waits until about half the hands are raised, then she calls on Pat.]

Fig. 13. Problem solving throughout the school day

Pat: There are 4 days before our trip.

Ms. Frances: How did you figure that out, Pat?

Pat: I counted 17 [pause], 18, 19, 20, 21. [Holds up a finger with each count.] So the answer is 4.

Ms. Frances: Good job, Pat. Did anyone solve the problem another way?

Mike: Well, I know that 17 plus 3 is 20, and 1 more than 20 is 21, so 3 and 1 is 4.

Ms. Frances: Good thinking. Did anyone solve the problem another way? [Children explain the various strategies they used to solve the problem. Most of the time Ms. Frances just listens.] Four days before

our trip. Is that more or less than a week away? [Class discusses using the calendar, counting, and comparing 4 and 7 to decide on the answer.] Let's see. We must take care of our lunch count now.

Later in the day a birthday party is held in Ms. Frances's classroom. The children have made cookies and have arranged them on 4 trays in a 3 × 5 array. After lunch Ms. Frances begins the discussion about organizing the party.

■ *Ms. Frances:* Well, there are many cookies for us to share. We must also remember to include Ms. Adams, our principal. How will we decide how many cookies each person will get?

Joan: First, we could count all the cookies.

Ben: Or we could just count the cookies on one tray.

Ms. Frances: Let's think about how each of those ways will help us figure out how many cookies we will each have.

Ms. Frances has engaged the children in real problem solving. They were realizing that problem solving extends beyond a special time of the day and that they have the skills to solve problems for which *they* wanted answers. They also shared ideas about how to solve the problems. The message is that mathematics is relevant and mathematical problem solving applies to many daily activities.

introducing symbols

Once children can easily represent and solve simple Join and Separate problems with objects or by counting, addition and subtraction symbols can be introduced and related to these informal operations. Before symbols are introduced for multiplication and division, children must be able to group and partition objects and distinguish multiplicative situations from additive situations. The symbols for the operation simply become a way of representing familiar operations. *The symbols +, −, ×, and ÷ should be clearly linked to children's informal procedures and presented as symbolic representations of operations that children have already learned.*

initial instruction

Work with number sentences should begin after children have successfully solved many types of problems. The symbols + and − should be introduced as a way to represent familiar problems. Unlike solution strategies, which children may develop naturally in a problem-solving environment, the writing of number sentences to represent story problems may require more explicit instruction. However, some children may already be familiar with the plus and minus signs as a result of other influences (e.g., parents, older siblings, or television). The following is an example of an initial lesson on writing number sentences in Ms. Santos's first-grade class.

Each child has an envelope containing two sets of numeral cards, with each card having a digit from 0 to 9 on it. The children can order the cards from 0 to 9 and use them in lessons on sequencing and counting sets.

■ *Ms. Santos:* Before we solve our first story problem, we are going to use our number cards to tell about the story. First we will need some different cards. [Gives each child 4 more cards +, −, =, and □ for the unknown.] Let's think about this problem. There were 5 eggs in the incubator. Mike put in 3 more eggs. How many eggs are in the incubator now? [Pauses.] Let's see if we can write down what happened in the story. How many eggs were in the incubator at first?

Kate: 5.

Ms. Santos: [Writes the number 5 on the chalkboard and has children find the card with the number 5.] Then what happened in the story?

Bob: Mike put 3 more eggs in.

Ms. Santos: Yes, Mike added 3 more eggs. To write that down we are going to use a plus sign. [Holds up the plus sign.] Pick up the card with the plus sign. [Looks around the group to see that they have all found the correct card.] Mike added 3 more eggs so we can write + 3. [Puts 5 + 3 on the chalkboard and has the children do the same.] We need a sign

to tell us how many we will have when we add 5 and 3.

Claire: I know, it's this. [Holds up the = card.] My mom told me.

Ms. Santos: Yes, that's the equal sign. We don't know how many eggs we will have when we add 5 and 3 so we will put the equal sign and a box. Five plus 3 equals what number? [Finishes the number sentence on the chalkboard and has the children do the same with the cards. Individuals then read their number sentences.] (See fig. 14.)

Fig. 14. Making a number sentence for a problem

Ms. Santos then continues this lesson by having the children solve the problem and talk about replacing the

□ with the sum of 5 + 3. Then the children use their cards to represent several story problems and discuss how they decided to write the number sentence. Although before this lesson the children had solved a variety of story problems, Ms. Santos decided to use Join (Result Unknown) problems to introduce the plus sign. Several lessons later she introduced the minus sign in a similar manner.

writing
open-number sentences

The difficulties that children have in writing number sentences to represent word problems arise because the symbols they have available ($a + b$, $a - b$, $a \times b$, $a \div b$) do not always correspond to their informal solutions with objects. For children performing addition and subtraction, $a - b$ may represent a separating action that corresponds to their solution of Separate problems like the following:

■ John had 8 marbles. He lost 3 of them. How many does he have left?

They have no difficulty writing a number sentence for this type of problem. But they solve the following Join (Change Unknown) problem by joining elements to another set and keeping track of the number of elements joined rather than removing elements from a larger set.

■ John had 3 marbles. He won some more. Now he has 8 marbles. How many marbles did he win?

Young children tend to view this problem as an additive situation, and their solution corresponds more closely to the open number sentence $3 + \square = 8$. They analyze the problem in terms of how many more are needed to add to 3 to get 8. Children naturally write number sentences that directly represent the action in the problem. This approach focuses on teaching children to write number sentences to represent problems rather than to solve open sentences.

Children relate number sentences to their modeling and counting strategies and solve them directly using these

strategies. Consider the following example where the children have just solved and discussed several strategies for solving Join (Change Unknown) problems. The children previously solved and represented Join and Separate (Results Unknown) problems and Part-Part-Whole (Whole Unknown) problems using the notation $A + B = \square$.

■ *Ms. Santos:* Let's think about how to write a number sentence for this story problem. Beth had 6 stickers. Her mom gave her some more. Now she has 14 stickers. How many stickers did Beth's mom give her? [Pauses.] How are we going to begin the number sentence for this story?

Jon: First, I would make a pile of 6, so put a 6 first. Then she got some but I don't know how many. . . .

Ms. Santos: [Begins the number sentence on an overhead projector with a numeral card showing a 6.] How might you write that?

Jon: I'd put plus, 'cause it said her mom gave her some. She's getting more, so it's adding. I don't know how many more stickers Beth got. Can we put the box (□) there?

Ms. Santos: OK. Beth had 6 stickers [points to the 6] and her mom gave her some more. We can write plus and put the box. [Continues writing the number sentence.] What's next?

Chris: She had 14, so put equals 14.

Ms. Santos: So 6 plus box equals 14. Laurie, I see that you made that number sentence. Can you tell us how you decided to write that for the story?

Laurie: Well, 6 stickers plus some more stickers equals 14 stickers. I was thinking about 6 plus what number is 14.

Ms. Santos: Did you figure out what number we can put in the box?

Laurie: Well, 8. I was thinking of 6 plus 4 more is 10 and 4 more is 14, so it's 8.

Ms. Santos: I like the way you explained that, Laurie. I would like everyone to make a number sentence for this story problem with your cards.

Representing the process of how children think about a problem is a transition stage. Open number sentences that model the strategy children initially use to solve problems gives them a way to connect their knowledge of problem solving to symbolic representations. Children should not be expected to perform operations with symbols that they do not perform readily with physical objects or counting strategies when solving word problems. Encourage discussions of the number sentences they generate for story problems. As they begin to see relationships among number facts, they will begin to write number sentences in the standard form, $a + b = \square$, $a - b = \square$, $a \times b = \square$, and $a \div b = \square$.

generating word problems

A curriculum that focuses on problem solving requires problems for children to solve. A variety of problems can be generated on selected themes or topics. Such themes can be a source of problems as well as a way to integrate mathematics, reading, language arts, social studies, and science. The themes are naturally flexible and adaptable and encompass any combination of solution strategies, problem types, and presentation styles.

The activities in this section can be adapted for whole-class presentations, small groups, or individuals, depending on instructional objectives. However, the best problem-solving activities are those that the teacher develops for students in her or his class. The best problems are those generated cooperatively with students. Throughout this chapter we have provided glimpses of teachers who used problem solving to develop the concepts of addition, subtraction, multiplication, and division. In each instance, the selection of the problem types and the context of the problems was relevant to the given situation. Similarly, instructional goals will determine the activities and the problems chosen.

We can make some suggestions for the selection of problems. Problem types can be clustered by level of difficulty (see fig. 11). Problems within each cluster are of approximately the same level of difficulty.

Children's progression through these levels is relatively predictable. Lessons should include a variety of problem types but only one new problem type from the next level of difficulty. Grouping and partitioning problems should be incorporated into a lesson once they have been introduced to the children.

Generating problems. Develop a routine with the class to generate problems. Ask the children to volunteer a topic, names, and numbers. If children give "dinosaurs," "Meg and Andy," and "5 and 9," a problem like the following can be generated:

Meg had 5 toy brontosaurs in her dinosaur collection. Andy gave her some more. Then Meg had 9 brontosaurs. How many did Andy give Meg? **a**

During the school day children have many opportunities to solve real-world problems, some of which may be nonstandard. Some problems may not be solved in one discussion because additional information may be needed.

Field trips. Find the cost for each child, total number of people, number of cars, number of parents, and so on. **a**

Lunch and milk money. Count coins to find a total value and various ways to use coins to make the total. **a**

Themes can be extended into other curricular areas, expecially science.

Animals. Classify by natural habitat, eating habits, location, length of hibernation, and so on, and use the classifications for counting, graphing, and problem solving. **a**

Zoo. Create a model of a zoo and the animals' natural habitats. Here are some sample problems: Some wolves are in their den. [One child puts some animals in the den where they can't be seen.] Three wolves are in the grass. [Places 3 in the grass.] There are 7 wolves altogether. How many are in the den?

There are 15 penguins on the iceberg. Eight penguins are in the water. How many more penguins are on the iceberg than in the water? a

Small creatures. Facts are gathered by students to generate problems: A honeybee has 6 legs and a spider has 8 legs. How many more legs does a spider have than a honeybee? Three honeybees each gathered 3 pounds of nectar to make honey. How much nectar did they gather altogether? a

Plants and seeds. Seeds and the growth of plants are important topics in the primary grades and can provide data for story problems. a

Children's literature is a rich source of story problems. Some stories deal specifically with numbers, whereas others can provide a story frame. Fables and folktales can provide a continuous story context. For example, one of the many versions of the story of Johnny Appleseed can be read to the children. After the story is read and discussed, the context is set for the following problem:

Story contexts. Johnny started on his journey to plant apple seeds. After he walked for many days and nights, he found just the right spot to plant his seeds. He planted 6 seeds by the stream and 5 seeds at the bottom of the hill. How many seeds did Johnny plant?

The next day . . . a

Bulletin boards are another medium that facilitates problem solving. Children can work with the information on the board and add to the display. During the week, after the class has discussed the material on the board, the children can devise word problems and put them on the board for others to solve.

Story extensions. As an extension of the Johnny Appleseed story children can describe, compare, and classify a variety of apples. The bulletin board can be used to display a picture or a bar graph of types of apples. The children can then generate such problems as the following: In a bowl are 8 Delicious apples and 5 Macintosh apples. How many more Delicious apples are in the bowl than Macintosh apples. a

Neighborhood map. Studying the neighborhood and the local community is a primary-grade social studies topic that can provide a stimulus for story problems. On the bulletin board, display a map of the neighborhood. The children can label the buildings, streets, and places where they live. After discussing directions, the children can generate stories for others to solve, for example: The post office is 5 blocks from school. The fire station is 8 blocks from school. How much farther is the fire station than the post office from the school? a

Scenes and words. The bulletin board can also be used as a resource for vocabulary words that children can use to generate story problems. The board can depict scenes (e.g., city blocks with stores and apartments, a circus, a jungle with prehistoric creatures, an aquarium, or a local event). The children can develop the theme and label their contributions. This will give the children the material to generate a variety of problems like the following:

A juggler was juggling 5 balls. She dropped 2 balls. How many balls is the juggler juggling now?

Four wagons are in the circus ring. Two clowns are in each wagon. How many clowns are in the wagons altogether? a

Story problems that develop from contexts that children are familiar with make mathematics more than a subject taught at a particular time. Instead, mathematics is integrated throughout the day and into everyday life. In addition, the careful selection of problem types and a knowledge of children's solution strategies will ensure success in problem solving.

The preparation of this paper was supported in part by a grant from the National Science Foundation (MDR-8550236). The opinions expressed in this paper do not necessarily reflect the position, policy, or endorsement of the National Science Foundation.

references

Carpenter, Thomas P. "Learning to Add and Subtract: An Exercise in Problem Solving." In *Teaching and Learning Mathematical Problem Solving: Multiple Research Perspectives,* edited by Edward A. Silver, pp. 17–40. Hillsdale, N.J.: Lawrence Erlbaum Associates, 1985.

Carpenter, Thomas P. and James M. Moser. "The Acquisition of Addition and Subtraction Concepts." In *The Acquisition of Mathematics Concepts and Processes,* edited by Richard Lesh and Marsha Landau, pp. 7–44. Orlando, Fla.: Academic Press, 1983.

_____. "The Acquisition of Addition and Subtraction Concepts in Grades One through Three. *Journal for Research in Mathematics Education* 15 (May 1984): 179–202.

Fuson, Karen. *Children's Counting and Concepts of Number.* New York: Springer-Verlag, 1988.

Kouba, Vicky L. "Children's Strategies for Equivalent Set Multiplication and Division Word Problems." *Journal for Research in Mathematics Education* 20 (March 1989): 147–58.

National Council of Teachers of Mathematics. *An Agenda for Action: Recommendations for School Mathematics of the 1980s.* Reston, Va.: The Council, 1980.

_____. *Curriculum and Evaluation Standards for School Mathematics.* Reston, Va.: The Council, 1988.

Rathmell, Edward C., and DeAnn M. Huinker. "Using 'Part-Whole' Language to Help Children Represent and Solve Word Problems." In *New Directions for Elementary School Mathematics,* 1989 Yearbook edited by Paul R. Trafton, pp. 99–110. Reston, Va.: National Council of Teachers of Mathematics, 1989.

Riley, Mary S., James G. Greeno, and Joan I. Heller. "Development of Children's Problem-solving Ability in Arithmetic." In *The Development of Mathematical Thinking,* edited by Herbert P. Ginsburg, pp. 153–96. New York: Academic Press, 1983.

Usiskin, Zalman, and Max M. Bell. *Applying Arithmetic: A Handbook of Applications of Arithmetic.* Chicago: University of Chicago Press, 1983.

carol thornton

7

strategies for the basic facts

6 + 3. 8 x 4. A child's ability to provide quick and correct answers to these and other basic number facts is a critical stepping-stone to success in other aspects of the school mathematics curriculum. Written and mental computation, computational estimation, and elements of problem solving rely on this skill.

What approaches to number-fact learning will help children move from counting to the memorized facts needed for "real mathematics" in day-to-day situations? This question has merited renewed interest by researchers and teachers in recent years (Baroody 1985; Fuson 1986; Rathmell 1981; Steinberg 1984; Thornton and Smith 1988). The questions these studies have asked include the following:

- Should we teach strategies for solving unknown facts rather than rely on drill alone?
- Should we group facts for recall by strategy, not by size of sum or factor?
- Should we delay memory work in subtraction until easy addition facts are mastered?
- Should we delay memory work in division until easy multiplication facts are mastered?

- Should we alter both the sequence and the pacing of number-fact work throughout primary school mathematics to accommodate these ideas?

Research and work with teachers and children suggest an affirmative answer to each of these questions, thus providing a framework for a sound basic-fact program. The underlying theme is that a child's *thinking process* is as important in number-fact work as the answers generated.

One result of a two-year subtraction study that included individual interviews with nearly 200 first-grade children in two number-fact programs (Thornton and Smith 1988) highlights this point. When children in the strategy-based program were given facts they had not studied, they generally were confident that they could work them out, and they did. Children in a control group who used a more traditional, drill-oriented program stated either that they had not studied the facts or that they found the facts too hard.

The strategy-based group used more sophisticated and varied strategies than the control group. The number of facts memorized by the end of the year and retained

by students in the next school year also was greater for the strategy-based group.

A strategy approach to teaching basic facts is supported by the National Council of Teachers of Mathematics (1989) in its *Curriculum and Evaluation Standards for School Mathematics.* Encouraging children to use efficient strategies to derive unknown facts *before drill* is better than "premature drill" (Brownell and Chazal 1935), and doing so increases both initial learning and retention (Leutzinger 1979; Rathmell 1978; Swenson 1949; Thiele 1938; Thornton 1978; Thornton and Smith 1988). Further, the thinking necessary in using strategies with facts is an essential ingredient for mental arithmetic and estimation.

framework for instruction

Effective instruction in basic facts progresses through six stages:[1]

1. *Concepts of the operations.* It is critical that children possess a firm understanding of number, of relationships between numbers, and of an operation itself before any attempt is made to develop number facts for that operation. Van de Walle, in chapter 4, provides a framework and activities for number sense and initial operation concepts. Carpenter et al., in chapter 6, give suggestions and examples for using word problems as a way to develop concepts of operations. When concepts are developed, children's thinking and explanations become a major focus.

2. *Prerequisites for thinking strategies.* The prerequisites for thinking strategies detailed below are skills that will later help children use efficient mental strategies to answer unknown facts. These prerequisites are outlined

---

1. This framework has been developed and tested in over 1000 classrooms with partial support from a federal grant administered through the Illinois Board of Higher Education, *Project Math, Good Beginnings, K–3.* Any suggestions or conclusions expressed are those of the author and do not necessarily reflect the views of the funding agency.

separately for addition and subtraction and multiplication and division.

3. *Thinking strategies.* Certain mental techniques that involve counting, number relationships, visual associations, or mental addition and subtraction can help children solve unknown facts. In terms of time and cognitive processing, some thinking strategies are more mature and more efficient than others.

Short mental counts can be carried out when one adds or subtracts 1, 2, or 3. Alternatively, children might think of a *visual* way to count (e.g., for the double 6 + 6, they might think of a dozen eggs, or 12). More sophisticated approaches involve *number relationships* (e.g., for 6 + 7, students can think "one more than 6 + 6"). Whenever possible, physical models should be used to introduce a thinking strategy. Thinking, not speed, is to be emphasized at this stage. With every thinking strategy, children should be encouraged to explain their thought process and to adopt strategies that make sense to them.

4. *Deciding on thinking strategies—use and choose.* Providing sufficient time for children to think through ways to find answers for facts serves the broader goal of helping them think mathematically. Hence, when children discover a useful thinking strategy for solving a group of unknown facts, it is critical both that they *use* the strategy accurately and that they can distinguish, or *choose*, when the thinking pattern applies and when it does not.

For example, children who count up to solve 11 − 8 often are one off in the count: "8, 9, 10, 11—the answer is 4." The goal is to avoid errors of this type, when students do not *use* the count-up strategy accurately. Another goal is for children to identify which facts fit the strategy: "11 − 2 is not a count-up because the forward count is too long; 11 − 9 is." Accuracy, not speed, is again the focus at this stage.

5. *Practice for fact mastery.* When it is evident that children are using correct and efficient thinking strategies for a set of unknown facts, drill or practice is required on the set of facts, along with others previously learned. Practice should be continued

systematically throughout the school year. The goal is an automatic response over time, or fact mastery.

6. *Assessment for fact mastery.* Ongoing assessment of children's level of number-fact mastery accompanies practice. The focus is to determine whether students can give immediate, accurate responses to basic facts and whether they are consistent in this performance over time.

addition and subtraction

concepts of operations

Memorization of facts should begin only when children reasonably understand the concept for each operation. To check whether children have developed "operation sense," the teacher can pose problems and listen to students' responses, for example:

- Can children solve word problems stated orally that involve the four operations? (See chapter 6 by Carpenter et al.)
- Can children directly model and give practical problems for such number sentences as 9 + 1 = □ and 8 − 2 = □?
- Can children use the part-part-whole language appropriately in addition and subtraction? For instance, they might say, "Part of the cube train is red—two cubes—and part is blue—three cubes. The whole train has five cubes."
- After children write an answer to a basic fact, can they use objects or draw a diagram to show that what they've written makes sense?
- Given a mix of oral problems based on familiar situations, can children tell which operation key to push on a calculator to solve a particular problem?

As children mature and have more experience with arithmetic operations, their concept of those operations also grows. Their understanding of each operation is broadened when children begin to compare one operation with another.

prerequisites for thinking strategies

When children can solve word problems orally and use physical models, written equations, and their own words to demonstrate their understanding of an operation (see chapter 6), and when evidence indicates that they have sufficient understanding of number and the relationships between numbers, as suggested by Van de Walle in chapter 4, then the instructional focus shifts. With a view to eventual fact mastery, emphasis now is placed on the development of thinking strategies that will enable children to answer unknown facts in an efficient manner. A check is also necessary for other prerequisites for thinking strategies. The most important skills for students to have are the following:

thinking strategy prerequisites for addition

- Ability to recognize when one, two, or three numbers are said orally, for example, "Eight, nine—*two* numbers" and "Eleven, ten, nine—*three* numbers"
- Ability to count on two or three more from any number, from 4 to 9
- Good visual imagery for the ten-frame (see chapter 4)

thinking strategy prerequisites for subtraction

- Mastery of addition prerequisites
- Ability to count back from any number, 12 or less
- Mastery of related addition facts, for example: for 9 − 3, students know 3 + 6

recognizing auditory counts

Is it necessary for children to finger count or touch numeral points as they count on to add or count back to subtract 1, 2, or 3? The answer is no *if* they can recognize how many numbers they've said in a count. The following simple activity can help children internalize these short counts, making finger counting unnecessary.

a *How many numbers do you hear?* Say two or three numbers in sequence (forward or backward) and ask students to tell or hold up fingers to show how many numbers they hear: "Six, seven, eight" (three numbers). "Ten, nine" (two numbers). Repeat for other sequences.   **a**

counting on and counting back

The immediate goal of counting on is to give students many examples in which the first number in an oral count is not "one." Display from three to nine objects, hide the initial set, and count on two or three more (see fig. 1). Using objects to model a count helps children be accurate and not one off in the count.

Because *counting backward* is difficult for many children (Carpenter and Moser 1982), in an initial activity children might start with up to twelve objects and then count backward as two or three objects are

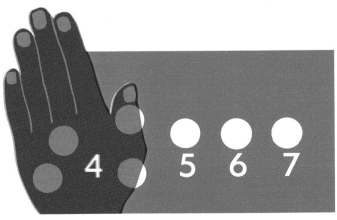

Fig. 1. Counting on from 4

removed (one by one). Next, they can move on to situations with hidden sets.

What's in my pocket? Materials: Nine small objects

In this activity, children establish the total number of objects, observe the teacher hide them, and then count backward as the teacher withdraws them, one by one, from the hidden set.

Teacher: How many here?

Students: Nine.

Teacher: Take out one; now there're how many?

Students: Eight.

Teacher: Take out another; now how many?

Students: Seven.

Teacher: Take out another; now how many do we have?

Students: Six.

Teacher: Nine, eight, seven, six. Are six objects still in my pocket? Should we check? [Note the effective modeling of the backward count by the teacher.] **a**

visual recognition with the ten-frame

Good visual imagery for the ten-frame can be very helpful for quickly solving unknown addition facts with a sum of 10 and the corresponding subtraction facts. The visual imagery is also helpful for using 10 as a bridge with addition facts such as 6 + 8 and 7 + 5 and subtraction facts such as 13 − 5 and 12 − 4. Two basic activities can develop this imagery.

Ten-frame flash. Materials: A set of ten-frame cards with one to ten stars on each card.

Show each card briefly, then remove it from sight. Ask, "How many stars did you see?" Repeat, emphasizing six to nine stars in the frame. It is helpful to make such comments as "Seven stars—that must be the top row and two; five—six, seven. Let's check." **a**

Frame fill. Materials: A set of ten-frame cards Flash the cards as above, then have children close their eyes. Now ask, "Can you see the

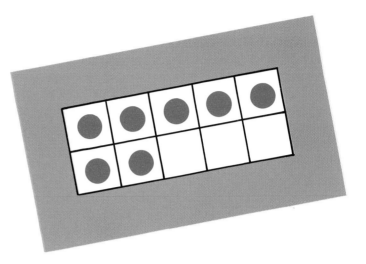

stars in the frame? How many would it take to fill the frame? Let's check." **a**

Counting on, counting back, auditory counting, and ten-frame activities can be initiated in kindergarten, continued in first grade and early second grade, and used in remedial or review programs. With one five-minute warm-up, children can sample each of the four activities. The goal is to assure that these counting skills are developed before children need to apply them in addition and subtraction thinking strategies.

thinking strategies for addition

Explicit intervention by the teacher can help children learn and use efficient thinking strategies for solving unknown facts (Baroody 1985; Fuson 1986; Rathmell 1981; Suydam 1985; Thornton and Smith 1988). One key is active learning of strategies, not just the telling of strategies. The other key is grouping unknown facts by strategy for recall rather than by the size of the sum. Major strategies for addition are summarized in figure 2 (Thornton 1982).

At first children use physical objects in a way that models the thinking strategy. As they internalize the thinking process, children can write or say their answers first, then use a physical model to check whether answers make sense and explain their thinking.

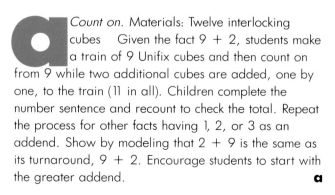

What strategies will help in addition?

Easy Facts

Count on when a fact
has an addend of **1**, **2**, or **3**.

Think of the ten-frame,
especially for "**10** sums."

Think of the picture
for each double.

Harder Facts

Think one more or one less
than a known addition fact.

+9 facts are one less than
+10 facts, which are easier.

Extend to other facts:
9 + 5 = 14, so 8 + 5 = 13 (1 less).

"**Make 10, add extra**"
especially for **7 + 4, 7 + 5,
8 + 4, 8 + 5,** and **8 + 6.**
(For **8 + 5: 8** and **2 = 10,**
and the three extra make **13.**)

Fig. 2. Thinking strategies for addition

The following activities are some addition thinking strategies that children find helpful:

Count on. Materials: Twelve interlocking cubes   Given the fact 9 + 2, students make a train of 9 Unifix cubes and then count on from 9 while two additional cubes are added, one by one, to the train (11 in all). Children complete the number sentence and recount to check the total. Repeat the process for other facts having 1, 2, or 3 as an addend. Show by modeling that 2 + 9 is the same as its turnaround, 9 + 2. Encourage students to start with the greater addend.   **a**

Adding 9. Materials: Ten-frame cards and 18 counters for each pair of students (see fig. 3) Students take turns for 10 + 4; one fills the ten-frame, the other puts four counters outside the frame. One student records 10 + 4 = 14. For 9 + 4, the first student then takes one counter out of the frame, writes 9 + 4 = 13, and says "One less." Children repeat the activity by placing a different number of counters outside the frame each time.   **a**

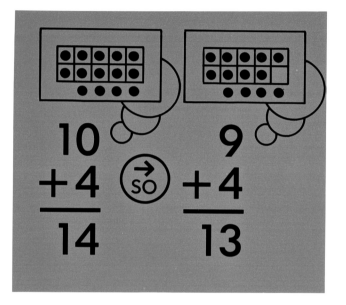

Fig. 3. Using 10 to add 9

Doubles. Materials: Picture cards and fact cards for doubles (fig. 4) and counters Have students give answers orally for the easy doubles: 1 + 1, 2 + 2, 3 + 3, 4 + 4, and 5 + 5. Ask, "Why is it easy to do doubles?" [Only one number to remember] Do the rest of the doubles (6 + 6, 7 + 7, 8 + 8, and 9 + 9), showing with counters that each is two more than the one before. "Why is 6 + 6 two more than ten?" [One more on each five]

Relate the doubles to picture cards and fact cards. Practice the doubles until students can give each answer in three seconds or less.   **a**

Doubles + 1. Materials: Picture and fact cards for doubles and double + 1 facts (see fig. 4)
Place known doubles facts with their pictures on the

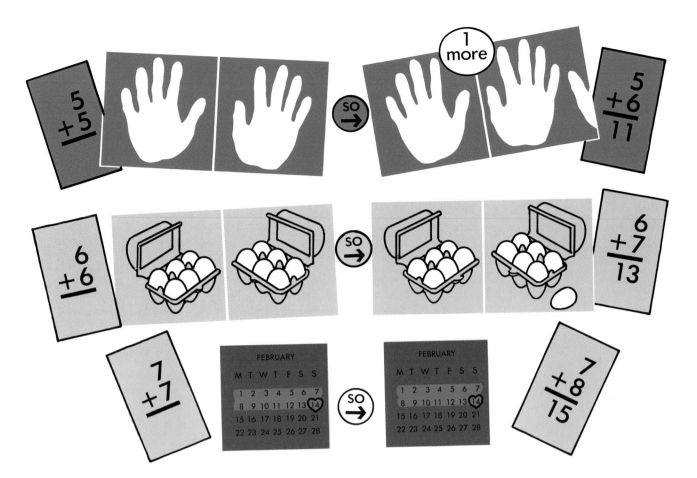

Fig. 4. Facts with doubles and doubles + 1 facts

chalk ledge. Point to each picture that shows a double + 1. The teacher points to the left and asks, "How many eggs do you see here?" [Six] "How many on the other side?" [Seven] "Can you see a double here? Which double will help you find 6 + 7?" [6 + 6] Write, "6 + 6 = 12, so 6 + 7 = 13."

Repeat for other double + 1 facts, especially 5 + 6 and 7 + 8. Extend the activity by starting with a double + 1 fact (e.g., 6 + 7), and ask children to tell the double they can use. Most children will identify 6 + 6 = 12, so 6 + 7 is 1 more (13). Some will identify 7 + 7 = 14, so 6 + 7 is 1 less. Be accepting of different ways students think. Use the doubles pictures to check. **a**

After children explore different strategies for particular groups of facts, follow-through activities help them use and choose strategies. Responses are then speeded up through practice (page 23). Before a new set of facts is introduced, a class "Cross-out Chart of Facts We Have Studied" (fig. 5) can be updated. Charting their progress helps children see how much they know, helps them set goals for the future, and lets them know that "this task has an end!" The figure shows the progress of a second-grade class in early fall after they had studied easier addition facts. Only eight more difficult facts remained to be learned: three double + 1 facts (5 + 6, 6 + 7, 7 + 8) and five others (7 + 4, 7 + 5, 8 + 4, 8 + 5, and 8 + 6).

First-grade classes typically would not cross off "addition 9s" until later in the year. For these students, the eight more difficult facts and their turnarounds might be shaded in some way to designate them as "second-grade facts." Most first graders are not ready to explore noncounting mental strategies for solving these facts. Instruction can be individualized at the end of the year to challenge those who are capable of learning other strategies.

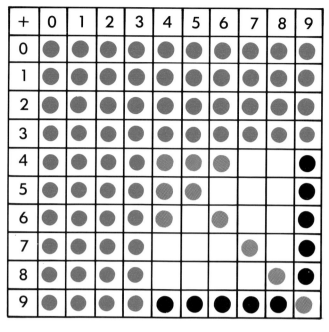

● Count-ons and zeroes
◐ Doubles and easy ten-frame facts
● Addition 9s

Fig. 5. Class cross-out chart of facts studied

pacing and sequencing issues

When subtraction work emphasizing fast recall is delayed until easier addition facts are mastered, then children can use addition facts in learning subtraction. An instructional sequence based on this philosophy follows:

1 Use a problem-solving context and direct modeling to teach or review the concept of addition.
2 Teach easy addition facts, using the overall plan given in this chapter.
3 Teach another curricular topic, for instance, geometry, measurement, place value, time, or money, as a major focus. Continue to review the addition facts as a minor focus.
4 Use a problem-solving context and modeling to teach or review subtraction concepts. (See chapters 4 and 6.)

5 Teach easy subtraction facts while reviewing easy addition facts.
6 Teach harder addition facts while reviewing other known facts.
7 Teach another curricular topic as a major focus while reviewing facts already introduced.
8 Teach harder subtraction facts and continue systematic review.

Within the parameters of an enriched primary school curriculum, steps 1 and 2 typically require two to four months in first grade and a few weeks in other primary grades. Step 5 typically spans the last half of first grade and part of second grade. Mastery of harder addition facts is an appropriate second-grade goal. Many, but by no means all, second graders also master harder subtraction facts.

thinking strategies for subtraction

The strategies listed in figure 6 are based on those commonly used by children to find answers for unknown subtraction facts (Thornton and Smith 1988). Lower-level strategies are given first. Mental counting and visual ten-frame or picture strategies can be learned and used by beginners and lower-level students to help solve virtually all the easy facts.

In early concept work in subtraction, children often use objects to show a whole, remove a part, and count what is left. When the instructional goal shifts to fact mastery, the next step is to provide experiences that develop higher-level approaches to solving unknown facts.

Because young children naturally tend to count, successful strategy-based programs for beginners focus first on the twenty-seven count-backs (-1, -2, -3 facts). This work, a natural extension of the prerequisite counting activity, links short, backward counts to the solving of specific subtraction facts.

A long-standing practice in many number-fact programs has been to present a count-back like $9 - 2$

and its related fact, 9 − 7, in the same lesson. This causes great difficulty to children who are not ready to use more sophisticated thinking strategies and must count. If a child counts back for both facts, then a tab of the counts for 9 − 7 is necessary, because the count is quite long. A similar tab for 9 − 2 is necessary if a child counts up for both facts. Most young beginners have difficulty selecting the quickest count, counting back versus counting up, and experience even greater difficulty in actually doing such a count. The counting movements are direct opposites. To complicate matters further, in one instance children must name the whole and count back from there. In the other, children must start with the part that is given and count up to the whole.

The sequence suggested in figure 6 specifically separates count-backs from count-ups with other easy facts. This sequence was used in a study by Thornton and Smith (1988) and has been replicated in many classrooms in the United States, Australia, and Canada. Thinking-strategy activities such as those that follow are basic to this sequence (Thornton and Toohey 1984). They involve direct modeling, discussion, and writing the fact. Extensions of these activities focus on writing answers first and then using a model to check whether the solutions make sense. Generally, facts are referred to by name, for example, count-backs, doubles, and count-ups.

Count-backs. Materials: Twelve Unifix cubes
The teacher writes 12 − 3 on the board. Taking turns, students form a train of twelve cubes and count back while they break off three cubes for their partner, one by one. Children write the complete equation, count the remaining cubes to check, and repeat for other count-backs. Later, they reverse the procedure. For a written expression, children establish the whole, 12, count back, write the part that is left, and then use cubes to check their answer. **a**

As soon as children demonstrate they can use a strategy accurately and efficiently to solve a group of unknown subtraction facts, "add to check" activities should be provided but never introduced on the same day as a new strategy.

What strategies
will help in subtraction?

Easy Facts

Count back when
1, 2, or 3 is being subtracted.

Think of the ten-frame for
subtracting from 10 and for
9 − 5 and 9 − 4.

Think of the picture
for each subtraction double.

Count up when the numbers
are close. (11 − 8, 9 − 7)

All Facts

Use the related addition fact:
13 − 5 = 8 because 5 + 8 = 13.

Think one more or one less
than a known subtraction fact.

Use the related subtraction fact:
14 − 9 = 5, so 14 − 5 = 9.

Fig. 6. Thinking strategies for subtraction

Understanding and applying the relationship between addition and subtraction is difficult (Steinberg 1984). Typically a time lag occurs between recognizing the inverse relationship and being able to use familiar addition facts to solve unknown subtraction facts. Repeated add-to-check experiences such as those below help children to internalize this relationship and increase the likelihood that they will use addition to solve subtraction.

Add to check. Materials: Twelve Unifix cubes
For 7 − 2 , children make a train of seven cubes. They establish the whole (7), break off a part (2), and complete the equation to tell the part that is left. Then they put the parts back together. Add

to check: "7 − 2 = 5 because 2 + 5 = 7." Repeat for other facts.

a

a *My favorites.* Materials: Twelve small counters
On a regular basis, invite students to circle two or three of their favorite problems on a worksheet and write the add-to-check fact beside each. Then, select one number pair on a page and ask the child to use counters to prove that what is written makes sense.

a

a *Ten-frame facts.* Materials: Ten-frame and ten counters for each pair of students
Write 10 − 5 on the board. Taking turns, students place ten counters in the frame; then they close their eyes to imagine "wiping out" the row of five and tell their partner what equation to write. Finally, they open their eyes to check. This process can be repeated for the other "ten" facts (subtracting from 10) and for the facts 9 − 5 and 9 − 4.

a

Many programs focus on fact families early in the subtraction program. It is better first to treat *pairs of facts:* (1) a subtraction and its add-to-check fact (e.g., 10 − 4 = 6 because 4 + 6 = 10) and (2) two related subtraction facts (e.g., 10 − 4 = 6 and 10 − 6 = 4), before associating all these as a "fact family."

 Count-ups. Materials: Twelve small counters for each pair of students
For 8 − 6, one child establishes the whole by laying out eight counters, touches the given part (six counters), and counts up to the whole: "6 . . . , 7, 8. I counted up 2: the other part has 2." The partner mimics with the written equation. "8 is the whole." [Says or touches the digit 6, and counts up]: "7, 8. I counted up 2: the other part has 2." Students repeat this activity with other count-ups—facts in which the numbers are "close neighbors" with differences of 1, 2, or 3. They can take turns using counters and writing.

a

thinking strategies for harder subtraction facts

Using known addition facts to derive harder subtraction facts is a powerful strategy. When add-to-check

activities are used with easier facts, most students develop a mind-set that enables them to use the addition strategy with harder facts.

Other options for solving unknown facts that students find helpful are presented in figure 6. Besides these strategies, older students in remedial classes often find it helpful to "subtract through 10" by actually using an add-on strategy. For "teen" minuend facts like 13 − 8, they start with the given part (8) and count up to 13 in two phases: "Count up 2 to 10; 3 more to 13, so we get 5."

deciding on the strategy: use or choose

Children need time to develop efficient thinking patterns. It is worth instructional time to nurture the development of number relationships, general number sense, and the kind of thinking students will use in mental mathematics and computational estimation. After students decide on a strategy that helps them solve a group of unknown facts, another important phase is necessary. It focuses (1) on children's correct use of the new strategy and (2) on children's ability to decide, or choose, when the newly learned strategy applies and when it does not.

To accomplish the first goal, such techniques as teacher modeling of correct counting, verbalization of the number or visual relationship, and other verbal hints are appropriate. The use of physical models is modified or eliminated, except for systematic checks to determine whether given answers make sense.

a *Write the helper: a "use" activity for doubles + 1.* Materials: Individual slates; flash cards for double + 1 facts
For each card, students write the double that helps them on their chalkboards and show it. Providing feedback helps: "Good! 7 + 7 is the helper. 7 + 7 is . . . ?" [14] "So 7 + 8 is . . ." [15]

a

One different—a "choose" activity for doubles + 1. Materials: Doubles + 1 picture cards (fig. 4); a mix of doubles + 1 cards and cards for known facts.

Use the picture cards to establish that the written addends are just "one different" from each other. Then, as each card is flashed, students make a happy face when a double + 1 fact card is displayed and a sad face for the other facts. Giving feedback helps: "Good! I see a happy face for 6 + 7! What double helps you?" [6 + 6] "And 6 + 6 = 12, so 6 + 7 is what?" [One more, or 13]   a

Count up: a "use" activity for subtraction count-ups. Materials: Count-up cards (fig. 7) For each card, ask, "What part do we know?" (e.g., "nine" in 11 − 9). The teacher counts forward from 9 to 11: "Ten, eleven. I said two numbers, so the other part is 2." Repeat for other count-ups. Sometimes you can switch roles with students. Model to check selected answers and to reinforce correct thinking! As students become more confident, replace the count-up cards with standard flash cards.   a

You find: a "choose" activity for subtraction count-ups. Materials: Individual slates; a mix of count-up and count-back cards Children copy and answer just the count-ups among the facts shown. To check count-up answers, call on one student to model the count. Disregard count-backs.   a

multiplication and division

concepts of the operations

A major focus in concept work for multiplication is having children directly model groups of counters with the same number in each group. Orally, groups are described, for example, as two fives or three fours, depending on the groups. The vocabulary related to the multiplication symbol (×) can be developed from

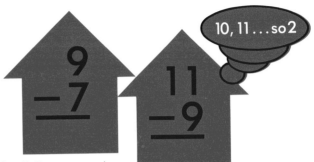

Fig. 7. Count-up cards

these models: Say, "I see a group of four once," pointing to one group. "I see a group of four three times," pointing to three groups. "So we can say 'three times four' for three groups. The symbol is ×. Three times four is 3 × 4." Eventually students complete number sentences for what they have modeled. With this emphasis on concept understanding, children use objects to model and check written multiplication sentences.

prerequisites
for thinking strategies

The skills listed below are frequently used for solving unknown multiplication and division facts. Beyond their usefulness in helping students derive answers to unknown facts, these skills are important in their own right with many applications to practical and mental mathematics.

thinking strategy
prerequisites for multiplication

- The student can "read" a standard clock to the nearest five minutes as "minutes after" (e.g., 2:15, 2:35).
- The student can subtract a one-digit number from a multiple of 10.
- Given a one-digit number, the student can add another to "make 9."
- The student can double two two-digit numbers mentally.
- The student can mentally add a one- and a two-digit number.

thinking strategy
prerequisites for division

- Students have mastered multiplication prerequisites.
- Students have firm mastery of related multiplication facts.

The prerequisite for "reading" five-minute intervals on a clock will be useful for both multiplication and division facts with 5. The next two multiplication prerequisites are needed for thinking strategies with 9s. Mental addition skills are included in the list of prerequisites because of their use with harder multiplication facts, where one fact can be broken into two easier facts.

Teachers committed to the effectiveness of the strategy approach to facts find it necessary to work on

prerequisites well in advance of their use. Such foresight precludes the need for students to learn prerequisite skills while trying to use them.

thinking strategies
for multiplication

When the instructional focus shifts to fact mastery, thinking strategies such as those presented in figure 8 are helpful.

Picture 2s are easy because most children know addition doubles. For those who don't, real-world objects can be used to introduce a visual mnemonic (Thornton 1982). If, for example, 2 × 7 is unknown, students can examine a calendar page on which the first day of the month is a Sunday. "Two times seven, that's two sevens, or two weeks: fourteen days." Students can circle the two groups of seven days and note that the first fourteen numbers are included in two weeks.

What strategies will help in multiplication and division?

Easy Multiplication Facts

Think of the picture for facts with **2** and turnarounds (of the related addition double).

Think of the clock for facts with a factor of **5**.

Use patterns for **9**s.

Harder Multiplication Facts

Break a fact into two easier parts.

Easier Division Facts

Think of the picture for facts with **2** (of the related double).

Think of the related division fact (14 ÷ 2 = 7, so 14 ÷ 7 = 2).

Think of the clock for facts with a factor of **5**.

Use patterns for **9**s.

All Division Facts

Use a multiplication fact you know (64 ÷ 8 = 8 because 8 x 8 = 64).

Fig. 8. Thinking strategies for multiplication and division

Turnarounds (commuting factors) can be presented relatively early with each new set of facts. The pictures themselves or array cards can be used to illustrate, for example, 7 × 2: "Think of the calendar. Seven twos:

Clock fives are quickly learned by students who can read a standard clock to the nearest five minutes in terms of minutes after. "Seven times five: Minute hand on seven; seven fives, or 35 minutes after." Over other alternatives, this particular mnemonic has proved most effective with learning-handicapped students both in this country and in Australia (Thornton and Toohey 1985).

Because of the many patterns for multiplication by 9, students typically select a usable solution strategy quite readily. Rathmell (1978) described a number pattern that many children use: "The sum of the digits in every product is 9. For example, since the product of 3 × 9 is in the twenties, by estimating that the product is a bit less than three 10s, then we know that 3 × 9 = 27 (sum of digits = 9). Similarly, 4 x 9 is in the 30s, so 4 × 9 = 36; 5 × 9 is in the 40s, so 5 × 9 = 45; and so on. Figure 9 presents a different number pattern that can be modeled using cubes or other counters.

3 x 9 = 30 − 3 (27)

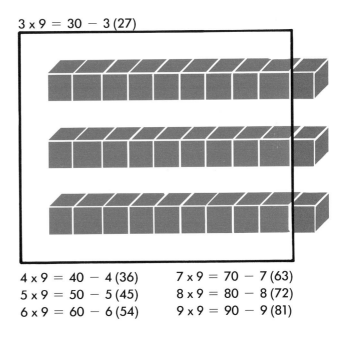

4 x 9 = 40 − 4 (36)   7 x 9 = 70 − 7 (63)
5 x 9 = 50 − 5 (45)   8 x 9 = 80 − 8 (72)
6 x 9 = 60 − 6 (54)   9 x 9 = 90 − 9 (81)

Fig. 9. A pattern for multiplying 9s

The 0s, 1s, 2s, 5s, and 9s, (and their turnarounds) make up 75 of the 100 multiplication facts and are quite easily learned using thinking strategies like those above. Only fifteen facts and their turnarounds remain: 3 × 3, 3 × 7; 4 × 3, 4 × 4, 4 × 6, 4 × 7, 4 × 8; 6 × 3, 6 × 6, 6 × 7, 6 × 8; 7 × 7; 8 × 3, 8 × 7, and 8 × 8. It can be great fun at this point to make a "Class Cross-out Chart" for multiplication like the one made for addition (see fig. 5). Students can then see how much they know and how little they have to learn!

strategies for harder multiplication facts

One basic strategy, which is based on the distributive property, is breaking each harder fact into two easier parts and combining the results.

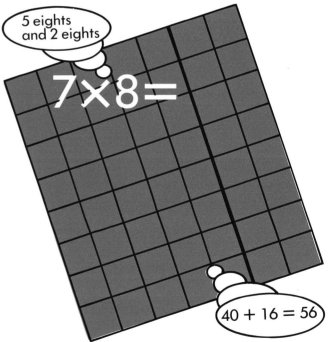

Fold and write. Materials: Graph paper, scissors, pad, and pencil for each pair of students.

For each fact, students cut a rectangle from the graph paper to model the fact, fold it to show two "easy" parts, talk about the solution, and complete the equation. For example, to find the product of 7 × 8, make an array that shows seven rows with eight squares in each row. Ask, "How many squares are in each row?" [8] "How many rows are there?" [7] "So you see seven 8s. What fact do you know with 8s?" [Five 8s is a likely response.] Fold the rectangle to show five 8s and two more 8s, as in figure 10. "What do five 8s equal?" [40] "What do two 8s equal?" [16] "How can you find seven 8s?" [Add 40 and 16.] "Then what is seven 8s?" [56] Have children complete the equation. It helps to involve students in summarizing big ideas. From the fold-and-write activity students can see the following:

- Most of the 15 facts are *break-apart* facts. Facts with even factors (4, 6, 8) can be split in half (e.g., four 6s = 12 + 12).
- Facts with factors of 6 and 8 can be broken at 5, resulting in an easy addition to a multiple of 10.

Fig. 10. Breaking a fact into parts

- Some facts can be found by folding the rectangle back and subtracting (e.g., "Nine 4s are 36. Fold down a four. So eight 4s is four less." [32] "We folded down one row."

a

pacing and sequencing issues

The easy versus harder fact breakdown in figure 8 is useful for instructional planning. Easy facts for both operations should be presented first, then harder facts for both operations. Children are more highly motivated when they can learn quickly. Further, avoid presenting multiplication and related division facts in back-to-back lessons or chapters. By not doing so, you increase the likelihood that children will learn a group of multiplication facts well enough to use them in checking or providing division answers. These two suggestions directly parallel those made earlier for addition and subtraction.

Techniques and sequences that have proved most effective differ from long-standing approaches for presenting multiplication and division facts. Emphasizing visuals in a meaningful way for 2s (pictures) and 5s (clock times) is a more efficient alternative to skip counting for multiplication. Because many 3s and 4s have developmentally harder solution strategies than 5s and 9s, these groups are not included among "easy facts." A Class Cross-out Chart can be updated, however, to highlight the number of 3s, 4s, 6s, 7s, and 8s that the class also knows. Encouraging children to label facts by strategy—Picture 2s, Clock 5s, Pattern 9s, Break-Apart Facts— helps them in both initial learning and recall.

thinking strategies for division

When the study of division facts is delayed until children have reasonable mastery of related multiplication facts, division facts are quite easy to learn. The main instructional goal is for children to use known multiplication facts to solve unknown division facts. If children have difficulty with easy facts, use models similar to those employed for multiplication, for example:

- 14 ÷ 2: Think of a calendar: 14 days, 2 weeks, 7 days in a week, 14 ÷ 2 = 7.

- 35 ÷ 5: Think of 35 minutes after the hour. Where's the minute hand? [On the answer digit, 7]

- 54 ÷ 9: In thinking of a pattern to help them, children commonly select from those suggested in figure 11.

- Children can model and sort division problems involving 0's and 1's (as is done in multiplication).

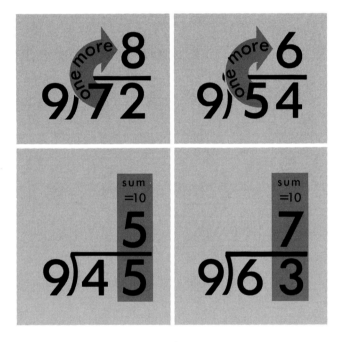

Fig. 11. Patterns for division with 9

After each group of facts has been presented, multiply-to-check activities should be done systematically to build or reinforce the division-multiplication relationship. As with addition and subtraction, formal work with fact families should be delayed until children have done extended activities with pairs of related division and multiplication facts.

Multiply-to-check activities are important in helping children understand and use multiplication as a strategy for solving related division facts. Incorporating these activities early in the study of easy division facts is the best method of helping children in the long run with harder division facts.

deciding on the strategy: use or choose

After developing thinking strategies for multiplication or division, students need activities to help them use the strategies and choose an appropriate one for given problems.

 Write the parts—a "use" activity for break-apart facts. Materials: Individual chalkboards; flash cards for break-apart facts; graph-paper transparency

For each fact students write the two helper facts on their chalkboards and show them. Occasionally, the teacher can project the transparency onto the chalkboard so students can show the two parts: "That's a good break for 6 × 8: Five 8s (40) and one more 8 (8) is 48." **a**

 Share and take back. Materials: Twenty Unifix cubes

For given facts, children model the sharing action (e.g., for 15 ÷ 5, 15 is shared among 5) and write the complete equation. Then they pool what was shared and multiply to check: "12 ÷ 5 = 3 *because* three 5s = 15." **a**

What checks? a "use" activity for harder division facts. Materials: Individual chalkboards; flash cards for harder division facts

For each fact students write and show the multiplication fact that checks. The teacher should provide feedback: "Yes, 24 ÷ 4 is 6, because . . ." [Child reads from the slate]: ". . . 4 × 6 = 24." **a**

 Check it out. Materials: A box of 100 counters so that at any given time about five children can use counters to verify a solution

On a regular basis, invite students to circle a favorite problem on a page in their books or on a worksheet and write the multiply-to-check fact beside it. Challenge a few students during each session to use counters to check that the correct multiplication fact was written. Within a week, all students can participate in this verification process. **a**

Is the answer 0? a "choose" activity for facts with zeros. Materials: Transparency or flash cards for facts with zeros using all four operations

Children hold their thumbs up if the answer to a fact is 0; otherwise, they signal thumbs down. Occasionally they model to check. **a**

Good practice is also *systematic* in that (1) only a few new facts are treated in any given setting, (2) previously memorized facts for an operation are rotated into practice sessions, and (3) short periods are found during the day for students to practice previously memorized facts from other operations. Until mastery of each group of facts is independently demonstrated, it generally is more effective not to mix facts from different operations in the same drill.

Good practice with success is *motivating*. The best route to motivation is to keep sessions short, three to five minutes, and to engage every student actively. Praising quality efforts as well as quality responses is equally important.

practice for fact mastery

Systematic, motivating, ongoing—these are characteristics of good practice for fact mastery or immediate recall of facts. The overriding goal is to raise the level of response until correct answers are given quickly (within two seconds) and consistently over time.

Good practice is *systematic* because it follows rather than precedes activities devoted to the development of thinking, use, or choose strategies. Children should sense when the focus shifts from "work it out" to "let's practice *remembering* the answers to these facts." Comments such as "I want you to try to memorize these facts today" create a mind-set that leads to success.

Students soon sense that strategy hints are rarely given during practice, that wrong answers are immediately corrected by the teacher, and that drill moves on. Reteaching occurs outside the drill, so group pacing and attention are unbroken.

Good practice is *ongoing*. In the spirit of distributed versus massed practice, "Less is best, more often." That is, it is better to have a five-minute practice every day than to schedule a half-hour practice session once each week.

Toward this end some teachers keep basic-fact flash cards in a shoebox on or near the chalk ledge. Whenever free moments occur during transition periods, the cards are handy for quick, motivating practice like that described above. As fact cards are used, they are placed at the rear of the deck or within the deck for reuse, depending on how well students responded.

If available, parental support can be very useful. The best results are obtained when short, specific lists of "facts to be studied" are provided, along with strategy hints to use as needed. Asking parents to verify that children practice a set of facts for two or three minutes each night during a two-week period is workable. Parents can show children how to set their own timer, and the time is short enough for uninterested students not to mind.

Popular extensions of practice work include the following:

- *Concept reinforcement:* Students use counters to show that one or two written answers on a practice sheet make sense.

- *Mental math:* "6 + 7 = 13, so 60 + 70 =?" "What's 7 × 8?" [40 + 16]

- *Applications:* Students write about a situation or draw a picture of one that shows a number fact.

assessment of fact mastery

Basic-fact mastery involves giving correct answers quickly, normally within two seconds and being consistent in this performance over time. Assessment activities, which usually take the form of short quizzes or timed tests, are the natural follow-up to practice. Young students who have been involved in many and varied practice activities enter the assessment phase quite naturally. Emphasizing short, six-to-eight-item focused quizzes has proved less threatening and just as effective as longer quizzes. Shorter quizzes can sample both the new facts being studied and others previously memorized. Telling students ahead of time which fact groups will be quizzed (e.g., 5s, 9s, or break-apart facts) makes them better prepared for, and less anxious in, the testing situation.

Timed tests with sixty to a hundred items have a very special but limited role in basic-fact assessment. These tests are most useful for diagnostic purposes and for occasional general testing of basic-fact mastery. For example, one might give such a test during the second or third week of school to determine the level of fact retention over the summer and to assist with instructional planning. At the end of a semester such tests might be readministered to determine long-term retention or progress. These tests should not be given on a daily or weekly basis.

Unless they are individually monitored, these tests reveal only the number of facts a child can correctly answer within a given time. They don't tell which facts were memorized or which were calculated. The tests do provide a good starting point by indicating which students are performing well and which need more help with basic facts. Many students like to do the problems they can in the time allotted, then take a different-color pen or pencil to complete others. It is important to keep students attuned to their progress and to involve them in setting goals for improvement. In addition to the class chart (fig. 5), personal charts of "Facts I Know" might be maintained. Alternatively, when a student's level of fact mastery is considerably lower than the class norm, personal cross-out charts showing only those facts the student does *not* know can be created. Individual testing can be used to determine which facts can be crossed off the list—those the student can answer within two seconds. Allow students to use the charts for seatwork and tests until all facts are mastered and crossed off.

summary

To help students keep pace with the demands of today's curriculum and to allow time for its more challenging aspects, the teaching and learning of basic facts needs to be more efficient. To help accomplish this goal, a conceptual framework for planning and implementing a sound basic-fact program has been presented.

A problem-solving approach to answering unknown facts is central. Children use simple strategies to learn easy facts, and then use known facts, number relationships, and other strategies to solve harder, unknown facts. As each new group of facts is studied, and it is clear that children are using correct, efficient thinking to derive unknown facts, practice is initiated to insure immediate recall. The goal is to have children learn facts more quickly and with greater retention. The result is not only better fact performance but also the introduction of the kind of thinking that is essential for all mental arithmetic and estimation.

references

Baroody, Arthur J. "Children's Difficulties in Subtraction: Some Causes and Questions." *Journal for Research in Mathematics Education* 15 (May 1985): 203–13.

Brownell, William A., and Charlotte B. Chazal. "The Effects of Premature Drill in Third-Grade Arithmetic." *Journal of Educational Research* 29 (September 1935): 17–28.

Carpenter, Thomas P., and James M. Moser. "The Development of Addition and Subtraction Problem-solving Skills." In *Addition and Subtraction: A Cognitive Perspective,* edited by Thomas P. Carpenter, James M. Moser, and Thomas A. Romberg. Hillsdale, N.J.: Lawrence Erlbaum Associates, 1982.

Fuson, Karen C. "Teaching Children to Subtract by Counting Up." *Journal for Research in Mathematics Education* 17 (May 1986): 172–89.

Leutzinger, Larry P. "The Effects of Counting On on the Acquisition of Addition Facts in First Grade." Ph.D. diss., University of Iowa, 1989.

National Council of Teachers of Mathematics. *Curriculum and Evaluation Standards for School Mathematics.* Reston, Va.: The Council, 1989.

Rathmell, Edward C. "Using Thinking Strategies to Learn Basic Facts." In *Developing Computational Skills,* 1978 Yearbook. Reston, Va.: National Council of Teachers of Mathematics, 1978.

_____. "Strategies for Improving Recall of Basic Facts." In *Mathematics, Myths, and Realities,* edited by Alan Rogerson, pp. 12–19. Melbourne, Australia: Acocia Press, 1981.

Steinberg, Ruth. "Derived Facts Strategies in Learning Addition and Subtraction." Paper presented at the annual meeting of the American Educational Research Association, New Orleans, April 1984.

Suydam, Marilyn N. "Improving Multiplication Skills." *Arithmetic Teacher* 32 (March 1985): 52.

Swenson, E. J. "Organization and Generalization as Factors in Learning, Transfer, and Retroactive Inhibition." In *Learning Theory in School Situations.* University of Minnesota Studies in Education, no. 2. Minneapolis: University of Minnesota Press, 1949.

Thiele, Carl Lewis. *The Contribution of Generalization to the Learning of Addition Facts.* New York: Bureau of Publications, Teachers College, Columbia University, 1938.

Thornton, Carol A. "Doubles Up—Easy." *Arithmetic Teacher* 29 (April 1982): 20.

_____. "Emphasizing Thinking Strategies in Basic Fact Instruction." *Journal for Research in Mathematics Education* 9 (May 1978): 214–27.

Thornton, Carol A., and Paula F. Smith. "Action Research: Strategies for Learning Subtraction Facts." *Arithmetic Teacher* 35 (April 1988): 9–12.

Thornton, Carol A., and Margaret A. Toohey. "Basic Math Facts: Guidelines for Teaching and Learning." *Learning Disabilities Focus* 1(1) (1985): 44–57.

_____. The Matter of Facts series. Sunnyvale, Calif.: Creative Publications, 1984.

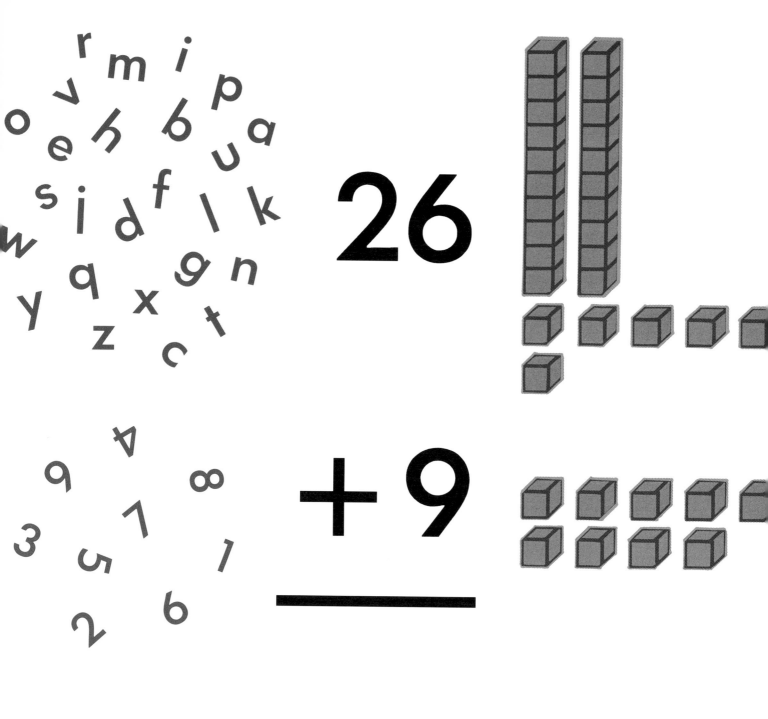

26

+9

35

whole number computation

edward rathmell
paul trafton

8

Computation has long been the driving force of the school mathematics curriculum at all levels and has often been viewed by educators and the public as the primary purpose for learning mathematics. As a result, the teaching of paper-and-pencil computation often consumes the majority of instructional time, dominates teachers' thinking about teaching mathematics, influences children's beliefs about what it means to know and do mathematics, and causes the omission of other important mathematics from the curriculum.

Today there is the potential for major change in many aspects of computation, including its role in the curriculum, the emphasis of instruction, the way it is taught, and how it is done. Significant questions, such as the following, are being addressed:

■ What are the purposes of learning to compute?

■ How does computation contribute to the development of mathematically literate citizens and workers?

■ How can the teaching of computation promote long-range goals for students as suggested by NCTM (1989) such as learning to value mathematics, becoming confident in one's own ability, becoming a mathematical problem solver, learning to communicate mathematically, and learning to reason mathematically?

■ What computational skills are important in a technological age?

■ Which paper-and-pencil computational skills, and what level of complexity, are still necessary?

■ How can computational goals be accomplished within a reasonable amount of instructional time?

The current reform movement in school mathematics is

a major force in the movement to rethink computation. Documents, such as the *Curriculum and Evaluation Standards for School Mathematics* (NCTM 1989), call for new curriculum goals and emphases and make recommendations about the content of the curriculum and approaches to instruction in order to prepare children more adequately to live and work in an information age. These recommendations are heavily influenced by the pervasive use of technology in today's world. The fact that most complex computation is now done by calculators and computers means that paper-and-pencil procedures can no longer be the focus of computation in the curriculum.

Another significant force influencing current thinking about computation is the rapidly growing body of research on children's thinking and learning in mathematics. This literature provides valuable insights about the way children develop and apply thinking strategies, about how they process information, and about their beliefs concerning mathematics and themselves as mathematics students. Recent knowledge about the relationship between conceptual and procedural aspects of mathematics learning provides direction for curriculum planners and teachers. Computational programs are possible that are more appropriate for children and result in better learning.

a new view of computation

For many individuals the word *computation* means using paper-and-pencil algorithms, a prescribed series of written steps to determine the correct answer. This is a narrow view of computation that does not reflect the context in which it usually occurs, the many ways in which it can be performed, and the reflective decision making that needs to be part of any computational process. Figure 1, which is adapted from the *Standards* report (NCTM 1989, p. 9), presents a more appropriate and useful way of viewing computation.

The need for computation usually arises from problem situations, as shown at the top of figure 1. The problem

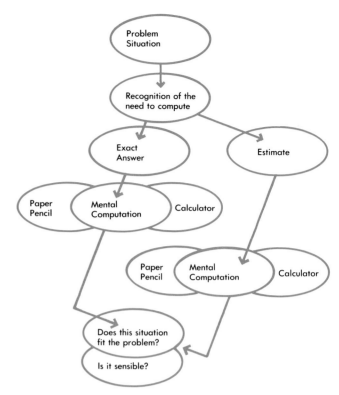

Fig. 1. An overview of computation

solver recognizes the need to compute as part of the problem-solving process. This same viewpoint should be reflected in the classroom. Currently, computational skills are often developed in virtual isolation from problem situations. Furthermore, students usually practice the skills for several days and receive a few contrived applications at the end of long sets of exercises. The curriculum needs to emphasize the contexts for computation and to provide computational experiences using real-world contexts.

The problem solver must first recognize that computation is needed and then decide whether one correct answer must be found or whether an estimate will be sufficient. Often an estimate is sufficient, depending on the context. A student who has $3 and wants to buy a ring binder and a package of notebook paper (see fig. 2) needs to know simply whether the total cost will be over $3 or under $3. The same student might also use estimation to find how much money would be left from the three dollars. For this student, an estimate is a quick and efficient way to help make shopping decisions. Of course the clerk who sells these items must find the exact total to know how much to charge.

Fig. 2. Estimating costs

Exact answers can be computed by mental calculation, by paper and pencil, or by a calculator, as shown in figure 3. Mental computation is appropriate when the numbers are easy to work with and there is no need to record partial computations. Paper-and-pencil computation is appropriate when an exact answer is needed, a written record is to be saved, or the numbers are too complicated to compute mentally but not so cumbersome that it would save time to find a calculator. Calculators should be used when the numbers are large or numerous. Estimation also needs to be part of the process of finding exact answers, since estimating is a valuable way of checking the computation. The following activity focuses on deciding how to compute.

How do you compute? Pose practical problems and have students decide how they would compute. "Suppose you and a friend are going to a movie and you have $10. It costs $4.75

"How much will 2 pens and a pencil cost?"

25...50...60 ...65. The cost is 65¢.

Mentally

"I want a ring binder and a package of notebook paper."

$1.39
+ 0.79

Pencil and Paper

Tom sold supplies to 8 students one morning. How much money did he collect?

Judy $0.65
Steve $1.83
Marsha $2.97
Booker $1.29

Calculator

Fig. 3. Ways to compute exact answers

for each of you. Do you have enough money? Can you estimate and answer the question? Can you find the total cost in your head? Can you calculate the amount of change in your head?"

Extend the activity to other practical situations such as buying items at the grocery store, mailing letters at the post office, or calculating monthly allowances.　**a**

Computation needs to relate to the original situation. "Does my solution fit the problem?" "Is my answer reasonable?" Checking an exact computation to see if it is reasonable is more than finding a specific estimate. It also involves sensing whether the answer "looks right."

Computing requires many decisions. Questions and discussion that focus children's attention on these decisions need to be integrated into all instruction, not treated in isolation. Children should come to accept and value all components of computation rather than view estimation and mental computation as add-ons to the "real" method of computation in school.

A change is needed in the traditional practice of teaching paper-and-pencil computation before doing any substantial work with mental computation, estimation, or calculators. Mental computation and estimation help children develop confidence in their ability to reason with numbers and provide a base for making judgments about the reasonableness of results. Calculators can, and should, be used prior to teaching paper-and-pencil algorithms.

Children have intuitions and strategies that enable them to find answers to problems in a variety of ways. Mental computation and estimation are extensions of children's number sense, counting abilities, knowledge of facts, thinking strategies for facts, and abilities to estimate quantities. When instruction for computing uses children's prior knowledge, the children's answers make sense to them, and their self-confidence as mathematics learners grows. The research evidence is limited but suggests that developing skills in mental computation and estimation prior to paper-and-pencil computation is both effective and powerful. Classroom experience indicates that children have difficulty with mental computation and estimation when learned after paper-and-pencil skills have been taught. When calculator

work is linked with an emphasis on recognizing sensible answers, it also reinforces computation as a tool for solving problems. Finally, early and ongoing emphasis on mental computation, estimation, and appropriate use of calculators provides a framework for developing paper-and-pencil skills.

mental computation

Young children are able to use counting strategies and relationships to solve the computational problems they later solve with paper-and-pencil algorithms, as shown by these examples:

- Five-year-old child:
  "1 hundred and 1 hundred make 2 hundred because 1 and 1 make 2."
- Six-year-old child:
  "I have 45 cents. I need 50 cents.

. . . 5, 10, 15, 20, 25, 30, 35, 40, *45*, 50.
So I need 5 cents more."

- Seven-year-old child:
  "16 + 16 is 2 tens and 2 sixes.
  2 tens is 20.
  6 more is 26.
  . . . 27, 28, 29, 30, 31, *32*."
  "Names for 8 . . . 2 + 2 + 2 + 2
  . . . 100 − 92
  . . . 1000 − 992"

- Nine-year-old child:
  "250 pennies for my brother and me—
  Half of 200 is 100.
  Half of 50 is 25.
  100 and 25 is 125.
  Each of us gets 125."

Sometimes the answer is found by applying a computational strategy; at other times it results from an intuitive awareness of relationships between numbers. Both approaches, which are often self-generated, are far more natural and sensible for many children than conventional paper-and-pencil algorithms.

Students who become adept at mental computation are able to use a rich variety of reasoning patterns in a flexible manner. Carraher, Carraher, and Schliemann (1987) investigated the written and oral performance of Brazilian third-grade students, ranging in age from eight to thirteen years, on computational tasks in different settings. The investigation documented the strengths of these children when computing mentally and the weakness of their paper-and-pencil skills. They gave interesting examples of reasoning, as in Eduardo's response to a store situation requiring subtracting 75 from 243:

"You just give me the two hundred (he meant 100). I'll give you twenty-five back. Plus the forty-three that you have, the hundred and forty-three, that's one hundred and sixty-eight." (1987, p. 91)

The student apparently viewed 243 as 2 hundreds and 43 more as shown in figure 4. He was aware that 100 could be partitioned into 75 and 25. He seemed to just

know that 25 and 43 is 68. He also remembered the extra hundred in his thinking.

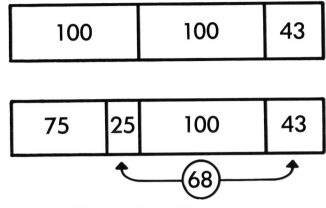

Fig. 4. A child's view of 243 − 75

Clearly, Eduardo was manipulating quantities that he could manage in a way that made sense to him. Reed and Lave (1981) suggest that mental computation is characterized by a manipulation of quantities as compared to the manipulation of symbols that may be an inherent part of our conventional paper-and-pencil algorithms. The varied and thoughtful ways children manipulate quantities when doing mental computation promote number sense as well as mathematical thinking. This kind of activity brings a dynamic quality to learning mathematics because children are actually *doing* mathematics rather than learning to repeat conventional procedures.

variety of strategies

Several approaches to adding two-digit numbers mentally are illustrated in figure 5. A variety of strategies occur with other operations, as illustrated in this activity:

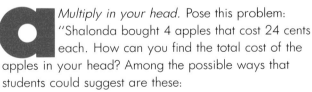
Multiply in your head. Pose this problem: "Shalonda bought 4 apples that cost 24 cents each. How can you find the total cost of the apples in your head? Among the possible ways that students could suggest are these:
". . . 4 × 25 makes 100. Subtract 4.

Fig. 5. Ways to do mental addition

. . . double 24 is 48. Double 48 is 96.
. . . 4 × 20 = 80 . . . 84, 88, 92, 96.
. . . 4 × 20 = 80; 4 × 4 = 16. 80 + 16 = 96."

Extend the problem to encourage mental computing with 25. "What if Shalonda buys only 2 apples? How much will they cost? How much change will she get back from a dollar? If the price goes up to 26 cents each, can she buy 4 apples with $1?"

a

Often a variety of strategies will be employed by the same student with the numbers and the situation influencing the choice of strategy. For 39 + 12, using an easier problem (add 40 and 12, then subtract 1) or transforming the problem to a related one (change 39 + 12 to 40 + 11) are frequently used strategies, but for 36 + 27, other strategies may be better. The intuitive reasoning required and the freedom to choose a strategy that makes sense are among the reasons that children tend to enjoy this work. As one teacher of middle school remedial students stated, "Mental computation makes them feel powerful." A third grader said, "It makes me feel smart."

Instruction in mental computation needs to reflect the spirit of computing mentally, that is, exploring different ways of reasoning as well as sharing and justifying solutions. In the early years of schooling, much of the work should be informal. Teachers should raise questions and listen to children's thinking as they work on activities. Thinking patterns that children have discovered on their own are a good beginning point for group discussion.

There are many ways to approach instruction for mental computation. Cobb and Merkel (1989), for example, describe a program in which children regularly work in small groups that generate and verify solutions to computational problems. The program does not attempt to develop specific strategies. The authors report the positive effects of this approach, including children's willingness to work on a single task for an extended period of time.

The following guided activities are the types to help develop mental computation.

skip counting

Skip counting by 1, by 10, by 25, and by 15 is helpful because adding on to a number often uses these strategies.

Count by tens on a hundred chart. Display a hundred chart. Point to a number and have children count by tens starting with that number. Begin with a multiple of 10, such as 20, 40, 70, or 90. Then use nonmultiples of 10, such as 48, and stop when 100 is passed (58, 68, 78, 88, 98, 108). **a**

Card-game skip count. Choose twenty numbers from 0 to 50 and write each on a card. Include multiples and nonmultiples of 10. Play the game with groups of three or four children. Shuffle the cards and place them face down. The first player draws a card, starts with that number, and counts on by 10 until she or he passes 100. If the counting is correct, the child keeps the card. Have children check the counting by using a hundred chart. The winner is the one with the most cards at the end of the game. **a**

Skip count on a calculator. Two children play the game. One child skip-counts orally by 25s while the other skip-counts with the calculator. [C 25 + = = = . . .] The goal is to reach 500. The first to get to 500 wins. The players should change roles and repeat the activity.

Extend their skip-counting work by having them count by 15s to 225. For younger children, use this activity to skip-count by 2s, 5s, or 10s. **a**

basic-fact strategies

Basic-fact strategies can be extended to mental computation with larger numbers.

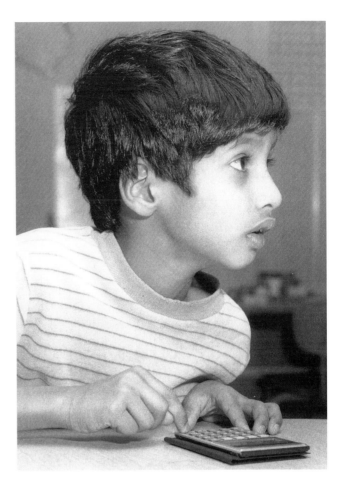
a

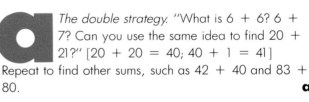*Count-on strategy.* Help students see how to use a count-on strategy. Write 9 + 3 and 45 + 2. "How do you count on to add 3 to 9? [10, 11, 12] How do you use the same method to add 2 to 45?" [Count on 46, 47.] Repeat to find other sums, such as 69 + 3, 81 + 2, and 17 + 4. **a**

The double strategy. "What is 6 + 6? 6 + 7? Can you use the same idea to find 20 + 21?" [20 + 20 = 40; 40 + 1 = 41] Repeat to find other sums, such as 42 + 40 and 83 + 80. **a**

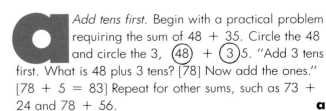*Add tens first.* Begin with a practical problem requiring the sum of 48 + 35. Circle the 48 and circle the 3, ⑭⑧ + ③5. "Add 3 tens first. What is 48 plus 3 tens? [78] Now add the ones." [78 + 5 = 83] Repeat for other sums, such as 73 + 24 and 78 + 56. **a**

The thinking suggested in these activities shows children how to use whole quantities, or familiar partitions of them, to do mental computation rather than the ones-tens-hundreds columns used in paper-and-pencil computation. Giving examples of possible ways to think must not be taken by students to mean that these are the only "right" ways to do the mental computation. In classrooms where children have been encouraged to explore and discuss different thinking strategies, this is usually not a problem.

using base-ten materials

When presenting or verifying a strategy suggested by a child, teachers will find that the use of base-ten materials often helps other children understand the thinking. In many situations strategies involve fundamental grouping and place-value ideas. Base-ten blocks can be used to model this thinking, relating mental computation to basic numeration ideas. (Fig. 6 illustrates adding 51 + 52.) Figure 7 presents an example in which counting back by tens and then ones is used to subtract. After showing 6 tens and 1 one, remove tens and then ones to show the counting back.

Fig. 6. Using base-ten blocks for mental addition

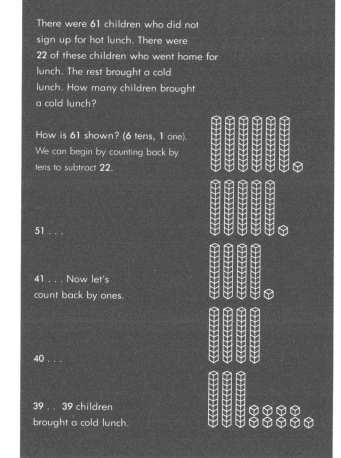

Fig. 7. Using base-ten blocks for mental subtraction

Patterns of thinking and confidence in using those patterns build gradually. Thus, mental computation is more appropriately viewed as an ongoing emphasis in a mathematics program than as a separate topic composed of subskills arranged in order and taught as separate lessons. Practice with mental computation should enable children to use the process naturally and confidently in appropriate situations.

Mental computation is the primary method of computing with multiples of ten, one hundred, and one thousand (e.g., 60 + 30, 1200 − 400, 3 × 150, 40 × 30, and 1200 ÷ 3), or adding or subtracting a single-digit number and a multidigit number (e.g., 148 + 6 and 97 − 8). There is little reason to emphasize paper-and-pencil methods, especially when computation is viewed as a tool for dealing with problem situations. Children should be able to use mental computation in situations where the numbers make it easy. With imaginative instruction, successful mental computation is possible for almost all children.

computational estimation

Mathematics and daily life provide contexts for mathematical thinking that do not involve finding exact answers. An estimate is often enough.

Incorporating estimation with numbers, measurement, and computation in the curriculum from the early years helps children accept estimation as a natural part of mathematics. These experiences should build on children's informal uses of estimation. Language like *about, a little more than, between, close to,* and *almost but not quite* is familiar to young children and is a part of their preschool experience.

As children make informal judgments about a reasonable range for a computed answer and use a variety of strategies to make estimates, they realize that mathematics involves exploring relationships, thinking flexibly, and making decisions. It is more than following the rules.

Estimation involves manipulating quantities in ways that make sense. There is no single prescribed technique used to derive an estimate. Estimation, like mental computation, brings a dynamic quality to learning mathematics and helps students broaden their view of mathematics.

Estimation builds on, and strengthens, children's number sense, mental computation skills, and place-value concepts, as illustrated in the next activity.

Estimate sums. Pose a practical problem: "There are 274 students in this school and 269 in the school close by. About how many students are in both schools?" Ask questions that encourage students to make informal judgments about a

reasonable range for the answer. "Is the answer more than 300? How do you know? [200 + 200 = 400] Is the answer more than 400? Why? Is the answer less than 600? How do you know?" [300 + 300 = 600] Students should be able to see that the exact answer is between 400 and 600.
Repeat with other estimates of sums, such as 423 + 522, 645 + 321, and 798 + 423. **a**

Much of the work with estimation will focus on the thinking strategies that can be used. However, consideration should also be given to recognizing when an estimate is sufficient and to recognizing the precision required—if it makes more sense to overestimate or underestimate. These decisions depend on the context of the situation, so it is important for estimation experiences to stem from problems.

Making informal quantitative judgments about a situation is a natural, intuitive way to promote estimation thinking with questions that focus on quantities and the reasoning process.

Model and estimate. Pose a problem and ask appropriate questions. "Danny has 48 cents and Marie has 34 cents. About how much do they have in all?" Then ask questions such as these: "Do they have more than 50 cents? Could they have as much as 100 cents? Why not? Do they have closer to 60 cents or 80 cents? [80 cents because there are 7 tens and some units] Do they have more than 80 cents? [Yes, because the units added together are more than 10.] Let's check with base-ten blocks." (See fig. 8.) Repeat with other problems and similar questions. Model with base-ten blocks as a way to check and to illustrate different ways to think. **a**

Over or under? Pose practical problems and have students decide whether they would overestimate or underestimate. "You have $5 and want to buy some grocery items. Do you overestimate or underestimate the total cost? Why do you overestimate? Suppose you are saving money to buy a new basketball. Do you overestimate or underestimate how much money you will get for your birthday?" [Probably underestimate]

48
+34

Fig. 8. Using base-ten blocks to estimate

Extend the activity by having students interview their parents or some other adult, asking similar questions of them. Have students share the results of the interviews and make a chart for overestimates and underestimates.

a

If children are using a calculator to find the sum of five items—$2.67, $4.69, $3.13, $1.49, and $3.65—they could first be asked, "Do you think an answer of $9.52 is sensible? What about $22.89? What do you think would be a sensible amount?"

reference points

Posing questions that make use of reference points is an excellent way to introduce estimation in an informal and natural way. Instead of producing a numerical estimate, children determine the relationship between a computation and a reference number, as shown in figure 9.

Target games are another type of informal estimation experience that builds number sense and produces interesting thinking patterns. Calculators are used to check children's estimates. In the example in figure 10, children are to find a number to add to 38 that will produce a sum between 70 and 75. After an initial estimate, such as 40, the sum of 38 and 40 is computed on a calculator. The children adjust their estimate on the basis of feedback from the calculator

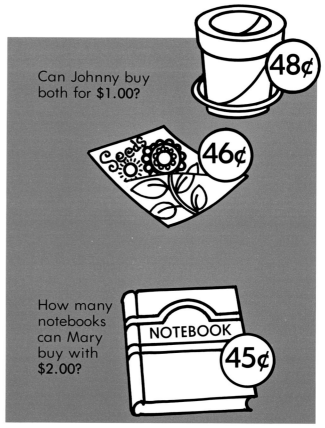

Fig. 9. Estimating using reference points

and check the new estimate. Calculators enable children to focus on relationships rather than on computational details.

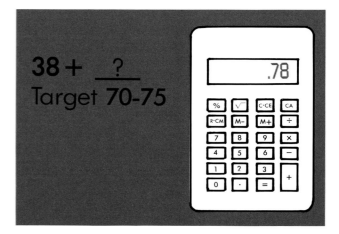

Fig. 10. Target estimation

Extended experiences with informal estimation activities should lead to more formal instruction that helps

children learn to solve problems by estimating. Children should be encouraged to use a variety of strategies and to share their thinking. Two important strategies are likely to emerge from this sharing: using "nice" numbers and "front end" estimation. The use of a particular strategy will depend on the situation, the numbers involved, and the relationships a child perceives. Often children will use a combination of strategies in the same problem. Teaching specific strategies should be handled carefully and should be delayed until children have explored and shared many experiences with estimation.

nice numbers

The nice-numbers strategy involves using numbers that are easy to work with. For addition, students might look for pairs of numbers whose sum is about 50 or 100, as shown in figure 11. For multiplying three items at $1.19 each, $1.25 might be perceived as being easy to use. Children can easily count, "$1.25, $2.50, $3.75."

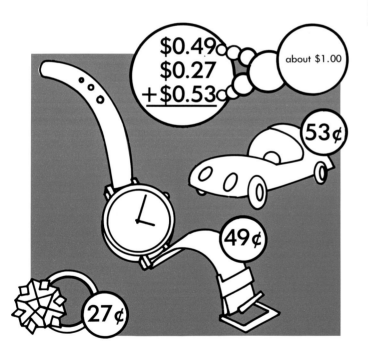

Fig. 11. Estimating using "nice" numbers

front-end estimation

In front-end addition, a student finds the sum of the leftmost digits and then adjusts the sum by looking at the rest of the number, as illustrated in figure 12. Initially a teacher might have children perform the first step noting that the total is more than the front-end sum. However, it is natural to informally discuss ways of getting closer.

Fig. 12. Estimating using front-end addition

rounding

Computing with numbers rounded to the nearest ten, hundred, or thousand has typically been the only approach to estimation that is taught. For 634 − 278, students would round each number to the nearest hundred and then subtract (600 − 300 = 300). For 3 × $1.19, students would round to the nearest dollar and find 3 × $1.00. Although rounding is a valid approach, it emphasizes following a prescribed series of steps to produce a single correct estimate. For most children, it also requires paper and pencil to record the rounded numbers so they can be viewed. When taught as the only approach, the rounding strategy is antithetical to the flexible type of estimation thinking that is important for children to develop. Children are simply learning another rule for manipulating numbers and fail to see the purpose of estimation as a useful and practical tool.

It is natural and important for children to have ongoing experiences with estimation in the primary grades and to have estimation be an integral part of computation. The work should be largely informal, with children encouraged to use, share, and compare several approaches to get ball-park estimates. This method encourages children to think about computation in a more holistic manner than with paper-and-pencil algorithms. Although specific strategies should be explored, the purpose is not to have students develop expert proficiency at this level.

paper-and-pencil computation

Paper-and-pencil computational skills must be taught carefully and meaningfully. Procedures children memorize without understanding do not further the development of number sense, the ability to judge reasonableness of results, and the flexibility of thinking with numbers. Meaningful computation instruction needs to be organized in the following stages:

1 Assess prerequisite understandings.
2 Provide experiences with manipulatives and develop appropriate language as a way to solve practical problems.
3 Relate concrete manipulations to symbols.
4 Practice, being sure to include special cases and concrete/symbolic connections.
5 Review algorithms, applications, and concrete/symbolic connections.

assess prerequisite understandings

Prior to formal instruction on a computational algorithm, children need to understand concepts of the operation, numbers, and place value and have some proficiency with basic facts. Without this background, children will be faced with frustration and failure or the likelihood of having to memorize rules by rote. In either event, the children will not be able to use computation meaningfully and flexibly. They will be unable to recognize appropriate computations or reasonable results. They will be unable to use their formal knowledge in informal settings because they will not have the understanding to make connections between mathematics and the real world.

concept of the operation

Each algorithm that children learn should initially stem from an action. For example, beginning concepts of the operations can be developed from the contexts of joining (addition), separating (subtraction), joining equal groups (multiplication), and sharing (division). Connections can then be developed to relate problem settings involving those actions to the corresponding operations (see chapter 6). For example, when asked a question involving equal groups of objects, children should recognize that multiplication can be used to determine the total, and they should also be able to use counters to represent the equal groups and explain their solution.

Children use these concepts with larger numbers, providing a meaningful link from their informal knowledge to algorithms. In summary, children should understand that an action corresponds to the operation and should be able to use manipulatives to show and explain that action for problem settings with small numbers.

number
and place value

Paper-and-pencil algorithms depend on breaking numbers into parts, operating on the parts, and combining the results. Understanding these processes necessarily means understanding place value and different representations of numbers (see chapter 5).

A concrete way to illustrate an algorithm uses base-ten materials to represent the numbers with manipulations to represent the operations. Since the actions on the base-ten materials stem from familiar ways to think with small numbers, the materials can also help make sense of thinking with larger numbers. Moreover, the materials can help prevent some of the common errors that children make with symbols. For example, some children do not bother to regroup when subtracting; they simply subtract the smaller number from the greater. With materials, it is impossible to perform this subtraction because there are not enough ones unless a ten is regrouped.

In summary, students should understand numbers, place value, and different representations of a number.

basic
facts

Mastering the basic facts is an important long-term goal (see chapter 7). It is not necessary, however, for children to have memorized all the basic facts for an operation prior to initial instruction on an algorithm. It is necessary that children know some facts and have an efficient way of thinking to keep from disrupting the flow of thinking when using an algorithm.

Unfortunately, children often do not possess these major prerequisites before algorithm instruction begins. Sowder (1988) found that it is quite common for children to use irrelevant cues to match an operation to a concrete problem setting. Lankford (1972) found that a majority of children in junior high school still have not mastered basic facts. Nearly half of all these students

were still using inefficient counting strategies for basic subtraction facts.

Children often have not developed the understanding of numbers necessary for them to partition numbers meaningfully or make good judgments about the reasonableness of an answer. A report on the Fourth National Assessment of Educational Progress (Kouba et al. 1988) indicates that fewer than half of the third-grade children tested in that study understood numbers beyond 100. In other studies it has been found that a majority of second- through fifth-grade children do not have a thorough understanding of place value. Children are commonly introduced to algorithms before they have the prerequisites necessary for meaningful learning.

use manipulatives
and
develop language

The major focus of the next instructional stage for a new algorithm involves using manipulatives to derive a solution concretely and discussing the step-by-step procedures used, the decisions made, and the reasonableness of results.

It is important to let children know what they are going to learn and why it is important. When new algorithms are introduced through practical problems or concrete situations familiar to children, the procedure is made relevant. Making the objective of a lesson clear, developing awareness that an algorithm is useful and relevant to the children's world, and relating the procedure to prior experiences all contribute to the focus and motivation for learning. Furthermore, by assessing prerequisite learning to ensure that the children are ready for instruction, teachers can promote success—a necessary ingredient for long-term motivation.

The step-by-step procedures that children learn in computing should arise naturally from problems with familiar language and settings. These situations allow children to make sense of the actions they perform on the manipulatives. The thinking they use later, when they perform the algorithm symbolically, stems from the actions they perform on the manipulatives. It is this thinking that enables children to bridge the gap from concrete to symbolic procedures. For that reason, it is important that children learn to verbalize the steps in the process and the reasons for making decisions at key points. Verbalization helps children focus on these procedures, and it helps them learn related thinking skills.

Figures 13 and 14 show examples for addition and division. The *talk* column contains questions that can be asked. Children should be encouraged to explain the process and demonstrate their actions with manipulatives. Their thinking and language needs to be guided to match the subsequent thinking in written form. This will enable children to make a meaningful connection between the concrete examples illustrated in figures 13 and 14 and the symbolic examples that follow.

Other, similar situations should be used to encourage children to talk through the procedures with materials before the written algorithm is introduced. This enables them to develop the thinking needed to make sense of the symbolic algorithm.

relate concrete manipulatives to symbols

After learning a step-by-step procedure with materials, children need to connect that knowledge to what gets recorded symbolically (see chapter 2). The steps that are performed in the symbolic solution of an algorithm correspond to steps used to solve the problem with manipualtives. Understanding these connections enables children to produce a written record of the manipulative process. The thinking they used to solve the problems with manipulatives can now be used to solve the problems symbolically.

Mrs. Ortez's second-grade class needs **28** cartons of milk. Mr. Olson's second-grade class needs **25** cartons of milk. How many cartons of milk are needed for the second grade?

What are we trying to find out? Do you think it will be more than **25**? . . **40**? . . **100**? How many cartons of milk did Mrs. Ortez's class need? How many did Mr. Olson's class need? How can we show that?

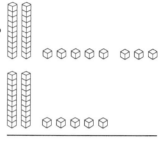

What do we combine first? How much is **8 + 5**? Are there enough ones to make a ten? How many ones are left over? What do we do with the ten?

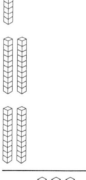

Now what do we combine? How much is **1 + 2 + 2**? Are there enough tens to make a hundred? How many cartons of milk did they need? Is this answer reasonable? Why?

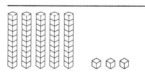

Fig. 13. Manipulatives and language for addition

Greg, Pam, and Misha collected aluminum cans for recycling. They got **7** dimes and **4** pennies to share. How much money should each get?

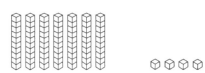

What are we trying to find out? Do you think each will get about **10** cents? . . . **20** cents? . . **50** cents? How many dimes do we have to share? How many pennies do we have to share? How many equal groups do we have to make? How many dimes does each get? How many dimes did that use? How many dimes are left over?

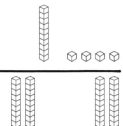

Is it fair for one of them to take the extra dime?

What could we do with the extra dime to share it? If we trade it for pennies, how many do we get? How many pennies do we have in all?

How many pennies does each get? How many pennies did that use? How many pennies are left over? Is it fair for one of them to take the extra pennies? How much did each get? How many extra pennies were there? What do you think they should do with these? Is this answer reasonable? Why?

Fig. 14. Manipulatives and language for division

Questions that encourage children to focus on connections between manipulatives and symbols are very important. Once children are able to describe what they are writing in the algorithm by referring to actions they could perform with the manipulatives,

relationships between the manipulative and the algorithm have been made, and the manipulative is no longer needed. They have internalized what they have been doing concretely. Figures 15, 16, 17, and 18 illustrate a way that connections to symbols can be made.

In the third-grade classes, there were **35** boys and **27** girls who signed up for hot lunch. How many children in third grade were going to eat hot lunch?

What do we need to find? Do you think it will be more than **40**? . . . **60**? How many boys are going to eat hot lunch? How many girls are going to eat hot lunch? How can we show that?

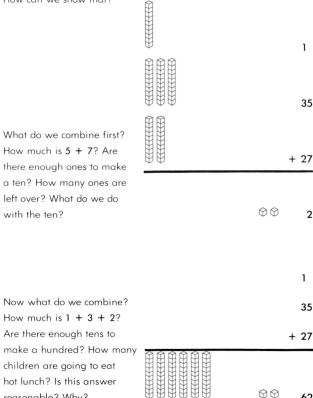

What do we combine first? How much is **5 + 7**? Are there enough ones to make a ten? How many ones are left over? What do we do with the ten?

Now what do we combine? How much is **1 + 3 + 2**? Are there enough tens to make a hundred? How many children are going to eat hot lunch? Is this answer reasonable? Why?

Fig. 15. Relating manipulatives to symbols for addition

There were **61** children who did not sign up for hot lunch. There were **22** of these who went home for lunch. The rest brought a cold lunch. How many brought a cold lunch?

What are we trying to find? Do you think it will be more than **60**? How many did not sign up for hot lunch? How many went home? How can we show this?

What do we subtract first? Are there enough ones to subtract **2**? How can we get more ones? If we trade a ten for ones, how many ones do we get? How many tens are left? How many ones are there now? How much is **5** tens and **11** ones?

Now are there enough ones to subtract **2**? What is **11 − 2**?

Now what do we subtract? What is **5** tens minus **2** tens? How many children are eating a cold lunch? Does this answer make sense? Why?

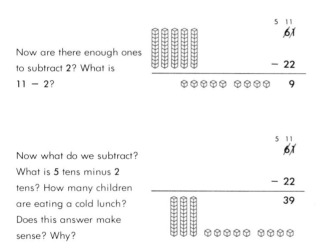

Fig. 16. Relating manipulatives to symbols for subtraction

It takes much longer for children to learn these relationships than is commonly planned for in classrooms. Textbooks often move to symbolic treatment of the topic before many of the children have been able to learn the connections. Teachers need to recognize the important role they play in the development of

The first-grade classes are taking a field trip. One bus can take **26** children. How many children can ride on **3** buses?

What do we need to find? Do you think it will be more than **30**? How many can ride on **1** bus? How many buses are there? How can we show this?

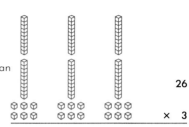

What do we multiply first? How much is **3 × 6**? Are there enough ones to make a ten? How many ones are left over? What do we do with the ten?

What do we multiply next? What is **3** times **2** tens? Do we have to add any other tens?

How many tens are there? How many can ride on the **3** buses? Is this answer reasonable? Why?

Fig. 17. Relating manipulatives to symbols for multiplication

paper-and-pencil computation and be prepared to provide extended experiences to facilitate the learning of these connections between the concrete situations and the symbolic algorithms.

practice

After children are able to compute symbolically, they need to practice on special cases and concrete/symbolic connections. This practice should not take the form of pages and pages of exercises. If children understand

There are 2 third-grade classes in Washington Elementary School. James needs to share the straws so that each class gets the same number. There are 5 packs of ten straws and 4 single straws. How many straws should each class get?

What do we need to find? Do you think it will be more or less than 50? How many straws are there? How many classes are there?

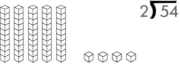

$$2 \overline{)54}$$

How many groups of ten can we give each class? Where do we write that? How many straws did that take? How many packs of ten are left over? Is it fair to give that pack of ten to one of the classes?

If we open that pack, how many straws are in the pack? How many single straws do we have?

How many single straws does each class get? How many straws did that take? How many straws are left over? How many straws did each class get? Does this answer make sense? Why?

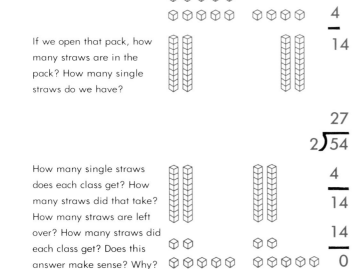

Fig. 18. Relating manipulatives to symbols for division

the connections described above, they do not need an overabundance of practice to achieve a high degree of proficiency. Practice for newly learned procedures should arise from problem-solving experiences applied to real-world situations.

The time for practice gives time to focus on special cases that have been associated with a high incidence of errors. For example, renaming across zeros in subtraction and coping with an internal zero in the quotient of a division problem need special attention. Children often confuse two different but similar procedures. Discrimination between the newly learned algorithm and previously known procedures is needed to clarify the distinction between the two. How are the procedures alike? How are they different? What is different about the situations for which each procedure is appropriate?

The time for practice also provides an opportunity for a daily review and reminder about the connections between the concrete manipulations and the symbolic algorithm. Children should be asked to explain these relationships. These explanations provide invaluable feedback to the teacher who can use them to make instructional decisions. They allow the teacher to judge the level of understanding, identify any misunderstandings, and determine the thinking used and the connections made between concrete and symbolic work. On the basis of this information teachers decide to review, reteach, provide extra practice, or move on to the next topic.

review

After children have learned an algorithm, they need planned systematic review to maintain applications and concrete/symbolic connections. Again, this review should not take the form of pages and pages of mindless drill. About once a week, children should review algorithms they have learned. They should be asked to explain their work, and quantitative questions should be asked to remind them of the connections between the earlier concrete manipulations and the current symbolic work.

regrouping and remainders

Problems involving regrouping or remainders have typically been omitted during the initial instructional period. For example, first-grade children are often introduced to two-digit addition and subtraction without regrouping. A year later they are taught to add and subtract with regrouping. Children develop their own way of thinking about these operations, often leading to a set of procedures that may be appropriate for problems without regrouping but not for those with regrouping. When children finally encounter problems requiring regrouping, they can have difficulties integrating the new decisions about regrouping into their previously constructed algorithm. Similar situations exist for multiplication and division.

In order to avoid these difficulties and to present an algorithm that works for all situations, problems that involve regrouping or remainders should be included when children are first learning a written algorithm. This focuses on the regrouping decisions that children have to make so that those decisions become part of their thinking from the start.

diagnosis

Despite careful treatment and meaningful instruction, some children still may have difficulties learning an algorithm. In those situations, it is important to check for prerequisite understandings, to ask the child to solve and explain problems with concrete materials, and to determine if connections between the concrete and symbolic procedures have been learned. The explanations a child gives in these situations will help identify any misunderstandings that might be causing difficulties.

It should be noted that errors children make are often consistent. Many computation errors involve basic facts. Teachers can help children who have these difficulties by identifying (1) which facts they know and which they

do not and (2) what thinking they are using to derive unknown facts. If their thinking strategies are immature or inefficient, activities should be used to help them learn new ways of thinking (see chapter 7). Another consistent error pattern involves using inappropriate procedures. Manipulatives can be used to help children with this difficulty develop appropriate thinking patterns. When that thinking is learned, instruction can then focus on making connections with the symbolic procedures.

the role of calculators

The role that calculators can play in helping children learn about computation is not well understood. Sometimes unilateral decisions are made to exclude the possibility of calculator use. It is clear that children who use a calculator as a substitute for understanding computation will not be able to compute effectively. However, calculators can be a valuable tool to stimulate thinking, explore ideas, facilitate problem solving, and investigate computation. When calculators are used thoughtfully, there are many positive outcomes and almost no negative consequences.

Calculators free children to engage in realistic and interesting problem solving. For example, as students gather data or note the prices of items they would like, the numbers often go beyond their paper-and-pencil or mental computation capabilities at that time. Calculators enable them to reason with numbers that arise in these situations.

Calculators also enable children to investigate patterns. For example, doubling patterns can be extended much further than would otherwise be possible without spending undue time on computation.

Calculators can be used to help develop estimation skills and number sense. For example, 10 threes can easily be found on the calculator by using keystrokes 3 $\boxed{+}$ $\boxed{=}$ $\boxed{=}$ $\boxed{=}$ $\boxed{=}$ $\boxed{=}$ $\boxed{=}$ $\boxed{=}$ $\boxed{=}$ $\boxed{=}$. This use of repeated addition helps children connect their knowledge of addition to the new operation of multiplication. But now questions that could not easily be answered without calculators can be asked. "How much is 20 threes? Is that the same as 3 twenties? Which is more, 4 twelves or 8 sixes? Explain."

Calculators need to be integrated into the curriculum in a way that helps children choose an appropriate way to compute. Children should not become dependent on calculators or mental computation or paper-and-pencil computation. They should learn to choose which method would work best for the situation on which they are working.

conclusion

Today there is a greater awareness that paper-and-pencil computation should not dominate the curriculum as it has in the past. A more balanced approach to computation is needed. There should be an increased emphasis on mental computation and estimation and on a natural integration of the calculator into the everyday mathematics classroom.

Whether it be paper-and-pencil computation, mental computation, computational estimation, or the use of calculators, curricular demands no longer permit teaching with minimal understanding and excessive practice. Procedures that children have memorized without understanding do not further the development of number sense, the ability to judge the reasonableness of results, a flexibility in thinking with numbers, or a comprehensive view of computation. In order to accomplish these broader goals, computation needs to be taught carefully and meaningfully.

Effective instruction for mental computation and estimation encourages a holistic approach. Flexibility is the key. Sometimes a quick estimate is sufficient to solve a problem. Depending on the situation and the numbers involved, different procedures may be used. Decisions about computing encourage reflection on the problem and the computation involved. Children with this

broader view of computation are more likely to notice unreasonable results. It seems likely that children should be encouraged to develop some mental computation and estimation strategies prior to receiving formal instruction on the written algorithms. When written algorithms are presented, children often focus almost exclusively on procedures. This leads to a restricted understanding of the algorithms and how they can be used. It can also contribute to a lack of awareness about reasonable results.

Everyday access to calculators as tools for teaching mathematics will change the flavor of computational instruction. It will not mean that conceptual understanding of the operations is ignored or becomes less important. Using the calculator should not involve aimless button pushing. Effective use should mean more time will be available for students to focus on understanding. It should free children to explore situations they otherwise could not experience. Realistic applications can be used because computation with numbers beyond children's paper-and-pencil proficiency are possible with the calculator. Furthermore, research indicates there is no need to fear that calculator use negatively affects the development of basic skills (Hembree and Dessart 1986).

Curricula designed (1) to place greater emphasis on noncomputational topics such as measurement, geometry, and collecting, organizing, and presenting data, (2) to introduce mental computation and estimation skills early, and (3) to have calculators available on an everyday basis will no doubt alter the grade-level placement of paper-and-pencil algorithms, the size of the numbers involved in them, and the way they are taught. Reasonable expectations for computational proficiency, including the size of the numbers and the level of accuracy, may also affect when and how written algorithms are taught. It is evident from both research and practice that when written algorithms are taught carefully and meaningfully with numbers children understand, children can learn to compute well. But questions remain. When should paper-and-pencil algorithms be introduced? When should children receive instructional attention with expectations of mastery?

Viewing computation in a holistic manner makes it a dynamic topic, not a static one that involves rote memorization of rules. Computation should encourage children to explore numbers and operations, seek relationships, and reflect on their work. Most important, computation should help children believe that mathematics makes sense.

bibliography

Carraher, Terezinha N., David W. Carraher, and Analúcia D. Schliemann. "Written and Oral Mathematics." *Journal for Research in Mathematics Education* 18 (March 1987): 83–97.

Cobb, Paul, and Graceann Merkel. "Thinking Strategies: Teaching Arithmetic through Problem Solving." In *New Directions for Elementary School Mathematics,* 1989 Yearbook of the National Council of Teachers of Mathematics, edited by Paul R. Trafton, pp. 70–81. Reston, Va.: The Council, 1989.

Hembree, Ray, and Donald J. Dessart. "Effects of Hand-held Calculators in Precollege Mathematics Education: A Meta-Analysis." *Journal for Research in Mathematics Education* 17 (March 1986): 83–99.

Kouba, Vicky L., Catherine A. Brown, Thomas P. Carpenter, Mary M. Lindquist, Edward A. Silver, and Jane O. Swafford. "Results of the Fourth NAEP Assessment of Mathematics: Number, Operations, and Word Problems." *Arithmetic Teacher* 35 (April 1988): 14–19.

Lankford, Francis G., Jr. *Some Computational Strategies of Seventh-Grade Pupils.* Charlottesville, Va.: Center for Advanced Studies, University of Virginia, 1972.

National Council of Teachers of Mathematics. *Curriculum and Evaluation Standards for School Mathematics.* Reston, Va.: The Council, 1989.

Reed, H. J., and Jean Lave. "Arithmetic as a Tool for Investigating Relations between Culture and Cognition." In *Language, Culture, and Cognition: Anthropological Perspectives,* edited by R. W. Casson, pp. 437–55. New York: Macmillan, 1981.

Sowder, Larry. "Children's Solutions of Story Problems." *Journal of Mathematical Behavior* 7 (1988): 227–38.

fractions and decimals

9

joseph payne ann towsley deann huinker

Fourth graders are working on the problem, "Which is more, $\frac{1}{2}$ or $\frac{9}{10}$?"

Brett uses paper fraction strips, starts counting the pieces to show nine-tenths, stops suddenly and says, "But nine-tenths is almost one whole. You only need one more tenth to make it a whole. So nine-tenths is much bigger."

Tony cannot do the problem using the symbols but shows some understanding when the teacher says the names. "In fractions a big number means a smaller piece, so the tenths would be real little and a half is a real big piece." Tony is concentrating on the size of the pieces but disregarding the number of pieces.

Sharon says, "Nine somethings is more than one, so

nine-tenths is bigger." When asked for further explanation, she replies, "Fractions, you know, halves," using the words *fraction* and *halves* as if they are generic terms for "piece."

Margaret answers the question successfully using her paper strips but is unable to show nine-tenths on a real candy bar. "The candy bar is not long enough to get nine-tenths," she notes and points to the paper strip that is longer than the candy bar.

There is great variation in the conceptual knowledge of these students. Brett showed that he has a sound grasp of fraction concepts. The other students have some understanding, but there are holes in their knowledge and incomplete connections between and among essential components of fraction knowledge.

175

nctm standards

The National Council of Teachers of Mathematics *Curriculum and Evaluation Standards for School Mathematics* (1989) speaks with clarity about a sensible instructional approach, an approach well supported by many research studies. The K–4 standards emphasize concepts, number sense, models, applications, and the exploration of operations:

Standard 12: FRACTIONS AND DECIMALS

In grades K–4, the mathematics curriculum should include fractions and decimals so that students can—

■ develop concepts of fractions, mixed numbers, and decimals;

■ develop number sense for fractions and decimals;

■ use models to relate fractions to decimals and to find equivalent fractions;

■ use models to explore operations on fractions and decimals;

■ apply fractions and decimals to problem situations. (P. 57)

The flow of the goals in the *Standards* begins by establishing a rich conceptual foundation in the primary grades and continues by building meaningful computation procedures in the middle and upper grades.

The major purpose of this chapter is to present a developmental sequence and classroom-proved activities for fraction concepts, for decimal concepts, and for concepts of the operations of addition and subtraction of fractions and decimals.

conceptual knowledge of fractions

Conceptual knowledge has many connections (see chapter 2). Conceptual knowledge of fractions involves connections between and among real-life experiences, concrete models, oral language, and written symbols.

connections

There are five major components of conceptual knowledge of fractions for students through grade 4, as shown in figure 1. All components need to be connected, so that if given any of the five, a child can give the other four.

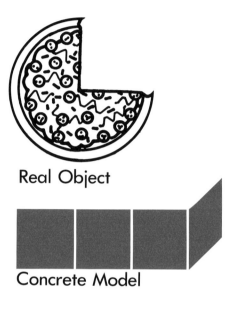

Real Object

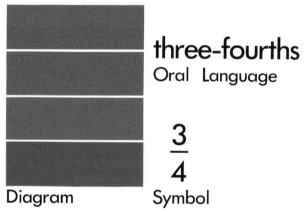

Concrete Model

three-fourths
Oral Language

$$\frac{3}{4}$$

Diagram   Symbol

Fig. 1. Components of conceptual knowledge of fractions

real objects

Fraction knowledge begins with parts and wholes of real objects—candy bars, cookies, pizza, spinach

oral language

Early language is likely to use the word *half* as a generic name for any part. This recognition that there is a special name for parts is a crucial first step. As children develop their knowledge of fractions, they learn the usual names for the fractional parts of real objects. Thus, the first major connection for a child to make is the connection between the parts of real objects and the oral names for those parts.

concrete models

As fraction activities become more formal, paper strips, cardboard circles, and geoboard examples act as models to represent a quantity. When these models are used, they can become pizzas, candy bars, or imagined spinach. The models make the perceptual examples clear, make showing a wide variety of equal parts easy, and involve each student in manipulative activities essential for understanding fractions. The concrete model is a representation of real objects and, like real objects, is related to the oral names for fractions.

(leave the big part on the plate). Initially, children see the parts with little attention paid to the size of the parts or the need for equal parts. Siblings and friends teach each other the necessity for fair shares, leading to the essential idea of equal parts. The foundational knowledge rests on practical experiences with real objects that are important to the child.

diagrams

A slightly more abstract model is a two-dimensional diagram, the kind that is prevalent in written materials. Initially, the concrete models are traced to draw the diagrams. When learning to interpret diagrams, children need special help to see the whole and to make a part-to-whole comparison of the part to the whole unit.

symbols

The fraction symbol itself is the final component that must be connected to the other four. Symbols come after substantial work with real objects, concrete models, and diagrams. Fraction symbols become a natural expression of the oral language that in turn is connected to sound quantitative ideas.

It is difficult to diagram the five components and the connections between them. If the concrete model and diagram are considered together (eventually they should mean the same, but for initial instruction, they are different), the components and connections can be shown as in figure 2. The figure is designed to show the foundational nature of real objects, concrete models and diagrams, and oral language, by showing them as the base of the pyramid. The base is solidly built first. Then the symbols are connected.

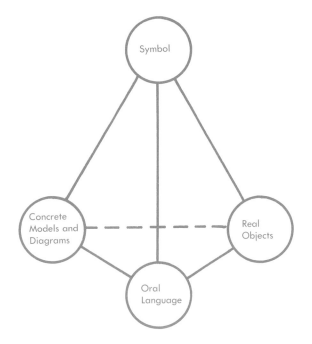

Fig. 2. Components and connections for conceptual knowledge of fractions

developmental sequence

A sense of the developmental sequence can be gained by contrasting the knowledge of the fourth graders illustrated at the beginning of this chapter with concepts held by a younger child.

Fourth graders: Know the difference between a part of a candy bar and a whole candy bar.

Two-year-olds: Call an apple cut into halves "two apples."

Fourth graders: Know that the amount of candy stays the same if a candy bar is broken into many small pieces or a few large pieces.
Four-year-olds: Break up crackers into many small pieces so they can have "more cracker" than a neighbor who has several large pieces.

Fourth graders: Carefully cut a candy bar into fair shares, meticulously comparing pieces to make sure they are even.
Five-year-olds: Pour milk into two identical cups, are satisfied if each cup gets "some," but are not concerned with even amounts.

The concept of parts and wholes is at the heart of fraction understanding. Parts and wholes lead to oral names and equal-sized pieces that in turn lead to symbols. What follows is a developmental sequence for the young child.

For children in preschool through kindergarten, ages three to five, the major goal is to develop the concept of whole, parts, and parts that make a whole. The key ideas are summarized in figure 3.

Wholes can be broken into parts and reassembled into wholes. Sometimes there aren't enough parts to make a complete whole.

Sometimes there are enough parts to make more than a whole or even several wholes.

There are big parts, small parts, even-sized parts.

Parts can be shared by cutting or breaking again.

Fig. 3. Part-whole ideas, ages three to five

For kindergarten through grade 3, ages five through eight, the emphasis is on equal-sized parts and oral names, as shown in figure 4. It is sufficient to concentrate on these aspects, leaving fraction symbols until grade 3. Gunderson (1958), in her insightful and provocative article, provided convincing evidence that fraction concepts can indeed be learned in grades 1 and 2, as long as the emphasis is not on fraction symbols. The work of Galloway (1975) provided support for Gunderson's position.

Equal-sized parts have special names. The names tell exactly how many even-sized parts fit into one whole.

Wholes are counted with the familiar numbers 0, 1, 2, 3, ...

The sizes of different parts, such as sixths and tenths, can be compared.

Parts, such as sixths and halves, can be counted. Sometimes there are not enough parts to make a whole.

Sometimes there are more than enough parts to make a whole or several wholes.

The special fraction names apply to all kinds of real objects, such as apples, clay disks, cups of juice, and pizza.

Amounts can be named using a whole number and a fraction name (mixed numbers).

Fractions and mixed numbers can be used to estimate amounts.

Fig. 4. Oral names and equal-sized parts, ages five to eight

For grades 3 and above, ages eight and older, fraction symbols are used to communicate quantitative ideas of part of a whole, as shown in figure 5.

informal activities

Playtime activities provide an excellent opportunity to

The symbol comes from the oral language.

The top number tells the number of pieces considered. The bottom number tells how many equal-sized pieces there are in one whole.

Fraction amounts can be close to the whole numbers, 0, 1, 2, ... Different fraction symbols can show the same amount (equivalent fractions).

Symbols show amounts, and these can be compared.

Symbols show amounts, and these can be estimated.

Fig. 5. Fraction symbols, ages eight and older

develop language and concepts for fractions. Important words include the following:

| part | whole | sharing |
| pieces | fair shares | almost a whole |

Informal exchanges with children should call attention to parts and the wholes they come from, to the comparison of big and little parts, and to amounts that are more than, or not quite, a complete whole.

 In the rice tub. As children play in the tub containing rice (birdseed, sand, water), use words that convey part-whole concepts. "Will you pour me a whole cup of rice? Now, how about pouring just a tiny part of this cup." After the child starts to pour, it may be necessary to say, "No, not the whole cup, just a tiny part."

"I think this teaspoon will fill only a tiny part of this bucket. Is there something else that would fill a bigger part of the bucket? Is there something else that holds more than the whole tub?"

Scoop up a pitcher of rice. "Shall we share this whole pitcher of rice? There are four of us. I hope we all get a fair share." Have a child pour rice into four cups. "Wait! Someone is getting too small a part. Can you even it out? Which cup needs a little more rice in it so that it's the same as the others?" **a**

Snack time. Share fruits or crackers at snack time for ideas and language of parts and wholes. "Here is a whole banana. Can you cut this banana into pieces? How many slices do you think there are in a whole banana? [A child says 'ten'.] OK, will you try to slice the banana into ten slices? I will cut mine into four pieces. [Teacher and child both cut, but the teacher makes equal-sized pieces.] Count your pieces. Are they the same size? [No] Which is your biggest piece? Are all my pieces the same size? [Yes] If I share my banana with four people, will each get a fair share or will someone get more? [Fair share] It is hard to cut into even pieces! Let's practice on a play-dough banana."

a

Clean-up time, art, water-play, and puzzle activities all offer good opportunities to emphasize whole sets of things, whole sheets of paper, parts of wholes, and completing the whole job. Informal activities provide a natural place for many mathematical concepts, including fractions, but structured activities are needed as well.

structured activities

In informal activities the word *whole* can refer both to discrete sets such as blocks and to continuous objects such as bananas. For young children, however, some objects have a more perceptually obvious or familiar

wholeness about them. A whole set of tools or a whole set of building blocks is arbitrarily defined and difficult to see. A whole apple, a whole person, or a whole circle is much easier. Although in their later elementary years children will be expected to handle the more abstract idea of the wholeness of a set of discrete objects, it is easier for children to begin structured activities with wholes and parts when the wholes are familiar and perceptually obvious to them.

For the most part, the following activities employ continuous and familiar wholes rather than discrete sets of arbitrarily defined wholes.

Toy person. Very young children (aged two to four) enjoy the toy kit in which a "person" is assembled using a vegetable for the head and plastic parts for face and body. Working with a small group of children, show a whole assembled person and then take it apart in front of the children. The parts are shared among the children, who hide them under the table or behind their backs.

"I have the head here. But it's not the whole person. I think I need a part. Mike, give me an eye for this person." [Mike gives the eye.] Ask for the various parts and gradually assemble the person. "Wait! I don't have the whole person yet! I'm still missing a part. Laura, do you have the part I'm missing? Do you have the mouth? [Puts mouth in place.] Now I have the whole person." **a**

For older children this same activity can include take-apart toy clocks or trucks or household items such as coffee pots, flashlights, ball-point pens, pencil sharpeners, food mills, or food processors. Science activities incorporate numerous opportunities to learn the parts of various wholes, for example, showing and naming the parts of a piece of fruit, the human body, or an automobile. Children also need the reverse experience of making wholes from parts.

For ages two to four, cut-outs of body parts of animals can be used—heads, tails, legs, bodies, noses, and wings of fish, birds, elephants, dogs, and insects. These can be made from magazine or book illustrations. The pieces can be mounted on tagboard and backed with flannel for flannel board use or with magnetic tape for use on a magnetic chalkboard.

Older children can use geometric shapes—circles, ovals, rectangles, and triangles—to build animals, people, or houses. Simple tangram puzzles can also be used.

Finger paints. Finger paints provide an opportunity for children aged four and five to draw wholes and cut them into parts of equal and unequal size. The concept of half is introduced informally.

Give children finger paints and paper. "First cover the whole paper with a big smear of finger paint. Now draw a big circle. Pretend that it is a pizza. Use your finger to cut yourself a big slice of that pizza."

"Look, Tommy has given himself half a pizza! That's a big slice. I'm going to give myself even more than a half. [Drawing a piece about three-fourths.] See, I get all of this around on this side. Can you give yourself a piece as big or bigger than that?" [They try.]

"Now smear your pizza up and draw a candy bar. Cut me a little, tiny piece of your candy bar. I'm trying to cut down on my candy. Ryan has certainly given me a tiny piece. Does that mean you get all the rest of the candy bar? Do you get all of this, almost the whole candy bar?" **a**

Four-, five-, and six-year-old children can practice cutting the pizza into the number of pieces they need for their families (larger pieces) or for all the children in the room (very tiny pieces). It is not necessary that their pieces be all the same size.

Six-, seven-, and eight-year-old children can practice cutting pieces of the same size, but they will need cutting strategies to make it easier. For instance, cutting into halves and then each half in half makes fourths. Thirds can be made by putting a dot in the center of the circle and drawing a "Y" so that the arms all meet in the center. Use the vocabulary of *halves* and *thirds* for children of this age when appropriate.

Play dough, equal-sized pieces. Give children, aged four to five, plastic knives and play dough. "Pat your play dough into a flat, round pie. Pretend you are going to share your pie with me. Try to cut it into two pieces. Try to make the pieces the same size. Remember, I get to choose the piece I want! Now pat your play dough into a pancake. Let's share this pancake among four people. Try to cut even shares. Can you put the four pieces back together again to make the whole pie?"

"Now roll your play dough into a hot dog. Can you cut the hot dog into two pieces? Are they the same size?"

Pieces should be laid next to or on top of each other to determine if they truly are equal sized. Circles and disks will have to be cut into wedges to get equal sizes, but squares and rectangles can be partitioned with parallel cuts. Cutting an item in two and comparing the resulting parts is appropriate for beginning cutters. **a**

Children aged six to eight are able to handle four and three equal-sized parts. Again, suggest cutting strategies for fourths, thirds, and sixths (sixths are halves first and then each half is in thirds). Fifths are especially difficult and will require help from the teacher.

Folding squares, equal-sized pieces. Give each child, ages six to eight, ten paper squares to fold into equal and unequal parts (fig. 6).

"Fold one of your squares in two. Be sure to match the edges and corners so that the pieces will be exactly the same size. [They try.] How would you fold another square into four pieces? [Fold in half and then fold each half in half.] When you open it up again, will the pieces be the same size? If you laid one piece on top of the other, would they match? [Yes, if you match corners and edges] Now fold a square into four unequal-sized pieces. You should end up with both big and little parts."

"Here's a challenge. Watch me fold my square. First I fold in half, and then each half in half, and then each of those in half again. Before I open it up, can you tell me how many equal-sized pieces I will have? [8] Now you try to fold eight equal-sized pieces with one of your squares. [They may use several squares to practice on.] Can anyone make sixteen equal-sized

pieces? Before you fold, can you predict whether they will be big pieces or little pieces?"

"Look over all the squares you folded and tell me which has the biggest pieces. [The square folded in two] Which has the smallest size pieces? [The square folded into sixteen pieces] But sixteen is such a *big* number! Why are the pieces *small*?" [Because you have to fit sixteen pieces into one square, and that makes each piece very small.] **a**

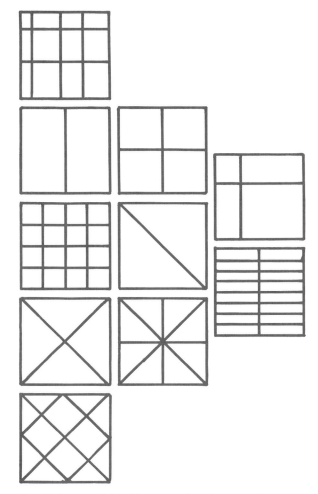

Fig. 6. Squares folded into equal and unequal parts

For older children, aged seven to ten, use circles and rectangular strips as well as squares. Thirds and fifths are easier to do on a rectangular strip. Tenths are especially important for beginning decimal work. They can be made on a rectangular strip by folding fifths first and then the fifths in half.

oral
fraction names

Previous activities included the names *halves* and *thirds* for older children and can be used to develop other fraction names. In second and third grade, conscious effort is needed to develop the language of fractions, as suggested in the following paper-folding activity.

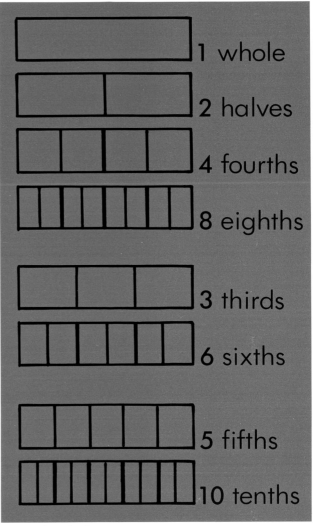

Fig. 7. Chart for fraction strips

a *Make fraction strips.* Each child needs eight rectangular strips of paper. (See fig. 7.) Different colors make oral work with groups of children easier. Each child needs one white strip, three of color A, two of color B, and two of color C. Strips 2″ × 8½″ can be easily cut from duplicating paper. Construction paper is more difficult to fold.

"The white strip is a whole. It is exactly one whole. Pretend that it is one whole candy bar. Pick up an orange (color A) strip and fold it into two equal-sized pieces. Remember to make fair shares. If you cut, I get to choose. [They fold.] What are these pieces called?" [Most children will know they are halves.] Write "halves" and "2" on the board. "Fold another orange strip into four equal-sized pieces. Who knows what they are called?" [Fourths]

The folding continues in this fashion until the set of fraction strips is complete and the chart on the board is finished, as shown in figure 7.

"The fraction names are like some names you already know for *third* in line or *sixth* grade. The one you have to watch out for is *halves*. *Fourths* sounds a little like *four* and *fourth* in line, but *halves* does not sound like *second* or *two*. Be sure to say the 'ths' when you pronounce the fraction names." **a**

In the following activities fraction strips are used to develop the oral and written names. Symbols can cause confusion if used before children are comfortable with oral names.

a *Show me, with oral names.* Each child has a set of fraction strips. Say the name and have students show the correct parts. "Show me your fifths strip. Show me 1 fifth. Show me 2 fifths, 3

fifths, 4 fifths, 5 fifths, 6 fifths . . . [We can't.] Can you pair up with another person to show me 6 fifths?" [Yes.] Continue asking for fourths, sixths, and so on. "Let's count backwards. Show me 10 tenths, 9 tenths, 8 tenths, . . ."

"Let's play a game. I'm going to count with fractions like we have been doing, and as I count, you show it on your strips. But here's a trick. Suppose I count, 1, 2, 3, . . . without telling you what *size* piece I'm counting? Did you know that '1, 2, 3' automatically means *wholes*? You will have to show me 1, 2, 3 *whole* strips when I count 1, 2, 3. Otherwise, listen for the size." Continue counting as before.

Reverse the activity. Show parts and have students give

the oral names. "Look at this fraction part. What is its name? [Fourths, for example] How many pieces do you see? [Three] What is the fraction name? [Three-fourths] I didn't hear the sound *th*. Can you try again?" Repeat with other parts. **a**

a *Compare sizes, with oral names.* Use the fraction strips and compare sizes using oral fraction names. "Look at all your strips and show me the biggest single piece. What is its name? [Half] Now show me the smallest single piece. What is its name? [Tenth] Which is bigger, a sixth or a third?" [Third]

Now don't look at your fraction strips. See if you can tell me which is bigger, a fourth or a tenth? [Fourth] Check your strips now to see if you were right." Continue asking for comparisons between single pieces of the fraction set.

Is there a rule that helps you decide without looking which is bigger just by listening to the fraction names?" [Yes, listen to the names. If it is a big number like tenths, then it's a small piece, because that's how many equal-sized pieces there are in the whole.] **a**

a *Make wholes, with oral names.* Use the fraction strips to reinforce the idea of which parts make a whole. "Look at your fourths strip. Show me 1 fourth, 2 fourths. How many fourths does it take to make one whole? [4] Show me 2 thirds, 3 thirds, 4 thirds. How many thirds does it take to make one whole?" [3] Continue to count with fractions, then ask how many it takes to make one whole.

"If it takes four fourths to make one whole, then how many ways can you use fourths to show less than one whole? [1 fourth, 2 fourths, 3 fourths] If it takes ten tenths to make one whole, then how many ways can you use tenths to show more than one whole? [11 tenths, 12 tenths, . . .] Is there a rule that can help you decide whether a fraction is more than or less than or equal to one whole?" [Yes. If both numbers sound like the same number, such as ten tenths, then it's equal to one whole. If the first number is less than the second number, then it's less than one whole. If the first number is more than the second number, then it's more than one whole.] **a**

a *Mixed numbers, with oral names.* Use the fraction strips to develop concepts and language for mixed numbers. Ask the children to hold up their wholes, counting them," one whole, two wholes, three wholes. . . ." Ask a number of children to each hold up a whole and one more child to hold up a half. "Let's count them together, starting with the wholes and being sure to count the half as 'and one-half.' " Young children may get caught up in the rhythm of the counting and continue counting in whole numbers, ". . . three wholes, four wholes, five wholes," when the number showing is four and one-half.

Connections with real-life examples of "four and one-half" are important to make. The strips can become "candy bars," "bananas," "sandwiches," or "crackers." Ask the children to make comparisons, "Would you rather have four and one-half cookies or four cookies? [four and one-half] Which side of the room has more candy bars (strips), this side with three and one-half or this side with five and one-half?" [Five and one-half] Repeat these activities with other fractions—fourths, thirds, eighths, and tenths.

Older children can illustrate oral addition and subtraction with the strips. Five children each hold up one whole and a sixth child holds up one-half. Play a rapid-fire game of "How many are there now?" [Five and one-half] by asking, "Three wholes sit down; how many are there now? [Two and one half] One whole stand up; how many are there now?" [Three and one-half] One-half sit down; how many are there now?" [Three wholes]

a

diagrams for fractions

Teachers must provide a deliberate and planned connection between real objects and diagrams. Children often misinterpret diagrams and give a part-to-part comparison. These errors are especially evident when several units are shown in a diagram (Muangnapoe 1975).

a *Diagrams for fraction parts.* Use fraction strips to draw diagrams and to help children interpret diagrams correctly. "Show me three-fourths with your strips. How can we draw a picture to show this amount? What do we need to show first?" [The whole]

Trace carefully around the whole strip on the chalkboard or overhead projector. "How do we show equal parts? [Draw lines where there are folds.] How do we show three parts?" [Shade the parts or color them in.]

As diagrams are drawn and parts are shaded have children give the oral names as they are shown in figure 8. A common mistake with the first strip is the children saying, "one-third," making a part-to-part comparison instead of part-to-whole.

a

These naming, counting, and comparison activities can be used with apples, clay disks, pretend pizzas, paper circles, and diagrams. Children should do activities that require them to use their fraction and mixed-number naming, counting, and comparison skills in many different contexts.

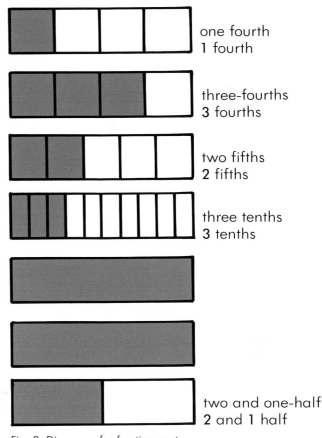

one fourth
1 fourth

three-fourths
3 fourths

two fifths
2 fifths

three tenths
3 tenths

two and one-half
2 and 1 half

Fig. 8. Diagrams for fraction parts

fraction symbols

Using the written fraction symbol is appropriate only after children can name, count, and compare using the oral language with facility. Writing symbols can be delayed safely until grade 3, with only oral language and models used with younger children.

Written symbols are developed in the same way as oral language. The same kind of questioning can be used, but now the model and the oral language are connected with the symbol. For example, the $\frac{3}{4}$ symbol is merely a short way to write the longer *3 fourths*. It is important to use both the long and the short form of written words together with the symbol until the children have mastered the connection, as shown in figure 9.

Symbols for mixed numbers can be introduced when children are familiar with fraction symbols.

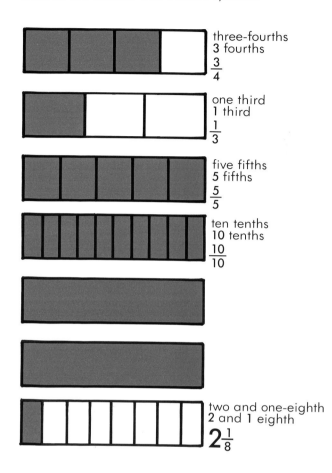

three-fourths
3 fourths
$\frac{3}{4}$

one third
1 third
$\frac{1}{3}$

five fifths
5 fifths
$\frac{5}{5}$

ten tenths
10 tenths
$\frac{10}{10}$

two and one-eighth
2 and 1 eighth
$2\frac{1}{8}$

Fig. 9. From models and oral names to symbols

comparisons

Fractions should be compared using real objects, fraction strips, or diagrams. The goal is for students to think of the quantities represented by the fractions and decide which amount is larger or smaller. Previous activities with oral names should have established a basis for this quantitative comparison.

 Compare the number of pieces. The easiest comparisons are with different numbers of pieces of equal size, probably because it is

so much like comparing whole numbers. (See fig. 10.) "Rebecca, show me $\frac{3}{10}$ with your strips. Jane, show me $\frac{5}{10}$. Who has more, Rebecca or Jane? [Jane] Who has less?" [Rebecca]

Later, such questions provide readiness for addition and subtraction. "How much more does Jane have than Rebecca? [$\frac{2}{10}$] How much less does Rebecca have than Jane?" [$\frac{2}{10}$]   a

a *Compare pieces of different sizes.* It is more difficult for students to compare fractions, such as $\frac{3}{4}$ and $\frac{3}{8}$, when the pieces are not the same size. (See fig. 10.) "Ryan, I have drawn a rectangle to show one whole candy bar. Can you come up and shade my figure to show $\frac{3}{4}$? Now, draw another whole candy bar underneath. Can you shade it to show $\frac{3}{8}$? Which is bigger, $\frac{3}{4}$ or $\frac{3}{8}$? [$\frac{3}{4}$] Why?" [It's a bigger amount.]   a

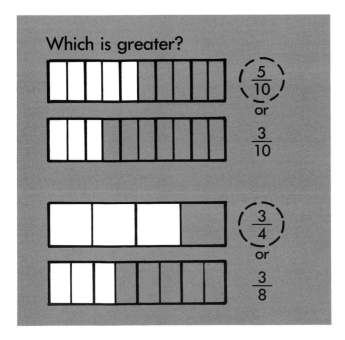

Which is greater?

$\frac{5}{10}$

or

$\frac{3}{10}$

$\frac{3}{4}$

or

$\frac{3}{8}$

Fig. 10. Comparing fractions using diagrams

equivalent fractions

Equivalent fractions show the same part or amount of a given unit. This quantitative basis for equivalent fractions is the rationale for all work through grade 4. Generalizations about multiplying or dividing numerators and denominators are left to the upper grades.

a *Equivalents for $\frac{1}{2}$ and 1.* Using the strips to find equivalents for 1 and for $\frac{1}{2}$ is appropriate for third graders. Younger children may have difficulty lining up the strips accurately to measure or understanding the concept of congruence. Use the strips and have children name one-half in many ways. "Can you show me that $\frac{1}{2}$ and $\frac{2}{4}$ show the same amount?" The strips can be stacked on top of each other and then clipped down the middle between two fingers. The strips can also be lined up in rows and one half pulled out to measure against all the other strips to find other equivalents to $\frac{1}{2}$, such as $\frac{4}{8}$, $\frac{3}{6}$, and $\frac{5}{10}$.

Finding equivalents for 1 is easy. "Hold up your fifths strip and count with me. Tell me to stop when I count one whole. One fifth, two fifths, three fifths, four fifths, five fifths," [Stop.] Follow these counting experiences with some thought-provoking questions, "Why does it take 5 fifths to make a whole when it takes only 3 thirds? Look at your strips and see if you can tell me why it takes more fifths than thirds to make a whole." **a**

a *Comparisons to 1, $\frac{1}{2}$, and 0.* Finding fractions close to 1 whole is the next step. "Show me $\frac{10}{10}$ with your strips. Fold back $\frac{1}{10}$. How much do you show now? [9 tenths] You have almost, but not quite, a whole. Use the strips and fold each back by one part to show a number that is close to 1. Are you closer to 1 when you fold back $\frac{1}{10}$ or when you fold back $\frac{1}{2}$?" [$\frac{1}{10}$]

Use this observation to develop comparisons between fractions close to 1. "Which is more, $\frac{3}{4}$ or $\frac{7}{8}$? Both are close to 1. [$\frac{7}{8}$, because it is $\frac{1}{8}$ away from 1; $\frac{3}{4}$ is $\frac{1}{4}$ away from 1] Which would you rather have, $\frac{9}{10}$ of a candy bar or $\frac{5}{6}$ of a candy bar? Which is closer to 1 whole?" [$\frac{9}{10}$ is closer to 1 whole.]

Combining the children's knowledge of equivalents to 1 whole and 1 half can help develop comparisons. Ask children to compare two fractions, one close to or equivalent to 1 and one equivalent to $\frac{1}{2}$. "Which is more, $\frac{4}{4}$ of a sandwich or $\frac{1}{2}$? [4 fourths] Why? [4 fourths is a whole.] Would you like $\frac{5}{5}$ of a paper or $\frac{3}{6}$?" [5 fifths, if I want the paper; 3 sixths, if I don't]

Comparisons to 0 use concepts of the size of the pieces. "Is $\frac{1}{4}$ closer to 0 or is $\frac{1}{10}$? Why? [$\frac{1}{10}$ is closer because it's a smaller piece.] Use your fraction strips. Can you find fractions that are closer to 0 than to 1? [$\frac{1}{10}$, $\frac{2}{10}$, $\frac{3}{10}$, $\frac{4}{10}$, $\frac{1}{8}$, $\frac{2}{8}$, $\frac{3}{8}$, $\frac{1}{6}$, $\frac{2}{6}$, $\frac{1}{5}$, $\frac{2}{5}$, $\frac{1}{4}$, $\frac{1}{3}$] How can you tell?" [If it's less than $\frac{1}{2}$ or more than $\frac{1}{2}$]

a

other models

Children understand fraction concepts most easily by using real objects and regions (paper strips and diagrams). This is also true for concepts of equivalent fractions and addition and subtraction of fractions. When should work begin on the linear and set models?

Difficulties with both linear and discrete set models were identified by Payne (1976) and Muangnapoe (1975). Later research corroborated the trouble with linear models, especially for teaching equivalent fractions. It is the firm conclusion of the authors of this chapter that neither the linear nor the set models are effective in teaching *initial* concepts of fractions, equivalent fractions, or addition and subtraction. These concepts should be taught first with concrete models and regions, either paper strips or diagrams.

When a linear unit is introduced, it should be related to concepts that are already well established. Using folded thin paper strips or straws can connect the linear model to the region model. Write fractions at the end of each piece to show the distance traveled from the starting end. If the linear strips are related to real objects such as licorice strips, students will recognize that the fractions should go at the end of the pieces because "you put the fraction to show how much you have eaten up." See figure 11.

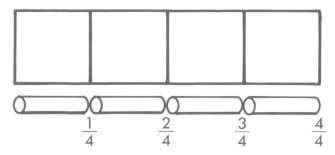

Fig. 11. Relating a linear unit to a region unit

Understanding linear units is necessary to be able to read rulers as shown in chapter 11. The key component is understanding that the marks show parts of the whole unit, not just points on a line.

The discrete set model has different difficulties: identifying the unit and eliminating the requirement that pieces be the same size. Using the fraction $\frac{4}{9}$ to show the part of the reading group that is boys requires viewing the group as a whole and counting the boys. Perceptually, the whole may be difficult to see, and the boys are not the same size. When the set model is introduced, these differences in views of fractions must be made clear and discussed. There are even greater difficulties in using set models for equivalent fractions for the same basic reasons. Equivalence with set models is best left to later grades when teaching ratios and equivalent ratios.

Finding a fractional part of a whole number, such as $\frac{1}{3}$ of 27, occurs sometimes in the curriculum as a fraction topic with the set model. Such problems are better dealt with as problems involving the division of whole numbers, dividing 27 into 3 equal parts. Make the connection to fractions as "dividing the amount into three equal parts and taking one of the parts."

conceptual knowledge of decimals

Fourth graders are comparing decimals. Here are Joe's responses when asked, "Which is larger?"

- 0.5 or 0.7? "0.7 because 7 tens is larger than 5 tens"

- 0.46 or 0.21? "0.46 because 46 hundreds is larger than 21 hundreds"

- 0.8 or 0.23? "0.23 because 23 hundreds is larger than 8 tens"

- 0.9 or 0.02? "0.02 because 2 hundreds is larger than 9 tens"

When the decimals have the same number of digits after the decimal point, Joe is able to give correct answers but for the wrong reason and with incorrect place-value names. When the decimals are uneven, his reasoning no longer works. Joe does not realize that the numerals to the right of the decimal point represent fractional parts of a whole unit, not whole numbers. Joe does not understand decimals.

Children can develop a conceptual understanding of decimals if they receive instruction that develops this knowledge. Decimal knowledge grows from, and relates to, fraction knowledge. Real objects, concrete models, and diagrams are used first with oral language for tenths and hundredths and are then related to symbols for decimals.

models and oral language for tenths

The study of fractions should always include tenths to serve as a basis for decimals. Proper development of fraction concepts requires about two weeks in either grade 3 or grade 4. If other work intervenes before decimals are taught, students will need at least one day reviewing fraction concepts for tenths with models and oral language. Readiness for decimal symbols is achieved through activities that distinguish between whole units and parts of whole units, establish the need for equal-sized parts, practice oral names for tenths, and develop decimal number sense.

Fair shares and tenths. "Let's pretend there are ten people at the party. Which cake in figure 12 should be served so that everyone gets a fair share? Why? "[The first or third because pieces are equal in size] "What is the name of one of the equal-sized pieces?" [Tenths]

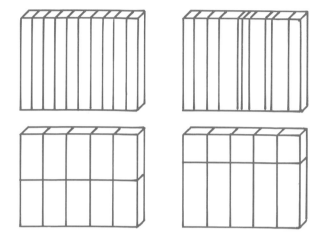

Fig. 12. Choosing fair shares for tenths

Give each child several paper strips that are marked to show ten equal parts. Define one paper strip as the whole unit and tell the children to pretend that it is a granola bar. "How many pieces are in each granola bar? [10] If I eat one of those pieces, how much of the whole granola bar did I eat?" [1 tenth] Now have the children color three of the parts red." If this is the amount you eat, how much of the whole granola bar did you eat? [3 tenths] How much of the granola bar didn't you eat?" [7 tenths] Repeat with other strips, having the children color in various amounts, including all ten parts. **a**

Children should have an understanding of tenths as quantities before they use decimal symbols. To help them develop this decimal number sense, they need opportunities to identify tenths that are (1) less than and greater than one whole unit, (2) close to one whole unit and close to zero units, and (3) less than, greater than, and equal to one-half.

Compare to 0 and 1. Use the paper strips. Tell students to pretend that these are granola bars. "If I give you 2 tenths of a granola bar, will I be giving you a little piece, a medium-sized piece, or a big piece of the granola bar? [Little piece]

Can you show me why with a paper strip? Is it closer to 0 or to 1? [To 0] Is 6 tenths closer to 0 or 1? [To 1] What about 10 tenths? 9 tenths? 13 tenths? 20 tenths?" Help students see that 13 tenths equal 1 whole and 3 tenths, and that 20 tenths make 2 wholes. Then ask the children to show and name amounts of tenths that are less than one whole unit, close to zero units, almost one whole unit but not quite, and more than one whole unit. Summarize the information in a table as in figure 13. **a**

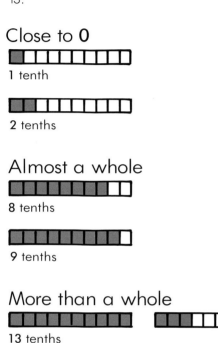

Fig. 13. Comparing decimals to 0 to 1

a *Comparisons and equivalents for $\frac{1}{2}$.* Give each child two paper strips, one that is marked with ten equal parts and one that is unmarked. Have them fold the unmarked strip in two equal parts to show halves and then color one half of the strip. "Use four strips and show an amount of tenths that is greater than one-half. What amount did you show? How do you know it is greater than one-half? [Compared with the half strip] Now show an amount of tenths that is less than one-half. How do you know it is less than one-half? [Less than the half strip] Pretend that these strips are granola bars. Would you rather have 5

tenths of the granola bar or 1 half of the granola bar?" Help the children understand that five-tenths and one-half are just different names for the same amount. **a**

symbols for tenths

When children are confident with models and oral language for tenths and express a sense of the quantities, they are ready for the decimal symbol for tenths. The written symbols are introduced with concrete models to help children connect the symbols to the quantities and real-world settings. Galloway (1975) found that decimals for tenths can be mastered by students in grade 3 if the decimal work is based on sound fraction knowledge.

a *Place-value chart.* Have children shade in 3 tenths of a paper strip, and then ask, "How much of the whole unit is shaded?" [3 tenths] Now tell the children that there is another way to write symbols for fractions that have ten equal parts in the whole unit. Present the chart shown in figure 14. Explain that we put a zero in the ones place to show that we do not have any whole units and we put a 3 in the tenths place to show that we have 3 tenths. Then have children show other amounts on the strips and let them help you record the numerals in the chart. **a**

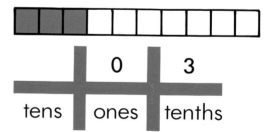

Fig. 14. Place-value chart for tenths

Once children are familiar with writing the numerals in the chart, ask, "What would the number look like if we took it out of the chart?" Erase the chart leaving just the numerals. "Does it look like a 3 or 3 tenths? We have a special way of writing these numbers when we take them out of the chart. We use a little dot called a decimal point to show us the ones place." See figure 15. Redraw the chart and place the decimal point in the ones place, then erase the chart again to show that now we can tell that the number means 3 tenths. After this, include the decimal point in the ones place whenever the chart is used.

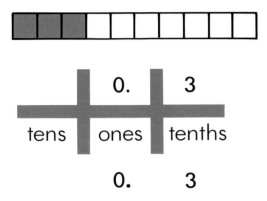

Fig. 15. From a chart to decimal symbols

Read the decimal 0.3 as "three tenths," *not* as "point three," with the name emphasizing the quantity. Three tenths gives a sense that this symbol means 3 of 10 equal parts, whereas point three gives no sense or feel for the quantity because the size of the unit is not named. Once children become familiar with quantities that are less than one, they should begin work with quantities that are greater than one. Read the decimal 1.2 as "one whole and two tenths" or "one and two tenths." Always read the decimal point as "and" to separate the whole number part from the fractional part.

Reading decimals. Have students use paper strips to illustrate decimal symbols and oral names. "Show this amount, 0.6, with your paper strip. How do you say the name of this number? [6 tenths] What does this number mean?" [6 of 10 equal parts] Repeat with other decimal symbols that are less than one whole unit. "Show me 3 whole units and 5 tenths. How can we write the symbol for this amount? [3.5] What does the 3 in the symbol tell us? [That we have 3 whole units] What does the 5 tell us? [That we also have 5 tenths of a whole unit] How do you say the name of this number?" [Three whole units and five tenths or three and five tenths]   a

When using models, children become adept at writing the symbol expressing how much of a whole unit is shaded because they can count the number of shaded parts and the total number of parts in the whole unit but this does not guarantee that they have developed a sense for the quantity expressed by the decimal symbols. Children should be given opportunities to tell how quantities relate to whole units, and they should be encouraged to explain or check their answers with models. Estimation is an excellent way to emphasize quantitative ideas.

Estimate with decimals. Use a can of pop and estimate amounts with decimals. "If I drink 0.2 of a can of pop, do I drink all of my pop or only some of it?" [Only some of it] Use a pop can and have a child show about how much is 0.2. "What if I drink 0.9, then about how much pop did I drink?" [Almost the whole can] Let the children use the pop can again to show this amount. "My friends and I drank this much pop, 4.7. About how much pop did we drink—less than one can, more than one can, more than two cans?" [You drank almost five cans of pop!]   a

It is important that children use models when they compare decimals initially, since symbols alone are more likely to produce misconceptions. A common error occurs when children begin working with decimal symbols and confuse them with whole numbers. They seem to see only the digits; they ignore the decimal point and treat the decimal as a whole number. Some children think of 0.7 as 7 whole units rather than 7 tenths, and 1.4 as fourteen instead of as one and four tenths. These children would think that 25.6 is greater than 72.

Compare decimals. Show children the two decimal symbols, 0.4 and 0.7. Have them secretly write down which decimal they think is larger. Then have the children show 0.4 and 0.7 using their paper strips. They can compare the quantities using the models and check their predictions. Repeat using pairs of decimals that are less than one and greater than one.

To extend this activity, use references to real objects.

For example, ask, "Would you rather have this much, 0.3, of the carrot or this much, 0.8, of the carrot? Why?" (If children do not like carrots, they may choose the smaller piece.) Repeat the questioning with items that the children do and do not like, always having them explain the reason for their choice. **a**

Another common error results when children do not recognize that decimals are just a different way of writing fractions. In the second NAEP mathematics assessment, less than 1 percent of the nine-year-olds were able to rename a fraction expressed in tenths as a decimal (Carpenter et al. 1981). For example, if the children were asked to write $\frac{2}{10}$ as a decimal, common incorrect responses were 2.1 or 2.10. Children at this level should know that the symbols $\frac{2}{10}$ and 0.2 represent the same quantity, 2 of 10 equal parts of a whole unit, and that the oral name, two tenths, is also the same for both. The following activity can help relate fractions, decimals, and models.

a *Relating fractions and decimals.* Prepare a set of cards for zero tenths through ten tenths , one card each for the decimal symbol, fraction symbol, oral name, and model, as shown in figure 16. Deal each child six cards. Place the rest face down in a pile. Then turn over the top card to start a discard pile. For each turn, a child must draw the top card from either pile and then discard one. The goal is to get four matching cards. **a**

Fig. 16. Cards for matching decimal, fraction, word name, and model

tenths and hundredths

Decimals for hundredths are appropriate for grade 4. Initial instruction should focus on naming the numbers

as tenths and hundredths. For example, at first 0.37 should be understood and read as "3 tenths 7 hundredths," not as "37 hundredths." This approach helps children make more sense of the decimal symbols and establishes a conceptual base for all algorithmic work, enabling them to make better connections between concepts and algorithmic procedures.

An initial model for hundredths can be the paper strip. Cut one of the tenths into 10 equal-sized pieces. Have students tell how many small parts are in a whole [100] and the name of the part [hundredths]. A more durable model is base-ten blocks, as shown in figure 17. This model can also be used for developing procedural knowledge in algorithms. The blocks must first be redefined with the flat representing one whole unit. Then the longs and small cubes are parts of the whole unit. If base-ten blocks are unavailable, ten-by-ten squares can be cut from graph paper, heavy card stock, or oaktag. Then tenths and hundredths can also be cut.

The large cube is used by some people to represent one, making the flat one-tenth, the long one-hundredth, and the small cube one-thousandth (Vance 1986). The major disadvantage is that it is more difficult to draw diagrams of decimals.

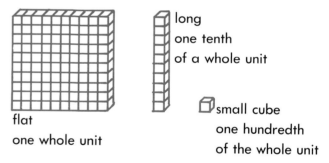

long
one tenth
of a whole unit

small cube
one hundredth
of the whole unit

flat
one whole unit

Fig. 17. Base-ten blocks as models for decimals

a *Base-ten blocks.* Using base-ten blocks, define the flat as one whole unit and tell the children to pretend that it is a cake. Then show one long and ask, "If I eat this piece of the cake, will I be eating a little part, a medium-sized part, or a big part of the cake? [Little part] How much of the cake will I be eating?" Let the children use base-ten blocks to determine that ten longs make one whole unit, so you would be eating one-tenth of the cake. Now show four longs and state that you plan to eat this much of the cake, then have the children determine that this is a medium-sized piece and is four-tenths of the whole cake. Repeat with other amounts, including those that are more than one whole unit, such as 12 longs.

Then tell the children that you are not hungry after all, so you have decided to feed the cake to the ants. Show one small cube and ask, "If I give this much to the ants, will they get a little part, a medium-sized part, or a big part of the cake? [A very little part] How much of the whole cake will they get?" Let them use base-ten blocks to determine that one hundred small cubes make one whole unit, so the ants would get *one-hundredth* of the cake. "Let's be nice and give them more."

Show 5 longs and 4 small cubes. "If we give them this much, will we be giving them a little part, a medium-sized part, or a big part of the cake? [A medium-sized part] Five longs is how much of the whole cake? [5 tenths] Four small cubes is how much of the whole cake? [4 hundredths] So we would be giving them 5 tenths 4 hundredths of the whole cake." Continue this questioning with other amounts.   **a**

When children are confident with models and oral language for tenths and hundredths, they are ready for the decimal symbols. To introduce the written symbols, explain that until now we have used decimals to tell how many tenths there are and that we can also use decimals to tell how many hundredths there are.

a *Place-value chart for hundredths.* Using base-ten blocks, show the flat and define it as the whole unit. Have the children show 4 longs and 2 small cubes, then ask, "How much of the whole unit is four longs? [4 tenths] How much of the whole unit is two small cubes?" [2 hundredths] Now show the chart in figure 18 and ask, "How many whole units do we have?" [Zero] Then write a 0 and a decimal point in the ones place. "How many tenths do we have?" [4] Write a 4 in the tenths place. "How many hundredths do we have?" [2] Write a 2 in the hundredths place. Then ask, "How much of the whole unit do we have?" [4 tenths 2 hundredths] Have children show other amounts and let them help you record the numerals in the chart.

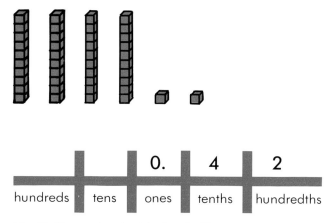

Fig. 18. Place-value chart for hundredths

When children are comfortable with recording the number in the chart, ask them if they remember why the decimal point is important. Help them realize that it shows us the ones place, so we can still tell what the number means when we take it out of the chart. Have the children show an amount and record it in the chart. Then have them take the number out of the chart, explain what the digits represent, and read the number as tenths and hundredths.   **a**

As children learn to model tenths and hundredths and write decimal symbols, continually emphasize the relative size of the numbers in relationship to the whole unit to help them make sense of these numbers. Children with well-developed understandings of decimals can associate the symbols with a sense of the quantities and can express this understanding with statements such as these: "That decimal is close to, but less than, one whole unit." "This decimal is close to, but greater than, one whole unit." "That decimal is close to zero." "This decimal is close to one-half."

a *Real-world decimals.* Collect examples of decimals used in real-world settings. Package labels and newspapers are an excellent source. Discuss the meanings of these numbers with the children. For example, a jar contains 0.95 liters of salad dressing, which is almost one whole liter. Other examples are shown in figure 19.   **a**

Computer disks	3.5 inches or 5.25 inches
Toothpaste	4.6 ounces
Nail polish	.5 fluid ounces
Paint	59.1 milliliters
Liquid paper	.6 fluid ounces
Note pad	38.1 mm × 50.8 mm
Tape	190.0 mm × 32.9 mm
Crayon box	9.2 cm × .79 cm
Meat	1.38 pounds
Bottle of pop	16.9 fluid oz
Popcorn salt	4.25 ounces
Pie crust mix	6.5 ounces
Cinnamon	1.12 ounces
Vegetable oil	1.41 liters
Salt	17.3 ounces
Glue stick	7.4 grams

Fig. 19. Real-world examples of decimals

Calculator displays. As children begin using calculators regularly, they will occasionally obtain decimal representations like 4.358976. To help them make sense of these decimals, cover up all digits to the right of 4 and use models to demonstrate that 4.3 is greater than 4. Then use the models to show that 4.35 is greater than 4.3, and then, by analogy, explain that 4.358976 is slightly larger than 4.3. Brief explanations like this will enable children to understand longer strings of digits in decimals. **a**

Comparing decimals. When children compare decimals like 0.07 and 0.4, the largest place value containing a nonzero digit should be considered first. "Which is the larger place value? [Tenths] How many tenths in the first number? [0 tenths] In the second number? [4 tenths] The second number is larger."

Working with partners and using base-ten blocks, one child can model 0.7 and the other can model 0.4. Now let them decide who has the larger number. Repeat with other pairs of decimals, such as 0.3 and 0.03, 0.7 and 0.72, 0.4 and 0.37, 0.8 and 0.09. **a**

tenths and hundredths as hundredths

When children understand decimals as tenths and hundredths, they are ready to learn that a decimal like 0.37 can also be understood and read as "37 hundredths." To learn this, children need to understand that 3 tenths is the same quantity as 30 hundredths, so that 0.37 = 30 hundredths + 7 hundredths, or 37 hundredths. This kind of understanding of equivalent decimals takes time. It appears easier because of the symbolism but is just as difficult conceptually as equivalent fractions.

Naming as hundredths. Use base-ten blocks to show how a decimal with tenths and hundredths can be named as hundredths. See figure 20. Ask children to show 1 tenth 3 hundredths with their base-ten blocks as you write the symbol, 0.13, on the chalkboard. "How many hundredths does it take to make one tenth? [10] Let's trade in our 1 tenth for 10 hundredths. Now how many hundredths do we have? [13] So, this decimal symbol, 0.13, tells us that we have 1 tenth 3 hundredths. What is another way we can say it?" [13 hundredths] Repeat with other decimals, such as 0.46, using models to show that 4 tenths equals 40 hundredths. If children are using models that are unscored on one side, they can first show the unscored side for tenths, and then turn it over

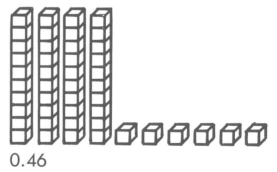

0.46

4 tenths 6 hundredths
40 hundredths 6 hundredths
46 hundredths

Fig. 20. Naming decimals as hundredths

to the scored side to find the equivalent number of hundredths.

a *Counting on a calculator.* Have children count by tenths orally and on a calculator. "Use your calculator. Press 0.1. Then press plus ($+$), then the equal key ($=$) nine times." After 0.9 is displayed, ask, "What do you think the calculator will show next? [10 tenths] What did it show?" [1.] Use base-ten blocks to show that 10 tenths equals 1. Continue counting by tenths, having students try to say the decimal name before it appears in the calculator display.

In a similar way, have students count by hundredths. Have them do keystroke counting by hundredths by pressing 0.01 $+$ $=$ $=$ $=$ . . . . "What comes after 9 hundredths? [10 hundredths] What does the calculator show?" [0.1, or 1 tenth] Use base-ten blocks to show that 1 tenth and 10 hundredths are equivalent. **a**

By developing this understanding of equivalent decimals, children acquire a better feel for the quantities and gain confidence when working with decimals. This knowledge should help them to make more sense of the symbols and be more flexible with computational procedures. This understanding will also set the stage for extending the study of decimals beyond tenths and hundredths.

diagnosing errors

A common error in working with decimals in the hundredths, as with tenths, is for children to ignore the decimal point and treat the decimals as whole numbers. In the second NAEP mathematics assessment, 59 percent of the nine-year-olds said that 7.94 was seven hundred ninety-four, whereas only 21 percent responded correctly (Carpenter et al. 1981). When comparing decimals, children might think that 1.4 is smaller than 0.39 because 14 is smaller than 39. This error can cause falsely inflated success rates when children compare or order decimals with the same number of decimal places. For example, although 0.17 is greater than 0.03 just as the whole number 17 is greater than 3, 0.17 is not greater than 0.3, but some children will think that it is.

Another common conceptual error occurs when children think that more digits to the right of the decimal point means a smaller number value. Because tenths are greater than hundredths, many children think that numbers with one decimal place (tenths) are greater than numbers with two decimal places (hundredths). These children would think that 0.4 is larger than 0.73. Children who make this error regard the smallest or "shortest" number as having the greatest value. If numbers have the same number of decimal places, some children think the larger number has the smaller value; for example, 0.83 is perceived as being smaller than 0.47. Others may argue that since digits added to the left of whole numbers make the number larger, so digits added to the right of the decimal point make the number smaller.

To help children correct these misconceptions, represent

numbers using base-ten blocks and emphasize that children should compare the whole number part first, then the tenths, and then the hundredths. For example, model 2.23 and 2.4 and compare them. Both numbers have 2 whole units, so next compare tenths. The first number has 2 tenths and the second number has 4 tenths; 4 tenths is larger than 2 tenths, so 2.4 is larger than 2.23.

Almost opposite to the error just discussed, some children will argue that 0.34 is larger than 0.5 because "hundreds" are larger than "tens." These children are thinking about whole numbers rather than the fractional parts that are pronounced with the "ths," as in "hundredths" and "tenths." The similarity between the whole number names and the fractional names causes problems for children. This similarity should be discussed with children and the names should always be clearly pronounced with added emphasis on the "ths."

Another conceptual error occurs when children read 0.15 hours as "15 minutes." They do not understand that 0.15 represents a fractional part of one hour and does not designate the number of minutes. This type of thinking also occurs when packages are labeled 3.25 pounds. Some children think this means 3 pounds 25 ounces.

addition and subtraction

If two weeks are used to develop fraction concepts in grade 4 relating real experiences and models to fraction symbols, it is easy for children to add and subtract like fractions. Payne (1976) reports almost 100 percent mastery in such a situation. Results were similar whether students were given a rule for adding and subtracting or whether they used their semantic knowledge of fractions to develop their own rule.

There have been recommendations that all fraction computation be delayed until grade 6 (Bezuk and

Cramer 1989). We agree that students should build a sound conceptual base of knowledge about the numbers themselves before doing computation, but it does not seem necessary to prohibit all computational work. Instead, it seems more reasonable to take a more deliberate approach to the development of computational procedures so that the procedures grow from the concepts of the numbers.

like fractions

The following activities for addition and subtraction with like fractions follow the sequence of oral work with models, written work with word names, and finally, written work with symbols. Note that there is no expectation that fractions be expressed in simplest form. Reducing to simplest form can profitably be delayed until later grades.

a *Addition and subtraction, orally.* Use the fraction strips and real-world problems to introduce addition and subtraction orally. "Ann has one-fourth of a candy bar. Sue has two-fourths of a candy bar. How much do they have altogether?" Have part of the class display one-fourth to show Ann's part. Have the other part of the class display two-fourths. "If we put the two parts together, how much do they have?" [Three-fourths] Repeat with other examples using different fraction strips.

"Suppose you have five-eighths of a beef jerky. Use your fraction strips to show that much." Have each student display five-eighths. "In one bite, you eat one-eighth. Fold down one-eighth. How much of the whole beef jerky do you have left? [Four-eighths] If you start with four-eighths and eat three-eighths, how much do you have left? [One-eighth] Can you show me with your strips?" Repeat with other fractions and similar stories. **a**

a *Addition and subtraction, with written words.* Use similar practical problems and write word names for problems two ways. "Mark used three-eighths of his sheet of paper for math and five-eighths for science. What part of a whole sheet did he use?" Have students demonstrate with their strips. "Can you tell the answer in eighths? [Eight-eighths] Can you tell the answer with wholes?" [One whole] Write the problem with words, and draw and shade a diagram as in figure 21. Relate the words to the diagram. Do similar problems with other fractions, including subtraction examples. **a**

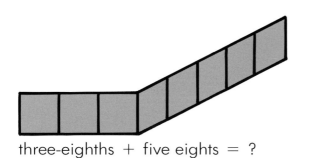

three-eighths + five eights = ?

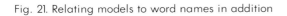

3 eighths + 5 eighths = ?

Fig. 21. Relating models to word names in addition

a *Addition and subtraction, with symbols.* "Chuck has seven-tenths of a liter of water. He drinks two-tenths of the liter. How much does he have left?" Have students demonstrate with their strips, then write the problem in words and show the connections among the strips, words, and fraction symbols, as shown in figure 22. "If we subtract two-tenths from seven-tenths, how much do we have left? [Five-tenths] How can we write it with fraction symbols?" Cover the word names and have students read the number sentence as "Seven-tenths minus two-tenths equals five-tenths." Insist on using the fraction names; never use "seven *over* ten" because of the need to emphasize the quantities in the problems.

Verbalizing a generalization is optional. If it is verbalized, use the phrase "Subtract the number of parts and write the size of the part" instead of the usual generalization about subtracting numerators and writing the denominator. **a**

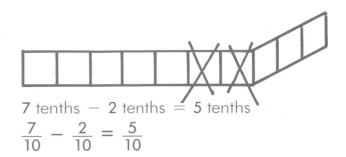

7 tenths − 2 tenths = 5 tenths

$$\frac{7}{10} - \frac{2}{10} = \frac{5}{10}$$

Fig. 22. Relating models, word names, and symbols for subtraction

related fractions

The same sequence works for adding and subtracting related fractions. Begin with fraction strips. Add and subtract, first using oral names, then written words, and finally written symbols.

a *Halves, fourths, and eighths.* It is easiest to begin with the related fractions halves, fourths, and eighths. "Use your fraction strips. Show me one-fourth of a candy bar in one hand. Now show me five-eighths in the other hand. How could we tell how much of a whole candy bar you have?" Someone might say, "One-fourth and five-eighths." "That is correct, but can we find a single fraction name for this amount? What do we need to trade? [The one-fourth for two of the eighths] Then how many eighths will there be altogether?" [Seven-eighths] Illustrate with two drawings, the word names, and the symbols, relating all three forms, as shown in figure 23.

Repeat with other examples, using both word names and symbols. As each example is completed, have students read the original and the final number sentences. **a**

a *Other related fractions.* Use similar examples with the related fractions thirds and sixths, and with fifths and tenths. Tenths are especially important because of their connection to decimals. "Show me two-tenths of a candy bar in one hand. Now show me one-fifth of the candy bar in the other hand. What do you need to do to tell me how

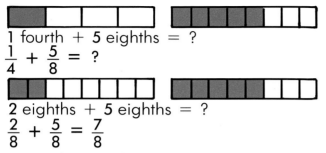

1 fourth + 5 eighths = ?

$$\frac{1}{4} + \frac{5}{8} = ?$$

2 eighths + 5 eighths = ?

$$\frac{2}{8} + \frac{5}{8} = \frac{7}{8}$$

Fig. 23. Relating models, oral names, and symbols for related fractions

much you have altogether using one fraction? [Trade one-fifth for two-tenths] How much do you have altogether?" [Four-tenths] Illustrate with a diagram, word names, and symbols as in figure 24.　　**a**

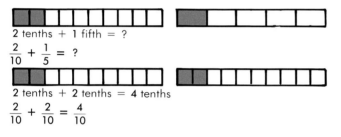

2 tenths + 1 fifth = ?

$$\frac{2}{10} + \frac{1}{5} = ?$$

2 tenths + 2 tenths = 4 tenths

$$\frac{2}{10} + \frac{2}{10} = \frac{4}{10}$$

Fig. 24. Adding related fractions using models

When adding and subtracting related fractions, emphasize needing pieces of the "same size" if the sum or difference is to be expressed as a single fraction. It is obvious from combining or separating with fraction strips that fractions of different sizes can be added and subtracted. The question is how to name the size of the resulting pieces. "Same size" is a clear way to say what must be done in a quantitative way.

decimals

Use the same sequence for adding and subtracting decimals. The importance of using concrete models and avoiding rules about decimal points cannot be overemphasized. Hiebert and Wearne (1986) provide convincing evidence that students who learn rules about operations on decimals without a quantitative background for the rules have great difficulty in

correcting errors and relating the rules to meaningful models.

The main idea is for students to add likes to likes—tenths to tenths and hundredths to hundredths. Reading two-place decimals as "tenths and hundredths" instead of just hundredths helps make the operations on decimals connect with the operations on quantities.

a *Add and subtract tenths.* Each student chooses a partner. "Will the person on the left hold up four-tenths? Will the person on the right hold up three-tenths? How much are you holding up together?" [Seven-tenths] Write each number in word form and in decimal form, relating the word names to the symbols, as shown in figure 25. Repeat examples, and include subtraction. Have students read the number sentence using the word *tenths*—not, for example, "zero point four"—to emphasize the quantities.　　**a**

4 tenths + 3 tenths = 7 tenths

0.4 + 0.3 = 0.7

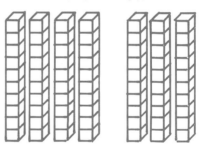

Fig. 25. Relating models, oral names, and decimal symbols for addition

a *Tenths and hundredths.* To emphasize combining like quantities, begin with tenths and with tenths/hundredths. "It rained 0.23 inches yesterday and 0.4 inches today. How much did it rain both days?" Illustrate the problem with base-ten blocks, and use word names and symbols as shown in figure 26. "Which pieces are the same size? [Tenths] Let's put tenths with tenths and hundredths with hundredths. How many tenths do we have? [Six] How many hundredths? [Three] How can we write a sum of 6 tenths 3 hundredths?" [0.63] Use other examples, adding and subtracting like units, and avoiding rules about decimal points.

a

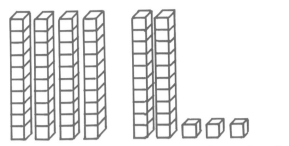

4 tenths + 2 tenths 3 hundredths
= 6 tenths 3 hundredths

0.4 + 0.23 = 0.63

Fig. 26. Relating models, oral names, and symbols for addition

suggestions for instruction

When teaching fractions and decimals, give more instructional time to the concept of the numbers themselves—relating real-life experiences, models, oral language, and symbols. Allow two weeks of practice at any grade level to achieve reasonable mastery. When children have had two weeks of development for fractions, it is easy to teach them decimal symbols and relate the symbols to models. Then, two or three days are needed to teach addition and subtraction of like fractions but substantially more for related fractions. The complexity of work on addition and subtraction in the upper grades can be reduced substantially by limiting the size of the denominators. Even so, at those levels, the development needs to be more deliberate and meaningless rules avoided.

Most textbooks will require major changes. Fourth-grade books often offer only a single lesson on the meaning of fractions then follow with fast-paced lessons on addition and subtraction. One lesson can barely scratch the surface of the conceptual

understanding needed to develop the operations. Teachers must adapt current textbooks to spend the needed seven to ten days on the meaning of fractions with lots of model work, oral naming, and connecting to symbols.

Also, more concrete model work is needed for decimals and operations on decimals. Rules are too easy to state and textbook exercises too easily rule-driven. Getting a sound foundation is the most important objective, since basic understanding is remembered longer and is more readily available for use in problem solving and applications.

The importance of helping students make connections among real-life examples, concrete models (paper strips), diagrams, oral names, and symbols cannot be overemphasized. In a study testing the multiplication of fractions with students in grades 4 and 5, Towsley (1989) found that students had much more difficulty correcting mistakes themselves when they could not make connections, especially when they were unable to connect to real-life experiences. The connections are not difficult to make. Learning how to make them requires time and practice.

There is overwhelming evidence that using the suggestions in this chapter can bring major improvements in achievement on fractions and decimals. It now will take determination and will to see these improvements take place in classrooms across the country.

bibliography

Behr, Merlyn J., Richard Lesh, Thomas R. Post, and Edward A. Silver. "Rational-Number Concepts." In *Acquisition of Mathematics Concepts and Processes,* pp. 91–126. New York: Academic Press, 1983.

Bezuk, Nadine S. "Fractions in the Early Childhood Mathematics Curriculum." *Arithmetic Teacher* 35 (February 1988): 56–60.

Bezuk, Nadine, and Kathleen Cramer. "Teaching about Fractions: What, When, and How?" In *New Directions for Elementary School Mathematics,* 1989 Yearbook of the National Council of Teachers of Mathematics, pp. 156–67. Reston, Va.: The Council, 1989.

Bruni, James V., and Helene J. Silverman. "Let's Do It: An Introduction to Fractions." *Arithmetic Teacher* 24 (November 1975): 538–46.

_____. "Let's Do It: Using Rectangles and Squares." *Arithmetic Teacher* 24 (February 1977): 97–102.

Carpenter, Thomas P., Mary K. Corbitt, Henry S. Kepner, Jr., Mary M. Lindquist, and Robert E. Reys. "Decimals: Results and Implications from National Assessment." *Arithmetic Teacher* 28 (April 1981): 34–37.

Coxford, Arthur F., and Lawrence W. Ellerbruch. "Fractional Numbers." In *Mathematics Learning in Early Childhood,* Thirty-seventh Yearbook of the National Council of Teachers of Mathematics, pp. 191–203. Reston, Va.: The Council, 1975.

Edge, Douglas. "Fractions and Panes." *Arithmetic Teacher* 34 (April 1987): 13–17.

Ellerbruch, Lawrence W., and Joseph N. Payne. "A Teaching Sequence from Initial Fraction Concepts through the Addition of Unlike Fractions." In *Developing Computational Skills,* 1978 Yearbook of the National Council of Teachers of Mathematics, pp. 129–47. Reston, Va.: The Council, 1978.

Galloway, Patricia J. "Achievement on Fractional Number Concepts, Ages Six through Ten, and on Decimals, Ages Eight through Ten." Ph.D. dissertation, University of Michigan, 1975.

Gunderson, Ethel. "Fractions—Seven-Year-Olds Use Them." *Arithmetic Teacher* 5 (November 1958): 233–38.

Gunderson, Agnes G., and Ethel Gunderson. "Fraction Concepts Held by Young Children." *Arithmetic Teacher* 4 (October 1957): 168–73.

Hiebert, James. "Children's Knowledge of Common and Decimal Fractions." *Education and Urban Society* 17 (August 1985): 427–37.

Hiebert, James, and Diana Wearne. "Procedures over Concepts: The Acquisition of Decimal Number Knowledge." In *Conceptual and Procedural Knowledge: The Case of Mathematics,* edited by James Hiebert, pp. 199–224. Hillsdale, N.J.: Lawrence Erlbaum, 1986.

Hollis, L. Y. "Mickey." "Teaching Rational Numbers—Primary Grades." *Arithmetic Teacher* 31 (February 1984): 36–39.

Kouba, Vicky L., Catherine A. Brown, Thomas P. Carpenter, Mary M. Lindquist, Edward A. Silver, and Jane O. Swafford. "Results of the Fourth NAEP Assessment of Mathematics: Number, Operations, and Word Problems." *Arithmetic Teacher* 35 (April 1988): 14–19.

McBride, John W., and Charles E. Lamb. "Using Concrete Materials to Teach Basic Fraction Concepts." *School Science and Mathematics* 86 (October 1986): 480–88.

Muangnapoe, Chatri. "An Investigation of the Learning of the Initial Concept and Oral/Written Symbols for Fractional Numbers in Grades Three and Four." Doctoral dissertation, University of Michigan, 1975. *Dissertation Abstracts International* 36 (1975): 1353A–54A. University Microfilms no. 75-20.415.

National Council of Teachers of Mathematics. *Curriculum and Evaluation Standards for School Mathematics.* Reston, Va.: The Council, 1989.

Ockenga, Earl, and Joan Duea. "Ideas." *Arithmetic Teacher* 25 (January 1978): 28–32.

Payne, Joseph N. "Review of Research on Fractions." In *Number and Measurement,* Papers from a Research Workshop, edited by Richard A. Lesh. Columbus, Ohio: ERIC/SMEAC, 1976.

Post, Thomas R. "Fractions: Results and Implications from National Assessment." *Arithmetic Teacher* 28 (May 1981): 26–31.

Pothier, Yvonne, and Daiyo Sawada. "Partitioning: The Emergence of Rational Number Ideas in Young Children." *Journal for Research in Mathematics Education* 14 (July 1983): 307–17.

Scott, Wayne R. "Fractions Taught by Folding Paper Strips." *Arithmetic Teacher* 28 (January 1981): 18–21.

Towsley, Ann. "The Use of Conceptual and Procedural Knowledge in the Learning of Concepts and Multiplication of Fractions in Grades 4 and 5." Doctoral dissertation, University of Michigan, 1989.

Vance, James H. "Estimating Decimal Products: An Instructional Sequence." In *Estimation and Mental Computation,* 1986 Yearbook of the National Council of Teachers of Mathematics, pp. 127–34. Reston, Va.: The Council, 1986.

Van de Walle, John, and Charles S. Thompson. "Let's Do It: Fractions with Counters." *Arithmetic Teacher* 27 (October 1980): 6–11.

_____. "Let's Do It: Fractions with Fraction Strips." *Arithmetic Teacher* 32 (December 1984): 4–9.

Zawojewski, Judith. "Ideas." *Arithmetic Teacher* 34 (December 1986): 18–25.

james bruni
roslynn seidenstein

10

geometric concepts and spatial sense

Early in their schooling children often conclude that whenever they do mathematics they use numbers. Mathematics programs for the young child tend to be dominated by arithmetic topics, with geometry representing a very small component of such programs. In one study of mathematics textbooks, for example, researchers found that, on average, *fewer than 7 percent* of the pages in K–4 texts were devoted to geometry (Fuys, Geddes, and Tischler 1988). Usiskin (1987) contends that currently no planned geometry program exists in the United States. Should we be alarmed that so little geometry is included in typical mathematics programs?

The answer is a resounding yes! For four main reasons, geometry *can* and *must* play a major role in mathematics programs for the young child, as indicated in the *Curriculum and Evaluation Standards for School Mathematics* (NCTM 1989):

1 Geometry relates to a child's world and is of intrinsic interest.
2 Geometry improves spatial ability, or "spatial sense."
3 Geometry is a vehicle for developing other mathematical concepts.
4 Geometry is a rich source for mathematics problems and of value in improving overall problem-solving ability.

Geometry, the study of shapes in space and spatial relationships, offers children one of the best opportunities to relate mathematics to the real world (Freudenthal 1973). Children's first experiences in trying to understand the world around them are spatial and geometric as they distinguish one object from another and determine how close or far away an object is. As they learn to move from one place to another, they use geometric and spatial ideas regularly to solve problems and make decisions in their everyday lives.

Spatial ability, or "spatial sense," can be improved through geometric activities. Spatial sense is essential in many tasks, such as writing letters and numerals, reading tables of information, following directions, making diagrams, reading maps, and visualizing objects that are described verbally.

The *Curriculum and Evaluation Standards for School Mathematics* includes geometry and spatial sense as major components of a quality K–4 mathematics program. Spatial sense is described as including "insights and intuitions about two- and three-dimensional shapes and their characteristics, the interrelationships of shapes, and the effects of changes to shapes" (NCTM 1989, p. 48).

The terms *spatial sense* and *spatial ability* can have many meanings. McGee (1979) described two broad types of spatial ability: (1) *spatial visualization*—the ability to mentally manipulate, rotate, twist, or invert a pictorially presented stimulus object; and (2) *spatial orientation*—the ability to comprehend the arrangement of elements within a visual pattern and the ability to not be confused by an object's changing orientation. Drawing on the pioneering work of Frostig and Horne (1964) on perceptual ability and the work of Hoffer (1977), Del Grande (1987) listed seven specific spatial abilities that have the greatest relevance to academic development. These are summarized in figure 1.

In a recent study Del Grande showed that the introduction of an activity-oriented geometry component into a mathematics program made it possible to improve the spatial-perception abilities of an experimental group of second-grade children (Del Grande 1985). Similarly, an earlier study by Perham (1978) indicated that developing general spatial abilities of first graders with a series of transformational geometry activities is possible. Perception is a learned skill, and appropriate teaching methods can modify and strengthen perceptual learning (Frostig and Maslow 1973). We can think of the learning of geometry and the improvement of spatial abilities as being interdependent (Del Grande 1987).

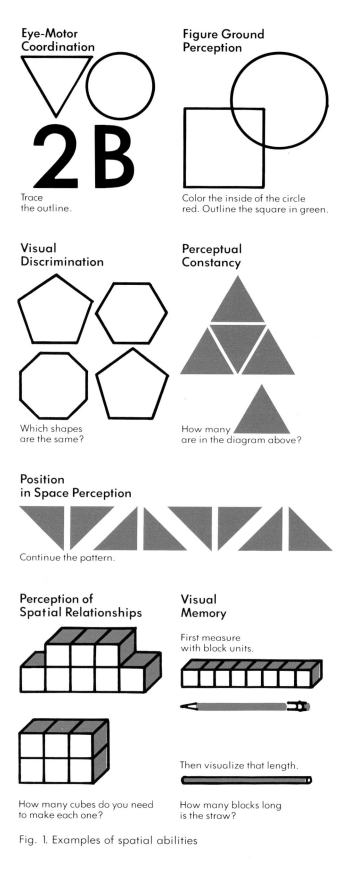

Eye-Motor Coordination

Trace the outline.

Figure Ground Perception

Color the inside of the circle red. Outline the square in green.

Visual Discrimination

Which shapes are the same?

Perceptual Constancy

How many are in the diagram above?

Position in Space Perception

Continue the pattern.

Perception of Spatial Relationships

How many cubes do you need to make each one?

Visual Memory

First measure with block units.

Then visualize that length.

How many blocks long is the straw?

Fig. 1. Examples of spatial abilities

Research suggests that mathematics achievement and spatial abilities are positively correlated (Guay and McDaniel 1977) and that spatial ability is related to problem-solving ability (Moses 1979). Geometry activities that improve spatial ability can also improve a student's success in mathematics in general.

As we develop mathematical concepts, we use more concrete materials such as multilink cubes, base-ten blocks, pattern blocks, fraction strips, and such representational devices as arrays, graphs, tables, charts, and diagrams. Geometric-spatial abilities are presumed when such concrete materials are used. For example, to use a cube to represent 1000, children need to visualize the large cube as being made up of 10 layers of 100 cubes each (see chapter 4). Spatial ability is evident in conceptualization (chapter 2), computation (chapter 8), measurement (chapter 11), fractions and decimals (chapter 9), and problem solving (chapter 3).

Bley and Thornton (1981) indicate that students who have difficulties with spatial relationships will also have difficulties in the visualization of the number system when presented in geometric ways. When determining the distance between two points on a ruler, children often count the line segments marking off units instead of the "spaces" between those markings. In the same way, in playing a board game, they often count the place where their marker is resting as the first step in making a move of a given number of steps.

When concrete and pictorial models are part of an instructional sequence, we cannot ignore the "hidden" geometric-spatial sense component of those models. Developing children's concepts of geometry and their spatial sense makes it more likely that they can benefit from the use of models and diagrams.

When we help children become better problem solvers, we often encourage them to visualize the problem or make a diagram. In doing so, we are encouraging them to use geometric concepts and spatial sense to solve problems. Experiences with geometric and spatial activities can nurture problem-solving strategies.

Some children find it easier to solve problems using a

geometric-spatial approach instead of an analytic approach (Krutetskii 1976). In studies of the mathematical abilities of students, Krutetskii identified two types of persons: those who approach problems analytically and those who approach problems geometrically. An analytical approach involves sequential, logical, symbolic, and verbal kinds of thinking. A geometric approach is more intuitive, spatial, nonverbal, and holistic.

Analytical thinking dominates traditional mathematics programs. This heavy emphasis on verbal and symbolic thinking can be especially disadvantageous for children for whom English is a second language. As the activities in this chapter indicate, geometric and spatial activities can develop more spatial and nonverbal types of thinking while being a source of genuine problem-solving opportunities.

This chapter includes a framework for planning geometry instruction, along with suggested experiences for the geometry and spatial-sense components of an exemplary mathematics program for the young child.

a framework for planning geometry instruction

In learning geometry, children need to be actively involved in investigating interesting problems using concrete materials in a carefully planned and sequenced program.

The work of two Dutch educators, Dina van Hiele-Geldof and Pierre Marie van Hiele (van Hiele 1984; van Hiele-Geldof 1984) showed that many students who have early success in mathematics frequently have difficulty with a formal course in geometry in high school. They identified five sequential levels of understanding of geometric concepts:

Level 0: Visualization. The student identifies a figure such as a square by its appearance *as a whole*. When calling a figure a square, the student focuses on the total figure and not the relationships of the sides or the angles.

Level 1: Analysis. The student begins to focus on specific properties of figures through observations and experimentation. For example, he or she can show that opposite sides of a rectangle are the same length and that its angles are all the same size. But the interrelationships among the figures is not yet apparent. For example, the student does not yet realize that a square can be thought of as a special kind of rectangle or that a rectangle can be considered a special type of parallelogram.

Level 2: Informal Deduction. The student can now use informal, logical reasoning to deduce properties of figures. For example, he or she knows that if one pair of opposite sides of a quadrilateral is congruent and parallel, then the other pair of sides must also be congruent and parallel. The student can organize discoveries about properties of figures and see how definitions are used. Middle school students might be at this level if they have had experience at the previous levels.

Level 3: Deduction and *Level 4: Rigor.* These levels refer to the more formal and abstract study of geometry typical of high school and college courses.

The levels are sequential. Success at one level depends on having the geometric thinking characteristic of the preceding levels. The van Hieles contend that the reason so many students have difficulty with geometry is that while students are thinking at one level, the instruction is geared to a higher level. American follow-up studies indicate that although high school courses in geometry may intend to present geometry at level 3, students are typically functioning at lower levels, even as low as level 0, and are doomed to have difficulty (Shaughnessy and Burger 1985).

Movement from one level to the next is not a natural, evolutionary process depending on a child's age or maturity. Consequently, the way a teacher organizes geometry instruction can make a significant difference in the student's advancement through the levels.

The geometric content and activities described in the remainder of this chapter are organized into two parts based on the van Hiele levels: (1) Introductory Geometric Experiences, with investigations beginning at level 0; and (2) Building on Introductory Experiences, extending investigations to level 1 thinking. Each part includes activities for exploring spatial relationships (location and direction), two- and three-dimensional geometric shapes, and spatial visualization. Children are encouraged to examine, describe, construct, transform, and identify special properties of shapes and how they relate to each other.

Although linear, area, and volume are important aspects of shape and space, investigations of these attributes appear in chapter 11.

introductory geometric experiences

Preschoolers, kindergarteners, and children in the early grades are generally at level 0, where they focus on the appearance of a shape *as a whole.* At this level, children need to be involved in the manipulation of models of geometric figures—direct, tactile, and visual explorations in which they draw, copy, trace, enlarge, combine, or modify physical objects (Crowley 1987). This geometric knowledge is used to extend investigations to level 1 thinking, with a focus on specific properties of shapes.

describing location and movement

Long before coming to school, the typical child has begun using terms for spatial relations. Children use words for location to describe the relative positions of themselves to another person or an object: "I'm in the house." "I'm on my bike." Through ordinary, everyday activities children learn many other terms: *front, back, above, below, between, next to, top, bottom, same side, different side*. Terms for movement describe how a person or an object moves to another place— *toward, back and forth, from here to there, frontward, backward, sideways, shortest path, longest path, straight path,* and *curved path*.

At first, the teacher's role is to encourage the children to use spatial terms in a variety of meaningful contexts, first to describe their own position and movements and then to describe the positions or movements of other persons or objects. Gradually, children can use representations such as diagrams and pictures.

Sides of a line for teams. To organize two teams, place a cord or strip of masking tape on the floor. Ask some of the children to stand on one side of the tape and others to stand on the other side. "All those wearing something red, stand on the side of the tape toward the door. If you are not wearing red, stand on the other side of the tape— toward the window."

Talk about who is standing on each side of the tape. "Who is on the same side of the tape as Martin? Is Scott on the same side of the tape as Jessica or on a different side?" The children can then form a line on each side of the tape, and you can talk about their order on line: "Who is in front of Jose? Who is behind Judy?" **a**

Similar ideas and language are used for classification activities.

A block fence as a line. Have children create a wall or fence using blocks or cubes and place their favorite objects or pictures of favorite characters on either side of the wall. For example, for a set of Sesame Street characters, ask, "Who is on the *same side* of the wall as Big Bird? Who is on the other side of the wall? Who is sitting *on* the wall?"

Use the same idea in reading stories to describe the location of characters. **a**

paths

Movements along a *path* can be described and translated into physical actions and then into pictures or diagrams. The children can also make up stories corresponding to a picture or diagram.

Paths in stories. Read a story, such as "Hansel and Gretel," and talk about how the children tried to remember their path into the forest. Act out the story by having two children walk among a "forest" of desks to a place on the other side of the room using a ball of yarn to make a trail or path. Then have them find their way back by following the path formed by the yarn. **a**

Paths in an amusement park. Tell a story about your visit to an amusement park. Give each child a sheet with a diagram of an amusement park with several rides indicated, along with an entrance and an exit. As you describe your visit, have children use a crayon to draw a path representing your journey through the park as you draw a similar path on the overhead projector (fig. 2). Give children another sheet with this diagram and have them draw a path representing the order in which they would go on the rides. In the beginning, it would be useful to limit how many rides they can go on. Once they have the idea, extend the number of possible rides or add a ticket office or refreshment stand. Highlight how the diagram tells the story of the trip to the park by having the children recreate the stories from the diagrams (fig. 3). **a**

The ability to follow a path along a flat surface is a skill needed as children learn to form letters and numerals. Current research emphasizes the effectiveness of helping children develop a motor plan, a description of the sequence of actions needed to form a particular numeral (Baroody 1987). The teacher first describes the movement for forming a numeral, then the children describe the movement before, during, and after writing it. Straight paths are needed for linear measurement and closed paths for area.

Fig. 2. Path for amusement park visit

Fig. 3. Path for ride preferences

a *Open and closed paths.* Create diagrams of "fences" using different curves, as shown in figure 4. "Pretend that a dog is chasing a cat but cannot cross over the fence. Can the dog catch the cat? Draw a path to show how." Having children build fences with blocks or a piece of string or yarn and place objects within those fences is a good way for them to act out the problem before drawing a path to record the strategy they used.   **a**

After learning basic spatial terms, children can learn directional terms such as *to the right* and *to the left*. Location and direction activities are fun on a geoboard

or dot paper. Working in pairs, children can help each other make sense of the spatial terms used.

Fig. 4. Open and closed paths

Find the hidden treasure. Place a washer on one of the pegs on a geoboard. Give clues to describe the location of the "treasure": "It's in the upper right-hand corner. It's in the third row. It's in the middle of that row. It's in the lower left-hand corner. It's at the beginning of that bottom row." Have the students place a washer on their boards to show where they think the treasure is. Take advantage of errors by having students describe the actual location of any misplaced treasures. **a**

 Simon says. Describe how you are putting an elastic band on the geoboard. Have children follow and do the same on their geoboards. Start with simple paths such as designs, letters, numerals, or combinations of shapes (fig. 5). A transparent geoboard on an overhead projector is helpful. **a**

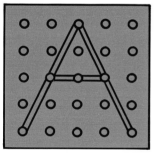
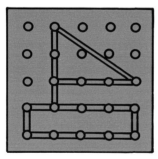

Fig. 5. Making designs on a geoboard

locating regions on a plane

Reading maps and tables requires one to locate a specific section or region on a flat surface or plane. For example, on a map, "A3" represents a specific region.

As children develop the ability to order numbers and letters, they can place them on a diagram in a corresponding "spatial" order (e.g., B above A, C above B, etc., and 2 to the right of 1, 3 to the right of 2, etc.).

Cubetown. On a large piece of posterboard draw a 5 × 5 grid (see fig. 6). Have children use cubes to build the city of Cubetown. Tell them that the streets in Cubetown are numbered 1, 2, 3, . . ., and run from left to right on the grid. The avenues are also numbered 1, 2, 3, . . ., but run from bottom to top. In Cubetown only one building can be on each section of land. The height of the building is the sum of the avenue and the street numbers. For example, the building on the lower left-hand corner is only two stories (cubes) high because it's on 1st Street and 1st Avenue (1 + 1 = 2). The building on the upper right-hand section of land is ten stories high because it is on 5th Street and 5th Avenue (5 + 5 = 10).

Variations include using dots instead of numerals and more or fewer streets and avenues. Examples of grid systems occur in seating charts, street maps, bulletin board displays, and so on. **a**

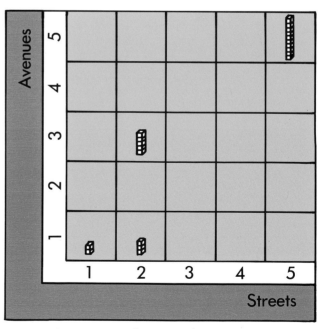

Fig. 6. Cubetown, sum of streets and avenues

starting with three-dimensional shapes

It is natural to begin investigations of geometric shapes by exploring three-dimensional objects in a child's environment. Children should have opportunities to describe and compare three-dimensional objects (e.g., "It rolls," "It has a pointed top," "It's flat on the bottom and on the top") and to sort and classify them. As the properties of specific figures are discovered and verbalized, you can informally introduce their names (e.g., sphere, cylinder, rectangular solid, cube, pyramid, cone) but only after they have explored and discussed their unique properties. Exploring and describing the characteristics of the shapes of objects should be the focus, not memorizing their special names.

Children need to have direct experiences with three-dimensional objects so they can see that two-dimensional shapes are components of three-dimensional shapes. For example, a rectangle is the shape of a face of a box. They need to visualize how real objects are formed, the relationships of their parts, and how they are represented in pictures and in diagrams.

The block building that many children do in preschool settings is a good introduction to investigating the similarities and differences among three-dimensional shapes and how they can be used.

 Sorting shapes. To extend informal experiences with shapes, have children make a collection of boxes and containers of all sorts—toothpaste, salt, cereal, cake mix, macaroni, soup cans, and so on. "Let's sort the shapes. Put the ones that roll here. Put the ones that don't roll there." (See fig. 7.) Have the children sort the containers in other ways—by size, category (food or not food), type of food, or whether a container has a top or not.

Since the dominant shapes in the collection of containers will be cylinders and rectangular solids, it is

Roll   Don't Roll

Fig. 7. Sorting boxes and containers

important also to use wooden or plastic geometric solids of other shapes, such as cones, pyramids, or spheres (fig. 8). Such a collection will allow children to work with many shapes, describe their characteristics, and sort the shapes in a variety of ways. **a**

Fig. 8. Geometric solids

Sort by "Alike" and "Different." Put one solid on a tray. Ask, "Can you find another solid that is like this one? Put it on the tray. How are the two solids alike? Can you find another solid that is like the first two in the same way?" (rolls, number of corners, straight edges, etc.)

Put a solid in a paper bag. "You can reach in and feel it but you can't look. Can you choose another solid like the one you felt?" **a**

At this point it is not important for children to use precise geometric terms, such as *rectangular solid, sphere,* or *pyramid.* A teacher can use those terms informally, but children should use more informal language. For example, although a child is likely to call a sphere a ball or describe it as "round all over" or "a shape that rolls," it is more important to observe the special characteristics of a shape and use natural language. If students use incorrect language like calling a sphere a circle or a cube a square, take advantage of the opportunity to point out the differences.

Encourage children to sort the solids in a variety of ways (e.g., rolls or doesn't roll, pointed or flat top, stackable or not stackable). As they begin to observe and describe the characteristics of different shapes using the solid models, have children relate those shapes to objects in their environment, the two-dimensional pictures, and diagrams of three-dimensional shapes.

a *Build a town.* As a social studies project, have students build a town with cardboard containers or blocks (see fig. 9). They will need to decide which containers are best to suggest the shape of different buildings, as well as the best arrangement for the buildings. "Where should the stores, firehouse, police station, houses, factories, and so on, be located?" By having them create the town with a grid on paper or posterboard, you can easily use this model to develop activities involving movement along a path as described in the previous section. **a**

a *Pictures of shapes.* Have children locate pictures in magazines or newspapers with shapes like the solid models and create a display of the pictures and the matching solids. **a**

Fig. 9. Using boxes and blocks to build a town

Have children talk about how some shapes are "almost" like one of the solids. A desk might be "almost" like the shape of a box, but the "top" is bigger than the "bottom." This discussion will help them observe more carefully the special characteristics of certain shapes (e.g., the opposite faces of a rectangular solid are identical or congruent).

As children work with these three-dimensional models, it is valuable to explore how these structures look from different perspectives.

a *Building structures.* Give children the opportunity to build structures with the solids. Take pictures or sketch the solids from different viewpoints (e.g., top, sides) and then use the pictures as task cards to build the original structure. **a**

a *Different views.* Place three shapes on a large piece of paper on which a 3 × 3 grid has been drawn, as shown in figure 10. Prepare cards that show four views for the three shapes, one from each side. Ask children to place a card on each side to show what the collection looks like from that side. The child can first do the activity by looking from each side and matching what he or she sees with a card. Then try to have the child put the cards with correct arrangements in each place before going around the square to check vantage points. **a**

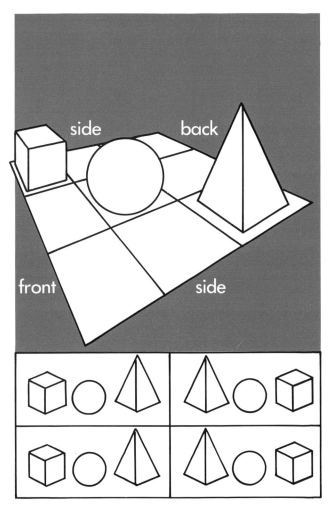

Fig. 10. Views of solids from each side of a grid

from three-dimensional to two-dimensional shapes: connecting activities

Investigations of the overall shapes of three-dimensional models lead naturally to an examination of the faces of those models and their shapes. When children sort geometric solids in different ways, they discover that some solids have all "flat parts," others have some flat parts, some have "rounded parts," whereas still others have no flat parts. After making this discovery, children can focus on the faces of three-dimensional shapes and the proper use of the term *face*.

a *Matching faces.* Point to the face of a shape. Have children find another face with the same size and shape. In building structures with blocks, children frequently need to match faces of solids that are the same size. **a**

a *How many faces?* Challenge children to guess how many faces each solid has and then count them, marking each face with a piece of tape to help them keep track of which faces were counted. **a**

a *Outlines of faces.* Trace the outlines of faces of solids onto posterboard cards and have the children try to determine from these outlines what block(s) have those faces. Have them check their guesses by placing the corresponding faces of the blocks they choose directly on the card (fig. 11). Some children may be able to make task cards like these. **a**

exploring two-dimensional shapes

Children's initial exposure to such shapes as triangles gives them only a superficial understanding. Given a diagram showing several shapes and asked to color only the triangles (fig. 12), many young children will consider only shape (c) a triangle because they think a

Fig. 11. Matching faces with solids

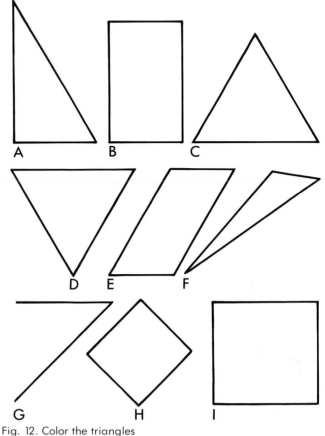

Fig. 12. Color the triangles

different orientations. Such activities suggest that a shape does not change when it is moved along a linear path (translated), rotated, or flipped.

triangle must have equal sides or a "bottom side going straight across" (Fisher 1978; Shaughnessy and Burger 1985). Also, children may consider shape (i) as a square but not shape (h). They may complete shape (g) mentally as a triangle, ignoring the need for a closed path with three sides.

To develop a more complete understanding of these geometric terms, children need to view two-dimensional shapes in different orientations. In completing a jigsaw puzzle, a child needs to find the correct piece for a specific location by visualizing the shape in different orientations. Similarly, when creating or copying a design or pattern with stickers or a rubber stamp as in figure 13, a child is organizing congruent shapes in

Fig. 13. Patterns: Shapes with different orientations

Shapes booklets. Have children look for examples of two-dimensional shapes in their environment (classroom, school, home, etc.) and find pictures of shapes within other shapes. Talk about how shapes look in different positions. Make booklets, a bulletin-board display, or a class collage displaying the collection of shapes. **a**

Covering with pattern blocks. Outline a figure on triangular grid paper as in figure 14. Find different ways the space within an outline can be completely covered with pattern blocks. **a**

Fig. 14. Covering with pattern blocks

Combining shapes helps children visualize shapes in different orientations. Tangrams and tangramlike activities are excellent for that purpose (fig. 15). For young children, a limit on the number of pieces allows greater success.

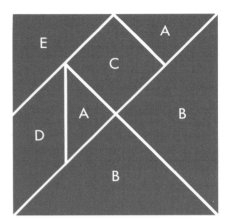

Fig. 15. Using tangram pieces to cover

Shapes from congruent right triangles. Give each child three paper squares, with each side about 8 centimeters. Have them fold each along a diagonal and then cut it into triangles. Challenge students to take two triangles and put them together so that the equal, or congruent, sides are touching. Have them experiment with different ways of doing this and discuss the three results (fig. 16). They may need to tape some models together and flip them

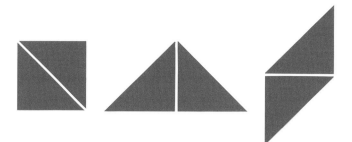

Fig. 16. Shapes from two congruent right triangles

to prove that a particular way is or is not different from one already used.

For an extension, have children use four triangles to make different shapes, as in figure 17.　　**a**

Children need many opportunities to construct different

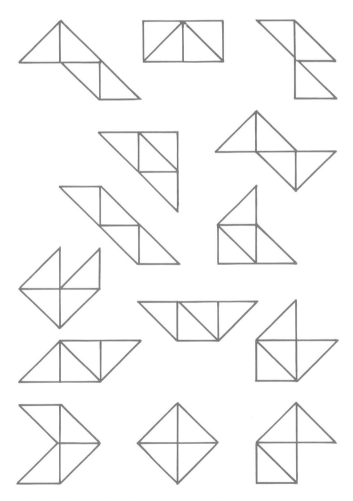

Fig. 17. Shapes from four congruent right triangles

shapes by tracing shapes from edges of blocks, using templates, cutting out paper regions into different shapes, and drawing shapes freehand and with a straightedge.

Geoboards are valuable tools for helping children construct and analyze models of two-dimensional shapes. After informal exploration, children can transfer the concrete model to a representational format on dot paper (fig. 18). It is easiest for children if the dots on paper are arranged just like the geoboard.

Fig. 18. Transferring geoboard model to dot paper

a *Investigate squares and triangles.* Use nine-dot geopaper. Ask, "What's the smallest square you can make? What's the largest square you can make? How many different squares can you make?" Talk about how the squares are different (e.g., in size or position). Then, conduct a similar investigation with triangles (fig. 19).　　**a**

a *Transforming shapes.* Use geoboards and have children make the shape shown under the "Start" heading in figure 20. Ask, "What can you do to make a shape that is a rectangle but not a square?" Demonstrate the figure under "Finish." "How is the new shape like the old? How is it different?" Encourage children to compare the number,

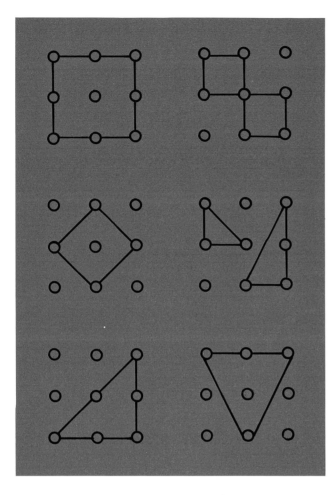

Fig. 19. Investigating squares and triangles

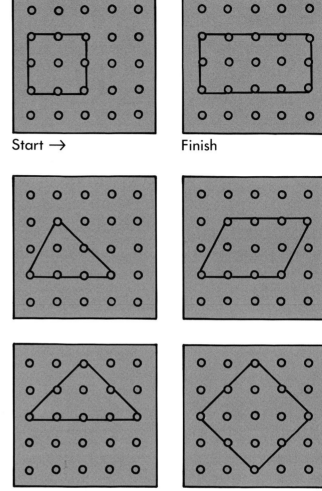

Start →   Finish

Fig. 20. Transforming shapes on a geoboard

length, and position of the sides and the number and position of the vertices (corners).

Logo "turtle geometry" activities on a computer are also helpful in constructing shapes (see chapter 13). As a child plans the steps needed to create a Logo picture, he or she needs to visualize the orientation of the shape to be made and how the Logo turtle must travel to create a path representing the shape.

symmetry

Symmetry arises naturally as children create designs and locate, examine, and construct shapes. A figure has *line* or *bilateral symmetry* if the figure can be folded along the line so that its parts match exactly.

Children often make pattern-block designs with line symmetry (fig. 21) and make paper figures by folding and cutting a sheet of paper (fig. 22).

Children can use a mirror to explore possible reflections and to develop an intuitive understanding of ways to "fold" a figure so that both sides match (i.e., find lines of symmetry). The emphasis is placed on finding out whether a figure has line symmetry and whether it can be shown in more than one way.

As children create designs and explore line symmetry, they may observe shapes and designs that they think must have a line of symmetry but do not, as in figure 23. Trying to find lines of symmetry may be frustrating because children realize a special pattern or balance is shown. That special property is indeed "symmetry," but

Fig. 21. Line symmetry with pattern blocks

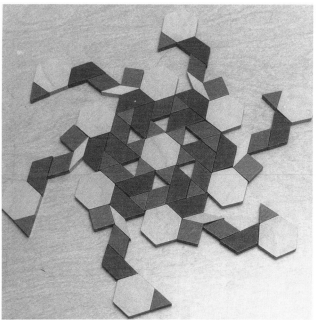

Fig. 23. Rotational symmetry but not line symmetry

visualize overlapping regions, and as they construct models.

Fig. 22. Line symmetry with paper cut-outs

it is called *rotational symmetry.* If you turn or rotate the shape or design, at some point or points during a complete rotation, the shape or design looks just like the original.

building on introductory experiences

Introductory experiences can be expanded as numbers are related to paths and coordinates, as students

creating paths as number lines

Although number-line models are evident in mathematics programs, teachers often find that children have difficulty with them. A child may count the markings along the number line instead of the number of spaces moved. Children will benefit by creating numbered paths in different ways and exploring movements along those paths prior to the use of the number line.

Building on their previous experience with paths, children can partition them in different ways, compare paths that have been partitioned, and explore problems by using more than one path at a time.

Begin with the creation of numbered paths on which children themselves can move. Then progress to diagrams as suggested in the following activities.

Giant postal carrier. Make up a story about a giant who is a postal carrier delivering mail to the houses along a "pretend" street in your classroom. Place several chairs (about 45 cm apart) in one straight row along the front of the classroom. At one end, label the first desk "Post Office." Have one child sit at each of the desks and get ready for the mail delivery. The giant starts at the post office. "How many giant steps to the first house (next desk)?" [One] "To the next house?" [One] Have one child be the giant and, starting at the post office, deliver a stack of "mail" to different people on the street.

Before each delivery, ask, "How many giant steps do you think it is to Eric's house?" Notice if anyone counts the desks from one house to another and not the spaces in between the houses.

Children develop an understanding of the unit and direction of movements along a numbered path—*five steps toward, in the direction of, away from, in the opposite direction from.* Follow up these first-hand experiences with a diagram representing the movements.

Diagram of postal carrier. Draw a line segment on the chalkboard or overhead projector to represent the "street" with houses all the same distance apart. Label houses for students who were not part of the dramatization as shown in figure 24. Ask questions to express movement and direction: "How many steps does the giant have to take to travel from Mary's house to Tom's house? In what direction? If the giant goes from Eric's house two steps *in the direction of* Adele's house, where will he be? If he went three steps in the direction of the post office and ended up at Sam's house, where did the giant start out?"

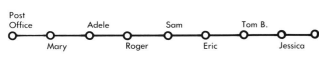

Fig. 24. Houses for mail delivery

numbered paths as coordinate grids

Numbered paths can be extended to coordinate grids to identify a specific location on a flat surface or plane. Children learn to move along two numbered paths in a specific way and are introduced to the concept of "ordered pairs" of numbers.

Mail delivery to streets and avenues. Arrange the desks as "houses" in a rectangular array (in rows and columns), with the post office at one corner, and make street signs for each "road." Roads going in one direction (e.g., vertically) might be named 0 Street, 1st Street, 2d Street, and so on, whereas roads going in the opposite direction (e.g., horizontally) can be named 0 Avenue, 1st Avenue, 2d Avenue, and so on, as shown in figure 25. Each house is located at the corner, or intersection, of two roads (e.g., a street and an avenue) and will have an address consisting of two numbers. The first digit indicates the street and the second digit denotes the avenue. Have "mail" ready to be delivered with only

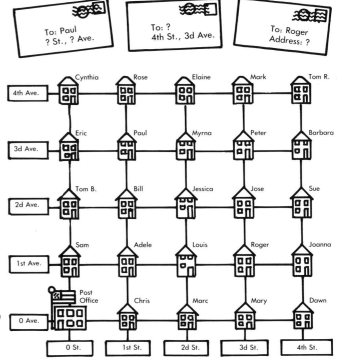

Fig. 25. Mail delivery to streets and avenues

the address given. Have students figure out which house the mail is to be delivered to and how to get there from the post office.

Many variations of this activity are possible (e.g., give the person's name and have him or her supply the address or have the person describe how to get from one house to another).

visualizing overlapping regions

Children need a facility with the concepts of "inside" and "outside" when they sort attribute blocks. Figure 26 shows that all the orange blocks go inside the

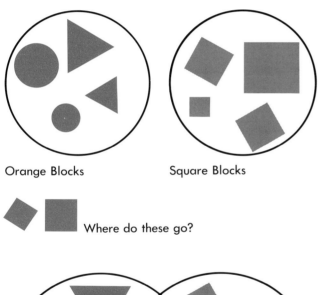

Orange Blocks   Square Blocks

Where do these go?

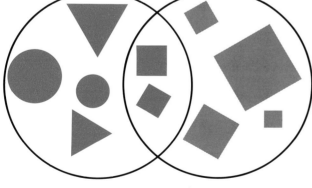

Orange Blocks   Square Blocks

Fig. 26. Deciding where to place orange square blocks

orange fence and all the square blocks inside the black fence. Ask, "Where do the orange squares go?" After moving them back and forth from one "yard" to another, children will begin to realize that they need to find a way to put those orange squares inside the black yard and the orange yard at the same time. A possible solution is shown. Children can see the region common to the two original "yards," that is, the intersection of the two circular regions.

A two-way classification diagram poses a challenge by making use of two spatial terms simultaneously, as shown in the example in figure 27.

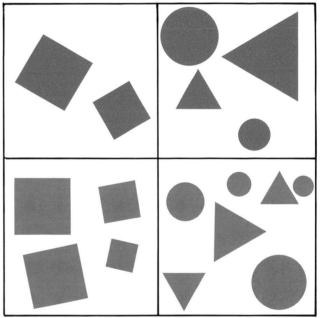

Fig. 27. Two-way classification with attribute blocks

constructing models of three-dimensional shapes

The introductory experiences with three-dimensional objects described previously form a basis for a more systematic investigation of the specific parts of three-dimensional objects or figures and the relationships among them. Such investigations include not only identifying and counting the faces, edges, and vertices of three-dimensional objects but also identifying faces

Geometric Concepts and Spatial Sense   219

that are the same size and shape (congruent), recognizing pairs of faces that intersect and the edge they have in common, locating faces in parallel planes (i.e., planes that would never intersect no matter how far they were extended), and exploring angles formed by intersecting edges and intersecting faces. Irregular shapes are explored, along with such standard three-dimensional shapes as spheres, cylinders, and rectangular solids. As children make, use, and transform models of such three-dimensional shapes, they visualize them from different orientations, relate the two-dimensional pattern, or "net," for making them to the three-dimensional shape, and connect the actual shapes with the diagrams depicting them.

Constructing a model of a three-dimensional shape focuses students' attention on its specific characteristics. Figure 28 shows a cube and Geo D-Stix models. Discussing how the models are like the cube and how they are different helps to develop children's understanding of specific characteristics of shapes. For example, a cube must have twelve edges all the same length and eight vertices, its faces must be squares, and its edges must all meet at square corners.

Children can use a variety of different kinds of commercial and homemade materials to construct

models. Some examples are Geo D-Stix, straws, or pipe cleaners, and Plasticine; or toothpicks and marshmallows or gumdrops, as illustrated in figure 29. Terms such as *perpendicular* and *parallel* can be introduced informally.

Fig. 29. Three-dimensional models with varied materials

Three-dimensional shapes can be made from paper, cardboard, or plastic regions. Some commercial materials have regions that snap together (fig. 30). By cutting, folding, and taping, children can make paper models from patterns, or "nets." This can improve children's ability to visualize the nets of polyhedra (Bourgeois 1986). Patterns are cut along dark lines already drawn on paper or posterboard, folded along dotted lines, and taped as in figure 31. These models can be used as boxes for special gifts, decorated as ornaments, or used in many different ways.

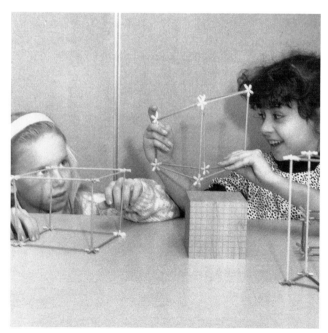

Fig. 28. Comparing Geo D-Stix models with a cube

Fig. 30. Plastic models

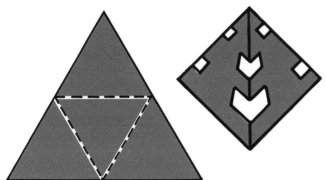

Fig. 31. Making a three-dimensional model from a two-dimensional net

Making three-dimensional models, as in figure 32, helps children visualize their parts. When challenged to match the nets to the models, children have the least difficulty in recognizing the nets of pyramids and triangular prisms where the triangular faces are arranged around the base (Bourgeois 1986).

More able students can be challenged not only to match nets to models but to find different nets that can be used to make a particular model.

Pentomino models. Have children draw pentominoes, a closed figure made with five squares attached with a complete side, as in

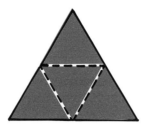

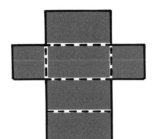

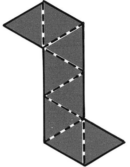

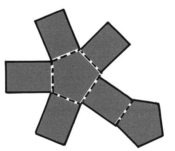

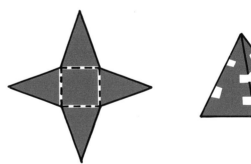

Fig. 32. Matching three-dimensional model with nets

figure 33. Squared paper or dot paper is helpful. "How many pentominoes are there?" [12] "How many can be folded to make an open box?" [8]

a

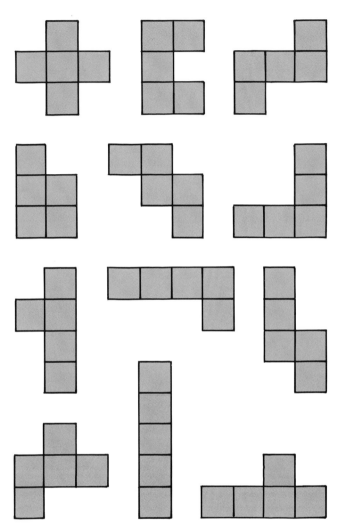

Fig. 33. Pentominoes

constructing dynamic models of two-dimensional shapes

Making models of two-dimensional shapes that can be easily altered or transformed is effective in developing students' understanding of the shape's essential properties (Bruni 1977). In fact, in constructing such models, learners can discover properties and relationships that they may not have been aware of when using a more static diagram.

Models of polygons made with cardboard or plastic strips (geostrips) and brass fasteners are shown in figure 34. In making these models, children will realize that it is difficult to keep the figures in place because the strips move and the model becomes distorted. Only triangles do not lose their original shape—they are rigid. This property of a triangle, its rigidity, makes it a very important shape in construction. Children can look for triangles in their environment and discover how their rigidity makes structures stronger.

Fig. 34. Nonrigid and rigid figures with geostrips

Children can also figure out how to make nontriangular models keep their shape. Using a strip to connect nonadjacent vertices, they can make the model rigid, in fact, they construct a diagonal of the polygon.

More convenient materials for constructing "dynamic" models of two-dimensional shapes are paper or card-stock strips that can be joined together with tape as indicated in figure 35. The advantage of these models is that the angles formed can easily be altered, transforming one figure into another. This process facilitates an understanding of the inherent properties of two-dimensional geometric shapes and begins to focus students on the interrelationships among these different shapes.

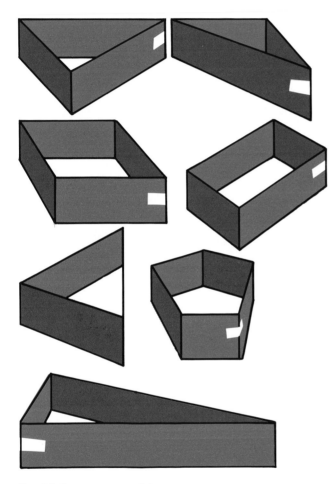

Fig. 35. Paper strip models

a *Paper geometry strips.* Have a group of children investigate how many *different* triangles they can make using paper or card-stock strips that are 2 cm × 24 cm. Have them describe the characteristics of, and the similarities and differences among, the triangles. Challenge them to sort the triangles into two sets in different ways. Then

have them sort the triangles into three sets in different ways.

Extend the activity by having children construct as many *different* four-sided figures, or quadrilaterals, as they can. Again have them sort their figures into two, three, or four sets and describe what characteristics they used to sort the models. **a**

As children make and describe these models, basic properties of two-dimensional geometric shapes emerge as an inherent part of the activities. Specific vocabulary can be introduced as children use their own language to describe properties. For example, they may describe some triangles as having "all the same sides" (equilateral), "two sides the same" (isosceles), or "no sides the same" (scalene). Some triangles may have "a fat corner" or an angle larger than a corner, or right angle (obtuse), whereas others may have "a square corner" (right angle). Still other triangles may have "only skinny corners" (acute).

Similarly, when children make and transform quadrilateral models, specific properties of such figures become apparent to them. Children can investigate and describe in their own words the properties of such special quadrilaterals as the *square* ("all sides the same"), the *rectangle* ("opposite sides the same," "four corner angles"), the *rhombus* ("crooked square," "diamond shape"), the *parallelogram* ("crooked rectangle," "opposite sides go in the same direction"), and *trapezoid* ("like a tent," "two sides slanted, two sides going in the same direction"). In this way, they can be guided to understand such special geometric terms as *vertex, side, intersecting, parallel, perpendicular, congruent,* and *angle.*

Such investigations will also lead children to consider the relationships among figures. For example, in trying to "straighten up" a model of a rectangle or of a square, they begin to see that a rectangle is really a special member of the family of parallelograms. Although the opposite sides maintain the same relationship (parallel and congruent), the relationship of the angles changes so that all angles are right angles. Similarly, a square can be thought of as a special rhombus (fig. 36).

Square → Rhombus Rectangle → Parallelogram

Fig. 36. Using geostrips to develop special relationships

visualizing angles

As children describe, construct, and transform models and compare shapes, they need to consider the angles formed by the sides of a plane figure or the edges or faces of a solid figure. An angle is a turn, or rotation, or the "shape," or "opening," formed by two straight line segments. The concept of a turn and different "amounts of turn" or rotation is used in describing a path. The "turtle geometry" component of Logo (chapter 13) is effective in helping young children develop the concept that an angle is an "amount" of a turn (Noss 1987).

Creating a tile pattern around a point can focus a child's attention on how the edges that meet form angles and the comparative sizes of the angles.

Tile pattern. Have children create tile patterns with pattern blocks. Focus their attention on the angles formed by the edges of the blocks: "How many corners does the orange block have? Are the corners all the same or different? How about the blue block? How are the corners different? Which corners are the same?" a

Parking cars. Pretend the pattern blocks are "cars" that need to be parked, so that a corner of a block touches a "post," or dot, on the paper as in figure 37. "How many orange blocks (squares) can you park around the post?" [4] "How many green blocks (equilateral triangles) can you park around the post?" [6] Do the same for each different block. "Why do only three yellow cars fit around a post?" "Why do so many more green blocks fit around a post?" a

In making and exploring models of shapes, place the

Fig. 37. Parking a car around a post with pattern blocks

emphasis on helping children (1) identify which parts of the shapes are referred to when the term *angle* is used; (2) compare the relative sizes of different angles (greater than, less than, or equal to); and (3) visualize a right, or corner, angle and estimate how another type of angle compares in size to a right angle.

These intuitive, exploratory activities are important *prerequisites* for measuring angles with a protractor. Although adolescents and adults may have been exposed to angle terminology and can measure an angle with a protractor, they often demonstrate only a tentative, rote understanding of the terms. They may only be able to recognize a particular type of angle, like a right angle, if one side is parallel to the bottom of the page, not if it appears in a different orientation (Fuys, Geddes, and Tischler 1988). Similarly, they might assume that a right angle must always open up toward the "right" (otherwise it would be a "left" angle!). Also, students are sometimes confused about the relationship between the length of the sides of a figure and the size of the angle they form.

a *Angles in a triangle.* Have children make three copies of the same triangle and mark the corresponding angles as *A, B,* and *C* (fig. 38). "Which is the largest angle? Which is the smallest angle? Prove your answer." Have them place one angle model on top of the other, matching one of the sides to show which is larger, as shown in the figure. (Adapted from *Developing Mathematical Processes* [1974].)

Extend work with angles. Have children put three different angles beside each other in different arrangements to discover that they always get a "straight" angle, as shown in the figure. **a**

a *Angles from a cut of a rectangle.* Give each child an index card or rectangular piece of paper and have them cut it along a slanted line segment that has been drawn from one side to the opposite side (see fig. 39). Ask them to compare all the angles that are formed and to use the same color to shade all angles that are the same size. "Which is largest?" [Angle *G* or angle *F* in fig. 39] "Which is smallest?" [Angle *E* or *H*] **a**

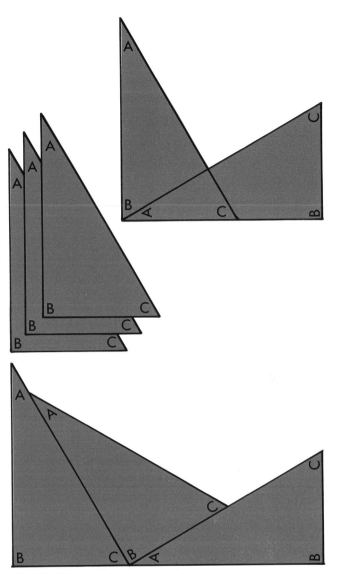

Fig. 38. Using angles in a triangle

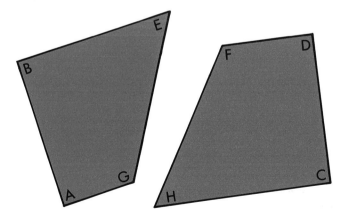

Fig. 39. Angles made by cutting a rectangle

a *Shopping for angles.* Establish a "price list" for different types of angles. Show a diagram of many polygons and have children decide how much each one is worth on the basis of the total "price" of all its angles (see fig. 40). **a**

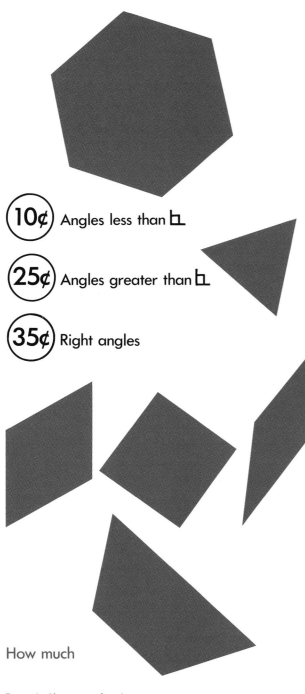

(10¢) Angles less than ⌐

(25¢) Angles greater than ⌐

(35¢) Right angles

How much

Fig. 40. Shopping for shapes

summary

Geometry must become a major component of early childhood mathematics programs. Geometry and spatial sense contribute to a child's success in learning mathematics. We have proposed a framework for planning geometry instruction at the early childhood level, along with an explicit geometry and spatial-sense curriculum and sample activities.

The suggested activities are organized into two parts. Each part includes activities requiring the exploration of spatial relations, properties of three- and two-dimensional shapes, and opportunities for spatial visualization. The first section, "Introductory Geometric Experiences," is a holistic exploration of geometric shapes, whereas the second part, "Building on Introductory Experiences," is a more detailed examination of parts of figures and relationships among the parts. All activities emphasize the importance of first-hand investigations and concrete experiences so vital for building an understanding of geometry concepts and developing spatial sense.

As we teach for "relational" understanding and make problem solving the focus of teaching, the need to emphasize geometry and spatial sense is more compelling than ever. A child's mathematical experiences begin with geometry. Carefully planned geometry and spatial sense development should be an integral part of the mathematical experiences throughout the years of the young child.

references

Baroody, Arthur J. *Children's Mathematical Thinking: A Developmental Framework for Preschool, Primary, and Special Education Teachers.* New York: Teachers College Press, Columbia University, 1987.

Bley, Nancy, and Carol Thornton. *Teaching Mathematics to the Learning Disabled.* Rockville, Md.: Aspen Systems, 1981.

Bourgeois, Roger D. "Third Graders' Ability to Associate Foldout Shapes with Polyhedra." *Journal for Research in Mathematics Education* 17 (May 1986): 222–30.

Bruni, James. *Experiencing Geometry.* Belmont, Calif.: Wadsworth Publishing Co., 1977.

Crowley, Mary L. "The van Hiele Model of the Development of Geometric Thought." In *Learning and Teaching Geometry, K–12, 1987 Yearbook,* edited by Mary M. Lindquist, pp. 1–16. Reston, Va.: National Council of Teachers of Mathematics, 1987.

Del Grande, John. "Can Grade Two Children's Spatial Perception Be Improved by Inserting a Transformational Geometry Component into Their Mathematics Program?" Ph.D. diss., Ontario Institute for Studies in Education, 1985.

_____. "Spatial Perception and Primary Geometry." In *Learning and Teaching Geometry, K–12, 1987 Yearbook,* edited by Mary M. Lindquist, pp. 126–35. Reston, Va.: National Council of Teachers of Mathematics, 1987.

Developing Mathematical Processes, Unit 44. Madison, Wis.: University of Wisconsin, Wisconsin Research and Development Center for Cognitive Learning, 1974. (Available from Delta Education, P.O. Box M, Nashua, NH 03061-9910.)

Fisher, Naomi. "Visual Influences of Figure Orientation on Concept Formation in Geometry." In *Recent Research concerning the Development of Spatial and Geometric Concepts,* edited by Richard Lesh and Diane Mierkiewicz, Columbus, Ohio: ERIC/SMEAC, 1978.

Freudenthal, Hans. *Mathematics as an Educational Task.* Dordrecht, Netherlands: D. Reidel, 1973.

Frostig, Marianne, and David Horne. *The Frostig Program for the Development of Visual Perception.* Chicago: Follett, 1964.

Fostig, Marianne, and Phyllis Maslow. *Learning Problems in the Classroom: Prevention and Remediation.* New York: Grune & Stratton, 1973.

Fuys, David, Dorothy Geddes, and Rosamond Tischler. *The van Hiele Model of Thinking in Geometry among Adolescents. Journal for Research in Mathematics Education* Monograph No. 3. Reston, Va.: National Council of Teachers of Mathematics, 1988.

Guay, R. B., and E. D. McDaniel. "The Relationship between Mathematics Achievement and Spatial Abilities among Elementary School Children." *Journal for Research in Mathematics Education* 8 (May 1977): 211–15.

Hoffer, Alan R. *Mathematics Resource Project: Geometry and Visualization.* Palo Alto, Calif.: Creative Publications, 1977.

Krutetskii, Vadim A. *The Psychology of Mathematical Abilities in Schoolchildren.* Chicago: University of Chicago Press, 1976.

McGee, M. G. *Human Spatial Abilities.* New York: Praeger Publishers, 1979.

Moses, Barbara E. "The Effects of Spatial Instruction on Mathematical Problem-solving Performance." Paper presented at the annual meeting of the American Education Research Association, San Francisco, April 1979.

National Council of Teachers of Mathematics. *Curriculum and Evaluation Standards for School Mathematics.* Reston, Va.: The Council, 1989.

Noss, Richard. "Children's Learning of Geometrical Concepts through Logo." *Journal for Research in Mathematics Education* 18 (November 1987): 343–62.

Perham, Faustine. "An Investigation into the Effects of Instruction on the Acquisition of Transformational Geometry Concepts in First Grade Children and Subsequent Transfer to General Spatial Ability." In *Recent Research concerning the Development of Spatial and Geometric Concepts,* edited by Richard Lesh and Diane Mierkiewicz, pp. 229–42. Columbus, Ohio: ERIC/SMEAC, 1978.

Shaughnessy, J. Michael, and William Burger. "Spadework prior to Deduction in Geometry." *Mathematics Teacher* 78 (September 1985): 419–28.

Usiskin, Zalman. "Resolving the Continuing Dilemmas in School Geometry." In *Learning and Teaching Geometry, K–12, 1987 Yearbook,* edited by Mary M. Lindquist, pp. 17–31. Reston, Va.: National Council of Teachers of Mathematics, 1987.

van Hiele, Pierre M. "A Child's Thought and Geometry." In *English Translation of Selected Writings of Dina van Hiele-Geldof and Pierre M. van Hiele,* edited by Dorothy Geddes, David Fuys, and Rosamond Tischler as part of the research project "An Investigation of the van Hiele Model of Thinking in Geometry among Adolescents," Research in Science Education (RISE) Program of the National Science Foundation, Grant No. SED 7920640. Washington, D.C.: NSF, 1984. (Original work published in 1959.)

van Hiele-Geldof, Dina. "Dissertation of Dina van Hiele-Geldof Entitled: The Didactic of Geometry in the Lowest Class of Secondary School." In *English Translation of Selected Writings of Dina van Hiele-Geldof and Pierre M. van Hiele,* edited by Dorothy Geddes, David Fuys, and Rosamond Tischler as part of the research project "An Investigation of the van Hiele Model of Thinking in Geometry among Adolescents," Research in Science Education (RISE) Program of the National Science Foundation, Grant No. SED 7920640. Washington, D.C.: NSF, 1984. (Original work published in 1957.)

measurement

werner liedtke

11

Measurement is an important part of the elementary school mathematics curriculum, too important to be postponed or omitted at any age or grade level. Measurement and the outcomes of measurement activities are ideal for reaching the five major goals suggested by the NCTM's *Curriculum and Evaluation Standards for School Mathematics* (NCTM 1989, p. 5): learning to value mathematics; becoming confident in one's own ability; becoming a mathematical problem solver; learning to communicate mathematically; and learning to reason mathematically. Two important questions are, What is measurement? and Which measurement skills and concepts might be most appropriate for young children?

Children learn to use numbers to show how many things are in a set of discrete objects, for example, "There are five toy animals on my bed." A system of assigning numbers to discrete objects motivates a child to use a similar scheme to express the magnitude of some continuous quantity, such as length, area, or time. It is helpful to think of something continuous as being made up of small, equal-sized discrete parts, or *units*, that can be put together to reconstruct the original quantity. Thus, to measure the top bar in figure 1, think of it as being composed of smaller units. Now we can apply this smaller unit along the length and see that six units are used up, so we say its measure is 6, using the arbitrary unit.

Fig. 1. Using an arbitrary unit

This simple example shows that measurement is a highly contrived process. The mathematics of measure includes a variety of basic ideas that may be obvious to an adult yet need to be developed and taught to children. The young child encounters or applies these ideas in an informal and intuitive way, with the generalizations and verbalizations not occurring until later grades.

foundational ideas

The important basic ideas for length can be generalized to other measurement topics.

- *Exactly one number is assigned by counting to describe the length of a segment.* Rather than counting repeatedly, we develop and read scales or calibrated instruments that do the counting for us.

- *A line segment, or a linear object, can be assigned a length of 1.* This makes possible the design of a measuring instrument for length or a ruler.

- *Additivity allows length to be treated as a number; we can add segments like we add numbers.* A young child may not realize what transformation will change the length of an object and what will leave it the same.

- *Iteration, the repeated application of a unit, allows one to use a number line and a ruler to find the distance between two points on a segment.*

- *Transitivity allows us to compare segments. We know, for example, that if Corinne is taller than Adam and Adam is taller than Beth, then Corinne will be taller than Beth.*

At what stage of cognitive development can children accommodate these fundamental ideas? Evidence suggests that these ideas are not understood by young children. Students need to begin by using nonstandard units to develop intuitive notions, and these include the basic idea of a "unit of measure." Hiebert (1984) concludes that regardless of their performance on tasks of conservation and transitivity, many first-grade children are ready to learn many measurement concepts. Wilson and Osborne (1988) suggest that teachers listen and watch children at work on

measurement tasks and adjust their expectations, teaching strategies, and evaluation procedures accordingly. "Most of the research about how children measure and think about measurement does not indicate specifically and directly how the teacher should behave or plan for instruction. Rather research has focused on what children cannot do and do not understand" (p. 109). They suggest that principles of instruction have to be inferred from existing research evidence, from the mathematics of measurement, and from information shared by those with experience in teaching young children. The following general principles are part of the summary by Wilson and Osborne (1988, p. 109):

- Children must measure frequently and often, preferably on real problems rather than textbook exercises.

- Children should encounter activity-oriented measurement situations by doing and experimenting rather than passively observing. The activities should encourage discussion to stimulate the refinement and testing of ideas and concepts.

- Instructional planning should emphasize the important ideas of measurement that transfer or work across measurement systems.

Even if teachers conclude that their students are ready for the presentation of measurement skills and concepts, another hurdle may need to be crossed. Many children may see no need to learn these ideas. Measurement tasks may not be part of their out-of-the-classroom experiences, and as far as they are concerned, the use of the overworked word *big* suffices whenever comparisons are to be made. It is advantageous for most young children if teachers base their teaching of measurement on the assumption that time will be needed to get young students to see a need for learning measurement skills and ideas.

preschool

In preschool settings, the main learning outcomes are defining different characteristics and making relative comparisons using appropriate terminology. Sorting activities and tasks are best suited for these children. Materials from the children's environment can be used in readiness activities to explore such questions as these:

- Which are the same length?
- Which are longer than this?
- Which are shorter?
- Who is the same height?
- Who is taller or shorter than this person?
- Which are the same size?
- Which is the biggest? Smallest?
- Which holds the most? The least?
- Which holds the same amount?
- Which is heavier? Which is lighter?
- Which takes longer? Which takes the least amount of time?
- Which is hot? Which is cold?

In the remainder of this chapter, a teaching sequence for length is presented in detail, including possible decisions to be made by the teacher. Because other measurement topics can follow a similar sequence, only the important concepts and issues are highlighted for these topics.

length

What are some of the major components of a teaching sequence on length? Before young children measure the lengths of objects or the distances between objects, a number of important skills and ideas must be developed. Sorting activities can be used at the intuitive level to define length as a characteristic of an object. The appropriate terminology is introduced: *as long as, longer than, shorter than.* Answers to such questions as How long? and How far apart? require learning how to measure to the nearest unit. Measurement skills are taught and then retaught as young children learn to measure with parts of their bodies (body units), with objects from their classrooms (arbitrary units), and finally with common standard units (customary or metric). An instrument to measure length is constructed

and used. These activities enable children to become familiar with the units commonly used for measuring length.

sorting and terminology

At the outset it is important to define the characteristics to be studied. This is a relatively easy task in the higher grades, but in the early grades it is rather difficult to define such characteristics as length, area, mass, and time.

One of the best ways of defining length and introducing young children to the appropriate terminology is through sorting tasks.

Sort by length. See figure 2. Do a two-way sort of a set of familiar objects. "Is the pencil *as long as* the mouth? What about the string? How can we tell if they are the same length?" [Put them side by side.] Now children demonstrate their choice, place the object in the correct pile, and use the terms *as long as* and *not as long as.* Follow the same process for "measuring" the length of an eye and the nose. Use the same objects for a three-way sort, *shorter, longer,* and *as long as.*   **a**

Important prerequisites for measurement of length are the ability to make comparisons, to impose order on objects and events, and to use appropriate terminology.

Tallest and shortest. Have a student choose something she thinks is *tall.* Then have her choose one *taller* and then the *tallest* in the classroom. Repeat for *short, shorter,* and *shortest.* Put objects in various positions. "Does it make the block tower taller if I put it on my desk? Why not?"   **a**

The next step in the teaching sequence begins with the question, How long? To answer this question, the teaching sequence is separated into three distinct parts: body units, arbitrary units, and standard units.

As young children are taught to measure, is it important to make use of the term *unit*? Is the term required or necessary? *Unit* and *standard unit* are abstract notions, too abstract for the early childhood setting. In the early grades these ideas are developed at an intuitive level and the term *unit* is reserved for later grades.

body units

Most children are able to represent the length or height of an object with parts of their bodies. When asked to compare the height of two towers on different levels, children initially may see no need to measure, relying on their eyes and perhaps using a hand motion that follows their line of sight. Measurement readiness is exhibited when children represent the height of one tower on parts of their bodies or use both hands to identify its height, as shown in figure 3.

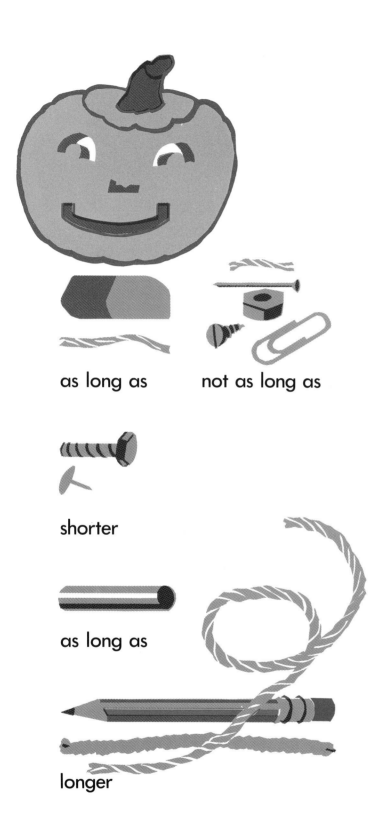

as long as   not as long as

shorter

as long as

longer

Fig. 2. Sorting objects by length

Fig. 3. Using body units to compare heights

The use of body units provides an informal historical perspective that can be integrated into the lessons. How did people of long ago solve problems in measuring length? How might they have measured the length of a tusk from a saber-toothed tiger? Why did they want to measure length?

Important measurement skills with body units include the following:

- Placing a unit consistently and correctly and giving reasons for doing so
- Simulating the use of many units by employing one unit repeatedly
- Measuring to the nearest unit by rounding up or rounding down

Examples and nonexamples can be used to show the importance of placing the unit consistently along the object to be measured. If, for example, students use a hand unit to find how long a table is, one student can spread out his or her fingers and another student can place one hand in a different direction. Are such actions appropriate? Why or why not?

Another important skill is the ability to simulate the measurement action with one body unit, that is, one hand or one handprint, and pretend that a sufficient number of units are available to cover the length of the object. Careful placement of the body unit and accurate marking or recordkeeping are important to describe the approximate length of an object.

Ruler introduction. At this stage young children can be introduced to a ruler in activities based on questions like the following:

What is a ruler?
Where do the markings on a ruler come from?
What do the markings mean?
Why is it an advantage to show numbers on a ruler?
What do the numbers on a ruler mean?
If the numbers are used, what rules need to be adopted for measuring the length of objects?

A strip of paper or cardboard can be used to make a ruler, shown in handprints in figure 4.

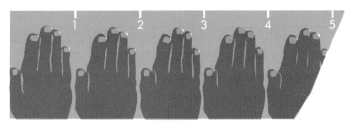

Fig. 4. Making a handprint ruler

The body-part ruler is used to find the lengths of different objects. Discussions about correct as well as incorrect uses of rulers can be based on examples of a thumb ruler, like those shown in figure 5. The rulers can be saved for later activities with arbitrary units. **a**

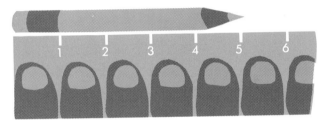

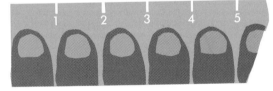

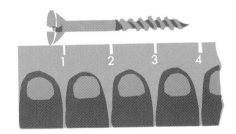

Fig. 5. Correct and incorrect ruler use

Since one important learning outcome is being able to describe the length of an object to the nearest unit, the proper usage of the term *about* needs to be taught. Children need to be involved in tasks that enable them to decide when it is appropriate to round up or round down to the nearest unit as in figure 6. The students can be asked to use the term *about* on every measurement activity sheet. As a result of examples and nonexamples, students need to be led to the generalization that when half or more than half of the unit is used, the measurement is rounded up to the next whole number.

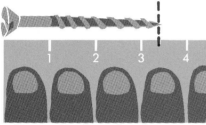

about 3 thumbs long

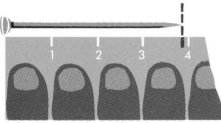

about 4 thumbs long

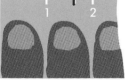

about 2 thumbs long

Fig. 6. Measuring to the nearest unit

Guessing and estimating can play an important role in teaching measurement of length with any unit when units are applied to events or objects from the students' experiences. A willingness to guess is an important prerequisite for estimating. Since the terms *guessing* and *estimating* connote different actions, children should be made aware of the difference.

a *Guess and estimate.* Use a story or dramatization to illustrate the differences between guessing and estimating. "About how many bicycles do you think there are at the school?" One child might respond, "Lots, about one hundred." Another child might respond, "Oh, I think there are about twenty on one side and about twenty on the other side. There are about forty bicycles." Help students see that the second answer is an estimate because it involves a pattern of thought and mental activity. Guessing is a statement made on the basis of experience that is often recalled without thinking.   **a**

Since estimation involves developing a mental picture of some basic part, it is advantageous to examine paths that consist of different parts. This process reinforces the idea of thinking of a whole in terms of parts.

a *Estimate using parts.* Use string or pipe cleaners to make paths with parts as in figure 7. "Estimate the short part in thumb units [2 thumb units]. Let's check with Ryan's thumb. How many times does the short path fit into the other part? Now, estimate the length of the whole path."   **a**

During the early stages of learning to measure with a new unit, students should be encouraged to make guesses. Later they are taught strategies for estimating.

It might be a disadvantage for students to measure with different units because of the temptation to make conversions. Instead, the focus should be on actual measurement skills, not on a measurement system. Students can be asked to make a decision about the unit they prefer or think most advantageous.

Fig. 7. Estimating using parts

a *Choose the unit.* Have students decide on the best unit for measuring various objects, as in figure 8. "To measure the width of this book, would you prefer to use a thumb unit or a hand unit?"

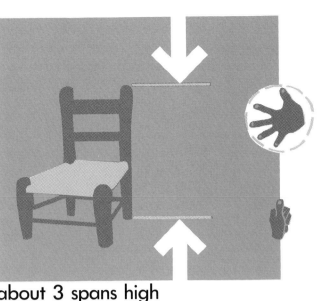

about 3 spans high

about 6 hands long

Fig. 8. Choosing a unit

[Probably a thumb] "When would you use a hand?" [For bigger things] "Why is it easier to use a hand than a step to find the length of the desk?" [Steps might not be the same size; hands will give a closer estimate.]

After a unit is chosen, estimate first and then measure. "About how many thumbs wide is the book? Estimate first. Now let's check by measuring." **a**

about 10 thumbs wide

How can students be led to realize that even if they correctly use the measurement skills they have learned, measuring with body units has disadvantages? Comparing different answers for tasks where the same body units were used, for example, a child's hand and the teacher's hand, helps them see the need for units that give the same answers.

arbitrary units

The concept of arbitrary units is introduced to solve the problem of having different numbers of hand units for the same object. Initially it is advantageous to adopt a small object, such as a paper clip, as a unit and reteach important measurement skills. One skill is using a single object as a unit.

Using many clips and one clip. Use several paper clips and measure objects in the classroom, as in figure 9. "How many paper clips can we place along the pencil to show its length?" [5] "Suppose we have only one paper clip. How can we find the length?" [Lay it off and mark it, like using your finger.] Note the need for accurate placement and careful marking.

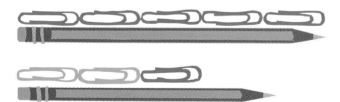

Fig. 9. Arbitrary units, many and single copies

Reteach measuring to the nearest unit, as shown in figure 10, and use the word *about*. "Is the length of the top pencil closer to three clips or four clips? Why?" [3 wholes; not as much as a half of another] "What about the bottom pencil?" [About 3, because there is more than a half left over.] **a**

A valuable experience in estimating is the follow-up, where children discuss and compare the strategies they

about 3 paper clips long

about 3 paper clips long

Fig. 10. Measuring to the nearest unit

used to arrive at their estimates. It is important not to evaluate estimates as poor or not good—all responses are good estimates. If some estimates are inadequate, record this information and plan further estimation and measurement activities to enable students to become more familiar with the units used in the estimation tasks. Games can provide experiences with estimation and units that have been introduced.

Peek and estimate. Draw a path with two or more straight parts on the chalkboard or a transparency but do not let students see it at first. Choose a piece of chalk as a unit. "I'll give you 10 seconds to peek at the path I've drawn. Then write your estimate of the length in chalk units." After 10 seconds, cover the path and have them write their estimate. Check by measuring. Repeat for shorter intervals as students become more proficient.

The game can become a group activity. Form groups of four or five children and make one student in each a recorder. The group discusses their estimates and agrees on what is to be written down. Always ask, "How did you think to get that estimate?" Record the results in a table such as the one in figure 11 and circle the winning group.

One simple but interesting variation is having each member in a group record an estimate. The results are then compared and discussed within each group before a value agreed on by the group is reported or recorded. This variation is more suitable for students in grades 3 and 4 and is ideal for developing an intuitive

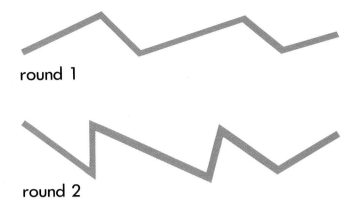

round 1

round 2

round	estimates				measurement
	group 1	group 2	group 3	group 4	
1	about ____	about ____	about ____	about ____	about ____
2	about ____	about ____	about ____		
3	abo				

Fig. 11. Group estimates of lengths of paths

need for knowing how to calculate and report averages. **a**

a *Draw a path.* Choose an arbitrary unit and have students estimate and draw a path that is a given number of units in length. "This paper clip is the unit. Draw a path that you estimate is 5 paper clips long." Have one student in each group use a paper clip and find the path that is closest to 5 paper clips. Repeat for lengths of 10, 20, and 30 paper clips. The results will show how familiar children are with a particular unit and how well they transfer information from one problem to the next. **a**

The teaching sequence with arbitrary units should conclude with a problem to highlight the inadequacies of these units. "How can we tell the second graders in another school or another country how tall we are? Would they know our paper-clip unit?"

standard units

Questions like these illustrate the necessity of adopting standard units for measurement to communicate with other people. The learning outcomes and the initial teaching sequence for the introduction of standard units are just the same for either measurement system, customary or metric. After students see the need for standard units, teaching strategies and activities should focus on reteaching and reinforcing important measurement skills and concepts like the following:

- Placement of the unit and using the term *about*
- Interpretations of markings on a ruler and proper use of a ruler
- Estimation as a way of becoming familiar with common units
- Stating simple relationships (e.g., 1 foot = 12 inches, 1 meter = 100 centimeters)
- Knowing some of the recording conventions for the system

Of these outcomes the last two are least indicative of a student's ability to measure lengths. The examination of a system, the relationships of units within that system, and any conversion of units within a system are more appropriate for the upper grades.

When several lessons with standard units are planned, the following questions should be kept in mind: Is it better to begin instruction with a small unit, such as the centimeter, or with a larger unit, such as the decimeter or meter? What are the possible advantages and disadvantages for either choice? What type of activities will best reteach important measurement skills and concepts? What type of activities and problems will result in students becoming familiar with the common units for measurement of length? How can their familiarity with units be evaluated? Is it advantageous to teach the customary and the metric system side by side, or should they be separated? The answers to these questions are likely to differ for students of different ages. Some hints and suggestions for possible answers follow.

Beginning with a small unit has some advantages. It is

easier to relate a small unit to objects from the students' environment—their papers, their desks, and so on—a small unit is better for developing an understanding of the marks on a ruler.

a *A centimeter ruler.* Use the same activity setting as for body and arbitrary units to construct a centimeter ruler. First use several centimeter blocks to measure. Then use a single block to make the ruler. "Why do we put numbers on the ruler?" [To show how many blocks long it is from the left end]

Illustrate proper placement and reading as real objects are measured (fig. 12). "Why don't we place the pencil to start at 1?" [Must start at the left end of the ruler, which means 0] **a**

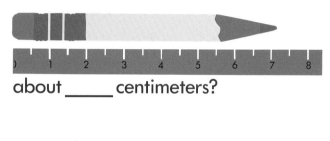

about _____ centimeters?

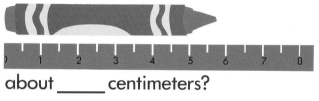

about _____ centimeters?

Fig. 12. Measuring to the nearest centimeter

Familiarity with a standard unit is gained by using that unit in a wide variety of settings and similar activities as done with arbitrary units.

a *Measure hunt.* Have students work in pairs or small groups and by estimation pick objects of given length. "Look around the classroom. How many objects can you see that are between 10 centimeters and 15 centimeters long?" After the list is made, have them check by measuring with a ruler. The winner is the pair or group of students with the most correct estimates. **a**

a *Mystery measure.* A mystery object is chosen by the teacher and its length written on the chalkboard. "Can you find my mystery object? It is 30 centimeters long. No rulers allowed." After students make their list of objects, they check by measuring. Make a special award to students or groups of students who included your mystery object.

An easier variation begins with the length of the mystery object drawn as a straight path on the chalkboard. **a**

The responses students give for estimation tasks will give an indication of how familiar they have become with centimeters. Being able to relate basic units to objects and events from their experiences should rank ahead of the ability to report the length of a given object in terms of two or more different units.

The meter, a larger metric unit, can be introduced with questions such as, How long is the chalkboard? How high is the door? How long is the classroom? How far is it from our classroom to the library? A few questions of this type should convince the students of the need and advantages of a larger unit.

a *Compare with a meter.* Display a meterstick. Ask, "Is the height of my desk less than a meter, about a meter, or more than a meter?" Make lists of objects for the three categories. Estimate first and then check with the meterstick. Other possible examples are the length of a table, height of a student, width of a window, and so on. **a**

After measuring only a few objects or distances, children will realize the advantages of measuring to the nearest centimeter and recording results in terms of meters and centimeters, for example, 2 m 16 cm. A recording format like 2.16 m should be used only after decimals are understood.

If the kilometer is introduced, children can pretend to think of one thousand metersticks laid end to end. Estimation can be done using known measurements.

a *Estimate a kilometer.* After students find the number of meters from the classroom door to the library door, ask: "How many times do we walk to the library and back to go one kilometer?" Find the distance in meters around the basketball court and the distance across the playground. "How many times do you walk around the basketball court to walk one kilometer?" Repeat for the playground.

"If we start at school and walk one kilometer north, for example, where do we end up? How would you go about finding a few places about one kilometer away from your house?" Diagrams and maps can be shown on the bulletin board to illustrate the solutions for some of these problems. The teacher or parents can assist by taking students in their cars, calling their attention to the odometer, and driving about 0.6 of a mile, the equivalent of 1 kilometer.

It may be tempting to construct a ruler that is 10 centimeters long and then to use this ruler as another unit, the decimeter, for measurement of length. Two possible disadvantages for introducing the decimeter or using a decimeter ruler in the early grades should be considered. The decimeter is not a commonly used unit and once the meter is introduced, the reference to three different units might be confusing for some young children.

The eye-hand coordination required for measuring the length of an object to the nearest millimeter is probably too fine for most children in the early grades. The introduction of this unit might best be postponed to the intermediate grades.

The metric system is used exclusively in Canada and almost every other country. In the United States, automobiles are manufactured to metric specifications, and international trade is forcing many businesses to "go metric." These economic reasons require that the metric system be taught in schools. For example, Michigan's *New Mathematics Objectives for Measurement* uses only the metric system (Michigan Department of Education 1989).

Since measurement skills and concepts are the major focus, the activities suggested for measuring length in one system are appropriate for the other system. On the one hand, the argument for introducing the inch before the foot or yard is similar to the argument for introducing the centimeter before the meter. On the other hand, a yardstick without any subdivisions is not suitable for children learning how to measure to the nearest unit. Students would have to measure large objects and might ignore parts of a yard.

If the children have constructed two rulers, one for inches and one for centimeters, at what age or at what grade level might they benefit from a comparison of these instruments: How is measuring with one ruler the same or different from measuring with the other ruler? How are the answers the same or different? The introduction of this type of discussion and activity may depend on the ability of the students.

From these teaching suggestions, it can be seen that knowing how to measure has nothing to do with the ability to make conversions between units. For young children, "thinking metric" should mean that they become familiar with basic units and be able to relate these units to their experience. Stating relationships within the system and examining the system will come later.

area

Since measuring area and length are similar processes, the same teaching sequence and many of the activities for length can be used with area. Consequently, only a few of the major ideas and outcomes are highlighted here.

The term *area* needs to be defined in examples that suggest the idea of an amount of covering.

a *Greedy paper monster.* Cut several pieces of paper of the same width but of different lengths, as in figure 13. "How are these alike? How are they different?"

"A greedy paper monster came by and saw all these

Fig. 13. The greedy paper monster

paper strips. Which did it eat first? Next? Last?" Have students put the paper strips in order, the way the monster would eat them.

Cut several new pieces. "Where does this piece go in the way we have them ordered? Tell me why you chose that spot." Put the new pieces so that the entire set is ordered by size.   **a**

a *Sort by area size.* Choose a "covering" unit, such as a sheet of paper. "Which covers more, the paper or an index card?" Choose other objects and compare their areas with the sheet of paper. Use such terms as *bigger than, covers more, has more area,* and *bigger size* and the corresponding units with *same* and *less.*

Present cut-out hexagons of different sizes as shown in figure 14. "Can you put them in order from smallest size to largest? Can you then put them in order from greatest area to least area?"

Then show the hexagon at the bottom of the figure. "Where does this one go so that the sizes will be in order? Can you tell me why you put it there?" Encourage students to say the ideas in their own words, using both *size* and *area* in conjunction with each other.   **a**

body units

When the teacher asks the questions "How big?" "What is the size?" or "What is the area?" about a given object, he or she might also present the problem of how people long ago might have measured or described the size or area of a skin or fur.

a *Area of a rug.* Sketch an outline of a "rug" on a large sheet of paper. The outline can be a rug of any shape. "Estimate the number of footprints needed to cover the rug. Write your estimate." One by one, have students stand on the rug and draw around their feet. Continue until the rug is covered with "shoe units," as shown in figure 15.

An alternative is to have as many children as possible stand on the rug at the same time and then count the number of "shoe units."

Footprints, or handprints, can be traced on construction paper, cut out, and then used to find the area of an object. Discuss the advantages and disadvantages of using footprints or handprints to measure area.   **a**

arbitrary units

To overcome some of the disadvantages that become apparent when using footprint units, choose arbitrary units such as triangles, squares, or rectangles. These units can then be used in activities for comparisons, ordering, estimating, and measuring. One important learning outcome for young children is that geometric shapes can be different but still have the same area.

standard units

After the need for a standard unit has been established, the square centimeter can be introduced. Since the square centimeter is rather small, measurement tasks should be completed by tracing the figure to be measured onto a grid of square

Fig. 14. Ordering objects by area size

centimeters or by placing a transparent grid onto the figure and then counting the number of squares.

Students also gain familiarity with a unit by estimating and measuring a wide variety of objects from the students' environment. Estimation tasks and games similar to those suggested for length can be adapted for area.

 Area in square centimeters. Cut a geometric shape from construction paper and tape it on the chalkboard. Have students estimate the

area of the shape in square centimeters. Discuss their estimates and their estimation strategies. Then show the students a square centimeter, tape it to the chalkboard

Fig. 15. Area in shoe-print units

next to the shape, and allow them to adjust their estimates. Again, discuss their estimates and strategies. "Is it easier to estimate when you can see the unit or when it is hidden? Why?" Then show the students a rectangle that has an area of 10 square centimeters and allow them to adjust their estimates again. Discuss their estimates and strategies. "How many of you changed your estimates? Do you think your new estimates are closer to the actual area of the shape? Why?" Now measure the area of the shape. Repeat this activity with other shapes. "Would you rather be shown the 1 square centimeter or the 10 square centimeters?"

Estimate the area of a rectangle the same way and show how to connect finding area with multiplication. "How many square centimeters are in the bottom row? How many rows do we have? Why can we use multiplication to find the total number of square centimeters?" Since the emphasis is on the concept of area, it is not appropriate to use length times width until later grades.   **a**

Geoboard gardens. Have children make a garden plot on a geoboard with a rubber band. "How are Jane's and Gary's alike? How are they different? Who has the biggest garden? The smallest garden?" Choose several students and have them display their gardens in order of size, as in figure 16.

Display a small rectangle and have them make a garden like the rectangle but larger (or smaller).   **a**

Geometric figures as units. Give each group or pair of children twenty congruent rectangles cut from cardboard or linoleum. The rectangle will serve as the unit of measure. On a prepared worksheet or on the chalkboard, list objects that would be appropriate to measure with the rectangles. Have the children estimate the area of each object and record their estimates on paper. For example, "How many rectangles do you think it will take to cover the top of your desk?" Then have them actually use their rectangles to cover each object and find its area.

Fig. 16. Geoboard gardens

Repeat with other shapes such as triangles and hexagons. For larger areas, such as the classroom floor, use larger units. Children should estimate first and then measure.

An activity sheet similar to the one in figure 17 can be used as a culminating task.   **a**

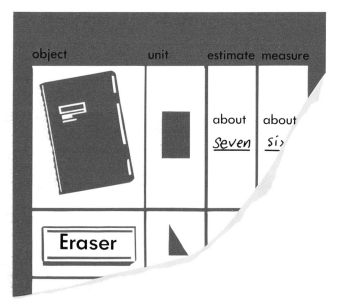

Fig. 17. Area with geometric units

capacity and volume

The main idea for capacity/volume is to find how much a container holds.

Different amounts, same-sized glasses. Use several glasses of the same size but filled with different amounts of juice or sand as in figure 18. "Which glass is the fullest? Which glass has the least amount of juice? Do two glasses have the same amount? Can we put them in order from least to greatest?"

a

Fig. 18. Glasses with different amounts

Different-sized containers. Use a collection of containers with different capacities, as in figure 19, and do a two-way sort. "Which

will hold less than this glass? Which will hold more?" A three-way sort can be done using *same, more,* and *less.*

A more difficult activity requires ordering. "Which one do you think will hold the most juice? The least juice?" Pour water, sand, or rice into the containers, and arrange them in order from the one that "holds the least" to the one that "holds the most." One important learning outcome is that containers with a similar appearance may not be the same size.

Since it is advantageous to display and use a wide variety of containers, students can be invited to supplement the collection begun by the teacher. **a**

body and arbitrary units

What kind of questions and problems can be posed to show students that long ago people determined the sizes of different containers by using a "handful" as a unit? To circumvent some of the difficulties of using a handful as a unit, a small container jar can be used.

Baby-food jar as a unit. Use a baby-food jar as an arbitrary unit of capacity. Display a bucket and ask, "Can you estimate the

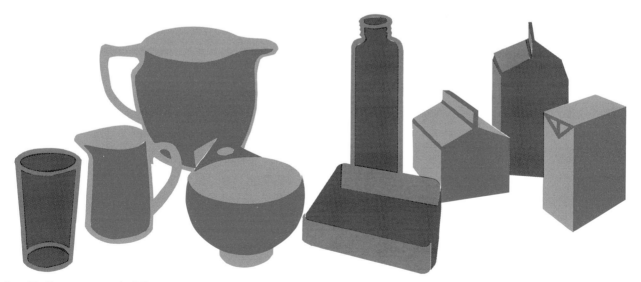

Fig. 19. Containers with different capacities

number of jars we need to fill the bucket?" Have students write their estimates. Then count jars as you fill the bucket about one-fourth full. "You know how many jars we have poured so far. Do you want to change your estimate?" When the bucket is half full, give students another opportunity to change their estimate. Repeat using containers smaller and larger than the bucket.   **a**

standard units

Which major learning outcomes should be accommodated as the teaching sequence is extended to include standard units? After students are convinced of the need for standard units, they should be able to identify from their experience various containers that have a capacity of a standard unit such as a liter (e.g., soda pop, family milk carton).

A familiarity with some of the more common units (pint, gallon, or liter) can be gained with a variety of sorting tasks.

a *Sort by capacity.* Choose several containers as in figure 19, including one with a standard unit such as a pint. Display one container. "Does this one hold more than a pint, less than a pint, or is it about a pint?" Sort the containers into three groups by size. As before, pour water, sand, or rice to verify estimates that students make. Repeat with other standard capacities such as 100 mL or 500 mL, gallon, and quart. Students need much experience to internalize the standard units and to see that containers can look different and yet hold the same.

As a variation, use magazine pictures of containers and sort them by capacity into three groups on the bulletin board. With pictures, encourage discussion of actual size versus illustrated size.   **a**

The primary units of *volume* are cubic centimeter and cubic inch. The distinguishing characteristic of volume (vs. capacity) is that it is measured in cubic units. (The connection between them is important in the upper grades, e.g., 1 liter is 1000 cubic centimeters and 1 cubic centimeter is 1 milliliter.) Activities for volume are

similar to the ones for capacity. A wooden or plastic block or a cardboard box can be chosen as arbitrary units. Then the volume of containers can be determined using those units.

a *How many rooms in your building?* Each pair or group of children is given a set of blocks, all the same size. "I want you to make a building. Each block is a room. When you finish, tell me how many rooms you have." Let one group make a different building. Discuss how they are different and how they are alike (fig. 20).   **a**

a *A block as arbitrary unit.* Use a wooden or plastic block as a unit. Display a container such as a shoe box. "Estimate and tell how many blocks are needed to fill the shoe box. Write your estimate." Then place one row of blocks on one side of the bottom. "Do you want to change your estimate? Write your new estimate." Fill the bottom layer of the box and have them estimate again. Repeat for other containers that are smaller and larger.

Fig. 20. Making rooms in a building

As a variation, use the desk as an arbitrary "box unit" and follow a similar procedure. "If you think of my desk as a box, how many boxes could I place along the front of the room? How many could I put on the wall in front of the room? How many could I put in the whole room?" Let students revise their estimates at each stage of questioning. One important learning outcome is that containers can have different appearances yet be the same size. **a**

weight

The following questions and problems can be part of an introductory teaching sequence for weight (mass).

a *Heavy or light?* Choose objects and hold them up one at a time. "Is it heavy or light? Why do you say it is heavy?" (Hard to lift; presses down on your hand, etc.) "Why do you say this one is light?" (Hard to feel; floats in the air like a feather, etc.) Provide enough examples and time for discussion on the meaning of *heavy* and *light*. "Can you tell whether it is heavy or light just by looking?" Point out that you need to feel the object or use a scale. **a**

a *Animals on a teeter-totter.* Draw a teeter-totter as in figure 21. "Let's think about animals on the teeter-totter, the same distance

Fig. 21. Animals on a teeter-totter

from the center. If we put an elephant on one end and a dog on the other, what happens? Which is heavier? Which is lighter? Why?" Repeat with other animals. **a**

a *Hidden weight.* Use five empty film canisters (free at almost any photo store). Fill each with substances of differing densities and label the canisters, as in figure 22. Give pairs of canisters to different groups of children. "Which is heavier? Which is lighter?" Check by feeling or with a balance scale. Have students order the canisters in order by weight, from least to greatest. **a**

Fig. 22. Film canisters for hidden weights

Balance scales are relatively easy to construct, as suggested by Bruni and Silverman (1976, pp. 5–6); see figure 23. Such balance scales are best suited for use with arbitrary units, since an ounce (gram) is too light and a pound (kilogram) is too heavy. "How can we use a balance scale and arbitrary units of some kind to find the weight of an object? Is it possible to tell how heavy something is by looking at it?"

Before introducing a standard unit, consider the following question: Is it more appropriate first to introduce the small standard unit (ounce or gram) or is it advantageous to begin with the larger common units (pound or kilogram)? Which of the units is more easily related to the students' experiences at a given age or grade level? Since rather delicate balance scales are required for the smaller units of mass and since it is easier to relate the larger units to a child's experience, a teaching sequence for the early grades should begin with the pound or kilogram.

The sorting tasks suggested for capacity can easily be adapted for weight (fig. 24).

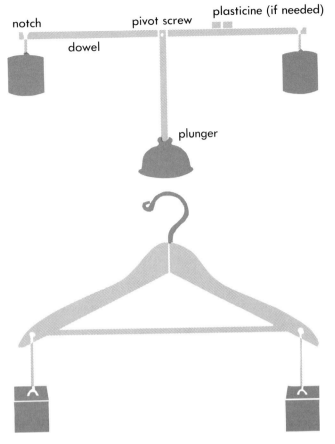

Fig. 23. Homemade balance scales

time

Many different skills and ideas are involved in being able to interpret the markings on a clock face, explain the functions of the two hands, or tell time. The skills and ideas that are re᠆ ᠆ed for conceptual understanding can be ᠆᠆esented in a teaching sequence similar to that suggested for the other measurement topics.

One possible teaching sequence for a grade 3 class is suggested. The teaching sequence outlined can be modified to suit different students, settings, or teaching styles. Then, of course, it is possible to modify the sequence or select a few parts of it to make it suitable for different age groups.

Identify events from the students' experience that can be used as responses to the following questions:

■ What takes a long time to do or to complete?

■ What takes little time to complete?

■ Which of two events takes longer to complete?

■ Who is faster or takes less time to complete a given task?

a *Sorting by amount of time.* Make a chart with headings as shown in figure 25. Write on slips of paper the names of various activities—brushing your teeth, playing a soccer game, taking a picture, building a house, and so on. Hold and read each slip. "Will it take a long time or a little time to brush your teeth?" Some activities can go in both categories, depending on the students, so let them vote on where it should go.

Extend the activity by choosing three events and having students order them from least to greatest times. Alternatively, have students choose three things that they do and draw a picture of each. Then have them

about 2 lbs.

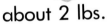

about 1 lb.

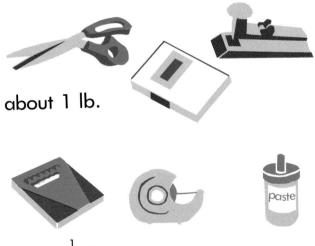

about $\frac{1}{2}$ lb.

Fig. 24. Sorting by weight

arrange the pictures in order by amount of time each takes. **a**

Deciding how long a given activity takes, for example, printing the alphabet or reciting a poem, can be determined by having students tap a pencil or clap hands and then count the number of taps or claps. Students can be encouraged to make guesses before they complete several tasks and then "time" each one.

A simple dramatization can illustrate some of the obvious disadvantages of this "timing" method. (A third-grade boy objected to the noise created by clapping hands and tapping pencils.) Use a metronome in a guess-and-check setting for various activities. The metronome can introduce students to a one-second interval. Can students identify events or tasks that take about one second to complete? What do people mean

when they say, "I'll be with you in one second" or "This will only take a second"?

Sixty of the one-second counts are then identified as making one minute. The minute is a basic unit and is commonly used: "I'll be with you in one minute"; "This will only take a minute"; "In a few minutes . . ."; "Just wait a minute." Throughout the year activities can be developed so students acquire an intuitive notion of the minute as a basic time interval. As suggested, this learning outcome should be a long-range goal. Once they begin a "one-minute-booklet," as shown in figure 26, students can add to it the remainder of the year. Events from various subjects in and around the school can be identified and then entered on the pages, where the student is asked to guess how many times a given task can be completed in one minute and then to carry out the task to check the guess.

Number line to 60. Make a number line from 0 to 60 on a strip of paper. "Each mark shows one minute. If it is 0 now, where will I point in 15 minutes? Twenty-five minutes? Forty-seven minutes?" Ask similar questions about the time from 0 until recess or mathematics class. **a**

Number-line clock. Make a circle out of the 60-minute number line. Fasten a minute counter (a pencil or stick) at the center. "If the counter starts at 0, where does it point after your

takes a long time to complete

takes a little time to complete

Fig. 25. Sorting by little time and long time

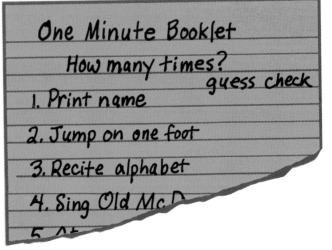

Fig. 26. One-minute booklet

favorite TV show?" Repeat for other events, always starting at 0.

Use the number-line clock to raise other questions. "Why is it an advantage to only show every fifth number?" "Why do most people know which numbers the counter or minute hand points to even if the numbers are not shown?" "If the minute hand points to the 5, do we know whether 5 minutes or 65 minutes have gone by?" "Why or why not?"   **a**

a *Hour hand.* A second counter, or the hour hand, and the numbers 1 to 12 are now introduced. Reading a clock or telling time is taught with reference to both counters, or hands. Looking at the position of the two hands, ask, "What time is it?" Explain the meaning of the answer in terms of the "movement" of the two hands. For the time shown in figure 27, we say that it is "3 o'clock" (of the clock) or that "three hours" or "three counts of sixty minutes" have gone by since both hands were at the "0 position" on the number line.   **a**

After students complete various activities that involve reading and setting clocks, new measures of time—day, week, month, year, decade—can be introduced.

Figure 27 shows both a standard clock and a digital clock. Developing a sense of duration is easier if a standard clock is used, since more visual information is available. The child is able to "see" a start and finish, or a beginning and an end.

Children who understand the meaning of the markings and numbers on a clock face and know the function of the two hands should find it easy to transfer their understanding to a digital clock. What disadvantages and difficulties exist in introducing a child to duration and the measurement of time with digital clocks?

If, for some reason, you decide to develop a unit on time by going in a direction opposite to what has been suggested, and doing so might be more appropriate for younger children, how would your teaching sequence be different? What are the possible advantages and disadvantages of introducing the hour hand before the minute hand? If you are preparing a unit on "telling time" for students below grade 3, which

Fig. 27. Relating a clock face and digital time

activities in the sequence suggested would you select or delete? Why?

temperature

If students recall past events, are they reminded of "cold" or "hot" sensations as the describe the events? Why? If the category "warm" is included in such sorting tasks, which events would be considered for it and why? Why might students disagree about some events or experiences? These questions suggest a bulletin board where students can categorize magazine pictures of events from their experience. Space between each category can be reserved for examples on which there is disagreement.

After the purposes of a thermometer are introduced

(e.g., How cold? How hot?), the students can identify various temperatures, or marks on the thermometer.

conclusion

The teaching and learning of measurement requires explanations, activities, and tasks that are not easily captured on a textbook page. Settings are necessary in which actual objects are compared and discussed with appropriate terminology. Using correct language is an important learning outcome.

For young children, measurement may seem to be a contrived process. Since many skills, ideas, and concepts are involved, it will take time and more than one exposure before students assimilate them.

Important teaching decisions must be made before the material for a given topic is presented to young children; thus, the teacher is the key. Printed materials can be a valuable reference, but it is the teacher who determines whether the topic, the teaching sequence, and the activities are appropriate for a given age level or for a certain classroom setting. As suggested in this chapter, the majority of activities that are related to learning how to measure are done without the use of the textbook.

We should remind ourselves that it is inappropriate to suggest to young children that one system of measurement is easier to learn or more natural to use than another. We also need to remind ourselves that years of experience may contribute to the false notion that one system or one set of units is somehow natural, whereas another system is difficult. The process of learning how to measure is the same in any system.

Some of the main ideas of a sequence for teaching measurement to the young child can be summarized by identifying the important skills and concepts for measurement of length:

■ Develop terms to describe the characteristics of length using sorting tasks

■ Use appropriate terminology while making comparisons and ordering using three or more objects

■ Find answers to "How long?":
Select an arbitrary unit
Place units appropriately
Measure to the nearest unit
Estimate using the units
Design a measurement instrument (ruler)
Interpret the markings and numbers on the ruler
Recognize the need for standard units
Become familiar with standard units
Estimate using standard units

■ Solve problems with standard units

■ Use the relationships among different units

Appropriate skills and concepts can be selected from this list and applied to teaching sequences for other measurement topics.

bibliography

Bruni, James V., and Helene J. Silverman. "Let's Do It: An Introduction to Weight Measurement." *Arithmetic Teacher* 23 (January 1976): 4–10.

Hiebert, James. "Why Do Some Children Have Trouble Learning Measurement Concepts?" *Arithmetic Teacher* 31 (March 1984): 19–24.

Holmes, Emma E. *Children Learning Mathematics: A Cognitive Approach to Teaching.* Englewood Cliffs, N.J.: Prentice-Hall, 1985.

Michigan Department of Education. *An Interpretation of the Michigan Essential Goals and Objectives.* Lansing: Michigan Council of Teachers of Mathematics, 1989.

National Council of Teachers of Mathematics. *Curriculum and Evaluation Standards for School Mathematics.* Reston, Va.: The Council, 1989.

Nelson, Doyal, and Robert E. Reys, eds. *Measurement in School Mathematics.* 1976 Yearbook of the National Council of Teachers of Mathematics. Reston, Va.: The Council, 1976.

Robinson, Edith, Michael Mahaffey, and Doyal Nelson. "Measurement." In *Mathematics Learning in Early Childhood,* edited by Joseph N. Payne, pp. 227–50. Reston, Va.: National Council of Teachers of Mathematics, 1975.

Romberg, Thomas A. "One Point of View: NCTM's Curriculum and Evaluation Standards: What They Are and Why They Are Needed." *Arithmetic Teacher* 35 (May 1988): 2–3.

Wilson, Patricia S., and Alan Osborne. "Foundational Ideas in Teaching about Measure." In *Teaching Mathematics in Grades K–8,* edited by Thomas R. Post, pp. 78–110. Toronto: Allyn & Bacon, 1988.

larry leutzinger

12
graphical representation and probability

The value of graphing statistical information is evident in figure 1. Which method—text or graph—does a better job of conveying the message that certain countries are growing faster than others?

Not only does the graph capture the reader's attention but it also conveys the message more directly and clearly. It allows the reader to make comparisons, study relationships, and draw conclusions more easily. A brief perusal of any newspaper or magazine reveals the increased use of graphs to present statistical information. With the advent of more effective and powerful computer programs, the prevalence of graphs and tables will increase.

Since more and more information will be presented in graphical or tabular form, children need to develop at an early age skills that allow then to read, interpret,

and analyze such information. Students should be able to interpret data in any form.

Another reason for including graphical representation in the mathematics curriculum is its excitement and appeal for children. Graphs can be incorporated in many mathematics topics to add zest and to provide problem-solving applications. Graphs, tables, and charts are most valuable when they are generated from data collected by the students themselves and when the statistics represented are useful in solving a real problem.

Graphing can offer a way to integrate mathematics with other content areas. In science, children can record the growth of plants; classify leaves, rocks, seeds, animals; record daily weather characteristics; or make a table of inanimate objects that float or sink. In

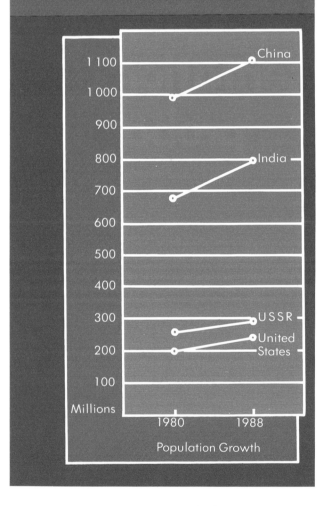

Some countries are growing at faster rates than others. In 1980 the population of the United States was 200 000 000. The estimated population of the United States in 1988 is 240 000 000. The U S S R had a population of 260 000 000 in 1980 and has about 290 000 000 today. The two largest nations in the world, India and China, had approximate populations of 680 000 000 and 995 000 000, respectively, in 1980 and populations of around 800 000 000 and 1 120 000 000, respectively, in 1988.

Fig. 1. Two ways to present statistical information

social studies, children can survey the characteristics of families and describe the population in their classroom or school. When studying the community, they can record, graph, and predict types of homes or stores and the number of phones, TVs, radios, hot tubs, and so on. The teacher can get a better idea of the characteristics of her or his students by surveying their likes and dislikes (e.g., food, music, friends, TV shows, or movies).

Graphical representation can be an all-school project with each classroom recording and graphing characteristics appropriate for their grade (for example, ways of getting to school, number of children eating lunch at school or bringing a lunch, favorite subjects, or number of books read). These graphs and tables can be displayed and a short paragraph describing the procedures, results, conclusions, and predictions can be posted nearby. Sometimes, school procedures have changed because of the results of such surveys, graphs, and written conclusions. For example, in one school the menu for an entire school year was modified to reflect the students' desires as indicated by a survey developed by fifth-grade students. The data were presented to the school board, who were so impressed that they recommended the changes. Collecting and recording data in graphical form adds much to any project and communicates more information than words alone. If the project answers a question or solves a problem, it is most worthwhile.

In addition to their importance in real-world applications and classroom motivation, reading, recording, and interpreting data aid in the development of problem-solving and thinking skills. Data representation skills are useful in solving many problems. Many verbal problems can be generated from each graph. Children can be asked to make up their own questions from graphs. The time spent on graphing, then, is time well spent.

A graph is a combination of numerical, visual, and verbal information. Many skills are necessary to understand a graph fully and still others are needed to construct one. A child must be able to compare and contrast numbers, associate verbal and numerical labels with the various components, draw conclusions, and communicate the information presented. To construct a graph requires such skills as counting, classifying, sorting, corresponding, labeling, and organizing.

Children should be led systematically from using concrete objects to represent data, as in the diagrams at the beginning of this chapter, to using colored squares to represent the information. Symbols can then be introduced in more abstract bar graphs, pictographs, and line graphs. Although most textbooks begin by having children read information from a graph, research indicates that children should construct their first graphs themselves with concrete materials. In this way they can better understand the process of collecting data and organizing a graph and communicate more when thinking about actions they have performed themselves.

uses of probability

Probability is closely related to graphical representation and statistics. Graphs can be used to estimate the likelihood of an event. The likelihood of an event occurring is the probability of that event and is represented by a number from 0 to 1 inclusive. For the young child, it is sufficient to use terms such as *likely, not likely, more likely,* and *less likely.*

Much of mathematics is exact, and this type of certainty appeals to many children. Probability, however, involves uncertainty. We cannot know for sure what events will occur, but we have to make decisions on the basis of what we know about their probability. Through probability activities, children can make decisions using known data to predict future outcomes.

Young children have many misconceptions about probability. They may expect all outcomes in an experiment to be equally likely, they may favor or avoid various outcomes solely because of preferences, or they may make inferences based on improper reasoning. Nevertheless, it is important for them to realize that although some aspects of mathematics require precision

and certainty, probability is concerned with choices that are based on the likelihood of an event. In real life, making a decision often involves selecting the best possible choice based on the facts available.

The remainder of this chapter contains ideas on using graphs and probability with special attention to their use in introducing other mathematical concepts. A final section includes extensions and grade-level placements.

early age children

Preschool and early grades provide an opportunity for classification, sorting, and counting.

classifying and sorting

Children should spend a portion of class time in preschool and kindergarten sorting and classifying objects in various ways. After children are familiar with the processes involved, they can learn to arrange the objects in an organized way.

a *Button sort.* On a strip of paper 3 cm wide, mark off ten 3-cm squares. Have children use these "ten-strips" to classify familiar items in the classroom. Then provide an assortment of buttons. After the children have sorted and classified them in various ways, such as by size, shape, number of holes, texture, or color, have them place each button with a certain characteristic into one square of the numbered strip. Place buttons with a different characteristic on another strip. Place the two strips next to each other, as shown in figure 2. Have children describe relationships using the concepts of one-to-one correspondence, more than, less than, and equal to—all prerequisites for meaningful counting.

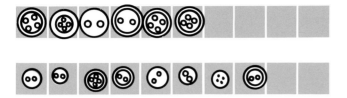

Fig. 2. Ten-strips for button sort

The teacher should ask such questions as, "Do the buttons match one to one? Are there more small buttons or large ones? Are there fewer large buttons than small ones? If I put two more large buttons on one strip, would the number be equal? If I take away two small buttons, will the strips be equal?"

Initially, place the ten-strips horizontally. Later have children position them vertically. Since many graphs have both horizontal and vertical scales, children should become familiar with both orientations. **a**

Tallies from ten-strips. Have children record in a table the data from the ten-strips. For each button, they make a mark in the table. Initially, they can use simple tally marks. Later, encourage children to make groups of five marks, as shown in figure 3.

Use the tally marks and ask similar questions: "Are there more small buttons or large buttons? How can I make them equal?" [Two more small buttons or change one small to a large]. **a**

Young children can also use ten-strips to investigate certain aspects of probability.

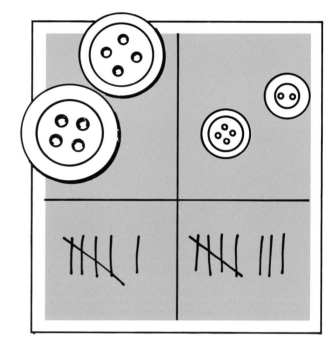

Fig. 3. Tally marks from a graph

Probability with ten-strips. Use red and blue chips to develop the concepts of more likely, less likely, and equally likely. Have children work in groups of three. Give each group an opaque container, such as a cup, holding 12 red chips and 6 blue chips. Have one child draw a chip from the cup without looking so that the choice is random. Have another child place the chip on a ten-strip marked "red" or on a ten-strip marked "blue." A third child makes a tally mark in the red or blue section of a table.

After they have picked 9 chips, have them compare and predict outcomes. "Did you draw out more red chips or more blue chips? Do you get the same answer from the strips and from the table? Which color is most likely to be drawn? Why? What color do you think the next chip drawn will be? Why do you choose that color?" Now have them pick a tenth chip, place it on the appropriate strip, and repeat the questions. "Do you think there are the same number of each color in the containers? Why?" Have them check the containers to verify their responses.

Repeat this activity many times with different numbers of objects in the containers. Sometimes put equal numbers of objects in each container and other times make an "unfair" setting (twice as many of one type). With each new trial, change the roles of the children in each group. Follow each experiment with class discussion. **a**

counting

Other experiences with graphing involve organized counting and can begin soon after the child has learned to count. As children count, they should move the counters from the original arrangement one at a time onto the first empty square on the ten-strip, as shown in figure 4.

The advantages of counting onto this strip are significant. First, many young children need to move the object being counted to make sure they do not miss it or count it twice. Fine motor skills are developed through such movements. The process of moving the object onto the strip reinforces the one-to-one correspondence between the object and the square on which it is placed.

a *Choose and count.* Display a handful of counters of one color. Ask, "Do you guess this will fill up the ten-strip? Do you think some spaces will be empty? Can you count out five of these and place them on the strip?" Repeat for other numbers up to 10. Provide counters of different colors. "Can you count out 6 blue counters and place them on the strip?"

Fig. 4. Moving and counting objects on a ten-strip

To develop their thinking skills, after the children have placed the objects on the strips, cover the first 4 or 5

counters on the strip with your hand. "How many counters are covered? Can you look at the empty squares to find out?" Then cover 3 or 4 counters in the middle of the strip, leaving 1, 2, or 3 objects exposed. "How many are covered? How many are on this side of my hand? How many are on the other side?" **a**

Sets of objects are easier to compare if they are arranged in similar ways. Children can begin to recognize the relationships between numbers without being forced to count by 1's.

a *Count and compare.* Use two number strips to count a collection of red and blue cubes, as in figure 5. Encourage counting on and counting back as they count and compare. "How many red counters are there? How many more blue counters than red? How many blue counters are there? If I take 2 of the blue counters away, how do the numbers of red and blue counters compare? Take one counter from the blue and put it on the red. How do the number of counters on each strip compare?" **a**

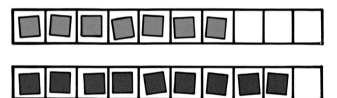

Fig. 5. Counting and comparing using ten-strips

After children have placed physical objects on a number strip, have them take an identical strip, place it below the first one, and color a square for each object. The colored squares in the second strip should correspond one to one with the squares on the first strip containing concrete objects. A label should be made for the colored strip to indicate what object was used. Then a different set of objects can be placed on the first strip and another strip colored to match the new objects. Again a label should be made to identify the objects. When four or five such colored strips have been made, the children can be encouraged to move their strips in various ways. Positioning the strips so the values indicate a stair-step pattern is the most effective way to compare and contrast the values.

a *Birthday seasons.* Prepare 4 ten-strips and label each with the name of a season as in figure 6. Then have each student color a square in the appropriate season for her or his birthday. Begin this activity with the questions, "Which season has the most birthdays? In which season do most children have birthdays? How may fewer children have birthdays in summer than in fall? If a new girl came into the room, in what season would you guess she was born? Why did you pick that season? How many children won't be in school on their birthday?"

The last question has an obvious answer of 3—those in the summer months, but is actually more complicated than that. Some birthdays in June, July, and August may fall on school days. Some birthdays during the year may fall on Saturdays, Sundays, or holidays. Fruitful discussions can result from analyzing these data. Perhaps the data need to be more specific. Ask the children how to do this. **a**

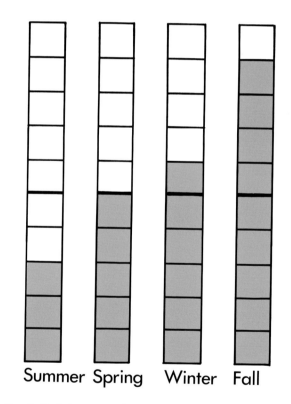

Summer Spring Winter Fall

Fig. 6. Birthdays in each season

The statistical measures range, mode, and median can be informally introduced through the movement of the number strips and the discussion of the number of objects represented on each strip. If the strips are arranged in a stair-step pattern, the largest and smallest values are apparent, as are the values between them. Ask children to describe the statistics before and after arranging the strips.

After the children have experience with representing data on number strips, they can begin to place objects on graph paper and later color the squares on graph paper. They should realize that each square represents a certain number of objects and that each row of the grid represents a different set of objects. The grid, then, is nothing more than a number of ten-strips aligned horizontally and vertically. Word labels are important so that children can keep track of the names of the items in each row or column, and numerical labels are important to indicate the scale being used.

A graph is not finished until it is properly labeled. Data can convey information and encourage discussion only if what they represent is well described and accurate. A title for the graph is needed. Labels should be attached to the graphs to indicate what data have been recorded. If children cannot write the name of the type of object being counted, cards with the labels already written can be provided.

introducing other concepts

Graphs and tables are most often reserved for the final sections of elementary school mathematics textbooks. Graphs and tables are a good way to introduce such concepts as addition, subtraction, numeration, or multiplication. A graph is even more significant if the children generate the information themselves. The following activities suggest graphs and tables that children can create. Such activities generate interest and foster language development.

numbers and number comparison

Before children make a graph, it is motivating and thought-provoking to pose a question that the data in the graph will help answer. The following activity begins with such a question.

Popular pets. Begin by asking, "What is the most popular pet of the children in this room?" A similar but related question— "What pets do children in the room own?"—may prove difficult because some children may not own pets.

Use the same color cube for each kind of pet. Let each child choose a colored cube for the pet chosen. Arrange the cubes in rows by color to form a bar graph, as in figure 7. Then have children count the cubes as the numbers are written in the table. "How many chose cats as their favorite? What number do I write in the table?" Then ask such questions as the following: "How many dogs are shown? Which pet is the most popular? What is the most popular animal? How many children voted for this animal? Which two pets are equally popular? Which animal is the least popular? Name a pet that is a favorite of zero children."

Cats	16
Dogs	8
Birds	5
Fish	2
Gerbils	2
Snakes	1

Fig. 7. Our favorite pets

Extend the discussion with probability questions. "If you went up to a house in your neighborhood, what pet would be most likely to greet you at the door? What would be the least likely pet at that house?"

Have children take the "graph" apart and compare the data by joining the cubes in different combinations. Ask questions about certain groups of pets that are illustrated by cubes of various colors. Use the cubes to ask questions related to fractions.

Combine all the cubes in a "train" with all cubes of the same color grouped together. This "graph" includes cubes for all the pets. The total number of children responding is represented by the total number of cubes. "Train graphs" provide children with an alternative way of examining data.

Have children guess the answer to the question before the graph is made. Then have each child select an interlocking cube for his or her favorite pet and place the cube on a picture of that pet or on a card listing the type of pet. Use the same color for each pet. "Half of the children like one kind of pet. What kind is that? One-fourth of you like another pet. What is it? What 4 pets together are liked just as much as dogs?" **a**

Investigating data in train form prepares children for later work with circle graphs, where the data are presented as a fractional part of a whole, and for statistics, where it is important to know the total number of cases, or outcomes. Children can reproduce the train on graph paper using appropriate colors. As the children mature, they can represent the numbers in a shaded rectangle by affixing numerical labels to the various sections. The children can reorganize the section for different effects, and comparisons can be made between the various sections.

addition and subtraction

In grades 1 and 2, the concepts of addition and subtraction can be introduced with the question, "What is your favorite subject in school?"

Favorite subject. Give each child a blank card and tell him or her to write the name of his or her favorite subject on it. Make a bar graph and table similar to the one in figure 8 for the data collected. "How many more children liked math than science? How many fewer children liked music than reading? How many children liked both art and gym? Write a number sentence relating the number of children who liked reading to the number who liked art. What two subjects together got just as many votes as reading? If you ask 12 other people what subjects they like best and they responded the way our class did, how many would like each of the subjects? If I asked you tomorrow, would your answer be the same?"

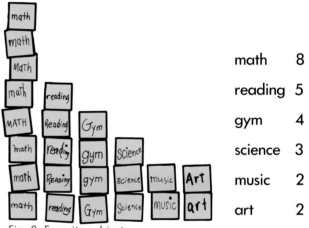

math	8
reading	5
gym	4
science	3
music	2
art	2

Fig. 8. Favorite subject

Have children create a train graph using colored cubes or color squares on graph paper to represent the data above. Ask questions that relate the number of children who like each subject to the total number of children in the class. "What fraction of the class chose math as their favorite subject? What fraction of this class did not choose math? Half of the class like two subjects. What are they?" **a**

Certain charts or tables contain data that can aid in children's learning. The addition table can be used to provide information to children as they start memorizing basic addition facts. As the facts are introduced, students can locate them on the chart and cross off the facts as they learn them. As thinking strategies are used to introduce basic facts, each is indicated on the chart. See chapter 6 for examples.

If timed tests are used to evaluate learning, each child can keep a record of his or her progress on a graph containing the date and the number of facts answered correctly in a certain time (see fig. 9). This procedure allows the child to monitor his or her progress without comparing the results to the class as a whole.

Graphs and charts can be used to investigate why certain addition facts are more difficult to learn and memorize than others.

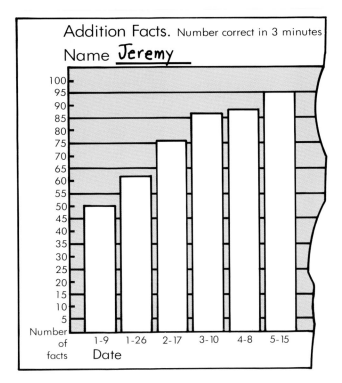

Fig. 9. Facts correct in 3 minutes

a *Graph of sums.* Give each group of three children two sets of number cards, with each card containing a number from 0 to 9. One child draws 2 cards from the 20 overturned cards. Another child adds the numbers shown on the cards and records the sum on a graph. The third child records the sum in a table. They replace 2 cards and mix them with the others after each draw. After each group of children in the class has drawn 20 pairs of cards and recorded the sums, show the results for the whole class on a graph and a table on the chalkboard. The results from one third-grade class of twenty-seven children (nine groups) appear in figure 10.

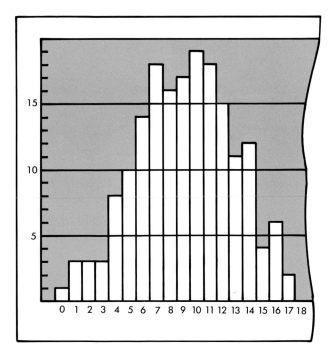

Fig. 10. Graph of sums for basic facts

"Which sum on your graph appeared the most?" [List the most frequently obtained sum for each of the groups. Make another graph showing the sums occurring most frequently in each group.] "How many times did you get a sum of 18? What cards would you draw to have a sum of 18? How does the shape of the class's graph compare to the shape of your graph? If we had 20 more draws, how many sums of 10 could we expect?"

Now have the children make a table listing the sums from 0 to 18 and all the two-card combinations that could yield each sum. The children should write each combination on a piece of paper (note that 3 + 5 and 5 + 3 are different combinations). They should place each card above the sum for that combination, as shown in figure 11. "How does the graph of the cards you drew compare to this graph? What is the most frequently occurring sum? How many sums are less than 10? Greater than 10? How do the number of combinations compare with the sums for the sums 1, 2, 3, 4, 5, 6, 7, 8, 9? How many combinations have a 1 as an addend? A 2? What conclusions can you draw? Which sums are the hardest for you to remember? Why do you think those are harder?" **a**

Fig. 11. Combinations for sums

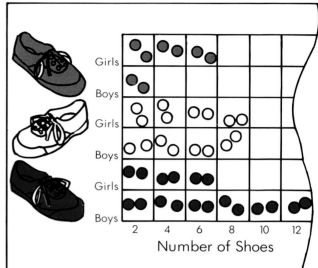

Fig. 12. Most frequent shoe color

The same type of table can be constructed for subtraction combinations. The result is much different, however. Each difference has exactly 10 combinations. The resulting bar graph contains ten bars of equal length.

multiplication

Begin by asking the children, "What color of shoe is worn by the most children in this class?"

a *Most frequent shoe color.* Have each student select two colored counters that correspond to the color of his or her shoes. Have each child come forward and place the counters in one square on the grid next to the name of the color. (See fig. 12.) The graph lists both boys' and girls' shoes on the bars. Each square stands for 2 shoes. "How many girls in the room have white shoes? How many children have brown shoes? How many shoes in the room are black? How many shoes are brown? How many fewer shoes are black than white?" **a**

Another multiplication example can be generated with a table to introduce ratios and rates to third and fourth graders.

a *Cost of marbles.* Pose a problem such as this to the class: "One marble costs 5¢. Sean bought some marbles. How much could he have spent?" Before any graph or table is made, discuss the problem with the children. "What does 'some' mean? Could Sean have spent 15¢? Could he have spent 8¢? Can you see a pattern in the amount he could have spent?" Have children suggest possible amounts that Sean could have spent and record them on a table (fig. 13). "If Sean bought 6 marbles, how much did he spend? If Sean spent 45¢, how many marbles did he buy? Sean went to the store with 10 nickels; he bought some marbles and left with 15¢. How many marbles did he buy? Sean entered the store with 4 marbles in his pocket. When he left the store, he had 11 marbles in his pocket. How much did he spend to buy the marbles? Sean bought fewer than 8 marbles and spent more than 25¢. How many marbles did he buy?" Extend the idea by having students make another table telling about buying something else. **a**

Using a table as just illustrated is a "double" problem-solving situation. A problem is initially posed that is clarified with a table and then additional specific questions are asked about the completed table. Research indicates that if students can be taught to

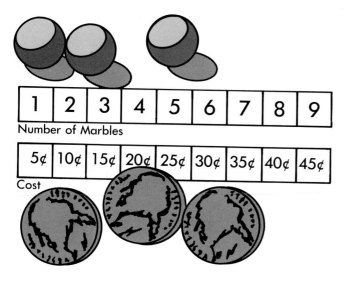

1	2	3	4	5	6	7	8	9

Number of Marbles

5¢	10¢	15¢	20¢	25¢	30¢	35¢	40¢	45¢

Cost

Fig. 13. Total cost of marbles

represent problem situations with tables or diagrams, they will become better problem solvers. They will also be better able to solve problems that involve a chart, table, or diagram.

projects

Graphs can not only stimulate initial discussion of a concept but also serve as extensions and applications of that concept. The following activities provide opportunities for class and individual projects as a way to collect, organize, represent, and interpret data.

Guess the number. On Monday, show the class a container with about 800 counters in it. Have each child guess the number of counters in the container. Record the lowest and highest guesses. Graph the range (highest guess minus lowest guess) and the middle number (range divided by 2) for Monday, using one bar for the range and another bar for the middle number.

On Tuesday, place a smaller container holding about 80 counters next to the original container and tell the children the number in the smaller container. Have the children make another guess as to the number in the large container. Again record the range of guesses and middle number.

On Wednesday, put about 200 counters in the smaller container and tell this number to students. Again record the guesses.

On Thursday, put about 400 in the smaller container; on Friday, use about 600.

At the end of the week compare the ranges and the middle numbers of guesses for each day. Have the children form a double line graph. One line should reflect the range each day and the other line the middle number. On Friday, tell the students the number of counters in the container. "Did the range of guesses decrease each day? Did the middle number get closer to the actual value each day? If you continue the guesses, what would the values for the range and middle number likely be? How do you determine those values?" **a**

Survey of the class. You can begin this extensive project by asking, "How can we describe our class?" Take a survey of the children, including personal characteristics (e.g., height, weight, hair color, hair length, glasses, shoe size, month of birth) and likes and dislikes (favorite TV show, color, actor or actress, holiday, movie, popular song). Have children keep track and graph the results.

Construct a variety of graphs of the data, including horizontal and vertical bar graphs, line graphs, pictographs, and tables. The values for girls and boys can be graphed separately.

Discuss each graph. Bring out comparisons of the numerical results and probable reasons for them. "Which is the most popular TV show? The least popular? What factors make a show the favorite?" [Type of program, time it is shown, amount of homework that night] For some of the data, have students find the median or mean (average). **a**

What's in a word? A good interdisciplinary project is analyzing reading passages for the length of words. Have the class work on this project in groups or individually, combining results for the total class. Have each group of children examine a 100-word passage from a book appropriate for their grade level and categorize the words by the number of letters. Have each group graph the words in each category, then share their results with the class. Make a large chart of the class results with individual group results noted. Compare the groups and their records. Ask questions to show how the results differ between the groups. "Does it make a difference which book you pick? What would the results be if you read 100 pages from a math or a social studies book?" Questions will also come from the children themselves as they compare their data with other groups'.   **a**

extensions and grade level suggestions

Making the transfer from bar graphs to line graphs is easy. Instead of shading in one square for each concrete object, the child simply places a dot on the square that represents the number of objects. Line graphs should be used only for data that are continuous, or nearly so, such as temperature, population, heights, or weights. Figure 14 shows temperatures for a week, with data recorded to the nearest 5°.

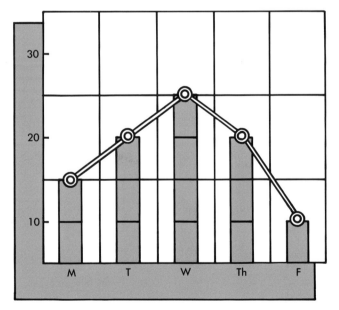

Fig. 14. Temperature at 9:00 a.m.

The introduction of the various types of graphs depends on the cognitive level of the child and the concept under study. Concrete materials should be used initially, but replaced later with representations only after the children understand one-to-one correspondences. Figure 15 contains recommended guidelines for the introduction of various types of graphs and tables.

One ten-strip containing objects (ages 3-4)

Two ten-strips containing objects (ages 4-5)

One ten-strip with squares shaded representing concrete objects (ages 4-5)

Two ten-strips with squares shaded (ages 5-6)

Table containing two sections (ages 5-6)

Pictograph (ages 5-6)

Multiple ten-strips with objects (ages 5-6)

Multiple ten-strips with squares shaded (ages 5-6)

Table containing multiple sections (ages 5-6)

Large-grid paper with objects placed in each square (ages 5-6)

Grid paper with shaded squares (age 7)

Grid paper with line graph (age 7 and over)

Fig. 15. Age guidelines for graphs and tables

summary

Statistical data and their representation in the form of graphs, charts, and tables, as well as ideas of probability, are basic skills that all children, starting at an early age, need to possess. In a world that increasingly relies on visual images to convey information, children need to learn how to analyze information in graphs and charts. They need to understand and interpret data to make decisions in and out of school and should be able to gather data, create graphs, and ask themselves questions about the results.

Graphing should be a tool for solving problems as well as a rich source of problem-solving activities. Statistics and graphing are important in developing and extending mathematical concepts. Statistics can serve as the focus of lessons on classifying, counting, addition, subtraction, and multiplication. The idea of events being more likely, less likely, or equally likely can introduce the topic of probability.

By bringing the real world into the mathematics classroom and having children collect and display real information and describe what they find, we can help children understand and appreciate the importance of statistics and their representation and the basic ideas of probability.

bibliography

Bestgen, Barbara J. "Making and Interpreting Graphs and Tables: Results and Implications from National Assessment." *Arithmetic Teacher* 28 (December 1980): 26–29.

Bruni, James V., and Helene J. Silverman. "Developing Concepts in Probability and Statistics—and Much More." *Arithmetic Teacher* 33 (February 1986): 34–37.

Dickinson, J. Craig. "Gather, Organize, Display: Mathematics for the Information Society." *Arithmetic Teacher* 34 (December 1986): 12–15.

Horak, Virginia M., and Willis J. Horak. "Collecting and Displaying the Data around Us." *Arithmetic Teacher* 30 (September 1982): 16–20.

Johnson, Elizabeth M. "Bar Graphs for First Graders." *Arithmetic Teacher* 29 (December 1981): 30–31.

O'Neil, David R., and Rosalie Jensen. "Looking at Facts." *Arithmetic Teacher* 29 (April 1982): 12–15.

Russell, Susan Jo, and Susan Friel. "Collecting and Analyzing Real Data in the Elementary School Classroom." In *New Directions for Elementary School Mathematics,* 1989 Yearbook, edited by Paul R. Trafton and Albert P. Shulte, pp. 134–48. Reston, Va: National Council of Teachers of Mathematics, 1989.

Shaw, Jean M. "Dealing with Data." *Arithmetic Teacher* 31 (May 1984): 9–15.

Slaughter, Judith Pollard. "The Graph Examined." *Arithmetic Teacher* 30 (March 1983): 41–45.

Smith, Robert F. "Bar Graphs for Five-Year-Olds." *Arithmetic Teacher* 27 (October 1979): 38–41.

Sullivan, Delia, and Mary Ann O'Neil. "This Is Us! Great Graphs for Kids." *Arithmetic Teacher* 28 (September 1980): 14–18.

Woodward, Ernest. "A Second-Grade Probability and Graphing Lesson." *Arithmetic Teacher* 30 (March 1983): 23–24.

patricia campbell
douglas clements

using microcomputers for mathematics learning

13

Laura was a determined first grader who wanted to draw a fish using the programming language Logo. With Logo commands she could move and turn the triangular cursor on the screen to draw straight lines, so she thought she ought to be able to use Logo to draw the curved lines of a fish. The teacher would not tell her how; instead she told Laura to work with James, who wanted to draw a snowman. The teacher gave them a large piece of paper with a big curve drawn on it and told them to think about how they would walk along such a curve.

James is now following Laura's directions for walking on the curve on the paper.

"You're off the line again!"

"You said forward 3, so I took three steps."

"Well, go back and this time only go two steps."

"Okay, okay. . . . I'm still on the line. But if I go forward again I'll be off the line. I have to turn," said James. "I have to turn to the . . . left."

"Okay, turn. . . . No, you're off the line again. Don't turn so much. Just do a little turn. . . . "Now go forward. . . . Don't go off the line."

"I have to turn the same way again."

"Okay, but just a little. . . . Now take one step again. Now turn just a little again."

"Wait," said James. "That's it! All you have to do is to go forward and then turn, and then go forward some more and turn again."

"Let me try it," said Laura, trading places with James and walking slowly along the curve. "You're right. That's it!"

"Let's try it on the computer," said James.

"Okay," said Laura, "but remember, I want to make a fish."

Later, the teacher prints a copy of their drawing, shown in figure 1. James tells the teacher that he wants to work with Laura again but next time he wants to draw a snowman.

Fig. 1. A "fish" created in Instant Logo

These young children were learning about curves and lines as they solved a problem that they had defined for themselves. This example shows the kind of mathematical learning that can be stimulated by a microcomputer. In this example, the children were actively thinking as they became aware of the conditions of the problem (What pattern of steps and turns produces a curve?) and the solution processes that they were using (How do you step and turn when you walk on a curved line?). Indeed, microcomputers offer a unique setting for young children in which mathematics can be presented as a field for investigation or as a time for examining or creating patterns, exploring possible relationships, or solving problems.

This chapter examines the potential of the microcomputer for promoting an enriched view of mathematics learning in geometry, problem solving, numeration, and estimation and cites some commercial software programs as exemplars. But first consider the issue of appropriate use.

Questions have been raised whether the microcomputer might foster the development of socially isolated children. Research indicates that even preschool children can profitably use a microcomputer without detrimental side effects (e.g., Fein, Campbell, and Schwartz 1987; Lipinski et al. 1986). Questions have been raised whether children who are not yet or just at the stage of concrete operations should be using a symbolic medium, such as a microcomputer (Barnes

and Hill 1983; Cuffaro 1984). Recent research indicates that preschoolers, given appropriate and meaningful tasks, are much more competent than has been thought. Further, much of the activity that preschool children engage in is symbolic. Young children use gestures and language to communicate; their play, songs, and art are replete with symbols (e.g., Gelman and Baillargeon 1983; Sheingold 1986). Technology can be in tune with the needs and potential of young children. But should it be? Isn't this an example of "hurrying" young children? (Elkind 1981)

The main issue is what is done with microcomputers. They are no more dangerous than books or pencils; all three devices can be used to push a child to read, write, or learn mathematics facts too soon. However, each tool can also provide developmentally appropriate experiences. The microcomputer offers a unique approach for enhancing academic and creative development in the classroom, fostering thinking and imagination (fig. 2). But it must be presented within an environment that simultaneously supports the active, social, and emotional needs of preschool- and primary-aged children.

Fig. 2. Working at a microcomputer

logo

Logo is a programming language that can be used by preschoolers or college graduates. It is an interactive language; with Logo the microcomputer will give you messages if a command cannot be processed. It is a procedural language; programs can be recalled, combined, and reused to make bigger, more complex programs. It can also be graphic; rather than just printing symbols, it can produce drawings. One component of Logo is turtle graphics. With turtle graphics, a child can give directions to a cursor, called a turtle, on the screen by using the commands FORWARD, BACK, LEFT, and RIGHT. The child can also use the commands PENUP and PENDOWN to indicate whether the turtle should or should not leave a drawing trail behind or REPEAT to indicate that other commands should be repeated. Interesting drawings can be produced with only these commands, but Logo can also be used to define new commands. For example, a common task is to ask second or third graders to write a program to make a rectangle. One second grader's solution is shown below, and the printout is shown in figure 3.

```
TO RECTANGLE
        FD 40
        RT 90
        FD 70
        RT 90
        FD 40
        RT 90
        FD 70
        RT 90
END
```

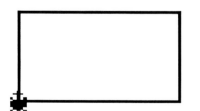

Fig. 3. Logo rectangle created by a second grader

Is this really mathematics? Or is Logo just an electronic crayon? The answer lies in how teachers use Logo in the classroom. Logo can be a setting in which children explore and learn mathematics or in which they want to learn more mathematics so they can do something else with Logo.

In the two prior examples, drawing a fish and drawing a rectangle, the children had to determine a listing of instructions to produce the geometric shape or figure they had conceptualized. They had to interpet that figure in terms of a few commands by breaking it into parts and, for the rectangle, specifying the measure of those parts. This process is mathematical problem solving. As children use Logo, they verbalize their goals and their strategies as they try to solve a problem. At the same time, they must consider "surprises"—when the commands do not produce the intended results—and then they must subsequently find and correct their errors. These are desirable problem-solving skills, but they can be difficult to foster.

Logo is a setting in which teachers can model and foster problem-solving strategies. In addition, Logo is mathematical. Logo permits children to use and create symbols to explore and extend their emerging knowledge of spatial relationships and geometric properties. It requires that children organize their ideas sequentially and logically as they think of number in terms of distances and angle measures.

The success of Logo instruction will depend on the effectiveness with which Logo is integrated into the curriculum because, as noted by Fein (1985, p. 22), "the importance of Logo is that it provides an unusually rich problem space within which children can confront important ideas; it does not guarantee that the confrontation will occur." An investigation of studies that report positive results reveals direct instructional procedures that provided just enough support, but not too much, along with the expectation that the children's work would show growth.

So what should be the characteristics of Logo instruction for young children if it is to foster mathematical thinking?

 How do you move? First, have young children consciously examine what occurs when they move about, for example:

"Where did you move?"

"How many steps did you take?"

"What if you took bigger or smaller steps?"

"How can you judge if your steps are the same size?"

"Did you walk straight ahead or turn as you walked?" (What is a straight line?)

"Are all turns alike in size and direction?"

"Can you record your motions by drawing a path?"

Next, help children begin to experience the exact nature of directions.

"How do you tell someone to move from one spot to another?"

"What if the person is already facing in the right direction?"

"What if the person is not facing the intended location?"

"Can more than one path exist between two points?"

"What would be the shortest path?"

"Does it matter if you tell a person to turn and then walk rather than to walk and then turn?"

"How do you tell a person to walk along a drawn path?"

"Is there only one set of directions possible?" **a**

In this process, children also experience what it means to assume the visual or spatial perspective of another person. If two children face each other, then what one child perceives as the left side of the room, the other child perceives as the right side of the room. With off-the-computer activities that focus on such questions, children experience what it means to move and to identify locations in space, to abstract physical motion with drawn figures, and to describe motion with a symbolic language that has directional (right or left) and distance (forward or back) commands. (See chapter 10.) Then, with such support devices as magnetic boards, command cards, and tracing paper, the children can transfer their interpretation of motion to the microcomputer using Logo. These activities also are a way to use Logo to attain mathematics curriculum goals.

Because many primary school children cannot cope with the complexity of the complete Logo language, there are a number of simpler versions of Logo available that use single keystrokes to direct the turtle (for an Instant Logo program as well as suggestions for instruction, see Campbell 1988). After gaining proficiency in a single-keystroke Logo, many second-grade and most third-grade children can advance to standard Logo. The support program *TEACH* is one possible bridge to standard Logo because it allows the child to define a procedure without exiting from the graphic screen (Clements 1983–84).

getting into shape: computers and geometry

Children learn about geometric shapes not so much from their perception of objects as from the actions they perform on these objects. Pierre van Hiele studied how children develop geometric ideas and hypothesized different levels of thinking through which children progress. (See chapter 10.) A quality geometry curriculum for young children should use action to facilitate children's development through these levels.

logo links

Performing physical actions on concrete objects is necessary if children are to develop geometric concepts. But they must internalize such physical actions and abstract the corresponding geometric notions. A powerful way for children to think about geometric objects is in the form of paths, as records of movement (Clements and Battista 1988). Children can first investigate paths by walking and drawing and then later by directing the Logo turtle. In this way, children can learn to think of the turtle's actions as ones that they can perform. We see evidence of this when in trying to figure out what a given set of directions will make the turtle draw, children turn their bodies in an attempt to figure out a turn. That is, they "project" themselves into the place of the turtle. In this way Logo environments are action-based. These actions are both perceptual—watching the turtle's movements—and physical—interpreting the turtle's movement as physical motion.

But why not just walk and draw? What does the turtle add? It allows the teacher to help form some crucial links.

linking the intuitive and the explicit

Having children visually scan the side of a building, run their hands along the edge of a rectangular table, or walk a straight path will help them abstract the concept of straightness. But this concept can be more explicitly developed with Logo activities.
Logo provides an environment for making paths and their components more conspicuous. It helps children link their intuitive knowledge about moving and drawing to more explicit mathematical ideas.

Building such links also facilitates growth through the

levels of geometric thinking. Consider the concept of rectangle. In the usual elementary school geometry curriculum, children only identify a rectangle, usually pictured with a horizontal base. In Logo, however, children can think at a higher level by constructing a sequence of commands to draw a rectangle. This helps them to make their concept of rectangle explicit. They analyze the visual aspects of the rectangle as a whole and make conclusions about its component parts and its properties. Thus, with proper guidance from the teacher, Logo allows children to consider and refine their intuitive expectations. The child can think about rectangles as paths created by movements of the turtle and, thus, develop a useful mental model for analyzing, talking about, and reflecting on rectangles. The building of such mental models deepens visual understanding and encourages descriptive and analytic thinking.

Drawing rectangles. A class of first graders working on a Logo-based geometry curriculum (Clements and Battista 1988) were constructing rectangles. In their own words, most of the rectangles were "lying down," that is, most of the rectangles had one side on a horizontal. After drawing several in that position, one student pondered, "I wonder if I can tilt it." She turned the turtle from its initial vertical heading, drew the first side, and then paused. She was unsure about how much to turn: Just enough to head in a horizontal direction? That was the direction in which the turtle had always headed before. Or should it move three turns? (Each turn was 30°.)

An observing teacher said, "How many turns did you have to use to make the corners on your other rectangles?" She thought, issued three left turns, and hesitated again. "How far? . . . Oh, it must be the same as its partner!" She then completed her rectangle. This child had posed a challenge for herself. The instructions to be given to the turtle at this new orientation were not obvious to her. With the help of indirect questions, she analyzed the situation and reflected on the properties of a rectangle. She also extended her visual ideas about rectangles.   **a**

linking conceptual and procedural knowledge

Logo can also help link two basic types of knowledge: conceptual and procedural. In Logo, children can be guided to link their conceptual knowledge of the properties of shapes to procedural knowledge by directing the turtle to construct those shapes. To draw a

figure in Logo, children must determine the measures of angles and the lengths of line segments, often using estimation and calculations to do so. They can also analyze a given figure and break it into smaller parts that are more easily constructed. Thus, with Logo, the children are constantly involved in problem solving, estimation, and arithmetic. When such links are established, children have constructed a richer and more flexible knowledge to apply to the solution of geometric problems.

Overall, then, Logo can link real-world manipulative experiences to more abstract mathematical ideas. Such an environment also emphasizes "doing geometry" and solving geometric problems, rather than learning geometry facts. Children seek questions as much as answers. They investigate rather than memorize. They are motivated to tackle significant geometric problems and given the tools needed for their solution.

shaping logo experiences: a logo-based geometry curriculum

Building such a geometric environment for children requires care. The teacher must ensure that these links are indeed forged by children. The key to presenting Logo to children in the primary grades is balanced instruction. Teacher-directed instruction must be given on aspects of the language, the mathematics of a display, or related geometric concepts. There must also be group problem solving, exploration of physical manipulations off the computer, and time for student projects. Teachers can define criteria for some projects, or they can encourage student-designed, teacher-approved projects. But primary school children must have time to create, discuss, and share their own displays.

introduction to paths

Paths begin with physical motion (Clements and Battista 1988).

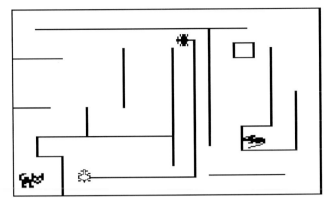

Fig. 4. Logo maze

Making paths. Have children walk on several paths made outdoors with chalk or indoors with masking tape. While they are walking the paths, encourage them to describe their movements. Then gather them around the paths and explain that a path is a record of movement by asking such questions as these:

"Have you ever followed a path drawn on the floor of a building? Where?"

"How are those paths and the masking-tape paths different? How are they the same?"

Next, discuss straight paths, bends, "curvy parts" (i.e., those created by continuous change in direction), and closed paths (inside, outside, and simple closed paths), always linking the path concept to the movement that created it.

"How do we know when a path is straight?" [When we keep going in the same direction.]

"How do we know we are going in the same direction?"

"What is direction?"

"What is a turn?" [Change in direction or heading]**a**

map paths

Game: The Turtle Says. . . . A small number of commands is given for the whole class to follow: "Forward, turn to the left." Discuss the paths created by these simple movements. Next, have pairs of children use Logo to direct the turtle through a map or maze loaded from the disk provided by the teacher or viewed from a transparency like the one in figure 4 that is taped to the screen. One child should enter instructions to the turtle while a partner records the path and commands on paper. **a**

Even though the children have experienced structured physical activities regarding motion, paths, and Logo commands, they need to transfer Logo motions to the screen. For instance, despite physical experiences and observations of the teacher demonstrating Logo commands at the computer, many children will still

believe that pressing L (for LEFT) will make the turtle *move* toward the left regardless of its heading. These children have not yet understood the two qualitatively different kinds of "moves" the turtle makes: changes in position (FORWARD and BACK) and changes in heading (RIGHT and LEFT).

Moving left or right. Two kindergarten boys developed the meaning of moving left with appropriate questions from a teacher. The turtle was facing "down," that is, at a 180° heading.

Steve: Let's make it go left.

Dave: Left is this way [points to his left].

Steve: [Presses L]

Dave: [in a disappointed tone]: Ohhh.

Teacher: What happened? What did the turtle do?

Steve: It . . . turned left.

Dave: But I want him to *go* left!

Teacher: Which way is the turtle heading?

Dave: Oh, yeah, *turn* him left and *then* go forward!

The teacher's questions helped the pair to reflect on the results of their actions and to attend to important features of the problem, but he did not directly tell the children what to do.

Later in the week, the boys seemed to have grasped firmly the idea of turning along a path. Typical was the following exchange:

Steve: He's facing this way, right? And we want him to go . . . [turning his head so that he's facing the same way as the turtle] . . . right!

Dave: So that would be . . . R [taps his head repeatedly and emphatically].

Steve [types R]: *Now,* F for forward!　　　**a**

When children turn their heads to align themselves with the turtle, it can indicate that they really "see" a change in direction occurring as a result of turning motion. Children did not construct this critical and surprisingly difficult idea simply by watching the teacher's demonstrations or hearing explanations. They used Logo as a tool to experiment with their own ideas. The teacher helped them reflect on their experiments.

At the conclusion of the maze activity, the teacher had several children show their work. He asked questions such as these:

"At what point(s) in your path was the turtle turning?"

"What can you tell me about the path you just made?"

"How many straight parts does the path have? How many bends?"

"Can you make a path with fewer straight parts? Fewer bends?"

"Were your paths simple paths?"

This last question yielded the response, "Ours are all simple. But nobody's is a closed path."

The teacher followed up by asking, "Why is that? How do you know for sure?"

A child responded, "Because the turtle always starts here and ends in a different place, over here. No matter where you go, that would never make a closed path!"

As a challenge, older children should be given more demanding "maps" and be asked to return the turtle to its starting position along precisely the same path. Children can solve this problem in many ways, but some find the elegant technique of "reversing" every Logo instruction that created the initial Logo path (e.g., to reverse the initial Logo commands FD 50 RT 30 FD 20, enter BK 20 LT 30 BK 50). This early experience with "undoing" can be linked to other inverse mathematical situations, such as "undoing" addition with subtraction.

shapes as special paths

Once the concept of path has been firmly grasped by children, move on to such "special" paths as angles, squares, and triangles. Viewing these shapes as paths will encourage children to start analyzing their components. With older children, this study of shapes as paths can be extended to include the concept of measuring interior and exterior angles. Writing procedures in Logo to draw geometric shapes encourages children to analyze and coordinate their perceptual properties. Logo also provides children a language for discussing their observations, analyses, and conjectures about shapes and their components.

Building squares. First have children build examples of squares in a variety of ways using a variety of materials. "Can two of you make a square with your two pairs of arms? How can you form a square with this string? What kind of sticks do you need to make a square? Using the tiles on the floor as guidelines, can you walk around a large square? How does your finger move if you trace a square in water or in the snow?"

After giving many examples of squares and talking about the essential characteristics (equal sides and angles, like the corner of this page), have children plan and write several "square procedures" in Logo using a different side length for each procedure, as noted in figure 5.

Discuss the procedures, having children relate the components of the square to the Logo definitions. "What part of the square is made by FD 40? [A side] By RT 90? [Turn of 90 degrees] By FD 40?" [The right angle and a side] Lead children to compare their various square procedures, listing the similarities (e.g., the pattern of commands) and differences (amount to go FORWARD, use of right or left turns). Discuss the properties of a square (e.g., four equal sides, four equal angles produced by 90° turns), relating them to similarities in children's procedures. Throughout this discussion, continue to relate the pattern of commands in the procedures to the properties of squares. For example, when a child responds that four FD commands have the same number as input, ask why this is true. Help them to see that it is true because the

Single-keystroke Logo (preschool to grade 1)

```
TO SQUARE1          TO SQUARE2
  F   F   F   F        F   F   F   F   F   F
  R   R   R            R   R   R
  F   F   F   F        F   F   F   F   F   F
  R   R   R            R   R   R
  F   F   F   F        F   F   F   F   F   F
  R   R   R            R   R   R
  F   F   F   F        F   F   F   F   F   F
  R   R   R            R   R   R
END                 END
```

Regular Logo (grades 2 and up)

```
TO SQUARE1          TO SQUARE2
  FD 40               FD 60
  RT 90               RT 90
  FD 40               FD 60
  RT 90               RT 90
  FD 40               FD 60
  RT 90               RT 90
  FD 40               FD 60
  RT 90               RT 90
END                 END
```

Fig. 5. Four procedures for creating a square

four sides of a square are equal in length. In these ways, Logo can help children link disparate areas of knowledge, with the goal of developing problem-solving and spatial-thinking abilities while constructing geometric ideas. Most computer-assisted instruction (CAI) programs tend to emphasize only one of these three abilities.

constructing geometric ideas: other software

Even very young children can use appropriate CAI geometry programs. One study indicated that computer lessons were more effective than television lessons for teaching preschoolers relational concepts such as above and below and over and under (Brawer 1984; cited in

Lieberman 1985). The most benefit may accrue, however, from computer programs that help the teacher extend children's experiences in constructing geometric ideas.

For example, the IBM/WICAT Elementary Mathematics series (WICAT Systems) is a complete sequence of geometry lessons for grade 1 and up that combines three construction tool kits with CAI-style assistance. With the first tool kit, CONSTRUCT, children can draw and label segments, lines, polygons, angles, and circles. With the second kit, TRANSFORM, they can alter figures. Commands include *translate, rotate, reflect, pull* (i.e., lengthen or shorten a figure along one dimension proportionately), and *scale* (i.e., make the figure larger than, but similar to, the original). The third tool kit, V-DRAW, is a simple Logo-like component of the system. Children are directed to use the drawing tools to construct line segments and shapes and the transformation tools to compare shapes and dimensions (see fig. 6). The CAI format allows children's work to be guided and checked; however, most lessons also possess an "explore" segment. In this segment children are encouraged to use the available tools to draw something, experiment with ideas, or meet an open-ended challenge. Such construction tools, used in a cycle of conceptual development, guided practice, and exploratory activities, can help develop understanding, problem-solving skills, and positive attitudes.

Another context in which the computer can provide geometric experiences that complement curriculum objectives is coordinates.

Find the Bumble. This program from *Bumble Games* (The Learning Company) presents a two-dimensional grid. Hidden somewhere on this grid is the Bumble character. A child chooses two coordinates (i.e., a column and a row), and he or she is shown that these coordinates correspond to one square that is highlighted on the grid. The object of the game is to find Bumble. Clues are given (e.g., "It's down and to the right," as are arrows). Bumble appears when found.

Bumble dots. In this program, children make dot-to-dot pictures. A child enters a sequence of dots on a grid by typing in pairs of

EXPLORE: When finished, press SKIP.
Use S for Scale to make the wheel
bigger.

Scale: use ↑ ↓; press ↵ when done.
Cursor is at the center of scaling.

EXPLORE: When finished, press SKIP.
Use S for Scale to make the wheel
bigger.

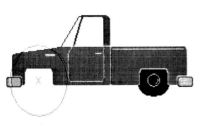

Scale: use ↑ ↓; press ↵ when done.
Cursor is at the center of scaling.

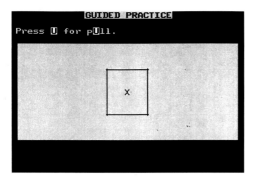

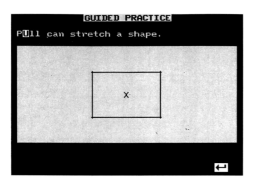

Fig. 6. Using the construction tools of the IBM/WICAT Elementary Mathematics series

numbers. As each new dot is entered, line segments are drawn to connect them. In this way, a picture is created, named by the child, and displayed with an electronic fanfare, as in figure 7. Because the children are pursuing a goal that is relevant to them, the usefulness of coordinates is highlighted and the feedback is understandable.

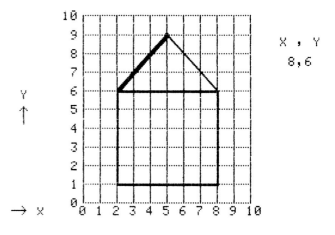

NAME DOT # 9

NUMBER PAIR IS: (X,Y <RETURN>)

Fig. 7. Creating a coordinate-based picture with *Bumble Games*

Other programs can create environments for creative, exploratory problem solving, which are particularly appropriate for younger children. For example, in working with preschoolers, Forman (1986) found that drawing programs offer a dynamic new way of exploring geometric concepts. For example, most of these programs provide a "boxes" function that allows children to draw rectangles by stretching an electronic "rubber band." That is, children might anchor the upper left-hand corner and then stretch the rectangle into shape. The program draws a rectangle between the anchored corner and the current position of the cursor on the screen. At any point, the child can freeze the rectangle by pressing a button. This stretching process gives children a different perspective on geometric figures, including new intuitions on the relationships between rectangles and squares.

Children can also have the computer fill enclosed regions with color. Many are surprised to discover that

274   Chapter Thirteen

what they had supposed was a closed boundary was not (the color "spills out" and continues to fill adjacent regions). This prompts them to reflect on such topological features as closure rather than on the mere characteristics of static shapes. The power of such drawing tools as "boxes" and "fill" lies in the possibility that children will internalize these functions, thus constructing new mental tools.

using mathematics software

Computers can also support mathematics curriculum goals besides geometry. In fact, much of the commercial mathematics software for young children has been designed to promote nongeometric problem solving or to provide drill and practice. These programs do not replace active teaching. However, they can reinforce skills or present challenging problem-solving tasks in a motivating fashion. It is important that teachers select software that complements their mathematics curriculum objectives.

problem solving

Many of the commercial problem-solving programs for young children can be enhanced if they are coordinated with manipulative activities. For example, in the preschool and primary grades, attribute-block tasks permit exploration of equivalence and difference relationships while encouraging logical analysis. Actual hands-on experience with the attribute pieces is necessary as the children become acquainted with the constraints of a given task and explore possible solutions. Although some of these activities are self-correcting, others require feedback about the accuracy of solutions from an adult because different solutions are possible. It is not unusual for primary teachers to decide that although their students enjoy attribute tasks and might benefit from further experience, the duration of these activities must be limited because of the need for adult supervision. Now, classification software is a viable addition to the curriculum.

Many software programs encourage classification according to such attributes as color, shape, or size. Tasks include sorting; identifying a similar, unique, or different characteristic; or formulating and testing classification rules. Good classification software permits exploration in a variety of settings at varying levels of difficulty while offering immediate feedback. Many versions of classification software are on the market, but one readily available version is *Gertrude's Secrets* (The Learning Company). This program contains three games in which children define and complete attribute displays; each of the games has two levels of difficulty. Immediate feedback is provided as a natural consequence of the child's action—correctly placed pieces stay put whereas incorrectly placed pieces "fall" to the border of the screen. Multiple solutions as well as alternative routes to any solution are possible. With this one disk, diverse attribute experiences can be presented to either individuals or pairs of students to complement classroom instruction. Simultaneous access to attribute blocks makes the classification software an appropriate stimulus for children as shown in figure 8. Teachers can encourage subsequent discussion of the problem-solving strategies used in the attribute-block tasks and the classification software, thus strengthening a connection between the manipulatives and the computer.

The main questions to ask when selecting educational computer programs are these: How does this software match my instructional goals? Does this software complement my instruction or is it incompatible? Studies have shown that computer programs can lead to increased achievement *if* they are carefully selected to match curricular goals (Kraus 1981). If they are not, these adjunct devices either make no difference or actually lower achievement (Baker, Herman, and Yeh 1981).

What are the characteristics of good problem-solving programs? The key is the ease with which they can be integrated with noncomputer problem-solving experiences. That is, how well does the software support the components of successful problem-solving practice? Good problem-solving software encourages children to interpret or understand a problem, represent or decipher a representation of the problem, explore and subsequently identify a solution strategy, implement

Fig. 8. Using the program *Gertrude's Secrets* with attribute blocks

the strategy, and then monitor the effectiveness of that strategy.

Good educational software also provides a context for problem presentation and solution that cannot be readily duplicated by a textbook or worksheet. Problem settings should be presented within a multisensory format, using an active screen display, not just written text. The context of the problem should be meaningful or realistic to the child, but fantasy settings are not ruled out. Good software permits children to explore approaches to a problem, providing clear feedback. This feature allows a teacher to assign pairs or small groups of students to work with the program, thus fostering a cooperative, engaged effort. Varying approaches to a solution should also be possible to encourage persistence, creativity, and alternative approaches. Finally, good problem-solving software is motivating. The goal is for students to build independence in problem solving.

The goal of independence will not be realized if the

students seek assurance before every keypress ("Is this right? What do I do now?"). Teachers must prepare students for the microcomputer activity, identifying and establishing prerequisites and providing concrete connections. Once that is accomplished, some effective techniques can build independence. These are noted in figure 9 (Pogrow 1986).

drill and practice

Microcomputer programs cannot and should not constitute the sole source of a young child's interactions with number and computation. Programs that present settings for the examination of number and computation are not meant to replace concrete experiences, nor can they serve as the managers of children's instruction within these areas. Properly chosen, microcomputer games can reinforce arithmetic skills, but they do not provide for conceptual understanding.

Prior to answering questions, determine if sufficient clues are already on the monitor screen

If clues are present, tell the students that the information is given and that they should figure it out on their own.

If insufficient clues are present, give only enough information to permit immediate progress.

If clues are present, but beyond a student's reading level, have the child read the clue aloud, with you supplying the unknown words. Explain only those words.

Do not make decisions for the children

If the children say they do not know what choice to make, tell them that they should try what *they* think is the right choice.

Once a choice is made, ask the children if that is what they wanted.

If they want to change their choice, have them make adjustments in the next response, or go back to where they made the last choice, or, when all else fails, go back to the menu.

Move about the computer area, scanning the children's work

Observe the children's use of the computer.

Praise children who are making progress.

Give the least amount of assistance possible to those children who are having problems. Ask for explanations about their strategies. Use questions, prompts, or hints. In this way you can model for the children the questions that they may eventually learn to ask themselves. Leading questions or small bits of information may guide the students toward their own solution.

Do not serve as the ultimate judge

Children will ask you about the quality of their work. Ask them to compare their results to their expectations.

Encourage the students to set and meet their own standards.

The goal is for the children to monitor their own work rather than rely on someone else to serve as their evaluator.

Fig. 9. Techniques for building independent problem solving

counting

There are probably more programs professing to teach counting and number-numeral recognition than anyone would care to count. Much of this software treats number and counting as a routine applied to fixed displays: See it, count it, say it, type it. This method is not the appropriate way for children to learn about counting and number. Most of the counting that young children do in school should involve real objects within meaningful situations. However, some interesting counting programs do incorporate feedback and challenging counting events of increasing difficulty.

Some general guidelines to follow when selecting counting software are these: First, look for programs that give the child control of object movement or that allow the child to respond by pressing keys in an iterative fashion. Counting is not a passive, observational activity. Programs that allow children to count on from numbers other than 1 are versatile additions to a primary school curriculum. Select programs that allow the teacher to decide if the objects should be randomly placed or ordered within clumps or arrays. Finally, good counting programs have several levels of difficulty and are not overly symbolic. They encourage active counting of displayed objects rather than the rote identification of numerals.

For example, *Counters* (Sunburst Communications) has five interactive levels that present either a one-to-one correspondence or the total set. At each level, items within sets are iterated using either sound or motion cues. The child can press any key when the correct correspondence between sets or between a numeral and a set occurs, which encourages active counting with the beeps or motions and not a reliance on keyboarding skills to locate numerals. Some counting programs are kinesthetic. They permit use of the space bar, or some other key, as a counter. With this feature children can define "five" as five keypresses, feeling the action of the count as their presses call up that many copies of a graphic object in a one-to-one fashion. However, no counting program replaces actual counting with objects.

computation

The most striking gains from the use of CAI have been noted in arithmetic skills for primary grade children, especially in compensatory education (e.g., Fuson and Brinko 1985; Kraus 1981; Ragosta, Holland, and Jamison 1981). However, drill alone is not sufficient. Consider the implications of a study by Alderman, Swinton, and Braswell (1979). Children using the computerized drill-and-practice software in this study outperformed the control group; however, an examination of items revealed that the children all made the same type of errors. The children in the CAI group had higher scores simply because they answered more items. They were more adept and efficient in responding, but they did not possess any stronger or deeper grasp of the concepts. Mathematics drill-and-practice programs can foster recall, but recall without understanding is worthless. Numerical drill programs can be a component of instruction, but the focus of the classroom instruction must be on conceptual understanding and the meaningful application of number and the arithmetic operations.

estimation

The use of computers and calculators has increased the importance of mental estimation skills. Teachers should search for computer programs that develop the basic computational estimation processes of reformulation, translation, and compensation (Reys, et al. 1982), as well as those involved in the estimation of area or distance. Research indicates that children can be taught to use valid estimation strategies in a short period of time, that computers can help deliver this instruction, and that replacing computational drill by estimation instruction does not decrease computational skills (Schoen et al. 1981). However, it is important to recognize that these skills must be taught explicitly.

computational estimation

What is the format of good estimation programs? One example of a computational estimation program is

Challenge Math (Sunburst). This program shows children three arithmetic problems and asks them to estimate which of their answers will be the largest. Children solve only that problem. Points are awarded both for correct computation and correct estimation. Thus, fast and accurate mental estimation is rewarded. Other estimation programs offer practice in both estimation and successive approximation. For example, the program *Power Drill* (Sunburst) presents computational problems using one of the four arithmetic operations at one of three levels of difficulty, for example, $78 + ? = 151$. If the child's answer is quite inaccurate, say 8, the program responds, "Way too SMALL" and provides a hint. If the child offers an adequate overestimate, for example, 80, the screen displays $78 + 80 = 158$ below the statement $78 + ? = 151$. An adequate underestimation, for example, 70, is displayed above the target statement, producing the following display:

$$78 + 70 = 148$$
$$78 + ? = 151$$
$$78 + 80 = 158$$

This process continues until the children "zero in" on the correct missing addend.

When using estimation programs, teachers must encourage children to estimate rather than compute; otherwise the children will not develop estimation strategies. An effective way to do this is to conduct whole-class discussions of solution strategies. Here are insights gleaned from such a discussion in one third-grade class.

- "I used to make my second estimate from scratch. But it's better to estimate how far your first estimate was off and work from there."

- "When it's an addition problem, making the missing number [addend] bigger makes the answer bigger. But when you're subtracting, making the missing number [subtrahend] bigger makes the answer *smaller*."

- "When you multiply, a bigger number gives a bigger answer. [$3 \times ? = 210$] When you divide, a bigger missing number gives a small answer." [$64 \div ? = 8$]

estimating
to develop number sense

Estimation activities can also develop children's number sense without dealing with arithmetic operations. For example, the software *Estimation* (Lawrence Hall of Science) provides several activities involving discrete and continuous quantities that are more appropriate for younger learners than the computationally oriented estimation programs described previously. The first activity has a train moving toward, and then through, a tunnel. See figure 10. The child attempts to stop the train when it passes over an arrow placed randomly by the program. The speed of the train can be varied. In "Junk Jar," children choose an object to fill a jar. A randomly sized jar is displayed, and the children estimate how many of the objects will fit in it. The computer then drops that number into the jar. The program "Bug Tracks" teaches estimation of linear quantity. Children guess how many bugs will fit along a "trail" or which of two trails is longer, or they draw a trail as long as one the program drew. For each, the program places bugs on each trail to provide feedback.

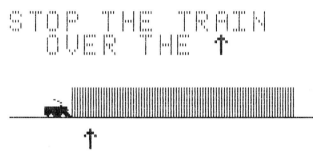

estimating measure

Logo can serve as a measurement context for an enriched understanding of number. Within Logo, children often create their own units to estimate the distance to an indicated point or to complete a figure: "I know this much [spanning two fingers] is a FORWARD 7 so I just have to put FORWARD 7, FORWARD 7, FORWARD 7 because it takes three of these [spanned fingers] to close in the edge." (See fig. 11.)

Fig. 11. Defining a unit of measure in a Logo environment.

Fig. 10. The *Estimation* program (Lawrence Hall of Science)

Another type of estimation activity involves ordering numbers. For example, in the IBM/WICAT series, children see a hole on a line between 433 and 535 and a hand holding a seed. They read: "Try to plant a seed in the hole. Type a whole number." For each wrong answer, a seed is dropped in the corresponding position and a plant grows, marked with a numeral. Thus, through successive approximation, the child determines the specific number required.

In this way, children build length representations of number as measure, without the distracting processing and dexterity demands associated with measuring instruments and physical quantity (Campbell 1987). As they gain experience with Logo, young children increasingly rely on and elaborate such self-constructed "standard units" of measure (Kull 1986). For example, one girl explained her "units" approach: "In your mind, if you had to go this far and you know about that much was ten turtle steps [holding her thumb and finger about a centimeter apart] . . . . That looks like 1, 2, 3, 4, 5, 6, 7 . . . . So what's 7 times 10? And that was 70" (Clements 1987). Research indicates that kindergarten and first-grade children who are taught Logo are able to estimate distance even when unit sizes vary. This is true even if the Logo instruction doesn't explicitly consider the inverse relationship between unit size and unit measure. With Logo, children can learn to adjust correctly the number that they assign to a distance when the unit for measuring that distance is changed (Campbell 1987). Logo helps children build a useful mental model, not unrelated to a ruler or a number line, for deepening understanding of number and measurement.

Even early, primitive strategies can lead to significant discoveries. For example, Noss (1984) reports a boy who turned the turtle through a right angle by "homing in" using the commands RIGHT 40 RIGHT 20 RIGHT 10 RIGHT 20. Having added the inputs, when it was necessary to create another right angle, he quickly announced the solution of RIGHT 90, much to the surprise of his peers and teacher. Teachers should watch for such surprising mathematical insights, so that they can be encouraged and extended.

teaching in a computer environment

Research indicates that teachers who use microcomputers effectively with young children take a positive, exploratory approach and emphasize cooperation rather than correct answers and competition. They are familiar with microcomputers, the programs they use, and, most important, with child development. These studies suggest that microcomputer work be introduced gradually. Actually, it is usually best to limit the number of programs used at one time to one, or at most, two. Similarly, expect independent work from students gradually. Prepare them for independence, clarify expectations for individualized or cooperative work, and increase the amount of such work slowly.

When you work closely with children and computers, it is unproductive to quiz students or offer help before they request it. Effective methods include prompting children to teach (e.g., by having the child assume a

teaching role or by reminding a child to explain his or her actions) and responding to specific requests for help (Paris and Morris 1985). Preparation and follow-up are as necessary for microcomputer activities as they are for any other form of instruction. Do not omit critical whole-group-discussion sessions following computer work. Consider using a single computer with a large screen or with an overhead projector for these discussions.

Research shows that the introduction of a microcomputer often places many additional demands on the teacher (Shrock et al. 1985). Plan carefully and use only those programs that will substantially benefit your students.

The following are some principles that can guide teachers as they begin to use mathematics software with young children.

Principle 1: Use microcomputers to enhance your curriculum goals, not for their own sake.

Class time should not simply expose children to computers so that they learn to "cope" with technology. Computers should support existing curricular goals for concept development, problem solving, exploration of relationships, and skill development. Microcomputers should be used only when they make a special contribution to children's learning of mathematics.

Principle 2: Use microcomputers to supplement manipulative activities, not to replace them.

Manipulative materials play a crucial role in the learning of mathematics. Software that stimulates shape recognition, counting, classification, patterning, ordering, and set transformation are ideal for young children, but these programs are not substitutes for active instruction and exploration with physical objects. The computer should be just one of many activities within a complete curriculum. Capitalize on the connection between physical manipulations of materials or the children's own bodies and the manipulation of graphic objects on the computer screen. Discuss with the children how these manipulations are similar or different. Strengthen links between off-computer and on-computer activities to foster concept development.

Principle 3: Use software that is developmentally appropriate.

Avoid programs with distracting color or sound or cluttered layouts. The reading level, the program-selection format, the attention span, and the required response routine should be appropriate for the age level of the children. Young children stay on task longer when a program shows their progress in a graphic display (Hungate and Heller 1984). Do not use programs that ignore incorrect responses or that do not revise a monitor display. These programs can be frustrating to young children, who often persist in reentering the same incorrect response or randomly striking the keyboard. Seek programs that allow multiple opportunities for success and provide informative feedback.

Developmentally appropriate software gives the child manipulative power (Kuschner 1985). Children should be able to change, modify, move, and rearrange any and all parts of what they are creating on the screen. They need an "undo" function that shows the "undoing" action. Programs for young children should

be designed so that nothing will happen if keys that are not to be used are pressed.

Related to both control and feedback are the concrete results children can see from their efforts. Good software generally provides a print option or at least the chance to save one's work.

Principle 4: Demand interactive software that capitalizes on the potential of the computer.

Microcomputer software must do more than simply mimic written materials. Children prefer programs that give them a feeling of control over the computer, particularly animated, interactive problem-solving software (Sherman, Divine, and Johnson 1985). The best software is flexible and permits more than one response or solution strategy. Do not use the computer as a substitute for teaching basic arithmetic facts or as a device for electronically presenting behaviorally defined arithmetic skill modules. Microcomputers should never be used to develop automaticity in the absence of understanding.

The microcomputer can assist teachers of young children. But the key is not what *can* be learned with a computer. The key is what mathematics *should* be learned. Do not have children use a computer only because it is there. Instead consider the principles and goals underlying mathematics instruction and focus on microcomputer use as a means of fostering students' construction of mathematical knowledge. Use computers because they challenge us to teach and children to learn in exciting and meaningful ways.

Portions of the work reported herein were supported by a grant from the National Institute of Mental Health, No. MSMA 1 RO3 MH423435-01, to the first author and a grant from the National Science Foundation, No. MDR-86551668, to the second author. Any opinions, findings, and conclusions or recommendations expressed in this publication are those of the authors and do not necessarily reflect the views or policy of the National Institute of Mental Health and the National Science Foundation.

references

Alderman, Donald L., Spencer S. Swinton, and James S. Braswell. "Assessing Basic Arithmetic Skills and Understanding across Curricula: Computer-assisted Instruction and Compensatory Education." *Journal of Children's Mathematical Behavior* 2 (Spring 1979): 3–28.

Baker, Eva L., Joan L. Herman, and Jennie P. Yeh. "Fun and Games: Their Contribution to Basic Skills Instruction in Elementary School." *American Educational Research Journal* 18 (Spring 1981): 83–92.

Barnes, B. J., and Shirley Hill. "Should Young Children Work with Microcomputers—Logo before Lego?" *Computing Teacher* 10 (May 1983): 11–14.

Campbell, Patricia F. *Measuring Distance: Children's Use of Number and Unit.* Final report submitted to the National Institute of Mental Health under the ADAMHA Small Grant Award Program. Grant No. MSMA 1 RO3 MH423435-01. University of Maryland, College Park, Md., December 1987.

————. "Microcomputers in the Primary Mathematics Classroom." *Arithmetic Teacher* 35 (February 1988): 22–30.

Clements, Douglas H. "Longitudinal Study of the Effects of Logo Programming on Cognitive Abilities and Achievement." *Journal of Educational Computing Research* 3, no. 1 (1987): 77–98.

————. "Supporting Young Children's Logo Programming." *Computing Teacher* 11 (December-January 1983–84): 24–30.

Clements, Douglas H., and Michael T. Battista. *Progress Report: The Development of a Logo-based Elementary School Geometry Curriculum.* NSF Grant No. MDR-8651668. SUNY at Buffalo/Kent State University, 1988.

Cuffaro, Harriet K. "Microcomputers in Education: Why Is Earlier Better?" *Teachers College Record* 85 (Summer 1984): 559–68.

Elkind, David. *The Hurried Child: Growing Up Too Fast Too Soon.* Reading, Mass.: Addison-Wesley, 1981.

Fein, Greta G. "Logo Instruction: A Constructivist View." Paper presented at the annual meeting of the American Educational Research Association, Chicago, April 1985.

Fein, Greta G., Patricia F. Campbell, and Shirley S. Schwartz. "Microcomputers in the Preschool: Effects on Social Participation and Cognitive Play." *Journal of Applied Developmental Psychology* 8 (April-June 1987): 197–208.

Forman, George. "Observations of Young Children Solving Problems with Computers and Robots." *Journal of Research in Childhood Education* 1 (August 1986): 60–74.

Fuson, Karen C., and Kathleen T. Brinko. "The Comparative Effectiveness of Microcomputers and Flash Cards in Drill and Practice of Basic Mathematics Facts." *Journal for Research in Mathematics Education* 16 (May 1985): 225–32.

Gelman, Rochel, and Renee Baillargeon. "A Review of Some Piagetian Concepts." In *Handbook of Child Psychology,* 4th ed., edited by Paul H. Mussen. Vol. 3, *Cognitive Development,* edited by John H. Flavell and Ellen M. Markman. New York: John Wiley & Sons, 1983.

Hungate, Harriet, and Joan I. Heller. "Preschool Children and Microcomputers." Paper presented at the annual meeting of the American Educational Research Association, New Orleans, April 1984.

Kraus, William H. "Using a Computer Game to Reinforce Skills in Addition Basic Facts in Second Grade." *Journal for Research in Mathematics Education* 12 (March 1981): 152–55.

Kull, Judith A. "Learning and Logo." In *Young Children and Microcomputers,* edited by Patricia F. Campbell and Greta G. Fein. Englewood Cliffs, N.J.: Prentice-Hall, 1986.

Kuschner, David. "A Study of the Possibilities for Reversible Actions in Software for Young Children." Paper presented at the Fifteenth Annual Symposium of the Jean Piaget Society, Philadelphia, June 1985.

Lieberman, Deborah. "Research on Children and Microcomputers: A Review of Utilization and Effects Studies." In *Children and Microcomputers: Research on the Newest Medium,* edited by Milton Chen and William Paisley. Beverly Hills, Calif.: Sage Publications, 1985.

Lipinski, Judith M., Robert E. Nida, Daniel D. Shade, and J. Allen Watson. "The Effects of Microcomputers on Young Children: An Examination of Free-Play Choices, Sex Differences and Social Interactions." *Journal of Educational Computing Research* 2, no. 2 (1986): 147–68.

Noss, Richard. *Children Learning Logo Programming.* Interim Report no. 2 of the Chiltern Logo Project. Hatfield, England: Advisory Unit for Computer Based Education, 1984.

Paris, Cynthia L., and Sandra K. Morris. "The Computer in the Early Childhood Classroom: Peer Helping and Peer Teaching." Paper presented at the Microworld for Young Children Conference, College Park, Md., March 1985. (ERIC Document Reproduction Service No. ED 257 555)

Pogrow, Stanley. *HOTS Curriculum.* Tucson, Ariz.: Thinking with Computers, 1986.

Ragosta, Marjorie, Paul Holland, and Dean T. Jamison. *Computer-assisted Instruction and Compensatory Education: The ETS/LAUSD Study.* Princeton, N.J.: Educational Testing Service, 1981.

Reys, Robert E., James F. Rybolt, Barbara J. Bestgen, and J. Wendall Wyatt. "Processes Used by Good Computational Estimators." *Journal for Research in Mathematics Education* 13 (May 1982): 183–201.

Schoen, Harold L., Charles D. Friesen, Joscelyn A. Jarrett, and Tonya D. Urbatsch. "Instruction in Estimating Solutions of Whole Number Computations." *Journal for Research in Mathematics Education* 12 (May 1981): 165–78.

Sheingold, Karen. "The Microcomputer as a Symbolic Medium." In *Young Children and Microcomputers,* edited by Patricia F. Campbell and Greta G. Fein. Englewood Cliffs, N.J.: Prentice-Hall, 1986.

Sherman, Janice, Katherine P. Divine, and Betty Johnson. "An Analysis of Computer Software Preferences of Preschool Children." *Educational Technology* 25 (May 1985): 39-41.

Shrock, S. A., M. Matthias, J. Anastasoff, C. Vensel, and S. Shaw. "Examining the Effects of the Microcomputer on a Real World Class: A Naturalistic Study." Paper presented at the annual convention of the Association for Educational Communications and Technology, Anaheim, Calif., January 1985.

software publishers/distributors

Lawrence Hall of Science
University of California, Berkeley
Mathematics/Computer Education Project
Berkeley, CA 94720

The Learning Company
545 Middlefield Road, Suite 170
Menlo Park, CA 94025

Sunburst Communications
39 Washington Avenue
Pleasantville, NY 10570-2898

WICAT Systems
P.O. Box 539
1875 South State Street
Orem, UT 84057

14

planning for mathematics instruction

the teacher as a decision maker

For a long time everyone has known that every teacher makes hundreds of decisions daily, indeed, sometimes hourly. But only recently has the role of the teacher as a decision maker been viewed as significant. The teacher must decide what, when, and how to teach and, moreover, interact with a class of children while carrying out these decisions, a process that demands countless other decisions. Teaching is a more complex activity than we have ever believed.

This chapter examines the critical role to be played by the classroom teacher in making decisions about content, lessons, and classroom management.

philosophy

A teacher makes a decision, partly on the basis of his or her philosophy about how children learn and about how to teach so they will learn more effectively. For the most part, this philosophy is not a conscious factor in decision making, that is, few teachers say, "Now let's see—what's my philosophy, how does it apply to these circumstances, and what does it indicate that I should do?" Rather, the philosophy is incorporated into the teacher's behaviors or set of beliefs that underlie everything he or she does in the classroom.

Because a teacher's philosophy is ingrained, it acts as an instantaneous "rudder," guiding his or her response to a particular situation. The teacher rarely has time to do more than respond immediately because the events in a classroom move too quickly, one following another all day long. Occasionally, the teacher can say, "I'll think about that and talk with you later," but generally, the teacher must respond immediately—or lose control of the class. Teachers are bombarded all day, every day, by myriad events that call for instantaneous decisions.

Some of these decisions pertain to behavior: one child is misbehaving, another needs encouragement, a third has given an unexpectedly thoughtful response, and yet another needs help. Sometimes decisions must be made about curricular concerns, for example, when a topic arises unexpectedly. Sometimes decisions must be made about teaching methods because children do not always respond in ways we anticipate. Their responses might show weaknesses and gaps, and teachers must be prepared to change their plans so they can help the child overcome the weakness or fill in a gap. Or the class might unexpectedly show that it knows the concept that was to be taught, thus requiring the teacher to extend or modify the lesson.

planning

The fact that decisions in the classroom must be made continuously does not alter the importance of planning

before a lesson is taught. Planning is decision making that takes into account the teacher's knowledge of the children, their abilities and interests, what they have learned, and what they will learn, so that content can be taught effectively.

The planning that precedes a lesson focuses the teacher's attention not only on the purpose of the lesson but also on the reasons for teaching a particular topic in a particular way. When decisions must be made as the lesson proceeds, planning aids the teacher (albeit unconsciously) in making decisions consistent with his or her philosophy.

types of planning

Every teacher must do three major types of planning: how to organize content, the classroom environment, and the children. Each type of planning pertains to organizing part of the curriculum to make it manageable for instruction. Unfortunately, some teachers do little or none of this planning: they rely solely on the textbook, following it slavishly, day after day. Fortunately, textbook authors and editors and publishers have realized that such teachers exist, and they endeavor to organize the material in a plausible fashion. Yet publishers do not know the individual children in a class—what those children already know, what they need to learn, and how they learn best. All that a textbook can do is present a lesson for the "average" child, as if one knew what such a child would be like.

Many textbooks suggest how and for how long each topic should be taught. An involved teacher will use such suggestions only as suggestions. More important to a teacher is the knowledge about children, curricula, and methodologies that he or she brings to teaching.

organizing the content

The content to be taught by any teacher in any classroom must be arranged or organized so that it can be presented efficiently as well as effectively. This involves considering not only what is in the textbook but also what is in the school's curriculum guide and any district or state requirements. Even more important is considering what the children are bringing to, and what they are expected to take away from, the classroom.

for the year

The first task is to establish clear goals for the year, decide what is to be taught, and for how long. Such planning is broad, that is, the curriculum is not broken down into subobjectives; rather, the major topics— place value to thousands, metric measurement, estimation strategies, mental arithmetic, geometry—are sufficient.

Also important in establishing goals for the year is considering not only what is in the textbook and what will be tested but also what *should* be taught. What do the children need to learn during the school year? Many mathematical topics are neglected in textbooks and tests: consider geometry—what can be more important to children than understanding the world around them?—or data analysis—every child is exposed to data every single day. We have long had a curriculum in the elementary school, particularly in the primary grades, that is dominated by computation. Certainly computational skills are important, yet the emphasis on paper-and-pencil computation belies the fact that in today's world, most computation is not done with paper and pencil. Calculators and computers, including those machines in the checkout line of stores, do the computations that were the primary goal of the elementary school mathematics curriculum for hundreds

of years. Instead of paper-and-pencil computation, more emphasis is needed on mental computation and on estimation because these are the skills needed to "check" the machines. As teachers organize the content for the year, they should make sure that such topics are receiving enough emphasis. Such planning ensures that children will be educated for the year 2010, not 1910 or 1810. The *Curriculum and Evaluation Standards for School Mathematics* (NCTM 1989) offers much additional guidance on what and how to teach.

After the topics are listed, teachers must formulate a plausible sequence in which to teach them. Again, the textbook can serve as guide, but many textbooks are oriented toward a "keep things moving" sequence, where it is deemed necessary to keep children's attention by continually changing topics. As a result, many children don't spend enough time on a given topic to learn it. The "one night stand" curriculum has done a disservice to children, and it promotes the insidious idea that mathematics consists of one topic after another, which have little, if any, relationship to each other.

Conceptual knowledge is too often short changed, both in terms of time spent and the necessary work with manipulatives. As is evident in chapter 2 and others in this book, the development of conceptual knowledge takes time. Developing the connections between conceptual and procedural knowledge takes much effort and careful work by teachers.

Some teachers are uncomfortable rearranging the sequence of lessons or units in a textbook, even when they know that the sequence is not effective for their students. They say that the authors and publishers should know about sequencing, even when it is evident that they do not. Some topics should be taught in a particular sequence; for example, it is difficult to teach multiplication if children have no idea of addition. But three lessons on subtraction with multidigit numbers can be grouped together, even though a textbook places them ten pages apart. Teachers need to use their professional judgment about the reordering of topics, deciding whether their children can learn better with successive days of instruction rather than a series of

discrete blocks of instruction. Opening the school year with a new topic, such as graphing, measurement, or geometry, is more interesting for students and alerts them that they will learn something new this year. Furthermore, the topic can often be used as a continuing theme in teaching other topics.

Finally, the teacher should determine about how much time to spend on each topic. This decision is not final but serves only as a guide to make sure that the school year does not end with half the topics untaught. With some children, however, it is plausible to omit some topics (e.g., subtraction across zeros).

for
the unit

After the teacher has developed a broad plan for the year, it can be divided into smaller parts. For example, the teacher may have decided to teach subtraction. How much time is needed first with manipulative materials? How many digits will be used? How much estimation and mental arithmetic will be included? These decisions are crucial because they form the foundation for children's opportunities to learn. If children are not taught something, it is unlikely that they

will learn it on their own. If they are tested on content that has not been taught, they probably will not do well on the test. It is important that children have an opportunity to learn, whether or not they are tested on the material.

for the day

Every teacher knows that the vital stage in planning is "What am I going to do tomorrow?" Some teachers leave the decision to the teacher's manual that accompanies their textbooks. Some teachers just rely on what appears on a given page in the child's textbook. Such teachers are particularly prone to conduct every mathematics lesson in the same way day after day. No wonder some children consider mathematics boring!

But other teachers take this task seriously: they actually spend more time planning lessons than they do correcting seatwork! They decide not only the focus or objective of the lesson, but also how they will introduce the topic, whether they will have children work individually or in groups, what materials the children will use, and what activities will be done. They consider what content they might have to review before the children begin on a new topic because they want to assure that children are successful. They also consider how to evaluate children's progress throughout the lesson because they know the children can't afford to wait until a paper-and-pencil test to find out how well they're doing. Such teachers think back over what the children have had difficulty with in the past and try to plan around such difficulties or prepare to respond to the need should it arise again.

Teachers also must respond to the need of children to know why they should learn what is being taught. Children need to know the relevance of a new topic—its relevance to previous topics, to future topics, and to the real world. Such depictions of relevance do not always need to be overtly stated. A problem with a sales receipt can be used to introduce a multidigit subtraction topic: even with nothing being said, most children will understand the relevance.

Children need to experience a high rate of success. To assure this level of success, teachers should not use only content that would be easy for the children. Rather, the content should be taught so that children grasp it readily. Often, this means the use of manipulative materials to introduce new ideas at all grade levels. It also means connecting new content to that previously learned. Children are continuously "constructing" their learning, adding to previous knowledge or modifying prior ideas, so we need to make it easy for them to construct a clear image of mathematical content.

organizing the environment

Most early childhood teachers realize the importance of organizing the environment to encourage children to explore, develop, test, discuss, and apply ideas. The classroom, both its furniture and its materials, connotes a certain type of environment the minute children walk in the door. If you walk into a kindergarten with chairs and desks arranged in rows, what do you think? If you walk into a kindergarten with a sofa and rug in one corner and tables in another corner, what do you think? If materials are tossed on shelves or in closets, what might be expected of a member of that class? If all the bulletin boards and walls are bare, how welcome would you feel? And what does that emptiness say about learning?

arranging the room

Once upon a time, all schoolrooms had desks and chairs nailed or screwed into the floor or onto long boards, a convenience for teachers in keeping the rows neat and a bonus for whoever cleaned the room. Some classrooms of today seem to emulate this model. What impression do you receive from such a classroom? You may think, "This classroom is really organized for work!" Or, "This classroom will mold children." What are some alternatives to the rows of desks that have appeared even in some preschool classrooms? The chances are that they are arranged in this way so that children can do a certain amount of sitting and writing. Even preschool classrooms have begun, in some instances, to teach what was once considered content for first grade and beyond, perhaps suggesting erroneously that learning requires this rigid arrangement. Many kindergartens have been trapped into this mold. The children must be given a "head start" on the curriculum. There is too much to learn, so

we have to start earlier. An alternative is to omit some topics, such as symbolic work or computation done prematurely without adequate conceptual development. More oral work and experiences with manipulatives are needed to build stronger conceptual knowledge. Mathematics needs to be taught at the child's level of understanding. Pencil and paper is not a necessary ingredient. An equal amount of learning can occur when the teacher provides problem-solving situations. (See chapters 3 and 6.) Most of all, young children need an environment that stimulates learning.

Tables, desks, and chairs of appropriate heights are adaptable to various classroom arrangements throughout the primary grades. They can be moved and rearranged easily by both adults and children. They provide sufficient space on which to spread out and facilitate cooperative work. They are adaptable not only to mathematics instruction but also to most other subjects and interests. They should be arranged so that children have a clear view of the teacher, the board, and bulletin boards, but traffic areas are kept clear.

Floor space should be also available, some of it carpeted. Listening to a story, planning group work, constructing and working with concrete materials are activities best done in such an area.

The rug area is one center for young children, but other centers for mathematics are also needed. One center contains measurement instruments; another might focus on the calculator, with a set of cards giving instructions so that one or two children can work at a time. The computer corner provides a quiet environment. Most children can work with computers with minimal instruction and supervision, but a teacher, aide, or a knowledgeable child needs to be available to help if necessary. Space is also needed so that children can work with manipulative materials, use calculators or computers, or record with paper and pencil.

collecting and storing materials

Because concrete manipulative materials play such a large role in any up-to-date mathematics instructional program, having an array of such materials is imperative. Many of these can be collected by children or parents at the teacher's suggestion: for instance, bottle caps, boxes, cards, egg and milk cartons, magazines with colored pictures, wallpaper samples, wrapping paper, pebbles, shells, Popsicle sticks, string, tubes from paper towels, or buttons.

One of the greatest difficulties that a teacher faces, however, is how to store the materials so that they can be found and used easily. Low shelves or "pigeonholes" are essential. Children should be able to

reach and remove things easily themselves rather than have the teacher come to help. The following are some teachers' ideas for storing these materials:

- Color code or label the materials and put a matching code or label on the appropriate storage space.

- Prepackage manipulatives into sets for one student, two students, or a small group.

- Put extra pieces into a "spare parts" container.

- Package sets of materials in durable individual containers, such as heavy plastic bags or transparent containers.

- Store individual sets of materials in "trays," such as box lids, shallow plastic pans, or stackable vegetable bins.

To help children who are "disorganized," consider using materials with built-in organization, such as bead frames, an abacus, or materials that fit together, such as Unifix cubes, rather than separate objects like lima beans or blocks. Or use containers that keep counters separated, such as egg cartons, muffin tins, or mats with clearly delineated spaces.

than others. Some children need more work with manipulative materials than others.

Grouping is not likely to be needed for geometry, measurement, graphing, concepts of number or numeration, and especially not with the proper use of manipulatives. Grouping on the basis of achievement may be needed for topics with many prerequisites such as subtraction with regrouping, two-digit multiplication, or division with remainders.

Sometimes we'll teach in one large group because all the children need to be introduced to a topic. Sometimes we'll insist that each child work alone because we want to see how he or she attacks a task independently. But at other times we'll want them to work together, taking advantage of how they learn in nonschool activities. Children learn from each other, and for schools to try to keep them from doing so is foolhardy.

Cooperative learning groups involve children of varying abilities working together to attain a goal. Often scores or grades are given for the group as a whole. The pressure for scores or grades may not be necessary with young children because they usually want to learn. Encouraging children to work cooperatively in groups is a primary goal throughout the early years.

creating the scene

How the classroom looks when children walk through the door greatly determines how the children will act and react in the room. Another factor to be considered is how the teacher wants the children to interact.

organizing children to differentiate instruction

Differentiating instruction to meet the needs of students is essential. One way to differentiate instruction is to group students for different activities and topics. Just as a grouping of students for reading will not suffice for mathematics neither will a grouping for a numeration topic be appropriate for geometry.

In kindergarten and preschool, groupings will likely be more spontaneous, perhaps based on the children's wishes to work or play together. As they progress through grade 1 and beyond, we'll want to group children by achievement on a certain topic. Some children are ready to learn a particular topic earlier

planning for variability

Plans for organizing content and the environment should both recognize the variability in how and what children learn.

lessons for different purposes

Mathematics is often taught in a manner different from other subjects, and unfortunately so. We need to consider how children learn mathematics most effectively. It is interesting enough to note that although we talk about problem solving in mathematics, we make more use of problem solving in other content areas. In reading, for instance, we ask, "What word might fit?" or "How do you sound that out?" In social studies we ask, "Why do we need people who will do this job?" or "Why is that city located where it is?" More of such problem-solving approaches need to be used in teaching mathematics.

Different lessons serve different purposes. Some lessons introduce a topic, some relate a topic to what's been learned previously, some extend ideas, some consolidate what children have learned, and some review what children have already learned.

What makes these lessons different from each other? When you walk into a classroom, can you tell what type of lesson is being taught? If the teacher has let the children in on the "secret," there's a higher probability that the lesson will be more clearly defined. There's likely to be more exploration when a new topic is introduced, more discussion when the goal is to relate topics or extend ideas, and more practice when the object is to consolidate or review, although the type of practice will differ.

direct instruction and exploration

Young children learn through exploring. *Play* is often another word for *exploring*. Play is not something that merely fills time; through play children learn about materials, and ideas, and relationships among ideas and people. This is not to say that we should inculcate the idea that all school is play, but we should make use of play as a medium of instruction.

Schools that discourage play in kindergarten in favor of worksheets and flashcards are doing children a disservice. Children might lose the knowledge and understanding they gain from experimenting with and exploring actual materials and situations. They need these as a foundation on which abstract ideas are later built.

Direct instruction has its place. We want children to extend their counting ability, to learn about counting on. So we read a story about ten mice, which involves counting over and over and sometimes counting on. We ask them to draw four objects and then some more, enough to make nine. But direct instruction has its limitations: soon, the children take over and explore those ideas we've already presented directly. Direct instruction seems to be efficient, but it needs to be backed up by other, more child-centered methods of instruction.

a problem-solving approach

A problem-solving approach is more than presenting problems to children and then solving them. It means that children are not simply shown how to solve a problem, as is often done in both textbooks and classrooms, but are involved in actively exploring ways to reach a solution. For example, consider an alternative way to introduce $83 - 19$ to children who have not learned regrouping or 37×42 to children who have had experience with one-digit but not two-digit factors. Instead of showing the children how to solve such problems, the teacher can simply ask, "How can we find the answer?" Let children use manipulatives or what they know about place value and subtraction or multiplying one-digit numbers. Make the task mirror real life, where mathematical ideas often must be manipulated to come up with an answer. Children will develop confidence in *their* ability, not just the teacher's. Inherent in the use of a problem-solving approach is that the teacher answers questions with questions, encouraging children to think.

lessons that motivate

It might be more appropriate to say "get the attention of" rather than "motivate." For children to learn efficiently, they need to focus on the point of the lesson. So we need to plan introductions, especially to important mathematical ideas, in out-of-the-ordinary ways.

Unfortunately, many teachers follow the same pattern every day for mathematics instruction: "Open your books to page 27." Mathematics becomes a sterile, read-it-from-the-book procedure rather than a process of construction.

capturing attention

What should teachers do instead of beginning mathematics lessons by opening the textbook? Think about how to make a topic capture children's attention. Suppose the teacher holds up a paper bag, rattles it, and says, "I have more than twelve counters in the bag but fewer than 50. Listen to the sounds and guess how many." The students are certain to be interested as you count them by tens to see how many are in the bag. Children will end up counting, just as if they had been told to count a set of objects on a worksheet, but with more attention to the objective of the lesson and to the reasonableness of their estimates and answers.

maintaining interest

Once children's attention is captured, it must be maintained. For many children and many materials, that process is automatic. For the others, the teacher must be ready with challenging questions and activities, with manipulative materials, or with group work. When children are involved in learning, their interest is maintained, so the teacher needs to strive for the goal of involvement, which cannot be achieved simply by telling children to pay attention.

lessons to encourage thinking

As most teachers know, a variety of programs and strategies have been proposed to help children develop thinking skills across subject areas. Most of these methods emphasize what the teacher can do in terms of speaking and action.

questioning strategies

Questions have a variety of purposes. Thus, to spark curiosity and stimulate investigation, we might ask, "What do you think will happen if . . .?" ("What happens if we change $498 - 362$ to $500 - 364$?") To develop comprehension, we might ask, "Why is that step necessary?" ("Why do you write the 2 on top when you multiply 4×36?") To detect faulty reasoning, we might ask, "How could you check this?" ("Why do you say that a square is not a rectangle?") To help children verbalize mathematical ideas, we might ask, "Can you tell the class why you did that?" ("Use base-ten blocks and show me why 62 is the same as 5 tens and 12 ones.") To encourage children to verify their conclusions, we might ask, "Can you prove that's the right answer?" ("Can you show that $12 \div 4 = 3$ is correct using these counters?") To promote progress, we might ask, "What will you do first?" ("To count on to find $2 + 8$, what do you do first?") The teacher's goal is to say as little as possible, listening to students' ideas. These ideas give clues about how learning is proceeding and what teaching is needed.

Our questions should encourage the children to *think* about mathematics as they are actively *doing* mathematics. Mathematics is a "reason-able" subject: children can learn many mathematical ideas without being shown how to *do* something. In elementary schools attention all too frequently has been placed merely on *how*: how to count, how to add, how to divide, how to subtract fractions, how to find the area. The idea that one might be able to *figure out* an answer is alien, for so much of mathematics instruction has emphasized memorizing the one way to solve a problem. Most people do not even realize that there's more than one way to find an answer to a mathematical problem. This perception must be changed.

interactions of pupils and teacher

Many interactions result naturally from how children are grouped for instruction. When children work in groups of two or four, pupil-to-pupil interactions will

abound. Most young children have few inhibitions about talking to each other about what they're doing; we need to encourage them to do so when working on mathematics in school rather than working alone.

Most interactions in most mathematics classrooms are between teacher and pupil: the teacher asks a question, the child responds, usually by recalling a mathematical fact. Only a small part of the time do most teachers ask questions that require the children to think, relate, interpret, or evaluate. Only rarely is time allowed for such replies. Instruction on basic facts is but one example of many questions with no encouragement to think and reason. See chapter 7 for numerous examples where time is essential for students to work through the thinking strategies. If mathematics is to be considered as something more than mere recall, a higher-level question calling for higher-level responses (the "why" type of questions) must be used.

Students only occasionally initiate interactions with the teacher. How can the teacher encourage such interactions? First of all, children are more likely to initiate interactions if they know they have the teacher's approval for doing so. The teacher's obvious pleasure that the child has raised a topic for discussion conveys more than just a mere, "Talk to me." Teachers also need to set the scene so that children will initiate discussion, for instance, when a teacher labels a "discovered" conjecture with the child's name, other children are encouraged to think of and describe their own ideas.

coping with variability

For some teachers, it is less a question of encouraging children to learn as it is a matter of coping with the variability evident in any group of children. The term *individual differences* is used so frequently that it has become jargon. We need to make it mean something for all children, not merely those with learning disabilities.

ability, achievement, and learning behaviors

Ability differences among children are evident in their behavior. Some children approach a new idea with curiosity, others with apprehension. Some of these reactions are affective associations with mathematics instruction, whereas others reflect the child's natural ease, or lack of it, with mathematics. How much a child learns in a mathematics classroom is influenced by the importance the teacher places on reassuring and motivating students and enhancing their learning.

Teachers can assess differences in achievement not only by tests but also by daily observations of behaviors and work. Helping each child achieve more, no matter what his or her starting level, should be a primary goal, not merely emphasizing what is to be tested.

How children learn is still a puzzling issue in many teaching situations. We need to try new ways continuously to help children learn. Often when a topic must be retaught, a teacher uses the same lesson or approach the second or third time as he or she used the first time. Most children didn't learn the first time because they didn't understand the initial approach, so clearly a new tactic is needed. We need to keep in mind the developmental level of the child, besides the other information we have gained from observations.

Teachers react differently to students, depending on student characteristics. Research has indicated that teachers react to students with low ability or achievement records in certain ways. As a rule, teachers do not allow as much time for slower students to answer questions as they do for more capable students. Slower students may need more time, not less. Even when teachers state that they know two classes differ in achievement or ability, they do not take this into account as they plan, nor do they vary the instruction for each group. Perhaps just knowing about these tendencies may help more teachers realize the importance of considering the needs of individual students in their classrooms.

diagnosis and pacing

We want to help children learn "right" the first time, without needing remedial help later. To do so, we must make diagnoses. Diagnosis helps us to ascertain ways in which teaching will be most effective. Diagnosis provides clues about the difficulties children are having as new ideas are introduced.

Lessons need to be paced to meet a child's ability level. They need to interest children, and they need to fit the content. Some content is more difficult than others to teach and to learn, for example, regrouping in subtraction and long division. Presumably, proceeding slowly and carefully with such content has a payoff in making sure that children know what common errors they should avoid.

"grabbing" teachable moments

There are times when children are ready to learn new ideas, and we need to take advantage of such "teachable" moments. Students may bring up a question the teacher did not consider when planning the lesson, such as a newspaper clipping with data on a recent event. Teachers can precipitate such moments by arranging the environment in a new and exciting way. The teacher must know what concepts he or she wants to teach and how these develop and then recognize the teachable moment when it arises. Such on-the-spot decisions arise daily.

managing the classroom

Classroom management is the foundation of sound learning. In a well-managed classroom, learning can proceed more smoothly because fewer distractions occur. Handling small groups, managing materials effectively, using time efficiently, and evaluating progress are all aspects of management. Underlying them all is, of course, control or discipline.

handling small groups

What happens when children are divided into small groups is a measure of how smoothly children will learn.

flexible groups

When groups are formed, they should be formed for a specific purpose; for example, four children need extra help in distinguishing between perimeter and area; six children have shown, three days into a nine-day unit, that they can divide with remainders. Thus, reteaching or enrichment are two reasons to form groups. Often it is necessary to regroup students with each new topic. Children can initially be grouped on the basis of their knowledge of a particular mathematical topic and then regrouped when a new topic is started, since achievement will vary by topic.

Each child needs to be taught appropriate mathematical content in each major curricular strand regardless of progress in other strands. The whole class can be introduced to the same topics. Then, small groups can work in depth on a small set of ideas, while other groups go into greater depth. Small groups thus can work at levels appropriate to their members, changing as those levels change.

independent activities

Because of their work with reading groups, most primary grade teachers recognize the need to provide activities for groups not currently working with the teacher. Such activities should be more than "busy

work" because this is valuable classroom time. Among the possible activities are those involving group work on a project, using a problem-solving program on the computer, reading a library book containing mathematical ideas, or working at a learning center. Some teachers have a "grab bag" that contains suggested activities; children usually enjoy the excitement of picking out something unexpected, even though it might be just what the teacher would have suggested verbally.

Whatever their nature, activities should be geared to the level of each child and related to previous instruction. Merely running off worksheet masters on the copying machine day after day fills time, the teacher's as well as the children's, but its effect on mathematics learning is limited.

group leaders, folders, and feedback

Children like to assume the role of the teacher and being a group leader lets them do that. In addition, teachers gain a valuable insight into how they themselves teach. How can young children assume the role of group leader effectively? Preparation is critical. They need to have a clear idea of what is expected of them, and the teacher can move around the classroom, observing and being ready to intervene if necessary. Finally, evaluations by both teacher and students can indicate where improvement is needed and how it can be attained, as well as ways in which the group work was successful.

A folder should be maintained for each child with samples of the child's work. This folder not only enables both teacher and child to look back over past achievement and assess progress but also serves as a valuable aid in talking with parents about the child's progress.

Feedback to the child is vital. The folder serves this purpose in one way, but what is said to the child every day as he or she answers questions, works on activities, or interacts with others is another form of feedback. The emphasis should, of course, be positive, but clearly less-than-positive comments cannot be ignored.

peer tutoring

Because children learn from each other, peer teaching or tutoring is a way to promote such learning. Peer tutoring not only involves two children working together

but having one child teach another. Children frequently communicate with each other in different and more meaningful ways than teachers. Different words, combined with a different awareness of where a difficulty may lie, help one teach another.

managing materials efficiently

Some teachers do not use manipulative materials partially because of the problems associated with managing them. They take up space and time.

manipulative materials

The interaction of a child with objects in the classroom forms the framework on which mathematical concepts are built. Mathematics instruction should place major emphasis on concrete, hands-on investigations. Young children do not learn mathematics by being told about it; they invent mathematics as explanations for their experiences. The adult mathematical world often deals with abstractions, whereas the child's mathematical world involves physical realities from which abstractions will ultimately be formulated. Examples of such abstractions are evident in all chapters, with chapter 6 focusing on word problems.

A stimulating classroom has a host of materials that young learners can manipulate. Physical materials can be used to explore such processes as describing, classifying, comparing, ordering, equalizing, joining, and separating.

Children should experience mathematical situations in a nonthreatening exploratory environment. Both nondirected and directed experiences should employ physical materials as vehicles for conceptualization. Directed experiences should be appropriate to the children's level of cognitive development. The sequential development of activities should move from concrete and pictorial to oral language and symbols.

Early in the year, when manipulatives are first used, teachers should discuss with children some rules for their use. These rules include (1) naming several students to distribute materials and collect them later; (2) having students check sets of materials for completeness (and complete them from the spare parts box); (3) giving students an exploratory period with new materials; (4) describing the purpose of the manipulative; (5) emphasizing that each child should work and talk quietly.

The teacher needs to select materials with their mathematical purpose in mind. It is also important to consider the use of materials that will engage the various senses. Seeing seven elephants, hearing seven beats on a drum, touching seven "holes" in an egg carton, taking seven steps—all these activities can strengthen understanding of the meaning of "seven."

The teacher should ask numerous questions to clarify ideas as materials are used, and children should talk among themselves as well as with the teacher about what they are doing. A primary goal is to keep the attention of the children focused on the mathematical goal. The use of manipulatives should not be hurried. Neither should the children be rushed from the concrete stage to symbolic work. It is vital to connect symbols and procedures to the manipulatives, for instance, by relating the numeral 32 to the word *thirty-two*, to base-ten blocks, and to the result of counting that many objects by ones. (See chapters 2, 4, 5, and 8.)

Evaluation has a role in the use of manipulatives as it does in every other aspect of teaching. Some teachers put each child's name on a card and make notes on five or six children a day. Others keep a clipboard handy and jot down questions, answers, problems, or interesting thoughts. A checklist of commonly observed behaviors, such as "began work promptly," "looked for other solutions," and so on, is worth considering.

other materials

Children also need to work with semiconcrete materials—pictures and diagrams of all types. Work

with both concrete and semiconcrete materials builds a firmer foundation for the development of abstract ideas or the memorization of important facts.

printed materials

The pictures in printed materials—textbooks, workbooks, and worksheets—are one example of semiconcrete materials. Printed materials also serve as a guide for the child in learning mathematics. Manipulative materials must be used in conjunction with printed materials. The textbook can't provide hands-on exploration; it can, however, reinforce mathematical ideas through pictures and activities and provide practice, especially when the children are ready to work with symbols.

demonstration materials

To focus a child's attention on a mathematical idea, the teacher can use demonstration materials, rather than have each child manipulate materials. For example, a teacher might use a book to demonstrate properties of a rectangle, show how tens are traded for a hundred, or how to fold a strip of paper to make "fair shares" for fractions. For most teachers, however, letting children get their own hands on the materials, either before or after the demonstration, is essential.

overhead projector

The overhead projector is a valuable tool in the mathematics classroom. Children's attention is drawn to the screen as they watch to see what will appear. Children enjoy participating in moving objects or writing on the overhead.

instructional television

Instructional television is one of the most neglected tools available to classroom teachers. Fewer than 15 percent of all teachers use television in their classrooms, many because they are not aware of the possibilities. A range of programs is available for presenting new ideas in ways that teachers cannot duplicate in the classroom, with the mere presence of the television screen also motivating the children. An increasing number of classrooms now have videocassette recorders (VCRs) available, so that teachers can use programs when they want. Moreover, with the VCR, teachers can stop at selected points to discuss ideas with children, even to consider what might happen next.

calculators

Calculators can be used to teach, explore, and reinforce many ideas in mathematics. The belief that calculators should not be used until after children have mastered computation is still a common one. That is, some teachers think that children should struggle to learn and *then* be shown (as if they didn't already know!) how quickly a machine can do what they've

been struggling to do. Why this method is believed effective is not clear, but it appears to stem from outdated ideas about building character.

computers

Computers are far more acceptable in most mathematics classrooms than calculators, yet they are used most often for one of the least important tasks, drill-and-practice programs. Clearly, many other programs are available, as indicated in chapter 13.

Some schools house computers in a computer laboratory, rather than in the classroom, where they can form an interest center. This approach makes efficient use of limited computer resources. Networking several computers should be considered, connecting them to one large hard disk for efficient loading of programs, management, and so on.

Possible disadvantages of having a computer laboratory include scheduling problems, lack of integration with classroom work, and teachers' feelings that they are not in touch with the computer program. Ways of overcoming such disadvantages need to be resolved with other teachers. Parent helpers can be used when a large group of children is interacting with computers.

resource materials

The teacher needs to develop files of useful materials, such as games and other activities, examples of good printed materials, lists of library books, and articles offering background information or suggesting new teaching strategies.

using time efficiently

The relationship of time and achievement is logical: the more time spent on tasks, the more likely children will learn. Using time efficiently has been considered a prime need ever since research indicated that much time is wasted in the classroom.

Making the best use of time means that the attention of the children must be focused quickly on the topic. Throughout the lesson, the pace must keep up with the reactions of the children.

flexibility

Teachers must let children be flexible in their thinking. If a child between the ages of two and five is placed in a preschool or kindergarten program that stresses academics, including mathematics, the child will probably learn more mathematics earlier. But why rush? Isn't it more important to stimulate the child's curiosity so that he or she will want to keep on learning in the future?

A less intense learning approach achieves better results in the long run, with more motivated children who will improve their skills in later years. Research indicates that only 10 percent of five-year-olds are ready to learn to read and do paper-and-pencil work with

mathematical topics. In contrast, 90 percent of seven-year-olds are ready.

Early childhood education can develop children's interest in school and learning. Having children attack worksheets when they can hardly control a pencil is not the way to inspire interest and confidence in mathematics.

using extra time

Inevitably, times will arise in the classroom when a lesson proceeds more quickly than expected and extra time becomes available. How can a teacher make the best use of this time? Being prepared with a set of review or practice activities is helpful: "Let's see how far we can count by 5s before it's time to go," or "Who can tell what number is 10 more than 27? 20 more than 44?"

involving all children

Keeping all children involved in a lesson is of utmost importance. "Blanks" in their learning will occur unless this happens. Yet keeping the attention of all children is not easy. One way is to let all children do something in the lesson. When drilling on number facts, for instance, have each child hold up a card with the answer, rather than go around the room calling on one child at a time.

evaluating process and progress

Evaluation is an important facet of teaching. Care must be taken that what is evaluated is what is important. If facts are important, then facts will be evaluated. If how the children get the answer is important, then evaluating the processes they use is important. If the focus is on problem solving, then problem solving must be evaluated.

A variety of evaluation procedures can be used. Tests leap to mind first but for the early childhood teacher, it is more important to consider observations, interviews, inventories, checklists, descriptions by students, anecdotal records, and attitude measures, as well as paper-and-pencil tests.

The major purpose of evaluation is to provide continual feedback on how well a teacher is helping the children learn and develop good attitudes toward mathematics.

conclusion

This chapter has considered various aspects of planning mathematics instruction for the young child. Among the decisions a teacher must make are those relating to content, environment, ways of coping with children's variability, and methods of managing the classroom. The teacher's role will change as curricula are modified, as more complex technology becomes available, and as teaching strategies that enable the teacher to act as a facilitator of learning become more widely used. Today, the teacher's role is more complex, and decisions to be made are more complicated, but we also know more about how to teach so that children learn—that is the goal of this book.

bibliography

Bain, Richard. "Let's Talk Maths!" *Mathematics in School* 17 (March 1988): 36–39.

Baratta-Lorton, Mary. *Mathematics Their Way: An Activity-centered Mathematics Program for Early Childhood Education.* Menlo Park, Calif.: Addison-Wesley Publishing Co., 1976.

Bohning, Gerry, and Marguerite C. Radencich. "Math Action Books for Young Readers." *Arithmetic Teacher* 37 (September 1989): 12–13.

Burns, Marilyn. "The Role of Questioning." *Arithmetic Teacher* 33 (February 1985): 14–16.

Clements, Douglas H. "Computers and Young Children: A Review of the Research." *Young Children* 43 (1987): 34–44.

Driscoll, Mark J. *Research within Reach: Elementary School Mathematics.* Reston, Va.: National Council of Teachers of Mathematics, 1980.

Duke, Daniel L., ed. *Helping Teachers Manage Classrooms.* Alexandria, Va.: Association for Supervision and Curriculum Development, 1982.

Evertson, Carolyn M., Edmund T. Emmer, Barbara S. Clements, Julie P. Sanford, and Murray E. Worsham. *Classroom Management for Elementary Teachers.* Englewood Cliffs, N.J.: Prentice-Hall, 1984.

Fennell, Francis (Skip). "Mainstreaming and the Mathematics Classroom." *Arithmetic Teacher* 32 (November 1984): 22–27.

Kantrowitz, Barbara, and Pat Wingert. "How Kids Learn." *Newsweek* (17 April 1989): 50–56.

Larson, Carol Novillis. "Organizing for Mathematics Instruction." *Arithmetic Teacher* 31 (September 1983): 16–20.

Mueller, Delbert W. "Building a Scope and Sequence for Early Childhood Mathematics." *Arithmetic Teacher* 33 (October 1985): 8–11.

National Council of Teachers of Mathematics. *Curriculum and Evaluation Standards for School Mathematics.* Reston, Va.: The Council, 1989.

Starkey, Mary Ann. "Calculating First Graders." *Arithmetic Teacher* 37 (October 1989): 6–7.

Suydam, Marilyn N., and J. Fred Weaver. *Using Research: A Key to Elementary School Mathematics.* Columbus, Ohio: ERIC Clearinghouse for Science, Mathematics and Environmental Education, 1981.

Index